SENTENCE: SIBERIA

Ann Lehtmets was born in southern Estonia in 1904
and educated at a girls' college. She settled with her
lawyer husband in Rakvere, Estonia's third largest city. In
1941 she was arrested and transported to Siberia, where
for seventeen years she was forced to live and work in
appalling conditions.

Douglas Hoile was born in South Australia in 1924. He
served in the RAAF as a Spitfire pilot during the second
world war, and later graduated in medicine at the University
of Adelaide. He married Ann Lehtmets's daughter, Tiiu,
in 1953 and has worked for many years as a general
practitioner involved in community service.

Reviews of 'SENTENCE: SIBERIA'

"...with pellucid, vivid and almost palpable near-total recall, Ann Lehtmets tells her story of seventeen years of living in Siberian exile."
Australian Book Review

"....reminders of the innate courage and resourcefulness of those who, when tested, emerge from the contest whole."
Serge Liberman, Literary Editor — *Australian Jewish News*

"Sentence Siberia is the story of how Ann Lehtmets survived the Siberian labor camps because of her sense of character and her desire to be reunited with her children."
News Weekly

"Ann Lehtmets is an international treasure. *Sentence: Siberia's* remarkable narrative force derives from the authors' imaginative reconstruction of dialogue around the remembered events."
Frank Campbell — *The Australian*

"What makes this book such grimly fascinating reading is its clear-eyed, relentless depiction of the casual brutality of village life and the implacable, primaeval harshness of the land."
The West Australian

"Sentence Siberia is a chilling document of how imperial regimes sacrifice minorities to enrich the dominant group."
Sydney Morning Herald

"...recalls experience in vivid detail. The book's fascination does not lie in its technique but in its tone, which blends comedy with tragedy."
The Age

SENTENCE: SIBERIA

Ann Vinnal (Lehtmets), 1922

ANN LEHTMETS AND
DOUGLAS HOILE

Published by D. Hoile Nominees Pty Ltd

First published by Wakefield press in Adelaide, South Australia, in 1994
Reprinted 1995 by Wakefield press, 2003 by Sid Harta, Victoria

Copyright @ D. Hoile Nominees Pty Ltd.
dehoile@bettanet.net.au

Cover design by Ann Wojcuk
This edition typeset by Chameleon Print Design
Printed by OU Greif, Tartu, Estonia

Cataloguing-in-publication data

Lehtmets, Ann, 1904–2000
Sentence: Siberia

ISBN 1-877059-18-8

1. Lehtmets, Ann, 1904–2000. 2. Prisoners of war – Estonia –
Biography. 3. Women prisoners – Russia – Siberia – Biography.
4. World War, 1939–1945 – Concentration camps – Russia – Siberia –
Biography. 5. Prisoners, Transportation of – Russia – Siberia –
Biography. 6. Forced labor – Russia – Siberia – . I. Hoile,
Douglas, 1924–   . II. Title.

940.531757092

Cover and title page photograph: Ann Vinnal (Lehtmets), 1922

To the memory of my husband
Elmar Aleksander Lehtmets

A.L.

CONTENTS

PREFACE

New Year's Eve ball: Elmar on left, Ann second from right

BEFORE THE TIDE

On the night of 14 June 1941, Ann Lehtmets was forcibly removed from her home in the city of Rakvere, Estonia, and transported to Siberia. In 1959, when she was reunited with her daughter in Australia, she became one of few to survive this other holocaust and rejoin the western world.

■

The June 1941 action by the Soviet Union, involving tens of thousands of Baltic citizens, was one ruthless step in the Kremlin march to demolish Estonia, Latvia and Lithuania as sovereign states and incorporate their territories into the USSR.

Each of these three nations, across the Baltic Sea from Finland, has a language and culture distinct from any in Russia. Each had no ties, ethnic or otherwise, with that country and no desire whatsoever to become a part of it.

The Ribbentrop-Molotov pact had been signed two years earlier, in 1939, on the eve of Hitler's invasion of Poland. Hitler's and Stalin's foreign ministers had been authorised, in exchange for 'peace' on the eastern front and in anticipation of non-intervention from the west, to tear central Europe apart and divide it between Germany and Russia, like spoils between raiding wolves. Perhaps the supposedly stronger wolf thought to satisfy its voracious rival for a while by allowing it the tasty offering of access to the Baltic Sea.

On 15 June 1940, almost exactly a year before the mass deportations, with central and western Europe in turmoil, the Russian dictator Stalin claimed his share. An ultimatum was presented virtually simultaneously to the individual Estonian,

Latvian and Lithuanian governments, demanding for the ussr the right to send troops anywhere in their territories. The ultimatum also demanded that the present governments 'retire' and new governments friendly to the USSR be formed. On the same day Soviet troops poured into Lithuania – the closest Baltic country to Germany, thus isolating all three – and within forty-eight hours into Latvia and Estonia.

The only possible allies against this invasion, Britain and France, were by then totally engrossed in their own desperate struggle. There was no hope of assistance; certainly none of surviving physical opposition.

Thus the elected governments of three nations were no more, 'retiring' to avoid bloodshed. The same applied to Latvia and to Lithuania as to Estonia, where President Päts, General Laidoner and all other members of the Estonian parliament were deposed. Local communists took their place, occupying all the important positions in parliament and soon in any civic institutions left. The Soviet legation in Tallinn gave Moscow's orders: the puppets had them carried out.

Those deposed were now nothing. Except marked.

Newspapers and radio stations were seized and controlled. It became an offence to receive overseas broadcasts, the only remaining contact with the outside world, and all 'news' was communist-issued.

■

President Päts and Laidoner, the Commander of Armed Forces, were arrested and deported. The judiciary was discharged, police and militia scattered, banks and news media taken over, and parliament dissolved. Hundreds of once-influential people now had no money, no income, and, in many instances, no home.

This was Estonia's and Estonians' uneasy state for the year before Ann Lehtmets's removal from her home.

■

Elmar Lehtmets, Ann's husband, a lawyer by profession, was editor-in-chief of Rakvere's principal newspaper at the time of the occupation, and a member of Estonia's democratic parliament. Ann was a commissioner of Girl Guides and active in local community service.

W e wish to thank Tiiu, daughter of Ann, wife of Douglas. Without her collaboration – as translator, typist and interpreter – there would have been no book.

■

Inevitably, some people met on the way through the years these pages cover are just that – transients: temporarily substantial before dissolving into mists of time and distance. No invention has been employed to achieve a neat ending; no apology is offered for the inability to tie up loose ends infinitely more unsatisfactory to writer than to reader.

All people in this book are – or were – real people. Some names have been changed, some abbreviated, as at the time of writing there was fear of reprisal, embarrassment or retaliation to friends and relatives behind the Iron Curtain. It is largely this fear that has held her chronicle back some thirty years from Ann's liberation, and even now is not entirely dispelled.

The Russian political turmoil of 1994 warns us that imperialist ambitions are far from forgotten in the Kremlin, and that Ann's unease is justified.

1994

■

We are deeply indebted to Viiu Vanderer of New Jersey, USA, a distant relative of Ann. This edition of `Sentence Siberia' is largely due to her vision and enthusiasm.

And we thank the Estonian American National Council for its assistance in funding.

Tiiu and Douglas Hoile
2008

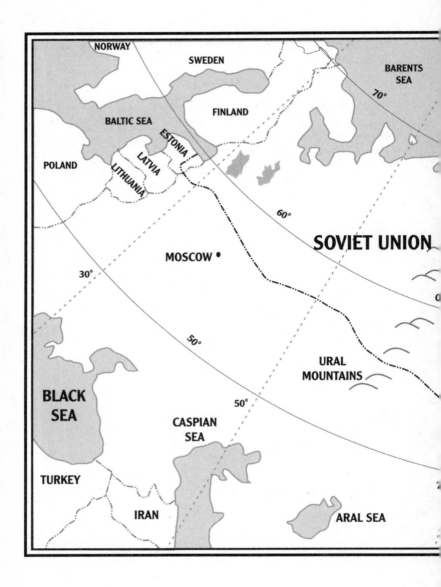

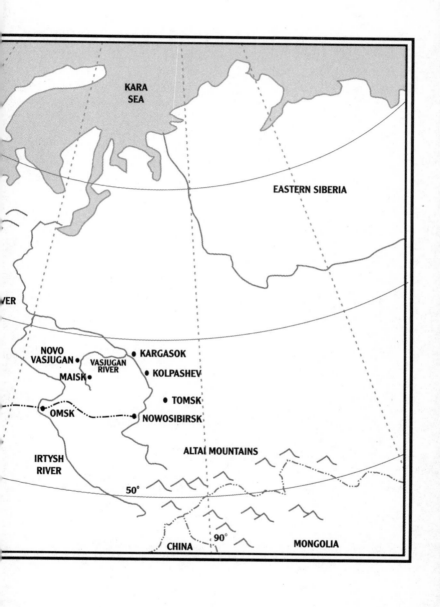

DEPORTATION

Last family photograph

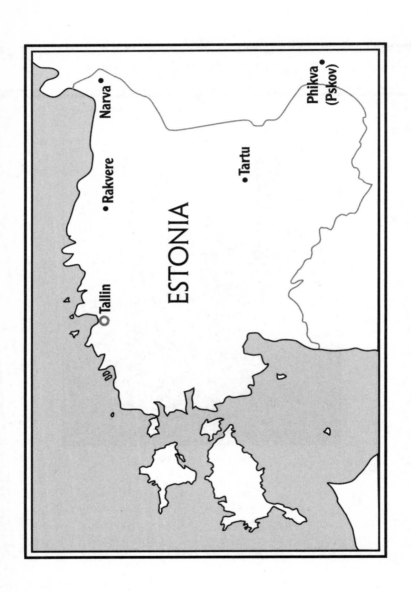

1

ARREST

It was well after midnight, and my husband was out. I could only guess where, and the best guess gave no comfort. If a tenth of the rumours being whispered around Rakvere had foundation, however slight, it was enough to send shivers up and down the least imaginative Estonian spine. Mine had never been one of those.

The window was open and the curtains a quarter drawn, moving gently in what breeze came through from the gardens beyond. The flat was small, but with two bedrooms comfortable enough. We had had to count ourselves lucky to find anything with a roof on after we had been pushed out of our own apartment, and doubly lucky to have a view over the park – though I was soon to wonder about that. The bedroom was barely adequate: a dressing table and salvaged wardrobe crowding it, the window no more than three steps from my pillow. There was no sound to come through, as there was no traffic. They had killed that, like so much else. There was no life in the city, no light, no breath, no heartbeat. It was as though a blanket had been thrown over it.

Something in the soft stillness made me look up. I felt a shock, as I still do recalling it so many years later, and my body stiffened. There in the window, still and silent as the shadows around him, was the shape of a man. He must have been tall, looming huge above me as he stood close and high in the frame, all the more fearsome in his heavy dark coat with collar and lapels turned up to keep light from his face. He remained motionless as I stared, momentarily paralysed. I shut my eyes, wanting to scream but unable to get sound past the thump of my heart in my throat,

3

knowing all the time that screaming would do no more than wake and frighten my mother in the next room. In the few seconds it took to move a muscle he was gone again, noiseless as a ghost, and everything was as before, peaceful as any summer night.

I put off the light and pulled the sheet over my face, trembling. It was two o'clock in the morning, the city's blanket heavy as a shroud, a long night to come, and a longer day before I could unburden my fears to my husband.

■

We arrived home simultaneously after, for me, a terrible next day, Elmar coming straight from his job as a clerk for a small factory, I from mine as an assistant in a frock shop. As with the flat, we had been fortunate in employment, for work of any sort was difficult to find after the occupation. Those who didn't work needed relatives or friends who did, or they starved. For a year now we had been living like this, day to day, dispossessed but hanging on.

There had been the preliminary moves before the invasion – the unlocking of the gates, as it were, tolerated because of incredible unawareness of the plans and preparations behind them, and which in any case we were in no position to prevent – and then the flood. Overnight we were a nation no more. Suddenly it seemed we were no longer people. Along with thousands of others, Elmar and I had been evicted so that Russian officers could move into our home. We were given two days to clear out of the place where we had spent most of our married lives and brought up our children – with detailed instructions as to what of our belongings we might take, what must be left behind – and find somewhere else to live, if we could. If not, too bad. Go we must.

In the quiet of the bedroom I told Elmar about last night's visitor. I was expecting disbelief. Imagination, he would say. The curtains blowing in the wind. Or a peeping Tom, a harmless pervert. We had them even before the infestation, he would remind me. Not to worry.

But I had my answers prepared, for I had been out early this morning before Mother was up and had seen two large footprints made by big feet placed carefully between the tulips. They were still there, if he cared to look. Oh no, I would say, that was no peeper, that was a professional at work. But Elmar was thoughtful and silent, obviously disturbed.

4

He put his arm across my shoulders. 'All right, Ann,' he said finally. 'Don't worry too much. We are only a couple of quiet suburbanites now. We can't be of interest to them.'

'Something brought him here! Elmar, we can't ignore it!'

'We'll keep the blind down in future.'

'And you – not home at that hour. Won't that make them suspicious?'

'Of what, my love?'

'I don't know. Of whatever you do when you stay out all night.'

'We're not doing any harm.'

Meeting other men with the same convictions. Talking. Trying to plan opposition. Trying to work out a future. Until now I had agreed: perhaps they could achieve some good, perhaps the risk was small.

'But they are still making arrests,' I reminded him.

'Only of those engaged in subversive activities.'

'Subversive?' What irony!

'That's what they call them. Don't worry, Ann.'

'Are you sure?'

I was unconvinced of both the innocence of his nocturnal meetings and the necessity of pretexts for arrest. There were many reports that reasons weren't needed.

'If they wanted me, my dear, they could have come twelve months ago when they took Päts and Laidoner. Or any time since. I may have been of some interest to them then, but I'm only a most unimportant clerk now.' Elmar smiled, and took my arm reassuringly. 'So I don't think you need be too upset about that fellow. They won't worry us at this late stage. There's just no point in it.'

So we misled ourselves for another day.

■

The doorbell rang. One ring, short and sharp, and I was awake.

So soon! I thought, as I forced myself to open the door. The very next night. If they'd only given us time – if we'd thought about it just a little longer, a little more seriously – if they'd left us even another day, we could have been well away from all this, perhaps in Sweden, an empty apartment behind us. But I knew it would never have been. Another day, another week, another month, and we would still have been here, still afraid, still optimistic, still hoping that by staying we could make the old ways come back.

And now it was happening. They were here. Come for Elmar.

What would I tell them? How explain my husband's absence at three in the morning? Only the truth. I did not know ... Where is he? I don't know ... What is he doing? I don't know ... Do you expect us to believe that? Yes. No. I don't know ...

I opened the door. It was Elmar.

Relief was momentary. My heart leapt, only to plunge again. He was more agitated than I had ever seen him. In the poor light from the tiny hall globe he looked utterly lost. My husband lost? Bewildered? Never before in our sixteen years of marriage. I froze.

'I can't remember where I left my key,' he said vaguely. His hands were wandering over his pockets. He had shrunk, and his eyes were dull and restless.

'What is it, Elmar?' Fear wrapped fingers around my throat. My voice was barely a whisper. The street was silent, some faint pallor in the night sky making sinister shadows all along it. Our own dim light suddenly made me feel we were under floodlights. I tugged at his sleeve. 'Come in. Quickly.' The cool night air was cold now.

Elmar sat wearily on the bed. 'Palgi. You remember?'

He looked pale.

'Of course I remember, dear.' A school friend, and editor-in-chief of Elmar's opposition newspaper. 'What has happened? What about him?'

'There are armed Russians all around his house. All the lights are on. I've just come from there.'

We knew then that the illusion was over. It was only a matter of time, hours at most.

'Elmar, what are we going to do?'

There was less than two hours' darkness left.

'I don't know. I just don't know. I'm very tired, Ann, and there's nothing now. Nothing to do. Nowhere to go. Later perhaps. First I must get some sleep.'

■

At 5.30 the doorbell rang again. I went to the door and in scarcely more than a whisper called through, 'Who is it?'

'Open up.' The voice was Russian, loud and demanding.

I left the door and ran to the bedroom, picking up Elmar's

overcoat on the way. 'The window, Elmar,' I pleaded breathlessly. 'Get out through the window!'

'Go and let them in, Ann,' he said quietly. He was already up and dressing. 'There is no sense in trying. The house will be surrounded.'

My legs would not function.

'Open the door, my dear. There is no way out.'

They were hammering and shouting commands. The din in the silence was shocking. I forced myself to move along the passage. Reaching for the latch, I stood aside to let them in. Three of them. It had sounded like an army. A captain of the NKVD, the dreaded Russian secret service, with a revolver; a Red Army soldier with a gun; and an Estonian. I recognised the Estonian. His name was Reinstein.

■

Local communists had crawled from their holes when the Soviet military had installed itself twelve months ago. The first Russian troops had been peaceful enough, although shabby, ignorant and somewhat bewildered; but the fellow-travellers were soon noticeable by their arrogance. Reinstein was one. He became well-known in Rakvere.

The pattern of establishing communism, until now not seen in practice, was becoming clear. First, example: Look, we have thrown off the shackles; you can, too – then propaganda: Capitalism is dying, the new world is for the masses – and subversion: Workers unite! Strike! Down with the bosses; wealth is for sharing. So far, the results in the young and progressive Baltic states had been dismal. Then veiled threat: A few regiments on your border, a few aircraft in your skies for protection – and open threat: Your government is your enemy; we know what's best for you, for the world; you *will* join us! – and finally, invasion: Occupation, forcible removal of leaders, planting of puppets, destruction of order, takeover of communications and services.

There remained loose ends. In 1940, it was unthinkable that all potential opposition could be simply eradicated, loose ends destroyed.

■

We knew Reinstein. We knew several Reinsteins. I saw Elmar

7

turn away from him, his lip twitching.

'Have you any weapons?' the captain bellowed.

We knew him too. Not personally, but by caste. We had come to know them all since last June. There was the Red Army soldiery, unkempt and noisy, parading in rollicking groups reeking of sweat, bad vodka and worse louse ointment. And, in contrast, the officers of the secret police, who had polished boots and shining hair and moved in scented clouds of their own with a kind of furtive insolence. Perhaps hardest to take of all was their new 'police force', the Red militia culled with a few exceptions from the ranks of local drunks, petty criminals, and small-time hoodlums, who now strutted the streets with the brutal arrogance of moronic authority in uniform.

'No.'

The captain flourished his revolver rather than pointed it. He strode instead of walking. He yelled when he spoke. He was not a big man and it seemed he had to emphasise everything he did. He motioned widely with his revolver and the soldier pushed the gun into my husband, prodding, working him over to the wall. I found myself taking a protective stance in front of the children's room.

Mother, incredibly, had not stirred. Children, mother, husband. A hammer was beating in my head ... Where will they take him? What will they do with him? What can I tell the children? How will we manage without him?

'Open that door!'

'Can you leave it till last? My mother is still asleep. Please.'

Surprisingly, they complied. The search was quick, but thorough. There was little enough to search. We had nothing they wanted; no documents, no weapons.

'Open it now. Wake her up.'

I began to do so, but my hand hung in the air. I could not think what to say. Elmar started across to help but the Red captain stepped in front of me and threw the door open himself.

I have never been able to recall exactly what I did say to Mother as I helped her dress, or she to me. I do remember her quiet dignity both then and during the next hour. Outwardly she was calm. She gave the appearance of being detached, as though the whole proceedings had nothing to do with her. I believe it disconcerted them as much as it relieved Elmar and me. I have remembered it often since, when I needed something more than I had within myself to console and encourage and give me strength.

It was in this room the searchers were busiest. The drawers were full of coins, medallions, rusty springs, bullets, caps, pipes, model boats, and toy guns, cars and wheels. Even a tiny box of gunpowder. Useless treasures that can never be discarded.

'What are these?'

'Just what you see,' I said.

'What are they for?'

'I don't know. They are my son's.'

'How old is he?'

'Thirteen.'

'Where is he?'

'He and my daughter are in the country.'

'What about her?' He indicated Mother, standing quietly in her robe watching. And the two single beds, one undisturbed.

'She stays here while they are away. It's summer school holiday.'

I almost made up my mind to say I did not know where in the country, which would sound a ridiculous lie. Would they interrogate them? They mustn't! Fortunately, I was never asked, for the soldier just then gave a loud exclamation of surprise and the captain, the question poised on his lips, turned his way. I remain in the soldier's debt. He was looking on top of the wardrobe and had found a picture of Stalin. He handed it down.

'Why is this picture of our leader up there?' the captain asked excitedly. 'Whose is it?'

'It's my son's.'

'Your son's?'

'He was given it as a prize. For editing the wall newspaper at school.' We had not wanted to get him into trouble by throwing it away. 'Last year,' I added lamely.

'But it's so dusty!' He seemed genuinely bewildered. 'Why is it on top of the wardrobe?'

'I work,' I told him. 'I have little time for dusting.'

The soldier shook his head. The captain smiled thinly. The picture was put on the table, facing us all.

The search was soon over. My husband was ordered to dress. 'And pack a bag.'

9

I went to help him, mechanically taking a few of his things out of drawers and getting out a suitcase.

'You! Stop that and start packing yourself.'

'Me?'

'Of course you.'

'Do you mean I have to come too?'

'Naturally.'

It took a minute to sink in. We were back in our bedroom and I was still in my nightdress. 'Would you turn around, then?'

'Don't play coy.' His look was almost contemptuous. 'Just hurry.'

Something snapped in me. I pulled off my nightgown, flung it from me and began to dress, suddenly furious with them all.

When at last I met my mother again, she told me the gown had flown right into the face of the nearest Russian. The three had then turned around quietly.

'Separate bags,' the captain barked.

'Why?' asked my husband. 'Where are we going?'

'Narymm, of course,' the soldier answered. The captain glared at him.

We packed as well as we could. I was dazed, I think Elmar the same. We said nothing, taking out clothes and putting them in suitcases. They watched, the soldier closely, the officer aloof, Reinstein propped in the doorway with a look of triumph. I put in frocks, underwear, shoes, stuff that just happened to get into my hands. Coherent thought was impossible.

'Take winter clothes as well,' the NKVD man said. 'Warm ones.' Probably the light nightdress at his feet had prompted his advice. Perhaps he only wanted to talk, to show authority; perhaps he wanted to air his knowledge of our destination. Who knows? Perhaps he even had a pang of conscience.

Elmar, at the wardrobe, took down the robes he had worn in court. The soldier laughed. 'You can throw them away,' he cackled. 'You won't need fancy dress where you're going.'

Elmar put them back quietly.

'No razor,' the captain snapped a moment later. He made an impatient show of looking at his watch. 'Come on, hurry it up.'

'Could I use the telephone?' My mind was beginning to turn over. 'Please?'

'What for?' The suspicious little eyes darted.

'Just to speak to the children.' I had to get in touch with them somehow, to let them know. I was suddenly desperate. We could not simply pack up and leave, with them thinking we hadn't even tried. They wouldn't understand. They didn't know this sort of compulsion. The more I thought of it, the more the desire for contact was overwhelming. 'Just for a little while?'

'No!'

He didn't look up, that stone-faced little man – I wanted to take him by the hair and bang his head down – busying himself at our table. He was pretending to make some kind of inventory.

'Not even one call?' I had no idea what I would say, either to them or to my sister. But I *had* to hear them once more, to say we loved them.

'What are these?' He picked up some papers and waved them at my husband.

'The children's school reports,' Elmar said. 'You can see the rows of fives.' I caught his tone of pride at their achievements of top marks. It meant he was thinking of them too. How could we go without a word? For a moment I held his eyes, as close to tears as my own. I thought I would choke.

'Leave the children be.' The captain looked up at me, briefly human, and bent over the desk again. 'It's no place for children,' he muttered.

I knew he was right. I suspect Elmar wanted no more attention drawn to them either, but I persisted. 'I only want to speak to them. Only a word?'

'Leave them alone,' the captain roared. 'You hear me!' He was NKVD again. His face flamed. 'Get on with it!'

I finished my packing. It would be useless to say more.

Warm clothes, he had said, and like an automaton I packed warm clothes, almost exclusively warm clothes, in the middle of summer.

The paperwork was soon done. How little we amounted to. My mother was asked to sign, as she was remaining in the apartment. She picked up the pen, but for all her outward calm she was unable to hold it, so badly was her hand shaking. Remorse swept through me: I had all but forgotten her. The Russian reached over impatiently, but I was quicker; I could not bear him to touch her. I steadied her hand while she signed the outrageous document. Where the inventory would finish we didn't know. It

11

didn't seem to matter.

'Say goodbye. Come – *davai*!' The captain pointed at the door.

I hugged and kissed my crying mother. Elmar embraced her gently. I had a final look about our small flat – such a short time ago so inadequate, now suddenly so attractive – patted Kupi the cat, and kissed Mother again. We stepped out into the street and were immediately sandwiched. Waiting armed escorts fell in on either side, the search party behind. Then, with the soldiers' footsteps ringing along the lightening and silent street, we trudged off to the accompanying sound of Mother's sobs and her broken call: 'I'll pray for you. I'll pray and wait for you.'

■

We were marched a kilometre or so at gunpoint, suitcases in hand, heavy-hearted, Mother's weeping blessing still echoing in our ears.

'I am sorry, Ann,' my husband said, 'terribly sorry you have to go through this for me.'

'Oh, Elmar!'

His eyes misted in their anguish. The bravest of words can come at the least brave of times. I knew what he meant by 'for me': that if he had been of some other profession I should not have been here now.

I answered, 'I am proud, my dearest, to be able to accompany you.' I should then have taken his arm and walked head up. But we had heavy bags, one in each hand, and a grubby Russian soldier at our heels prodding with his rifle and yapping, '*Davai, davai* – Come on, come on.'

My husband asked the soldiers if they could help with my luggage. He asked the men themselves, twice. He would not ask Reinstein. The captain heard, and pretended he didn't. One mumbled, 'I would, but I can't, I'm on duty,' and gestured uncomfortably with his rifle. The captain said, 'No talking.'

I stopped myself from stumbling and did not look at him.

My legs were failing, my arms numb with strain by the time we reached an army truck parked several blocks away. It was in front of the house of friends of ours, the Falks, Paul and Ella, who were a few years younger. I do not know if we met there by design, or whether the timing was accidental. Whichever way, it was fortunate for me. I needed rest; I couldn't carry the cases much longer.

The sight of Ella Falk coming out of the house with their two small children – baby Peter asleep in her arms – lifted my morale. Although no greetings passed, we were no longer alone.

We were told to get in. All together. 'Plenty of room. *Davai*!'

I felt the contraction in my chest relax a fraction. Not the dreaded NKVD building and summary execution for us, it seemed. It could still be possible, I supposed. But hardly with children, when they could so easily have been left behind ...

Although we had been told a destination, we had learned to accept anything, however official, with reservation. Narymm, Siberia? Possibly. Or would it yet be NKVD headquarters? Or both? No other alternatives appeared likely. Whichever, it was a terrifying enough prospect.

How to reach the children? What was to happen to Elmar and me? There was so much to think of, so much we had to say to each other, and no knowing how much time to say it. So we sat together and held hands in the back of the truck in silence while the Falk family was bustled in, leaving another crying mother and grandmother behind. There was no conversation, no greeting, not even a goodbye.

The vehicle moved off. The few who had witnessed the dawn commotion stood helpless in the street or watched from narrowed doorways and windows. Mai Falk cried loudly for her grandmother. Her mother shushed the child. 'Don't cry, darling. Amamma will be there when we get back.'

I do not know if Amamma was. I don't know if the child was consoled at the time. I don't remember. I was thinking of my own children and recollect little of that truck ride. Only that I sat beside Elmar.

■

The railway station was bedlam. In the first cool light of a clear summer day the air was clean and fresh and still. The scene that met us was all the more shocking for that. It might have been more tolerable if we *had* all been screaming mad. We were led between platforms, over sleepers and cinders and rubble, to the goods section, Reinstein pointing the way over crisscrossing tracks, between piles of timber, to a siding. A goods train of immense length stood there, a train that was a mobile prison in dozens of square sections, an engine panting idly at its distant head. The goods – Estonian people, hundreds and hundreds of them, listed by lots, numbered like cattle on a cargo manifest – were being crammed into barred and locked cages. The loading was in full swing, efficient as an everyday practice. There was no sign of hurry. My feet dragged, and no-one noticed.

'*Davai, davai!*' They kept us moving along the line in front of the rolling stock. Some of the big square doors were open and though all wagons looked full more people were being herded on. Most were quiet, but the noise of crying children rang everywhere, and occasionally the furious shout of a guard. Faces looked out of small, square, heavily barred windows, high up, one to each wagon. They peered between white knuckles gripping bars. Some looked fearful, some already hopeless, a few defiant, all scarcely believing. Only hours ago these thousands of people had been sleeping in their own beds, ostensibly free.

A thin crowd of relations and friends had gathered. A few were allowed by their nearest guards to go forward singly or in small groups to talk from a distance. Some of the guards enjoyed themselves by threatening and prodding distressed people – grandmothers, youngsters, adults and wailing babies alike – with gun butts and bayonets, refusing children contact with parents, parents with children.

We went past carriages of dismal human freight, past their keepers. We knew many people. No greetings were exchanged, only forlorn recognition. We came to a stop near a wagon where I recognised Linda Roos behind the bars. Her son was with her, scarlet, bleary-eyed from measles. Dr Kuldsepp, Rakvere's well-loved paediatrician, was trying to get into the carriage with medicine for him. The doctor was remonstrating with a brutish guard, waving at the child, brandishing his bag. His fair hair was tousled. As we came opposite the door the guard was shoving the defenceless man backwards across the rails and sleepers and stones with his rifle. That was where I saw him for the last time, tears streaming down his face, pathetic bag useless in his gifted hands.

Finally we were stopped, Elmar and I, by the captain who had brought us. We stood before one of the wagons. Close up, it was big and high off the ground. The door was open; inside was dark. I didn't want to look closer. I put down my bags and

14

turned to Elmar.

'Say goodbye,' the captain commanded.

We didn't understand.

'You.' He pointed at me. 'Up.'

We stood close, staring into the black hole.

'Men in separate carriages,' he said. 'If you want your children' – he was addressing me – 'I'll be back tomorrow. Tell me then. Think carefully.'

'Not together?'

'No.'

A last look about our home town – from a part of it new to me; I had never been here before – one last kiss and caress from my husband. Then he was jostled away.

The captain picked up my bags and threw them into the gaping doorway. I followed, scrambling, ignoring his help.

2

PARTINGS

The carriage was not as big as it had looked from the outside. As I scrambled in, it seemed to be completely filled with women and children, bags and parcels. All were strangers to me, apart from Ella Falk and her two children. I didn't know her well, either. Never since childhood had I felt so alone. Somebody put her arms around me. 'You too, Ann! I'm so glad we're together. Where are your children?'

Mrs Sein was a slight acquaintance; suddenly, she was an old friend. But mention of the children set a thousand needles stinging at my eyes. Several of the mothers were soothing theirs, and my heart ached to comfort my own. Elmar had said it was better not to take them. Even the captain had said it. In desperation I turned to friends I did not yet know.

'No,' counselled one. 'No,' from another. Non-committal gestures and head shakes. But each pulled her own close. No and Yes. I decided, felt better for it, and was immediately assailed by doubt. Not see them again? No. Bring them to this? Never! But to leave without word?

I knew I must make a decision. And it must stand.

There was really only one.

My brain cleared a little and I took a more critical look about me. One end wall of our wagon was furnished with two wooden shelves a couple of metres deep, one above the other. Bunks presumably, and not nearly enough to sleep everybody. There were no other fittings. In one corner, just under the roof and above the top shelf, was a window, square and barred, depressingly small. In the diagonally opposite corner a small triangle had been sawn out of the floorboards. The boards were scuffed and worn by the feet and hoofs and claws of previous passengers, and were soiled from their droppings. The triangular hole and the shelves were new. It took a little time and a gasp of nausea to realise what the hole was for.

The shelves, the only places to sit, were occupied by whimpering children – one wanting a drink, one to go home, one crying over and over for 'Daddy' – and in the corner by the triangle a vacant-looking girl squatted, talking and cursing at no-one, demanding to go home.

We had introduced ourselves in the early confusion. Some names stuck; others came back later. There were twenty-five of us all told: eleven women including the mentally retarded Inge; twelve children under ten years old; Edgar, thirteen; and a young man of nineteen, apparently registered as a child.

The morning wore on, warm and humid, with nothing happening, and no-one knowing. The carriage was airless and half-dark, the solid doors barred shut. No-one complained. In that time, while looking after the children, talking little, thinking much, I felt a little strength, a little hope and a great hatred gather in me, such hatred as I had never believed possible. I had detested Russia and Russians in a general way before. Now it was clear and specific: I hated them all.

About lunchtime, the door was opened, and some luggage thrown in. It was labelled 'Mrs Malla'. Nobody knew her, and we could only pity one who was yet to join us. The woman herself never arrived; we heard later that she had been put into a men's carriage and sent to a special security labour camp with them. We never heard why, never heard any more. We were yet to learn that mistakes were frequently made, seldom admitted, never corrected. The door was closed again, and stayed that way the rest of the day.

The first night was wakeful. Only the small children slept, curled on the shelves. We took turns watching at the window, listening at the crack in the door, waiting for the order that might come from somewhere to save us. But there were only the noises of the night and the guards' footsteps. In the morning the door was opened, for no reason that we could see except to let the guards peer in to menace us with scowls and rifles. Perhaps it boosted their morale. Good for them, we decided cynically, because it did help ours a little. We had been through a full day and night of miserable nothing, locked in a square blank cell. A lost, long, miserable day. The open door put us back near the living.

People stood outside, heads wilted. They had been pushed beyond the station yard fence out onto a field, and I could see a high wall and city buildings in the distance. Most of the silent watchers had obviously been there all night, waiting. They looked weary: the men were unshaven, the women bedraggled. They were more than quiet – a sense of doom seemed to have overtaken them. An old woman sat on a heap of planks inside the fence. I could hear her crying as though her heart would break.

One of the guards halted before her. 'What have you got to howl about?' he growled.

'Oh, nothing,' she threw back at him. 'I'm the flower seller at the market, that's all, and now my customers are gone.' But when he turned away she hissed at his back, 'Bloody murderers!'

Doors were banging along the train. This time the sound was more urgent. Guards strode by purposefully. A couple of them stopped at our carriage to check inside and count us. We turned our backs on them, but as they left I craned to see through the gap of the closing door. Mrs Falk's mother came running up. She had been among the watchers yesterday and had not appeared this morning, which had been a worry to Ella. She wasted no time now, coming right to the crack of light in the doorway.

'Peter!' she called urgently through the crack. 'Give me Peter. I can look after him.'

There was no doubt where he would be better off. The baby's mother was desperate. Even now he was due for a feed, and there was no feed to give.

The guard had not latched the door properly. We widened the gap and quickly passed out the boy and a basket of nappies, Ella Falk nodding assent through tears. She was frozen to her seat on the floor. A guard saw the transaction from two or three carriages away. He ran up with a yell, grabbed the child from the older woman's arms, threw him back among us, banged the door shut and slammed its iron latch-bar across. Clang!

We heard the woman outside cry out, and the guard swear. Inside, Peter's mother collapsed on a pile of luggage. The basket stayed out. So did his blanket. Someone went to support Ella, while I held in my lap a crying Peter, clad only in the thin night-dress he had been put to bed in two evenings ago.

Until now we had held on to some primitive hope of a miracle, which had prevented us from thinking beyond today in anything but the vaguest terms. Tomorrow? We envisioned all sorts of possibilities to be tackled as they arrived. With that clanging door, and with dreadful certainty, we realised we had no say in the future. We were completely at the mercy – what a word to use! – of dreaded 'father' Stalin, with the assistance of the Red Army. We could, and would, be denied the most elementary of human rights. Suddenly, clearly, we knew it, and there was nothing we could do about it. With the knowledge, a swelling wave of protest rose in me, in every one of us. For some, it would never dissolve.

Peter's mother recovered. The crying children gradually quietened when Mrs Elk, with more courage than enthusiasm, began on fairy stories. Even Inge had been shocked to silence by the episode of the baby. She had never seen any creature treated like that.

We talked briefly after a while and reached our first voiced decision. Unanimously, we decided never at any cost to show tears to our gaolers. An odd resolution perhaps, but to us, at the time, it was immensely important as an expression of our new spirit. Often in the future it would be of great value – to me, at least – in helping preserve pride and sanity. I was thankful in a way that I had been put among so many children. As it was, there was little time for thinking, an example to be shown, and less chance of breaking down.

The iron bar fell noisily. The captain who had arrested us was there. I walked to the doorway and looked down at him. He was in uniform. He was all the guards, all Russia – all Stalin – rolled into one. I calmly hated the loathsome little man standing beneath. He had to look up to me, which seemed right.

'Do you want to take your children with you?' he asked, without preamble.

'No.'

'It is better so.'

He nodded his head in some kind of approval, and left.

Later, in Siberia, in pain, in hunger, I remembered him. I remembered hating him and I almost regretted it. I remembered his advice and his nod. I even prayed for him. And his children.

When all was said and done, he was human and, although NKVD, he had not condemned my children when I believe he could have.

We stayed one more full day in Rakvere station, and I had visitors. One, a family friend, hearing of the mass arrests and that we were among the victims, left his job for the day to pack parcels of food and bring them to us. He brought me a note from Elmar, too, which I treasured for later, and left me all the cash he had with him, one-hundred-and-thirty roubles. I was grateful, for I had no money, although I had no idea whether it would be of value. It was to cost my friend more than roubles, as he spent two months in gaol for leaving his post at the department of railways without permission. Later, one of the girls from the frock shop came. She had called at home to see why I had not been at work, and brought with her a heavy package prepared by my mother. I took it, shoved it in a corner, and forgot it. If I had known what it contained I might have sent it back. And if I had done that I doubt I would have survived.

In the evening one of the children called from the window. 'You have another visitor, Aunty Ann; there is someone outside asking for you,' she said as she made way for me.

I clambered up and looked out. It was my nine-year-old daughter, with a family friend. As if I had never had sight before I looked at her, aching, seeing nothing but her fair hair and puzzled eyes, her trembling mouth and firm little body. The rest of the world vanished. 'Tiiu, my darling. Don't cry,' was all I could say.

We looked at each other in silence.

I heard the quick steps of a guard and, kissing my fingers, reached my hand out between the bars. My friend held her up. A touch, a finger-kiss. Then the guard was there, irritably shaking his rifle. '*Davai! Davai!* Move off!'

There was silence in the carriage. All eyes were on me, I knew. The children had moved instinctively away from the window to their own mothers, watching. I had no tears. I stayed at the window, looking at the empty space where my daughter had been. I felt dead. My child was gone. My son was not even this close. I might never see either of them again.

Later in the evening, with a series of bangs and jerks, we moved.

■

21

The second evening came and went. We did not notice. We had grown accustomed to gloom, as even one head in the window almost blocked it. A degree less sun and suddenly it was dark. The children on their shelf-beds shuffled fitfully in half sleep. We sat, stiff with discomfort, shutting our eyes for no more than a few minutes at a time, rocking with the train. A few whispers over the distant roar of the engine, the constant rattle of wheels, the rush of wind through our now-invisible floor hole, an occasional dry sob from the children on their planks; all became one continuous sound in dulled ears.

On and on we crawled. Occasionally a draught of clean smoky air gushed up through the triangle, reminding us of the stench we no longer noticed otherwise, a combined stench of ourselves and the people and cattle before us, animals all, living, breathing, sweating, excreting. On and on.

I found my way over the silent figures on the top shelf and squatted by the window opening. A small boy at my heels stirred. I reached out a hand to comfort him, but he did not wake. I was seeing again the pale, round face of my daughter, and fancied I heard the sobbing call of my son from under the carriage: 'Mother! Dear Mother! Dear Mother!'

The train slowed. Stopped. I peered hard. Was it a familiar silhouette? A guess? Somehow I knew. Whatever the connection, I had no doubt we were in Tartu. Beautiful, historic Tartu, with its centuries-old university so much a part of our lives. I thought of Elmar. We were in Tartu, in the dark, most likely in the farthest corner of the goods yard. And we might as well be buried in the earth beneath.

A woman joined me. We could see nothing, not even stars. I peered into the blackness and gripped the bars, near hysteria at being so close to a beloved place I might never see again, and could not see now. I could tell from her breathing that my companion felt the same.

We heard the sound of footsteps and talk in the distance. I listened carefully but could catch no more than the occasional word or syllable. They were speaking Estonian. Then there was nothing again – no voices, no noise outside in the total darkness. Then footsteps once more, quick and quiet. Closer. Right beneath us.

'Tartu!' A man's urgent whisper. 'Throw out any letters you

have. No need of stamps, we'll see they get there. But hurry!'

We passed the message to the others, all in whispers. In the excitement and darkness I could not find writing materials. I searched my bag two, three times over – it did not take long – my pockets, everything. Perhaps I'd forgotten to pack them, I realised in panic. Someone offered paper and pencil. I took them gratefully, only to find that I was so afraid that the messenger would be back before I had finished, I could think of nothing to write. Finally, in the light of several matches, I scribbled a few meaningless words. Then the addresses of my nearest relatives, my dearest friends, eluded me. I changed my mind and scratched out names, rewrote and, with trembling fingers, finished two short letters. They were to reliable acquaintances, hardly people I would normally write to, saying nothing. Why not to the children? Or my mother? Or the closest of friends? Who knows? There was no deliberation on my part, yet there was no doubt. Perhaps even then some part of my mind knew I had to cut myself off from everyone I loved. I could harm people merely by being related to them or by writing an intimate word. I was already dimly reconciled to the fact that I was an exile.

We threw the letters from the window and awaited the messenger breathlessly. Would he be back? Would he get them? Would he see them all? Would he pick up mine? Send it on? It seemed terribly important.

In place of the expected stealthy footsteps there came instead the sudden sound of running feet, a hoarse shout and a single rifle shot. The feet stopped abruptly at the report, there were a few excited voices in the distance, and that was all. We strained to hear. Nobody in the carriage stirred. Even the children were still. Yet we heard nothing. The silence was appalling.

An age passed and the familiar footsteps stopped by our window.

'The letters are there,' I whispered urgently. 'What happened?'

'Someone tried to escape from the men's half.' A hoarse whisper back. 'He'd pulled the bars out. I have the letters. Be brave. See you soon.' No more. He had gone.

Who was it? Who had got out?

Our friend had said 'tried'. Whoever it was had failed, then. Had he been killed? Hurt? Left alive on the ground?

Who was it?

By the time we had courage to ask, it was too late.

For the first time we cried, together, aloud, and without shame. Each one of us had someone there – husband, son, father, brother – and he might be only a few metres away, lying on the ground. Dying, perhaps dead now. And we could not go to him.

We lost restraint as we wept, and talked of our husbands, families, people and places, old homes and trouble-free times. We tried to ignore the man lying outside, to subdue weakness, to find strength. Our vow not to show tears to our gaolers was reasserted as we reassured each other and cemented friendships.

In the quiet later, I remembered Elmar's note to me, and read it to the others. He had said that they were in good spirits. Be brave, he had said, we'll meet again – at home – soon! The note had brought hope to me when I had first read it, even given me strength enough to console others who had not heard from their men. But now, after that gunshot ...

The train shuddered to a stop early the next morning. We heard the bar being removed and thrown down, then the door slid open with a bang.

'*Davai, davai!* Come on, get out!'

All did, except Mrs Balter and I. Wordlessly, we agreed we would not set foot on Russian soil until we had to. The children picked at grass and some of the women called to others from the next carriage once their eyes had adjusted to the unaccustomed light. There were no men to be seen, only flat grassland and clear sky.

'*Davai*! Get back!'

The door slammed shut again.

'Someone out there was saying they think war's going to break out.'

'War?'

'The men think so, from a few carriages up. They said to pass it on.'

It was something to try to believe in, something to hang on to. The Germans would annihilate the Russians, we theorised; they were far stronger. It was just a matter of how long. They might annihilate each other if we were really lucky, and leave the British victorious, which would be better still. Any other result was inconceivable. The Russians couldn't match anybody with proper armament and anything like equal numbers, could they? Their army was pathetic. Look at what the Finns had managed to do to them in the Winter War!

■

I awoke to hear Peter crying at his mother's empty breast. From the next carriage came the sound of singing: *The Land And People Of Estonia I Love With All My Heart.* It was a brave sound.

We wanted more than bravery, however. We wanted more than song. For once, it stirred nothing in us. The children in our compartment were thirsty. As well as Peter, one or two others were whimpering. For the first time in their lives, they had asked for something they needed and been denied.

The water problem became the worst of torments. Our prison walls were hot. What little air that came in was warm and dry, and skin, eyes, lips and throats were parched. Only dry food remained in the pooled collection, and there was frighteningly little. All that could be found was shared, and as much as possible put aside for the future. Most adults were beyond hunger. Meals, like time and place, had no meaning any more. There was only the endless rock and clatter of our smelly, dark, airless coop.

Twilight outside, and all the children but Peter went to sleep. Mrs Balter and I took turns to walk with him while his mother had some rest. She was easy to manage as we took her baby from her, a docile automaton, her beautiful grey eyes sunken and staring. We put her down and she curled up like a child.

Well after midnight the whole carriage was startled awake as a piercing, prolonged burst of screaming began near the door. It went on and on eerily without pause, accompanied by a furious rattling of the doors. 'I am not an animal! Let me out! I want to go home!'

Goose flesh came up on my arms. The back of my neck prickled. The so far very quiet and patient Inge, the retarded sister-in-law of Mrs Holm, had broken down. There was nothing we could do to pacify her, no reason in her. The children were crying, and it seemed there would never be sleep again, never daylight. We gave up trying to placate Inge after a time and let her rock and chant in peace. It was less wearing on us all, and composure was wearing thin.

In the morning Inge slept at last, and we decided to take inventory of baggage. It turned out to be a depressing exercise. Mrs Holm had only her husband's clothing. Mrs Lohvard displayed a full bag of pots, pans, crockery and – perhaps reluctantly – several lengths of smoked sausage. She expressed shock that she had no spare clothes for the children. Mrs Randin had packed a large box of assorted household articles, including one loaf of bread, now gone, bedding, and summer wear. The captain of our arresting party had told Elmar and me to pack separately. We had done so, and had neglected food and utensils entirely. All I had was clothing. Mrs Nommik had only her husband's work-box full of carpenter's tools; she had had no time to gather clothes.

I remembered the package delivered at the station and riffled through an unlikely assortment of more clothes. Poor Mother must have been distraught. Why else would she have packed no food, but included a handful of garden soil tied up in a toilet bag, and a linen table cloth of all things?

My entire stock of food was what had been handed me at Rakvere by our railway engineer friend, and it had almost gone.

And Elmar? What of him? I knew he had no food either, unless he had also been given some at Rakvere. What if he had not? I felt guilty. I should have thought of it.

About midday the train stopped. We shouted, kicked the walls, and banged on the door, demanding that the pen be opened. The veneers had worn thin now. Primitive instincts were shaking loose the mantles of manners. Of what value was restraint against self-preservation? Good manners against protection of the young? We needed water and we hollered for it.

The door stayed shut and we saw no-one to shout to. All that was visible from the window was a large storehouse and many rail-tracks.

'Pihkva?' somebody said.

We thought it probable. Pihkva is on the border, a sizeable rail centre, almost into Russia. We hadn't come as far as I had thought.

The train moved in jerks, seemed to turn, stopped again. We heard footsteps, a few words spoken in Russian. There was more movement, a series of jolts both ways. We posted observers at the window, upsetting the children, who had been allowed to monopolise it during daylight so far.

26

It was my watch when we moved off after shunting. As we rolled slowly out of the yard we passed a stationary goods wagon with wide open doors and I had a long clear view of its interior. There was a table in the middle, facing the door, with two chairs at it. The walls were lined with shelves of yellow, green and blue paper. Files? Official forms? They must be. This was an office on wheels. The wagon, empty of people, was part of a long train of boxcars. Like ours, I thought, except that all the doors were thrown open and guarded from outside by alert-looking soldiers with rifles. We still moved slowly, no more than walking pace. The other train was full of men. My interest quickened. Open doors? I could see into the cars. Our men! Standing in clusters now in the gaping doorways, faces strained, anxiously scanning our line as we went by.

I caught sight of Elmar at a door, shirt neck open, face stubbled. He was looking strangely content, almost smiling. Our eyes would not meet, try as I did to will him. He was serene among those desolate men, as we rumbled on out of range.

That last brief glimpse of my husband will remain with me the rest of my life. Like Mona Lisa's, his smile seemed to hold a secret which, though not quite aimed at me, was for me. I know this. I know he knew I was watching and was saying something to me – 'There will be war and we shall all be home soon' was all I could think at the time – and I felt stronger. The train from Rakvere had been divided into two. We had now left the men's section behind, and sadly I shall never know the real reason for that smile.

Their part was to go to the Oblast (political region) of Sverdlovsk, just east of the Urals, to the slave camps of Sossva and Verhorturje. We did not know that, of course, and the names would have meant nothing to us if we did. I learned later that the carriage I had seen, with the table and papers, was the court where the men were sentenced. Five hundred in two days. One judge. All were given hard labour – some for fifteen years, some ten, some five – 'without correspondence privileges.' Privileges! What a joke.

Why did the Soviets sometimes, certainly not always, adhere so solemnly to the procedures of 'trial' and sentence? Perhaps to bolster claims of righteousness, although no prisoner was ever given an opportunity to plead or defend, none ever acquitted.

Records, if ever kept, were never released. But communist justice was served. Men were 'tried', convicted under its astonishing articles, and, apparently, never in the first instance sentenced to death. That, presumably, would have been unjust. All were earnestly sent to the same places, however, and the survival rate from those special regime camps at Sossva and Verhorturje was less than one in a hundred, irrespective of 'crime' or length of sentence.

Our own 'trials' were yet to come. Or if they had been held already – which, in the light of things, was quite possible – we were yet to hear the results. Meanwhile, it appeared, sentence had already been passed.

Leaving the men behind caused intense depression among us. Though beyond seeing or speaking distance, there had been comfort in their nearness. We were alone, our last supports knocked from under us. Even the brief platform left by my husband's smile soon melted. And courage, I found, needs something, however nebulous, to stand on. Fear came into the eyes of each of us, and stilled our tongues. The children too, small as they were – only five or six of the thirteen were of school age – were quiet. They sensed without being told that something terrible had happened. There were no requests for fairy tales that night.

During the evening, Peter's three-year-old sister Mai became ill with gastroenteritis. We had little to ease her misery. Somebody gave her some dry rice, which she took after hesitating because the other children were watching hungrily, and I had a little dried white bread for her. She looked like a shrunken mouse as she curled up in her corner to nibble furtively at the scraps. Except for the eyes. A mouse's eyes are bright, while hers dulled by the minute as she lost fluid we could not replace.

We had had, as the Siberian saying goes, the blossom of our suffering. The fruit was yet to come.

3

BEYOND THE URALS

Flat treeless plain stretched kilometre after kilometre to the Ural Mountains, green and blue and orange in the violet haze, and I remembered their reputation for surpassing beauty. You must see them at sunrise, they used to say. Enchanting. Marvellous. Unforgettable.

The sun shone on them now, bright on the peaks and flowing down, which meant we were to the east and must have passed through them in the night. I looked out past the bars of our slow-moving box as dawn touched the grass, rippling gold and free in the fresh air. Lucky grass!

Behind me on the plank bed one of the children cried sharply and I heard the now familiar short, wet noise. Mai again. Her mother was cradling Peter, so I turned from the Urals with some regret, and went to help. This meant changing her; she had another pair of pants, soiled of course, but dry. I talked to soothe her. She whimpered still, but more quietly. Together we rocked in mechanical torpor with the movement of the train.

We halted soon at another small station, surrounded by steppe. We crowded the window. As far as the eye could see there were no fences, no trees, nothing but waving dry grass. Then, to one side, the young man Enn spotted the smoke-blackened wooden station building and a few clay huts. We started hammering on the sides again, using shoes, knife handles, anything that would make noise, clamouring for water. Those mothers not banging began preparing breakfast, if you could call it that. The children were told they could eat their meagre rations only if they promised not to ask for drinks. We would have to

29

quench their thirst with fairy tales again.

There was no response to the noise – and no surprise in that – so we gave up and resumed our corners.

Near midday we were still at the station on the bleak side of the Urals. Was it a week we had been in this thing? It seemed half a lifetime. There was no sign or sound of movement anywhere and we were drooping in the heat. A noise outside, followed by the ringing crash of the iron bar dropping from the door, startled us upright. We blinked into the glare as Tintooth, the guard, climbed in. We looked again as he turned to assist a young woman, solidly built, in the uniform of a nurse.

Our spirits should have soared. We had been praying for someone with a claim to humanity for days. But the uniform seemed to be her only qualification. 'The children,' she said without a glance at them. 'Do they have lice?'

She spoke rough country Russian. The children, and all but two adults, did not understand her.

'You won't find lice here,' I said. 'But we have a sick baby and one child with dysentery. And all the others are thirsty. We need water and medicine and the door left open for some fresh air.'

She turned and left without further word.

The guard left with her, but after a pace or two he dropped behind. We had seen him several times before, trotting about busily every time we were stationary. It seemed he had charge of our carriage, and some of those near us. His distinguishing feature was a mouthful of metal teeth, which he showed now. Not an attractive sight.

'A bucket,' he demanded gruffly. He rubbed finger and thumb impatiently. 'Come on, a bucket!'

We had only one. It was Mrs Lohvard's, and naturally she was reluctant to part with it. We had no reason to trust a Russian guard. However, Tintooth marched off with the bucket, even leaving the door open while he did so, and returned in a few minutes with it brimful of clean, cool water – and a pot of ointment for lice, despite our assurance.

We made tea for all, our spirits higher than for several days. We dipped out a cup of water for each person and smeared two heads with the ointment, for – clever Tintooth! – the national insect of mighty Russia had made its debut among us.

We were clean, or nearly so. We had been refreshed by a slight breeze before the door had been shut again. Little Peter had gone to sleep satisfied after a bottle of sugar and water. His sister had shown signs of improvement, and the other children were contented.

I retired to my corner, the comforting arm of Mrs Sein around my shoulder, envying the women who had their children, sympathising with them at the same time, loving my own and hating the man who had made me leave them.

I hated him for what he was, what he represented, what he had done to us. I hated him most for the decision he had pressed me into making, for forcing the most fateful single word of my entire life from me – 'No' – and leaving me for an unknown number of days or years to wonder constantly why I had said it, and whether or not I had been wrong.

There was no more I could do for Mai, who had settled for the moment. Nor for the others. There was nothing left but to think. There was washing to be done and we had no water. Exercising and we had no space. Meals, and no food. Treatment, and no medicine. I could only try to conserve my own strength and avoid thinking of what ought to be rather than what was.

We were moving again. I could not raise the effort to look out. Beyond the black wagon wall I knew there was only the plain.

Was it real? Could children possibly be caught up in anything like this? What were we doing here? Where did it begin?

■

It might have begun 5000 years ago. That cannot be told with certainty. All that is known is that the Estonian people were settled in their present territory on the eastern shore of the Baltic Sea for many centuries before history began. They have been there since, on land they claim their own by right of countless generations of continuous occupation.

Tacitus, we were taught, mentions the *Aesti* as local inhabitants in his *Germania*, compiled at the end of the first century AD, and archaeological finds place them in the same area more than a thousand years earlier still. Five thousand years? Perhaps.

One thousand years, then? The native tribes were invaded by Vikings, the first of the despoilers, on their way to the land of the Slavs. Invaded, but not conquered. In the succeeding half millennium they fought off Russians, Germans and Danes, the last-named building their famous castle on the site of Tallinn, later our capital. Eventually, early in the thirteenth century they were conquered by the more numerous and powerful Germans. Then began a long period of serfdom under German and later Swedish masters until 1721 when the latter ceded their Baltic territories to Imperial Russia following Tsar Peter's defeat of the Swedish army in 1709. Two hundred and fifty years ago.

Two-hundred-and-fifty years of Russians. For a quarter of a millennium the might of our eastern neighbour has borne down on us.

I was a baby when Estonians first attempted to break away – in 1905, with Russia in revolutionary chaos. Sadly, the bid was defeated, and even harsher martial law imposed. Even so, as through all the previous centuries of domination, the individuality of the Estonian people persisted – in language, culture and national pride.

Lessons taught, epics learned, books and pages read and discussed, old resentments inherited through the ages: all flashed in disorder across my brain as I shivered in my hot corner. Always a sentimental student of history, the past had never seemed so alive to me, never been so close, as now. For most of my life the old dates, the lines from books, were vague and distant, between musty pages. Now I *knew* the oppression of my ancestors, *felt* their frustration.

I was still at school when our great national milestone was achieved. In 1917, with the world ravaged by the Great War and Russia again in the turmoil of revolution, a hastily formed Estonian Army fought and won our War of Independence, driving out all foreign troops. I recalled now the euphoria of that glorious victory and the heady years that followed.

In 1918 we were a nation; by the end of 1919, our land was cleared of usurpers; in 1920 there was the peace treaty with the Kremlin, declaring that Russia 'voluntarily and forever renounces all sovereign rights over the territory and people of Estonia'. For the first time in 700 years we were masters of our own destiny, rid of foreign oppressors, free in the land of our fathers. And I was a part of living history. For the next twenty years – all my adult life – I lived in a new and vibrant country in freedom and prosperity Russians had never seen.

Then they came again, ignoring the pact. Sleep would not come as events of the past, distant and recent, slid in and out of my mind. I recalled the dynamiting of the symbolic freedom memorial by the invasion troops just a year ago, the destruction of plaques honouring the heroes of that 1918 War of Independence, the removal of the blue, black and white tricolour from the historic tower of Toompea in Tallinn and its replacement by the detested red rag . . . the arrogant, ignorant troops everywhere . . . later the arrests of protesting students and the escorted trips to NKVD headquarters for interrogation. I remembered the disappearances and rumours of torture. All these passed through my mind: the acts of perfidy, vandalism and terrorism of the past year mingling with the rancour of the centuries of subjugation before. And now: experience.

4

WAR

We stopped again. We had not long to wait this time before the door was thrown open. Tintooth appeared, counted quickly, signalled us to be silent, and stood aside respectfully. Such courtesy! Something momentous was about to happen.

The train commandant entered. We guessed his rank by his appearance – clean shaven, groomed, combed hair slick and sweet-smelling – and his mean, authoritative face. Uniform insignia meant little to us, but there was no doubt: here was Authority.

The instant attention we gave him must have been gratifying. Here at last, we knew, was someone with power to help us. He posed inside the door, eyes half-closed and focused somewhere over our heads. Not an auspicious entrance, but . . .

We scarcely breathed.

'Is everybody present and healthy?'

My heart dropped. Someone groaned. He was of no use to us, it was apparent to all. He had the warmth of an arctic wolf.

'We are all here,' I replied, turning away from him. 'Where in the devil's name else?'

'Any lice? Who is your leader?'

We were a full day beyond the Urals. Our first day in Siberia.

■

Three or four nights ago, the night that the men had gone their separate way, with the kilometres increasing between us and home, I had crouched in the dark, looking over my fellow travellers. Ordinary human beings, desiring nothing but the freedom we had lately enjoyed. Why, then? We had harmed no-one, wanted nothing but to be left alone. Why this? Subjection, humiliation, separation. Now starvation. God knew what next. Worst of all was this terrible caging. I decided with an unchristian passion that I hated the concept that had begun this barbarism, and the regime that enforced it. I hated the people and the entire country that suffered its existence. And I swore aloud I would never allow myself to surrender to them.

During that night I believe we passed Moscow.

Two mornings further on we had screeched and clattered to a halt at a small, grubby station consisting of an old building, a semblance of a platform and a part-fenced yard. Beyond the yard was a ditch with a wooden bridge and neglected-looking wood cabins on rough stone foundations. Not much to see, but we crowded, one after the other, to the window to look. A broken-down village. It was different from the endless sea of open plains, that was all. And the noise and the rocking had ceased, for a change. Rows of stacked timber ran parallel to the tracks on either side of the buildings and, beyond, women were working the ground with picks and spades. People! That *was* different. Our carriage had stopped opposite a dilapidated hut with patched-up windows, plainly still lived in, surrounded by mud and pools of water. Water!

'Look!'

We began the usual hammering and rattling on the door.

'Water!' we called in Russian. 'We need water. Our children are dying of thirst!'

Elderly women suddenly appeared beneath the window, bringing bottles and tins out of hiding from behind aprons. There were children dressed in rags, barefooted, with ancient faces. One small boy stretched out his skinny hand. 'Bread,' he whined. 'Give me some bread, in the name of the Lord.' Begging from us! Russians! A day or two ago I might have done differently; today, facing the boy, I could not refuse. This child was starving. Hate him? How could I? Or the silent women bringing water? How could anyone? I slipped one of my remaining stale rusks out through the window, tossed it, and then he was gone. Mrs Balter saw and nodded. I was glad no-one else had.

Trading went quickly. Money was passed out, and in its place we got a bottle of milk and some carrots. The carrots went to the children, and the milk to Peter, though he hardly cared for it any more.

As the children divided the carrots – with a selflessness and precision that brought tears to every adult eye, the older ones giving the younger the bigger portions – I turned from the window and went to the farthest corner, away from the excitement. The picture of the Russian boy would not leave my mind. That pale little, old-looking face.

Was there someone – anyone? – left to care for my children? Or were they, too, begging crusts and drinking water off the ground? I turned my back, put my head against the iron wall and wept. Silently, I hoped.

It was hot and humid, becoming unbearable. The little water I had had was making me damp with perspiration. My skin itched. Worse, several hours ago I had finished my last half-cigarette.

∎

My attitude to Russia and Russians might have modified where small boys and old women were concerned. In the main, and certainly towards NKVD officers, it had not. It took a scant second to decide that. Just for a second, when the commandant had appeared, I had hoped. The teetering moment had passed and now he was merely an enemy.

No-one had asked me to assume the position of spokeswoman. I can only think that I was goaded by his supercilious attitude – I can't abide people who don't look you in the eye – and his stupid question. Besides, few of us spoke Russian, and the others had reason to guard their tongues. Being childless gave me licence to be rash.

'We have not, and never have had, any lice.' I kept my eyes from the ointment-smeared heads and matched him in haughtiness. 'We most certainly have no medicines, however, and the children are sick from the heat and lack of water. We have no leader. We have no need of one.'

'You will be given warm food.' A little more respect? I made a mental note. 'Make a list, the children separately, and choose a representative.'

He turned and left, leaving behind not only a sickly smell but, to our intense delight, an open door.

'Look!'

How marvellous is light and air. How little we need of God's bounty to give us joy. The first time in two days.

'Sh! Someone might hear and close it.'

'We'd better make out that list.'

■

Free use of Estonian Christian names has always been a familiarity reserved for high levels of intimacy. Even in our circumstances we observed the courtesies of custom, and called each other 'Mrs Falk' or 'Mrs Balter'. Except for me. Possibly because I was 'single', largely because of the idiosyncrasies they noted, the children early on found out and used my given name. I remained 'Ann' to most, young or old, Estonian or otherwise, for ever after.

■

The first nomination came from one of the eight-year-olds. 'Aunty Ann can speak Russian. And she smokes and wears pants,' she added. 'Let her be leader.'

I had never before been voted into office on a platform of cigarettes and slacks, but as there were no other acceptances I agreed. Gladly. Now, perhaps, I would be in contact with others on the train: there must be some purpose in wanting a delegate. Maybe I would meet the others, maybe get news of outside. Even – my heart beat faster – a chance of escape!

I made the list. Soon there was a call for all leaders to take with them buckets for water, pots for food, and their lists. I asked Tintooth, by shouting from the doorway and making elaborate gestures, if I could take Enn with me. He nodded. I thanked him, and he hawked and spat, embarrassed at being such a good fellow.

A queue was already forming next to the train. Two people were getting out from each carriage. So Tintooth had granted no special favour at all. Good fellow my foot! There were thirty-three or thirty-four carriages, I counted, of which we were number twenty-eight. Allowing twenty-five people to each carriage, I calculated there were something like eight hundred and fifty people on the train. Almost all were women and children, the few men apparently those who would not be classified as heads of families.

My feet were on the ground for the first time in eight days. I marked time, slowly, feeling it under me. I freed my eyes out into the distance, to the wide horizon and the sky. It was a clear blue sky with a few fluffy clouds. Down here was flat ground covered with dry grass, nothing on it but us, our train, and the line running forever ahead and behind.

In the queue I saw several friends and acquaintances. Among them were two men from Rakvere, but we could speak only to those next to us in the line.

'No talking there. *Davai!*'

The guards, most of them middle-aged, probably too old for active military duty, had rifles slung loosely over their shoulders. They busily shuffled us on. '*Davai! Davai!*' Why the hurry out here, where there was plenty of time and space, we never discovered.

Large coppers had been set up in a big log-walled building, a barn of a place with ticket-window-sized holes cut out of the near side. The guards called it a 'diner'. Through the windows we were ladled out our first ever rations of porridge made from millet and peas, one serve per registered person, with oil and tomato puree poured over. We were also given our ration of black bread for three days: nine-hundred grams for each child, fifteen-hundred per adult, roughly measured. We were then expected to move on, but I held my ground. Two surly men swore and waved us on with their ladles. I told them we had thirteen children with us, and must have water. I was cursed as I had never been, as only Russians know how to curse, with a self-conscious Enn beside me. Fortunately he did not understand the words, though the meaning was plain. They tired of this when I refused to budge. We got our bucket filled, and Tintooth escorted us back, even helping to carry the pail of boiling water.

On the way we were watched by a crowd of women in tattered work clothes; local, obviously, though we could not see where they came from. They were railway workers, our future experience would tell us. Russian navvies. Although the guards tried to shoo them off, they stayed nailed to the ground, looking us up and down with frank curiosity.

'*Davai!* This isn't a stage show!'

It must have been that and more to these simple people. That they had never seen women in slacks was apparent by their pointing and nudging. Pretty dresses took their eye too, and silk summer blouses. Our hairdos were still holding up, and our footwear had not yet been sold and 'eaten'. All claimed attention.

The porridge and bread were not received with half the same delight as the water. Only Mrs Nommik and her children ate heartily. They had used their food earlier than the rest of us and had hardly any left now. I also had very little, but I was not so interested. We had water. The door was open. Things could be worse.

We decided to try and get aid for the children. Enn and I had heard on the grapevine that there was a special carriage for the sick. Perhaps there was even a doctor on board. I called the nearest guard, who promised to ask the commandant, then went away. We did not see him again. I asked Tintooth. He, too, left, but soon returned.

Tintooth marched straight to our doorway. Silently, distrustfully, we watched his approach. He was a tall man with wiry hair and uncouth speech. He stood framed in the doorway with his cap pushed to the back of his head, looking uneasy, teeth gleaming. 'Yer can get out and have a walk,' he said. He seemed to be peering in all corners at once. 'All of yer.'

I relayed the message. Most heard it apathetically.

'Hurry up now.'

'You mean we have to?'

'Them's the orders.'

'But what about the children? They're sick.'

He shrugged.

'And how about that doctor? Is there one here?'

'I don't know. You'll have to wait and see. *Davai.*' We could get no more from him. 'Out yer get.'

This time I left the carriage with the others, all except Mrs Balter and Peter. Tintooth tried to shift her but she refused point blank and he gave up. We were formed in a column and marched behind the station to the edge of the vast plain. There was no sound, no sight or sign of animal life outside our ranks; and here we were, far out in the middle of nothing, being moved along slowly by armed men. It was uncanny. We all felt it. We talked in whispers, throwing glances at the train, now all of two hundred metres away, and at the men with guns. One of them unslung his rifle carelessly and we fell silent. He hefted it back on his other shoulder.

'Halt!'

We halted, standing quietly in fearful silence. Nothing happened for long drawn minutes. A train appeared from the other direction, puffed in, stopped, and spilt a few passengers carrying parcels wrapped in cloth. They disappeared, Lord knows where. The train chuffed off and the order came to march back. We breathed again.

With the station cleared of possible contacts we were allowed in the building. Peter's mother somehow managed to buy a bottle of milk. There was nothing else to be had, and no news.

Back at the carriage I asked Tintooth again, 'What about the doctor for the children?'

'There ain't no medicines anyway,' he said soothingly. 'So what good would a doctor do yer?'

He was a simple fellow, not much affected one way or the other by suffering. He was certainly not prepared to go out of his way to help, but at the same time wanted not to be disliked. A fence-sitter. What he said was no doubt true.

'Where are we going?' I asked.

There was clearly nothing to be gained by pursuing the subject of the doctor. I was surprised he answered this one.

'Novo-Sibirsk for the time being,' he whispered.

'How long?'

'A week at least.'

■

Our fears confirmed, we now became preoccupied with winter clothing. There was no point in deluding ourselves. Siberia was no place for the few clothes we had thrown into bags at the height of summer, and obviously we were not going to be home before winter. Siberia's climate was common enough knowledge. I was better off than most, thanks to Mother and our captain. The parcel Mother had sent was packed with the most unlikely items. It now seemed possible – and events proved it so – they would be welcome. The mothers of the smaller children were particularly depressed. We 'single' women did what we could to raise their spirits, but with little heart and less success. The icy chill in the very name of 'Siberia' pervaded the warm, smelly atmosphere of our carriage and stayed through another baggage search – this would be

41

the third or fourth: for what, we didn't now bother to ask – until well after midnight when, each in her accustomed place and each with her own dark thoughts, we awaited the mercy of sleep.

I had just dozed off when the train shuddered violently. We slid across the floor. The engine whistled, and the normal rocking changed to a frantic side-to-side sway. The train squealed and clanked to a stop. From the window I could just make out the shape of the landscape: flat, marshy, with water lying about. All was still. We had the feeling of a tilt to one side. A half-hour or so later we moved on again. Enn, who had jumped up with me to the window, told me to go back to sleep: he would keep watch.

When I awoke at daylight, Enn was still at his post, squatting by the window, unable to move. His legs had gone to sleep and had to be massaged painfully back to life before he could get down. Once off the plank he was little better off: the greater part of floor space was used in caring for the little ones; most of what was left was women's territory. The children's space was increasing as the gastroenteritis spread. Baby Peter had it now. Enn stood against the wall, moving his legs until they were back to normal before finally sliding down to sleep in a sitting position, legs stretched straight out in front.

The vigil had been for nothing. He had not seen a thing. And we did not stop again for two whole days and nights.

■

'Look! Look, a city!' Mai was calling from the window as if she'd seen a fairy castle. 'A real city! Perhaps we can get water and food.'

The train was slowing. It stopped quite near a passenger platform. We were in a sizeable town with a big station, near a large square. We could see the square plainly over the extended platform, and the tracks beyond. In the middle was a post with a loudspeaker on top, and around it buildings two and three storeys high. There was even a kiosk. Like Mai, we were impressed. But would they let us out?

Our water was gone. The children were restless. The carriage was polluted with their bowel-storms and the air was foul. There was nothing to clean with. We chewed spasmodically on the black bread carefully dried by Mrs Balter The sleepless nights had been trying, the untreated sickness pitiful to watch. But many times worse than either was the thirst.

The door opened. We hadn't even thought to bang on it.

'Leaders, get out for bread. Bring vessels for soup.' A tinny voice hailed us from the loudspeaker, repeating instructions over and over. 'Get out for bread. Bring vessels for soup.'

Enn and I climbed down after commandeering the biggest bag and pots we could find. The area between carriage and platform was splotched with spilt pea porridge, tomato slush and excreta, partly dried in the sun. Similar trains had been here before, some recently. Perhaps our men, I thought, but decided to say nothing.

We picked our way carefully over the fly-infested sleepers – though far from pure, the air we were breathing was better than that of the past two days – to where a queue was already forming. We angled swiftly across for position.

'*Davai! Davai!*'

We were stepping over the final track to the end of the queue when the loudspeaker again blurted to life. We had not noticed: the guards had been strangely quiet.

'Attention! All hear me! Citizens, members of our undefeated Red Army, all you imperialistic exploiters and suckers of blood.' The nonsense went on for several seconds. I glanced at Enn, who was impassive. I had forgotten he did not understand Russian. 'Our country has been violated. War has begun. We must defend our *rodina* [birthland] from the invaders.'

I dug my fingers into Enn's arm. 'War, Enn! There is war!'

They will surely be defeated, they can't withstand invasion. No more of this. We'll be free to go home again . . .

'*Davai! Davai!*'

The words did not touch us now. We could look at the guards with eyes of life. All the faces near us took on the same shine as the whispered word passed.

We moved on excitedly in spasmodic jerks – war or no war, we were still hungry, thirsty, and dependent – passing a small tended lawn next to the station building. There were women and children there, perhaps thirty or forty, in drab cotton coats, most of them asleep with their cloth-wrapped bundles as pillows. We looked at them, wondering; but said nothing. Groups of soldiers were standing about talking animatedly, swearing, looking our way malevolently. We were the imperialist bloodsuckers now, no longer just another trainload of deportees. Our status had changed. We were enemy.

Our progress was quick for a start, and down. A basement under the station turned out to be a storeroom. We bottlenecked at the stairs. Enn and I were last in the queue, despite our short cut, and it looked as though we would be here some time.

'Who are the women and children up there?' I asked a guard. Not Tintooth this time, but one who had been reasonably talkative on other occasions.

'Travellers waiting for a train,' he said. 'Don't be so inquisitive.'

None of the Estonians had time for talking. They could not get back quickly enough to pass the news. We shuffled on in silence. Finally only Enn and I remained, and our bread was in the bag. There was still one loaf left over.

'Ah, take it for yourself, *grasdonotska* [little citizen],' said one of the men to me.

'You'll be glad of a bit extra,' said the other.

'My bread is in the bag with the others, thank you,' I said. I was not going to take their miserable favours. I was at least their equal. Soon now I would be as free. 'I don't need it.'

They looked at me and at each other with astonishment. Mad! One of them picked up the loaf and thrust it firmly, if unceremoniously, under my arm, muttering an obscenity. 'Lunatic foreigners!' sighed the other.

I put my nose in the air and marched out firmly, Enn following. We had the extra bread, and we had neither taken it, begged for it, nor given thanks for it. Victory! But Enn's expression reflected the Russians' astonishment rather than my triumph. I shook my head. Men!

The broadcast had finished, but we had heard all we needed. War meant Germany versus Russia, and who couldn't predict the outcome of that? The Germans, in no time. They might not give us our independence back immediately, but there wouldn't be this. We would see our families, our homes, our men again. Passing the kiosk on the way back I noticed Estonian brand cigarettes displayed. 'Mikado'. 'Eva'. An omen! Estonia forever! I longed for one.

Near our carriage, Mr Pedusoo, from further up the train, was dawdling. He was waiting for us and smiled as we approached. I suddenly realised we had forgotten the water, but no matter; Mr

Pedusoo had three cigarettes and a whispered message: 'Share these. War, my dear! See you soon in Rakvere.'

We spent half the night in discussion. The possibilities were all favourable. Whatever happened, our lot must improve.

Mr Pedusoo was to be a source of information again; it seemed he was a natural collector of it.

■

In the morning we were still in the same place, no more than slightly dampened. Next to us was another train, carrying tall gaunt men in sheepskin jackets and high hats, women with veils and scarves, and dull-eyed children. They were in a worse state than we. They were defeated.

I called in Russian, 'Who are you? Where do you come from?'

A man answered but I couldn't understand his dialect. Bessarabian, we thought. I tried to pass on the good news, to tell him about the war. He did not understand. We all tried, but there was no contact. Their train moved on before ours, and we never saw them again.

Tintooth opened the door. 'Yer can get water now.' He stopped, and looked again. His little eyes widened in amazement. Everybody was cheerful. We were full of hope, even for the baby, who had lain without whimpering all morning. We neither wept nor complained nor even asked for a doctor. He stared suspiciously.

'Where?'

'Over there. You'll find it.'

The puzzled guard was reluctant to leave. He was trying to peer in, to find a reason. Enn picked up the bucket while Tintooth lingered.

'Why are we still here?' asked one of the women. I translated.

Tintooth shrugged, put out by our euphoria.

'Does anybody know what they're doing?'

He glared without answering.

'Can we get cigarettes?'

'No.'

He went off in a huff.

Enn and I went for the water. As soon as we had returned, the door was locked and bolted by a still puzzled, perhaps cautious,

Tintooth, who left again immediately.

He was back about midday. 'Who wanted cigarettes?' he demanded.

No-one answered. It was our turn to be suspicious.

'I'll get 'em for yer.'

I gave him ten of my hundred-and-twenty roubles and asked for cheap ones. Some of the women said I was foolish – and I agreed – but I desperately wanted a smoke. It was worth a try at ten roubles.

In the evening he was at the door again. This time he had with him several cartons of 'Paratroopers' at ten kopeks a pack, plus matches and five rolls of 'Lifesavers'. Incredible! I could have hugged him as he stood showing his great metal teeth. He was all but wagging his tail. He even apologised for the quality of the cigarettes. 'But with these yer get a lot more.'

I thanked him extravagantly and gave him a pack for his trouble. He looked more pleased, even a little embarrassed. I offered him the change but he would not hear of it. We were both in such good humour that I tried asking if he would leave the door open.

'All right. Only because of the children, though!'

I wondered about offering him money to let it stay open while we travelled, but discussed it with the others and agreed with the majority that it would be too risky. He did not seem to like bribery. Perhaps the penalties were severe. Later we found that the people in the next carriage had already travelled for several nights with theirs open, at the cost of a few roubles.

We talked a lot again that night; we smoked and even sang. We resolved to rename our favourite guard Silvertooth. Good old Silvertooth! We told fairytales to the little ones. We were fed. We had water. War had begun. And there were enough cigarettes for all the smokers for days.

■

We left before dawn. At lunch time we pulled off into a small siding while several army trains passed us, each crammed with young soldiers. There must have been many thousands. This was sobering news. So many men already mobilised so far from the front? So many units armed and ready? And so soon? Were they better prepared than we'd thought? Sobering, indeed.

Towards evening there was another stop, and heated talk out-side in Russian and Estonian. We heard a woman crying. Another louse hunt perhaps? But our door remained closed, we remained ignorant, and clanked off again, not stopping for another full day and half a night.

We hammered routinely. The bolt slid out. The bar dropped.

'What are you banging for?' A cheerful Silvertooth appeared. 'Can't you see I'm opening up?'

'Where are we?'

'*A vot!* – Well now! – In Omsk. Come out and get water.'

The grapevine here carried news of a different kind. A young woman in a carriage a couple up from ours had cut the wrists of her three-year-old son. She had been withdrawn for the past few days, they said, weeping when the boy had asked for water. Her companions had been alerted by the child's cries in the night, but they had only been able to stop her doing harm to herself. At that unexplained stop, mother and child had been taken off, the boy already dead for several hours.

The smiles of the past day or two vanished. We were reminded of where we were, not of where we would like to be. And of *what* we were – eight hundred head of cattle dependent for water, for our very existence, on an engine driver's whim. We were reminded of Siberia, our lack of clothing and food, the loss of our children, husbands, homes. A normal, healthy boy and his mother: one dead, one insane. Whatever our future, good or bad, this was our present. Enn looked murderous. I had a great urge to throw myself down in frustration, to scream and kick, to destroy something. Something Russian. Anything.

Instead, still trembling, we hurried along with the others in the chain of bucket carriers. I remembered the woman vaguely. She came from Narva, a particularly attractive girl. Nobody blamed her. Nobody in the line said what everyone thought. It is unchristian to wish for death, unfair to lay criticism on those who stopped her when any of us would have done the same. Enn and I decided not to tell our companions. Baby Peter's condition seemed hopeless, his mother already desperate; we did not want a repeat in our carriage.

We stayed at Omsk all day and the urge for violence slowly settled. Direct action was out of the question. The bottled-up fever cooled, and gelled into serious thoughts of escape. So far, though we had idly discussed the yearning, this had been out of the question. For the others it still was. But Enn and I, thrown together and broadened in outlook by our duties, simmered in a corner, and speculated. The guards were fewer now, doubtless because of the immense distance between us and home, and they were no longer carrying guns. Supervision was lax. The opportunity seemed close at hand, even if nothing else was. We decided we would be ready should the moment come; preparation, with the resources at hand, would be practically nil. What would happen after we got away – if we got away – was in the lap of the gods.

■

Nervous tension ran high. This could be it. We were well away from the train; close to cover; no guards close. We were in the queue and nearing the supply for the evening water, eyes constantly checking all the enemy within range. Enn was as jumpy as a young colt. My mouth was dry.

A young couple approached from the thin crowd of watchers, but company was the last thing we needed, and we turned away. They greeted us tentatively. In Estonian! Our heads flicked like puppets'.

They looked harmless enough. Indeed, they looked typically Estonian: fair hair, light complexions, distinctive among the darker local people.

I returned the greeting suspiciously. In Russian.

'Where are you from?' the young man asked.

He was persisting with Estonian. I thawed a little. 'Rakvere,' I answered.

'Where are you going?'

'Siberia.' Where else?

'Are you sure?'

'We think. Novo-Sibirsk for a start.'

'Why?'

What an odd question.

'Why do you think? We're prisoners.'

'Prisoners?' Their shock appeared genuine. 'But you're all Estonians.'

'Yes.' He had said 'Estonians' as he would have said 'friends'.

'We were told you were being evacuated from the war zone.

Why should you go to Siberia?'

There was little more to say. We told them briefly how we had come thus far, and why. It seemed important that they should know, despite our anxiety to be rid of them. It was getting dark, there were many people milling about, and guards were scarce. Those we saw were uninterested. This would be the time to try. And we were making no headway convincing these two.

'What about you?' Enn asked. 'What are you doing here?'

'We live here. Our parents lived on the Estonian border. They were deported in 1918.'

They seemed to accept this as normal. Perhaps it was.

'We want to escape,' I said bluntly. We were getting close to the tanks. Our new friends were keeping pace with us, with no sign of leaving, and such an opportunity might not occur again. Should we try now? It was the next few minutes or not at all.

'Oh no!' the man said quickly. 'Dressed as you are, and without a passport or identification card – you don't have them, do you? Or a lot of money?' I shook my head. 'You wouldn't get far.'

The girl cried. My enthusiasm faltered. Enn still fidgeted to be off. I had thought our dress would pass, as we had worn our most sober clothes. No slacks for me. Enn had put extra warm clothing on under his jacket, and I had brought an overcoat to help us keep warm on our long hike. We had on our sturdiest shoes, and had tied all our money around our necks, out of sight.

'You can stay a night with us if you try it,' the girl said through tears. 'Only one, though.'

It was brave of her, and probably did more than anything to dampen our hopes. She made it sound so impossible. Money, identification cards, passports. What else hadn't we thought about?

She told us where she lived, obviously distressed, I think more for us than for herself. We hesitated, and were lost.

'*Davai! Davai!*'

The bucket was unusually heavy on the way back. Uncomfortably warm and clumsy in my overcoat, weak from hunger and thoroughly dispirited, I spilt some near-boiling water on my leg. The wooden bridge seemed endless as I trudged on, trailing the others. Even Enn had left me behind.

'What are you stumbling for? *Davai!* Quicker, you fascist slut!'

My cup was full. I put the bucket down, slopping more scalding water on my feet. 'You call yourself a man?' I screeched. Tears of pain, rage and frustration nearly blinded me. All I could see was a Russian guard. He might have had a machine-gun pointed at me. I didn't care. 'Do you think you're half a man? Bullying women and children with a gun in your hands? Speaking to me like that?'

I could have gone on, but I was tired, and he forestalled me. He picked up the bucket and, grinning, carried it the rest of the way, lifted it in to the wagon and helped me up the step.

5

WINGS OF THE ANGELS

We could walk freely on the platforms now, drink from the tanks and wash our hands. There were no guards. Just before nightfall several days beyond Omsk we stopped at another small, clean station to let several more troop trains through. Depressing enough. And the further slackening of security obviously meant escape was considered impossible or useless, which was understandable, as the journey had gone on at the same unhurried pace for so many days across flat uninteresting country. No-one bothered to look out any more.

On my way back to the carriage, at one of these stops, I stumbled over a bolt and picked it up. Enn said it was the one used for locking the door from the outside. It could well have been, as I had found it close by. I hid it in my suitcase out of sheer perversity. It wouldn't prevent them shutting the door, but it would create a fuss. Let them look for it. Let them find another. This one would go down the hole when we were under way.

'Have you seen the bolt?' Tintooth duly asked.

We helped him search.

'*Ladna* – never mind – we'll leave the door open for a while. It's a bit stuffy in here anyway.' And off he went.

We changed Tintooth's name from time to time and mood to mood. He would have to do something special before earning 'Silvertooth' again. We had found out about our neighbours' door.

I felt minor triumph at my first act of stealing, and it had a happy sequel; we travelled the whole night with the door open. Several of us spent the dark hours sitting silently in the wide opening looking at the clear-shining stars. Outside the box, outside Russia, in our own familiar sky. Next morning the door was closed again and locked with a new bolt. The stolen one would travel with me until I threw it on the last I would see of Siberian soil on my way back to Estonia, seventeen years later, a purely private gesture witnessed by no other soul.

Many local girls were at the station to wave the soldiers past. They had taken time over their appearance, which was unusual. Not to be outdone, we – after a brief meeting, in a fit of contrariness – tidied our own hair, smartened our step, smoothed our clothes, put on airs and paraded. We earned more than shocked glances and laughter at our slacks; we also attracted admiring looks from the soldiers, and satisfying female envy at the quality of our shoes and clothes. When the soldiers had gone, we talked. They had called us evacuees, and it was soon apparent that that was what they were themselves – Russians from the western border areas, not locals at all. This gave us something to ponder about back in the carriage. Why were young Russians being evacuated to Siberia? Why so soon? And what about those thousands of soldiers? Was the war not going well for them?

On we rattled, day and night all the same now. Those who had food scraps left were embarrassed to eat, and did so in the dark. Those who had none pretended not to see. Nobody wanted to talk, think, or be reminded of anything; but it was impossible to be oblivious; the children saw to that. 'Why do we have to stay in this box? Where are we going? Why isn't Daddy here? When will we be home? When can we eat?' Our only answers were the fairytales, and they were losing appeal by the day.

■

Early one morning we rolled into another city. It had been two weeks. We had started to mark off the days on the carriage wall in Rakvere. Two before we had left, nine to Omsk, another five since. Two weeks and two days since we had had a bath or washed our clothes. The grime showed and, no doubt, smelt.

The suburbs we passed through were dirty and untidy. Fences were broken. Everything was drab: houses, the few people we saw, the occasional item of clothing on a backyard line. Even the ground was dull and dry, with no flowers and little greenery. We crawled to a halt with no station in sight. We banged and yelled, and the field outside the window looked back blankly. The door remained shut the whole day and night.

Mrs Lohvard offered me a hunk of salami. I hesitated, as she had her two children to feed. But she seemed to have plenty – she had begun with a bag full – and I had had nothing but my bread ration for five or six days, nothing at all for twenty-four hours. I accepted. Enn gave me a piece of dried bread. And, with the last of my water, a hint of green slime on the bottom of the bowl, I had a memorable breakfast. From our window we could see dusty streets in the middle distance closely lined with bleached grey wooden houses, all with the carved eaves peculiar to central Russia. No trees, shrubs, telephone poles or power lines. There were large shed-like buildings with smoking chimneys close by: factories, we supposed. Groups of women came and went from them, mostly dressed in patched, quilted jackets despite the summer heat. They were out of earshot.

Tintooth came in the evening.

'Open this damned door, come on, open up so we can get some water!'

'You know where we are?'

'If you won't let us out at least bring us some water.'

'Novo-Sibirsk.' He said it with pride.

'How nice. Here, take the bucket. *Please*, if that's what you're waiting for, bring us some water.'

Our lack of curiosity upset him, which served him right. Perhaps it was his home town. He brought the water with a scowl, locking the door immediately after handing in the bucket. Definitely a Tintooth day.

We were more interested than we had let him see. Where from here? Guessing games. We knew Novo-Sibirsk was on the Ob River, but not much else. What next? I think each of us secretly had 'Home!' in the back of the mind. This was all too unreal to continue; someone somewhere – perhaps in Novo-Sibirsk – must clear up this nonsense and pack us off back the way we had come. But no-one said this aloud.

There was excitement as it became clear to the children that, whatever else happened, we would have to leave the train. In the whole carriage, only little Peter and, to a lesser extent, his mother, remained untouched. He lay motionless on her lap, his eyes closed. Aware of his approaching death, she did not put him down for a moment; neither would she let us nurse him.

I would have sold my remaining cigarettes quite early in the night for a sleeping pill. Later, I'd have traded my soul for a few hours' release. It was one of the worst nights. In daylight it was possible to forget for a time; we could help, be cheerful, even have fanciful fits of hope as we busied ourselves and fed the children fabrications. The nights belonged to ourselves, however, to sleeplessness and despair. With my head pressed against the plank wall I was shaking with suppressed sobs when I felt a touch on my shoulder. 'You too, Ann?' It was Peter's mother, Ella. She put her arms about me. Her comfort, in the extremity of her own suffering, soothed me more than any drug. She had faced her realities. I had yet to do so. We sat together and closed our eyes.

There was abnormal movement when I awoke. Everyone was tidying up. Bedding had been cleared from the shelves, belongings packed, loose articles bundled. The children were gathered at the window, dressed and combed. I was surprised and annoyed by how long I had slept. 'What's going on?' I asked. Surely I could not have slept through Tintooth, and the door was still shut. 'Why are you all packing?'

Nobody seemed to know. There had been no direction.

I moved to the window to look out. Helju, fair and five, looked at me reproachfully. 'Auntie Ann! Don't you know daytime is the children's turn at the window? And you our leader!'

I looked over the children's heads but there was nothing to see. Only the same grey scene as yesterday. The building, the women. Now there were some bare-footed children, mainly small boys in dark shirts, pants halfway down their muddy, bare legs.

Soon we moved again, very slowly, no more than a crawl. An hour or more later we stopped. Beyond a narrow strip of land, we could see endless water gleaming flatly in the early morning sun. Our bodies prickled for it, but we stayed locked in our stinking closet.

■

The door opened. The train commandant entered, with his cold fish-eyed look at no-one and everyone. I held my peace, as did we all. 'Pack your things,' he ordered, 'and place them on the bank next to the track.' Place, not put. A sandy embankment raised the railway lines a metre or more above ground level. 'There's no hurry. You may stretch your legs, as long as you stay in front of the carriage.'

The children spilled out. They laughed, ran, and shouted, their memories blessedly short. How happy they looked. And how our hearts tightened that their freedom, their birthright, should be meted out in small doses by a miserable cold Russian as though he were granting a mighty privilege.

God's gift was now NKVD favour.

God, how could you let it be?

6

ON THE WATER

In the train we had dreamed of water – from a drop on parched lips to cool cupfuls; from a damp face-cloth to a plunge in clean sea – and the trickling streams and still lakes of Estonia, the 'land of the thousand lakes.' Now an endless stretch of quiet water with its little green islands seemed to mock us. So like home, so unlike it. We could only look at its sun-drenched surface and wonder where it would take us, dumped on the shore as we were, like a load of forest logs. It was peaceful and beautiful, yet I could not help remembering the words of the soldier arresting us: 'Don't think you're going on a summer holiday!'

We waited, wondered, and looked after the children, who soon tired of their games. And still we waited.

'It doesn't much matter which way we go,' was Mrs Lohvard's philosophy. 'It must be better than what we've been through already.'

∎

'*Davai!* What are you standing around for? Pick up your stuff and move. Get over to the gates there.'

We had seen the line of roofs, long and low, beyond the forward end of the train, apparently at the water's edge. They could only have been storage sheds. I had earlier tried moving along the embankment for a closer look. Enn, likewise restless, had joined me when he saw me leave the group. We did not get far, however, before a guard from farther up demanded to know where we had come from. Carriage 28. He had sent us back.

'*Davai!*'

Leaving the children and weaker adults to move at their own pace, we began lugging bags along the road to the landing gates four-hundred metres or so along a dusty track at first parallel to, and later diverging toward, the river from the railway. We shuffled back and forth for an hour until everything was transferred. I was for leaving my extra parcel – Mother's contribution – behind, but Enn insisted I might need it.

'But most of it's useless. Or duplicated. And it's so heavy!'

'You never know. I'll help you.'

Peter was scarcely breathing. He was the colour of milk, little blue veins showing, big eyes sunken. A couple of the other children were unsteady but they managed to walk. A visit from a woman doctor while we were on the move had left us with two white powders and a tin of the national ointment. No examination, no advice.

Enn and I, for want of something to do, and perhaps with some vague thought of sympathy for the next occupants, decided to clean out our carriage before starting off with the last of the baggage. The impulse was rewarded, for in the dark corner of the top shelf I found a heavy package of cooking utensils. It had been handed in at Rakvere for the Mrs Malla we never saw. The contents were voted to me, as I had found them and no-one else was interested. So I became the owner of a ladle, a spoon, a hand basin, a saucepan, a frying pan, an enamel mug, a primus stove and a small bottle of kerosene. I took them without much enthusiasm, already having more baggage than I could easily manage. We had no idea how valuable they would become.

Enn and I soon became fidgety again. Our duty to the group for the time was discharged, and we found sitting uselessly near a dying baby nerve-racking. We decided to slip off and explore, although we had been allotted a spot near the gates and forbidden to stray. I muttered something to the others about looking for a better place, though in truth we had no other motive than to get away from them all for a while. It had been a long time.

The huge open-roofed landing was a beehive. There were large groups of Latvians and other nationals, mostly women and children like ourselves, and a separate group of dark-skinned, dark-haired folk, whose language I did not recognise. There might have been two or three thousand people in all, grouped around baggage arranged in heaps by order of carriages. We must have been the last of at least four trains, and probably formed the biggest national group. Some of the units had brought pieces of furniture – they must have had advice – chairs, mirrors; I even saw a treadle sewing machine. Some of the people looked in good condition, others were worse than ourselves. A few were trying unsuccessfully to get into the harbour terminal building, a large timber structure surrounded by an iron fence, all under the same roof as the landing platform.

In the group of dark-skinned people was a fine-looking elderly man in a wheelchair.

'Where are you from?' I asked in Russian.

He replied in German. 'From near Tsernovits, Romania.'

'Romania?'

He turned away pointedly.

A Romanian who preferred to speak German! He must really hate Russians!

We pushed on through Babel. The loudest among the multitude of languages was Russian. They may not have had the numbers, but they were leaving no doubt who was on top. 'Come here!' 'Go there!' '*Davai!*'

Near the gate into the terminal was an old man sporting an old, black jacket and a red-trimmed cap that must have been stuck on the back of his head for years. It belonged where it was. So did he, and the three-day stubble on his wrinkled olive face. I put a rouble in his hand and asked if our ship was coming soon.

'Ship?' he cackled. '*A vot!* In an hour you'll be on a barge, that's what you'll be on.'

'What do you mean, a barge?'

'A barge is what I said. A barge is what I mean.'

'Will all these people fit on?'

'You'll soon see. It'll take you all right. Aye. We've seen 'em loaded before and sent up old Ob. Hundreds of 'em. Ever since '17.' He added, confidentially, 'Be quick getting a place near the forward hatch.'

'Where are we going?'

The ancient waved his hand into infinity and slipped through the gate. It occurred to me he had said nothing about any of those hundreds – each carrying thousands – coming back.

■

The gangway was lowered. A mass of people stirred.

They picked up belongings, urged on by shouting guards, and slowly converged on the steps, bottlenecking immediately.

From our site near the back of the landing we heard the hoot of a siren and the slow throb of an engine coming nearer. Over the heads of a listless confusion of people, beneath the landing roof-line, we saw the vague moving mass of a hull, slipping past, edging close, stopping. The harbour building blocked forward view, but we knew our transport had arrived.

Enn and I set off as planned, leaving most of our gear with the others. Using our elbows freely, we had little competition, no argument, and were among the first on board. Once on the wide, flat, open deck we picked our spot alongside the forward hatch. The old man was right. There seemed plenty of air here, a reasonable amount of light, the stairs were close by, and it was only a short walk to the lavatories.

I stayed guarding the spot while Enn went to get the others and the luggage. I chose these roles deliberately, overruling Enn with the excuse that he could carry more luggage, as I knew I could be tougher than he. Self-preservation was the thing now, good manners already relics of the past – as a new citizen of Siberia, perhaps I should say the 'decadent past'. With effrontery astounding even to myself, I set about dissuading others . . . Sorry! We had more children. They were younger. Sick with diarrhoea, at that. We needed this spot. We were here first. It's *ours* . . . I was prepared to battle, but the need didn't arise. There was no argument, only apathy, from the few who approached.

It was not until a couple of hours had passed, when most people and their chattels were aboard and more or less settled, that we noticed all our neighbours were Estonians. Where were the others? Where were the Latvians, Lithuanians, my crippled old gentleman from Romania? Enn went to look and found that our barge was being towed by a large motor ship. We had missed it in the crush when the dock gates were opened, having eyes only for our forward hatch. The ship was painted, with cabins and wash rooms, even a doctor on board. We cursed the old man with the cap. The early arrivals had been better informed. Now it was far too late to do anything about it. A lesson learnt. A rouble down the drain.

Peter's death was imminent. His mother was resigned to it.

She wished only for it to be over soon so her baby could be decently buried; we did not know what might happen once we were out on the water. Her silent dejection spread. Those around us hushed, talking little, and only in whispers. I, for one, had never been witness to death and I had more than one companion when it seemed I did hear the wings of the angel.

■

'You can get off for supper. Quick or you don't get none.'

We found the dining room, a large timber structure on stilts adjoining the harbour building. The interior was clean, the tables bare boards. We had to buy our food, a tin bowl of cabbage soup and a thick slice of black bread. The only utensils available were lacquered wooden spoons with flowers etched on them. I sat in a group of strangers, all women, and enjoyed eating. It was nice being without the children. The bread was satisfying, and the soup palatable, though I found a thick spoon difficult to manage.

I looked up at last from my empty plate. Nobody was in the least interested in me. On impulse I slipped the spoon in my sleeve, stood up and walked out. My second theft of retaliation. I now had one bolt and one wooden spoon and was surprised at the satisfaction it gave me to get such a little back; my own good cutlery had had to stay at our old apartment for the Russian tenants.

There was nothing to the barge but a flat deck some forty metres long, perhaps twelve wide. Below, on boards clearing the bilge and on the sloping plates of the hull, jammed between sharp-angled ribs, my fellow-travellers sought comfort. In the semidarkness I wandered away from boat and barge and stood alone on the edge of the wharf. Town lights across the river glittered in the distance, shivering on the water. Faint yellow blobs flickered from transports near by. My thoughts were far off, with my family. For a few precious minutes I had them to myself.

I was quite alone, as I had not been since that night before it began. I could have easily broken down. Realising this, I switched back to the present and, instead, looking numbly at those cold lights, the barge, the water, and listening to the silence, converted my thoughts to hostility. Two thousand people, a summer night, stars coming out. And there was silence. He was right, it was no pleasure cruise. How long I stood there I do not know. What frustrated impulse made me spit into the water I do not know either, as I had never in my life done such a thing. But I did. And a sudden movement next to me launched a second splat! on the river.

I jumped, mortified. A man! I felt myself blushing to the roots of my hair. I looked again, and it was Tintooth. 'You!' I burst out. Enough that he should encroach on my privacy, worse that he had seen my unlady-like performance. But to join in it! The nerve! 'You even have to follow me around here!'

It could have been even worse, of course. It could have been someone who mattered.

He mumbled and made a helpless movement with his hands.

'Do you have no semblance of pride?' I ranted on. 'An able-bodied man: a gaoler of innocent children! And now you want to track around spying on their mothers!' A little inconsistency was no obstacle to the release of a few inhibitions.

He spat again, let me go on for a time, looked cautiously about, then handed me his packet of cigarettes.

'Citizen, I am human too. I do what I'm told. I've seen what you've been through these last three weeks.' He swore in sympathy. 'And the children.'

I was uncertain. I shut up, my aggressive stance deflated.

'Do you have children?' he asked.

'Yes.' I took one of his cigarettes, and lit it from his.

'Here?'

'No.'

'You're lucky then.'

He spat in the river once more and disappeared, leaving me his cigarettes. Silvertooth. I never saw him again.

■

Before my foot touched the gangway I was reminded again: the soft crying of children, complaints of tummy-aches, smells of the results, calls for food and water. Everywhere the same. I had neglected my duties for a few hours. It was night now. A few more town lights, a few more flickers on the boats. My feet were lead weights.

Enn told me somewhat reproachfully that he had discovered a pantry in the centre of the barge. But it did not help much, he added: there was not a drop of drinking water to be had. We had been warned about the river while on the landing and forbidden

62

to drink from it. That glorious vision was no more than a mirage in the desert. We managed a mug of well water from an elderly Latvian woman, dividing it among the children. There were thirteen of them, however, and the drop each seemed to make them thirstier. We made beds for them on deck, and sat talking in whispers while they slept, hoping for relief in the morning.

The noises of the night were different to those of the train. No rattle and clank, no rush of air. Now we had the hum of mosquitoes to keep us from sleeping, the footsteps and voices of people queuing for lavatories, water sucking and slapping at the side of the barge in occasional puffs of breeze. We were accustomed to the sob and the whimper of children; there were simply more of them here, and closer.

With first light came the order to go to the tow-ship for boiled water, which must have been brought or pumped on board in the night. Enn and I were late, although we hurried right off with our bucket and saucepans. The order had been passed from group to group, each one sending its delegates as the word arrived, and we were well back from its source. The queue was long when we reached it, curling and doubling back untidily. We had been in it some time, moving slowly, before we realised we were in line for the latrine. One line had become intertwined with the other. A man from our 'neighbourhood', seeing our plight, beckoned me to stand in front of him. 'I saw you start off before me,' he said. 'It's all right. Come in here.'

I moved across gratefully. As we settled, a big dark fellow roaming the deck came up, yelling. Everyone turned towards him.

'Don't you know things are done in order here?' He was a Latvian, speaking Russian, and did not bother to keep his voice down. 'It's my job to see they are.' He jerked his thumb. 'On the end of the line!'

I tried to plead my case. Others helped, but he would not listen. Outshouting us all, he began pulling me by the arm.

'Leave me alone. Get out of my way!' I banged pots and bucket down on the deck at Enn's feet, shook myself free, and ran. Devil take him! I would find someone in charge, get some justice. There must be somebody here in authority. I pushed down narrow stairs, ducking under a sign saying 'No Admittance'. Somewhere in the middle of the vessel, in a passageway with neat cabins on either side, I nearly collided with a man in a threadbare dressing-gown. He was too surprised to protest, and I was too incensed for caution.

'Are you the captain?' I demanded.

He muttered some prolonged obscenity that ended with 'engineer'.

'Where is he then?'

A shrug and a grunt.

'Is there a doctor?'

Another obscenity. 'In this shitboat,' he mumbled, 'there aren't even sailors, let alone a doctor.'

I began to see he was no more pleased at being here than I. I also noticed his Russian was accented, and cooled a little. Biting his head off would get me nowhere.

'Where are you from?' I asked.

'Riga.' Another Latvian. They must have co-opted a crew of them.

'Is there a captain on board then?'

'Have to be.'

'Where?'

'I think I've seen it on a door but I don't remember.' I preferred this one to the one on the deck. 'Maybe down there.'

I finally found, in the direction he pointed, the door marked 'Captain'. It was next to the galley, the door locked.

I knocked, then hammered, but there was no response. I waited. Having got this far I was not going back on deck without a showdown of some sort. Luckily, I didn't have to wait long.

'I am the spokesman for our group,' I explained civilly. 'In charge of water supplies. We have thirteen children in the group, half of them ill. A baby is dying. We must have water.'

'All right,' he said indifferently. He was a small man with a weathered face, unreadable eyes permanently squinted into slits. He didn't even want to know why I was down here. 'You can get it in the pantry. Any time. Means you won't have to queue. Use the stove there, too, if you like.' He nodded at the galley.

'Would you give me a note to that effect?' I asked.

He scribbled a few words on paper, hesitated, shrugged, and signed it. Clearly easier than arguing. Who was first to the water was of little interest to him.

Back on deck I showed the paper, grabbed Enn by the arm, and went down for water. The Latvian guard, catching our desperation, followed us to the galley. He even helped us back to the barge with the bucket.

'I'm sorry.' Seeing the children, the Latvian apologised. He had not always been a warder. 'I didn't realise – '

'Look,' called Enn. He held his dripping saucepans high.

But nobody turned. In our excitement we had not noticed the quietness.

'Is Peter worse?' I was suddenly anxious. 'We have good water for him.'

Not for Peter. He lay, wrapped loosely in a white cloth on a suitcase. The sun beat gently on him and a light breeze ruffled the material. The dead baby's mother sat on the boards next to him, holding one tiny hand. Mrs Balter sat alongside rocking and patting her shoulder.

I picked my way back to the captain. He nodded distastefully, as if I'd reported dog litter on his deck. An hour later two orderlies came from the settlement.

I gave Mrs Balter a little of the soil from Rakvere Mother had sent me. She wrapped it in a lace hankie and slipped it inside Peter's nightdress.

'What's that?' barked one of the men.

'Earth,' I choked. 'Earth from his homeland. Let him lie in it.'

He curled his lip in a sceptical sneer.

The other, the younger of the two, bent and took the white parcel gently in his arms. Big tears were rolling off his cheeks. Peter's mother crumpled soundlessly into Mrs Balter's lap. Somewhere away from us someone started singing quietly. 'Please take me, O Lord, by my hand . . .'

■

The silver expanse sparkled clear in the sunshine, too bright to look into. I moved to the other side. The cool blue water was sprinkled irregularly with flat islets of lush green, ranging from reed-clumps to great hillocks several hundred metres across. Sometimes, as the pilot carefully picked his way, we nearly touched on one or other side. The banks were walls of sweet-scented black alders in full blossom. I stood at the rail, dully watching the Ob slide beneath us. As with the Urals, I failed to appreciate its undoubted beauty.

We had been moving steadily for several days. It seemed we

had never been on the train. The air was filled with the sharp cries of children in distress. The queue for the latrine lengthened and shortened, never ended, day and night, and the breeze drifted its foul smell through open ports and hatchways into every corner of the vessel. You could wonder why we bothered using the thing. People in all stages of undress walked tiredly to the queue or ran with silent purpose. Children bleated for help, some older ones swore. Many failed to hold on and cried out in their frustration.

As shutting the ports was out of the question, the only relief was on deck. And that was no picnic. It was impossible to move across it without having to step over something or somebody. Somewhere in the middle, I came across an acquaintance. Mrs – ? Goodness, what was it? We had last met at a banquet in Tallinn. I could no more remember the occasion than I could recall her name. I could visualise the scene, though. It had been a sumptuous affair – evening gowns, furs, food, wine, speeches, dancing. The picture flitted across my mind, like a dream. I don't think she recognised me, but she held my arm and begged me to get a doctor for her children. I said yes and helped her change and pacify them a little, a boy and a girl squirming helplessly on the rough deck in soiled clothes. Everyone who was able gave aid, but there was little to be done except clean up, boil water, change clothes and calm the hysterical. *This* was reality. Our change from the stuffy train to open air had been disastrous. With closer contact, the gastroenteritis had spread rapidly.

I still had my permit to use the stove in the galley. There was nothing left to cook, a fact we tried to ignore, but we constantly got water from the river and boiled it, even for washing, until the kerosene ran low. Innocent though the river looked, who knew how many had passed this way, polluting it, as we were? The same permit allowed us water from the ship's supply, but that was now useless, as by the second day there was none left.

The morning after we had moved off from Novo-Sibirsk we were visited by a worried woman from a group near us. They were concerned about a young mother and her six-year-old child who had been very ill the previous day. This morning neither had risen. Both were lying completely covered under one blanket, motionless, not responding to calls. No-one there had the courage to look, so they had come to us. Enn was given the task. Poor Enn, put among us as a child, now approached as a tribal elder. When he gently lifted the blanket he found the mother alive, clutching to her warmth the already stiffened body of her little wax-faced, fair-haired daughter. I caught Mrs Balter's look of compassion for them all, especially for her son. She stayed back and did not interfere as he detached the dead from the scarcely alive.

The child's body was taken off into swampy land in the evening, wrapped in a blanket; there was no stopping earlier. A few people gathered at the rail but, before a prayer could be said or a hymn sung, they were roughly dispersed by guards. Russians. The Latvians had gone. The people went back to their places with lips trembling, fists tight, hatred vying with the sorrow in their hearts.

Next came a suicide attempt by a young bride of three or four months. She had spent the best part of two days crouched at the rail before venturing the climb over. After she was pulled back we formed a roster to keep an eye on her, and in a day or two she informed us brightly that she was expecting a baby. This would keep her so happy and occupied during the following weeks we came almost to envy her her delusion. She was beside me now, smiling secretly into the distance. I put my hand on hers to share her joy.

Miraculously there were no more deaths on our cruise down the Ob. We were travelling north, in the direction of its flow, though there was little current at this time of year.

My knowledge of the geography of the area was limited then, and my later recollections of the 'cruise' little more than a confusion of water and green islands, of mosquitoes hunting singly by day and in swarms at night, of suffering and hunger and misery, and, above all, stench. There were no newspapers, of course, and no radio. We were in a world and a time of our own, as day followed monotonous day. At least I learned that the Ob is a mammoth among rivers. From bank to swampy bank was farther than the eye could see.

We lined the rail, those who could stand and could find a few minutes with little to do, and thought of absolutely nothing. That was the least depressing way of passing time.

■

A shrill whistle from the tow-ship roused us. A settlement caught the sun and glinted it back at us. Soon there were fields, reclaimed from marsh judging by the retaining earthworks, and later, buildings, even two-storeyed ones, and people moving about on the shore. We drifted in closer.

'My God!' I whispered as my eyes picked out a tall woman standing apart from the drably clad peasant folk. She was dressed in flowing black and wore a large veiled hat. She could not be flesh, I kept saying to myself. She belonged to another world.

'This is Kolpashev,' announced the loudspeaker. 'You are allowed ashore for one hour.'

The first people were off before the barge had been manoeuvred against the wharf. I had pangs of conscience as I hurried off with them, leaving behind the sick and the weak.

The figure in black was moving towards us, holding her hat. She flew to us, crying. I stepped aside to watch her and marvel. She was a handsome woman, about my own age. She embraced and commiserated with us in several languages, berating the Russians, and welcoming and advising us. I had stopped, and so could not now escape her. She explained that she was Polish, deported from Warsaw six months ago. She was working as a stevedore. Her children were dead, her husband taken elsewhere.

Her dress was her last article of clothing. The hat was a twig of willow twisted into a circle to support a once-elegant black veil, which she wore for protection against mosquitoes. She was bizarre, but real, which boosted my shaky confidence in my own mental state.

In her rush of information, she was pessimistic about the war. From reports they had received, the Russians seemed to be winning. I found this upsetting, and questioned her further. Where did the reports come from? Did they have a radio? Papers? But she either knew little or would not say much. Otherwise she insisted on doing what she could for us, even offering me a piece of her veil. By this time my co-travellers had drifted off. I accepted and thanked her formally. I believe she had been a very talented woman, certainly an accomplished linguist. She was aristocratic, not yet demented, not entirely sane. I could not bear to stay with her long and wandered along the unsheltered landing.

Here I was introduced to the latrine, Siberian style: a room on stilts, roofless, doorless, the floor covered with straw. I mounted the steps and looked in. Around the walls, at eye level from halfway up the stairs, the straw was dotted with excreta. Next step was nose level. I stopped two steps from the top and looked about. No other such structure was in sight. Apparently the same one served both sexes. What on earth would you do if . . .

A man appeared from behind the near wall. I had missed him. Thank God I hadn't gone in. He stood aside courteously, looking down at me.

'When it's all covered,' the worker explained on seeing me hesitate, 'we'll bring in new straw. Plenty of time yet. You off the transport?'

He was tucking in his shirt as he talked. He finished and patted himself comfortable. Then, satisfied, he tightened his twine trouser-belt.

I used to be fastidious. It seemed such a long time ago. I nodded, not batting an eyelid. He was a friendly-looking fellow.

'What happens to us from here?' I asked.

'The devil knows.'

Not God, I noted, as in most languages. I thanked him and went in.

The barge whistled the recall. I noticed only then that people were returning along the bank with cigarettes and other parcels. Idiot! I had wasted time looking around, talking to people, asking questions. And my cigarettes were finished! Not one left, the last half-butt from Tintooth drawn till it had scorched my lip more than twenty-four hours ago. Every minute of that time I had craved a smoke, yet the opportunity had come and gone and I had not given it a single thought. What a fool.

And food! I had none of that either. The whistle went again, and – 'Davai! Davai!' – there was no time.

■

The barge shivered ever so slightly, creaked, settled, and tilted to one side. In a flash I was alive to the situation. They're going to sink us! I knew it. Those devious Russians! They've brought us all this way, gone to all this trouble, put us through all this misery, just to tow us out into this godforsaken wilderness of water and sink us in the night. Devious, sadistic people – it would take them to think up something like this.

It was exactly two o'clock and not another soul was stirring, perhaps for the first time in the voyage. Enn and his mother were the only others of our group on deck, the rest preferring the heat inside to the mosquitoes out. I didn't have the heart to wake them. It was Enn who had announced in great glee quite early in the evening that whole groups of Latvians and the Romanians seemed not to have returned from the shore leave in Kolpashev during the afternoon. There was room on both ship and barge. We could spread ourselves. Enn had also bought plenty of cigarettes; noticing I was not shopping, he had thoughtfully got me four packets. Room. Cigarettes. What next?

We had decided to sleep up top, despite the insects whining in droves, as it was more peaceful there than below with the children. What luxury, sleeping in the open! My new veil was a godsend. But now this. Was it all a sick Russian joke?

I tiptoed – was it slightly uphill? and was that a gurgle? were we settling already? – heading blindly for the rail. It was pitch dark and silent as the tomb except for a persistent stealthy rush of water somewhere. It would be a watery tomb, silent because the tug's engine had stopped. The tug, our tow-ship! I had forgotten it. Had it sneaked off in the night? Were we completely alone? I could barely see the luminous hands of my watch – as if time mattered – and the only noise was the quiet lap and gurgle of water below, perhaps already slowly flooding the lower compartments.

I would sit it out alone, in peace, and let them die the same way. There was no good alternative. In some sort of contentment, disturbed only by the knowledge that four precious packets of cigarettes would go down with me unsmoked, I went to sleep.

In the morning we were alive and afloat, straining gently at the line whose tautening must have disturbed me in the night. We had turned into one of the Ob's tributaries and stopped, probably to avoid the hazards of nocturnal navigation. We were in the mouth, heading into its turbulent current. Behind us was the main stream of the Ob. There was a lot of speculating, no news. Somebody was sure this was the Vasjugan River, but that did not tell us much.

I had a more pressing problem. While others were preparing breakfast from the food bought yesterday, I had nothing. Enn's mother came to my rescue with some dried bread and a slice of raw salt pork. She had a whole jar of it, and I did not take much persuading. Oh my lack of foresight! Not only yesterday,

I chided myself, but even before that. I had left a whole barrel of the same stuff in the cellar of our flat back in Rakvere. There was salt pork and plenty of other food reserves, all carefully stored for an emergency, but I had not recognised one when it came. I tried to console myself with the thought that at least the children and my mother would be able to make good use of it. As it happened, they never did.

■

The transport was moving in very much narrower and more dangerous waters now. The banks of the new river were never more than ten to twenty metres away on either side, muddy and slimy, with many branches and inlets, so it was difficult at times to tell river from backwater. The course was shown where necessary by markers, rough weathered poles sticking out of the flat water like forgotten fence posts in a desert. At times our ungainly vessel scraped its bottom on sandbanks or rumbled over submerged stumps and snags. We even got stuck on some big ones and had to back and fill and manoeuvre over or around them. Plagues of mosquitoes, flies, and bigger marsh flies attacked us as we went through swampy areas. These patches were covered with low, scrubby growth. As far as we could tell they were uninhabited by humans. The drier parts, where the banks were higher, though still seldom above deck level, gave an occasional sign of people in the way of small clearings and the beginnings or endings of narrow foot-trodden paths between shrubs and full-sized trees. Some had a log or two for a landing. We decided that they probably led to small settlements or collective farms. They were few, however, and deserted, and increased rather than lessened our sense of detachment from the human race.

It was July, the time of receding waters, and of course we were travelling upstream now, away from the mighty Ob. The Ob, the geography books tell us, is almost 5500 kilometres long and flows from the Altai mountains in central Asia north and west and north again to the Gulf of Ob, a 1000-kilometre inlet of the Arctic Ocean. In its middle course, through the vast Western Siberian Lowlands, it is accompanied hundreds of kilometres away on its left by the Irtish, another great river which joins the Ob 800 kilometres from its mouth. Between these two, south of their junction, are 250 000 square kilometres of swamp-land – an area six times that of Estonia, almost the total size of Germany – in the middle of which is the Vasjugan, draining eastwards into the Ob. In winter the marshes are ice-bound, hard, and may be crossed. In spring they are flooded, and called the Vasjugan Sea. In summer they are neither land nor sea and are utterly impassable. That is what the books say, and it is the truth. The knowledge would come to us as it had come to few geographers.

It was summer. The sea was drying up and, as the water level dropped, the Vasjugan River's course was becoming more clearly defined, its banks closer and higher, with each succeeding day. We could only see the banks, some shrubby growth, and the trunks of a few tall trees on higher ground.

■

One evening we stuck fast for several hours into the dark. The tug roared and panted as it pulled, pushed, shoved backwards, forwards, sideways, every way. Water swirled muddy in the lights. The order came, with the accustomed yelling and swearing, for everyone but the youngest children and the very sick to leave the barge, which presented a problem in itself. The tug moved to the side of the barge and pushed again, angling it nearer the bank for us to get off. The guards hollered constantly. If their vocal energies could have been usefully harnessed, we'd have been kilometres upstream. At last they dropped the gangway into the darkness well short of the river's edge, and to shouts of '*Aidaa*' – 'Go!' – we were driven into thigh-deep mud and water. From there we made nervously for the bank in pitch darkness.

A thick rope was attached to the front of the vessel and brought ashore. A sailor from the tug took up position at the front of the line, holding up a lantern. 'All of you now. *Davai!* Take hold and pull!' Surprisingly, our effort, helped and balanced by the puffing tug, was enough. The barge moved. For half an hour, while it still dragged its bottom, we drove on in the blackness through the driftwood-tangled morass. Our feet stuck. Sharp hidden twigs and branches lanced at our legs, mosquitoes at the rest of us. A guard walked beside counting, 'One-two-one-two,' and swearing in between. If a foot was slow out of the slime it was trodden on by one behind; if too quick, it was jabbed by a hidden spike; if a body stumbled it recovered quickly for fear of the consequences of not doing so.

Finally we were back on board, faces and necks swollen from bites, legs bruised and bleeding, hands blistered, clothes torn. Worse for some, they had lost their foot-wear in the sticky mud. Jaws clenched, souls fuming, we tried to tidy ourselves up. It was hopeless. We were weak to the point of exhaustion, our resources of clean water and clothing quite inadequate. I saw no tears, for all that, and there was no complaining because there was no-one to listen.

Only when drifting off to sleep, still dirty from the stinking mire, did I remember to be terrified of snakes, bears and wolves.

■

Early on a fine morning, another baby went ashore in a wooden crate, tucked under the arm of a guard who swung a spade in his other hand. A few watched in silence. He came back from behind the nearest shrub in a moment, too soon to have dug even the smallest hole in the softest ground. Someone groaned and pointed at the dry spade. We began a hymn, which was answered loudly in the Russian language's best invective. Between profanities, they yelled threats to leave us, too, in the swamp. More people sang. Even the most irreligious joined in, to drown the guards and score a point for defiance.

■

'Everybody ready to go ashore. *Davai*! Pack, and get your things together in groups.'

As if on cue, there was a change in the weather. The sun disappeared, the wind dropped right away and the sky darkened threateningly. Lightning pricked at the horizon's gathering gloom. After days of oppressive heat the air was suddenly cool, still and humid. Our paraphernalia, tied up in bundles, thrown into bags, jammed into suitcases, lay in piles on deck. Grouping was still by rail-trucks.

Most of us, in the sudden coolness, and to reduce bulk to be carried, had pulled on as many clothes as possible. It was easy enough, they hung on us like sacks.

Thunder was suddenly on top of us. Lightning cracked open the sky and rain poured down in huge drops. As we rushed to get our things under cover, the barge stopped. The tow-ship whistle blew.

The guard commander posed at the head of the gangway. 'Off! *Davai!*' he shouted through the rain. 'Off you get, devil take you, and be quick!'

A howl of protest went up through the roar of the elements. Some tried reason. 'Just till the rain eases.' A few refused to budge. The result was the same. We were herded off with prods and kicks like a flock of mangy sheep.

Being in the van of the protesters I was one of the first off, helped by an elbow in the ribs from a guard. I went bumping and sliding down a cataract of a gangway, clinging to my precious possessions. I stumbled off the bottom and landed in mud, my drenched bundles scattered around. The suitcase thudded beside me, thrown by the grinning guard. No helping hand here. It was be quick or lose something.

I found a small piece of higher ground with some clumps of spiny grass. Collecting my soaked things, I dumped them on it and went back to help with the children. It surprised me to realise I was ignoring others in trouble in my haste to find our own group. We were family now; spare energy was not for strangers. The pile of baggage grew. We parked the children on it and spread our only two raincoats and a couple of blankets over a dozen thin, shivering bodies. Through the murk we glumly watched the tug turn the barge back the way it had come and disappear. A single toot floated back.

A strong wind had sprung up, driving the rain at us and tugging at anything loose. While we held down the children's roof, Enn opened his mother's umbrella and gave it to Mrs Toome, who was sick, exhausted, and unprotected. The wind whisked the umbrella from her fingers, and flung it into the darkness of the storm. We watched it bound away, calling half-heartedly to the next group to stop it, weighing its undoubted value against the effort of chase. Like us, they didn't move.

7

'DON'T TRUST ANYBODY'

'Wait till I come back?' I pleaded. A waste of words. Where else would Enn – or any of them – go?

Several hours had passed since we had heard the derisive farewell whistle of the tug and still we huddled in the rain, getting colder. Nobody was going to move unless forced. Not until there was somewhere to go.

We had been told nothing; hadn't seen a guard, hadn't even heard one. Which meant there definitely *was* none.

Since there was nothing to lose, I decided to investigate. Who knew? Maybe we were due for a change of fortune. And in any event I felt a thrill of adventure, stepping out on my own. No barriers, walls, rails, or guards.

Enn had been first to see the light flickering from the edge of the forest, a hundred metres in from the river bank. That made it 'ours' if we wanted it. It was no use him going, he admitted, knowing scarcely a word of Russian.

The light came from the window of a tiny cabin. As I approached I saw a small entrance porch with steps and handrails leading up. Both porch and cabin floor were half a metre above the ground, supported on thick, round posts. The outside walls were made of evenly, though roughly, trimmed horizontal logs; the porch, steps and rails were of sawn timber. The wall logs projected alternately at the corners, neatly finished. There was pride in this building. But what mattered was that there was a roof.

I climbed the steps and stood under the roof, listening to the steady drum of rain. The porch floor was dry. Wind whistled through the fluted corners on either side, not touching me. I was in heaven.

I knocked on a door whose only lock was a simple thumb catch, waited a few seconds and entered. The whole cabin was the size of an apartment bedroom. No partition or floor covering. A family sat in front of a large Russian oven: an old man, an equally old woman and a boy of about twelve. They looked up, unsurprised, in the light of their *smoka*.

'We have no cover,' I burst out. 'We are in the rain. Children too, some of them sick. And they are all soaked and freezing.' It occurred to me that they could refuse. 'Please! Could we put them in the porch? Out of the rain and the wind?'

The old man rose immediately, unhurried. He needed no explanations. He knew we must be under surveillance and he was not a waster of words. 'I'll find out from someone in charge,' he said, and passed by me into the storm.

The woman got up just as quickly. There was no authority high enough for her. It was her home. 'Bring them in!' she cried. 'Bring those poor children in! We can't leave them out in that weather.'

Her Russian, like her husband's, was scarcely intelligible to me. But there was no doubt about her message. I ran back.

The old woman's wrinkled face shook in sympathy and her slanted eyes softened with kindness as she greeted the children, patted and fussed over them, crooning in a weird sing-song. 'My dear little ones – my little doves – come and get warm. Come with me. Come into the dry.' She trotted back to the shore to help carry bundles, her short body strong and sure on the treacherous surface. We stowed our possessions on the porch, under it, under the house, under the eaves, wherever we could out of the rain. My large suitcase had been at the bottom of the pile. The sides were dented and water had run in. I tipped it to let the water squirt from the cracks.

I went to help our hostess. She was everywhere, beginning with the children, herding them in a cluster near the oven, alight even at this time of year. This single source of warmth in the building was straight out of Pushkin or Tolstoy; I could see it in any of a dozen stories I remembered from schooldays: a clay-walled box in the corner, about two metres square, chin-high, with a single square opening facing out across the room. From where I stood by the doorway, the glow from the open fire-pit shone between the children standing in front of it. Bare arms stretched out to the heat as clothes were thrown up on the solid warm oven top to dry. The old woman clucked about them while the rest of us handled the bags, crooning, working, scolding. By the time all the baggage was under cover she had tea ready. Then she produced sugar, followed by an assortment of cups and mugs. She saw to it that everyone from the youngest up had some of her hot brew. Never was tea better.

The old man returned. 'The horses have come,' he said. 'You'll be taken to where you'll sleep the night.'

'They will not,' his wife said firmly. 'They'll stay here.'

'But they can't!' He was worried, probably with good reason.

'You go back and get permission if you like.' She said 'permission' with a snort. 'But stay they will.'

There was no arguing with her. He shrugged and gave up cheerfully enough. He preferred it this way, obviously, so why protest a lost cause?

She busied herself hanging children's clothes to dry, getting drinks, moving among them, talking incessantly. 'Oh you little darlings, they made you get cold did they? I'll get you your little tea, then we'll dry your little clothes. Then you can get under your little blankets . . .' The diminutives fairly tumbled over each other.

Mrs Nommik tugged at my sleeve. 'Ann, who are these people? Are they Russians?'

I was as confused as she. Like her, I was determined to hate all Russians. 'I don't know,' I said.

Someone whispered, 'Ostiaks.'

Which relieved our dilemma – we could relax, let ourselves like them – but it had little meaning otherwise.

One of the three-year-olds climbed on our hostess's lap. She was openly delighted. The children slept dry and warm on the floor while we older ones huddled, damp heaps, on the porch and in the lee of the cabin.

■

We eventually discovered that the Ostiaks are native to the region. They call the Ob the As, themselves As-yaksh (people of the Ob). They are small people with black hair, dark skin, and dark eyes.

77

Their eyes are often slanted, faces almost beardless, noses broad and flat in the mould of the Mongols. They hunt, fish, and gather – cones from the pines and cedars, berries, seeds, birch bark – much as they have been doing for centuries, except that under communist rule they had to produce a quota for the State as well as enough to feed, warm and clothe themselves and their young.

The Ostiaks – except for some of the children – are determinedly illiterate. They dislike interference and are noted for stubbornness, stolidity, and resistance to change, particularly if this means being regimented. Hence they did not recognise the rules, and the State seldom got its share.

■

Shortly after daybreak we felt the sun's lifesaving warmth. Untangling ourselves, we hoped what we wore would soon dry, because nothing else was. Footwear would be the main trouble, as the ground was still wet. We might be better off barefooted.

'Look!' The bank was empty of people. There was just bare ground, the silent river, a clearing sky.

'Where shall we go?' And how? Perhaps we should have stayed with the others. Where were they?

We scarcely had time to speculate. A horse pulling an open dray plodded into the early light. The driver was not even curious. 'So you're ready now, are you?' He had been here before, gone home for a sleep and come back. No questions. He'd been told to pick us up. He hadn't been told when.

The Ostiak woman helped the children dress and plied them with titbits. Small salted fish, potatoes, a little milk. Grateful mothers offered her money, a pair of stockings and a head scarf they managed to rustle up between them. She refused money but took the other things, astonished at the magnificence of gifts for her simple hospitality, coming out to wave us goodbye as we trudged after the cart laden with baggage and children.

■

Three collective farms, together with the few Ostiak cabins scattered near the forests, formed the settlement. We would discover that it was fairly typical.

It did not take long to get to our new quarters, and the first glance showed how lucky we had been to have spent the night elsewhere. Our home had once been the office of one of the farms. It was built of logs and lined with plaster. Or rather, had once been lined. It had been submerged in recent floods, as shown by high water marks on all walls. The stove had crumbled, much of the plaster had fallen out of walls and ceiling, and the floor boards had been saturated and were beginning to rot. The only two windows were broken, most of the glass gone.

But the floor had been recently swept. And the place did have a door. *And* it had ninety per cent of a roof. It could have been worse.

We allotted duties besides housekeeping, which was to be shared by everyone. Enn was to get wood and try to light a fire in the stove; Mrs Balter was named cook; Mrs Sein and I, as the only speakers of Russian, were the 'communicators'. The rest of us would be busy enough coping with the children.

The floor had been cleared of sediment and rubbish but we decided to wash it again anyway. Who knew what had been on it?

We plugged holes in the windows, cleaned mud, moss and weeds off the walls, and even managed to patch the sides of the stove with clay. In the meantime Enn had somehow bought a load of dry wood from the Ostiaks. He started the fire. The wet stove smoked in great clouds at first, but it didn't matter; sitting in the sunshine we were settled as we had not been in weeks. There was solid ground underfoot, air to breathe, space to move.

The hut was in a dip in the ground between low hills. The country around had a gentle roll with the highest points not much more than building height above the lowest. We guessed that the hut had been sited in a gully to give protection from winter's icy winds, but the siting had been a mistake. It had been almost submerged, presumably by local run-off, and so had been abandoned, unfit for use. Except, of course, by such as us. Cattle trucks, barges, the naked elements, derelict huts. What next?

Bundles, bags and baggage were saturated. We took them out and emptied every last item on the grass. We wrung the wringable, and spread the rest, hanging clothing and bedding over shrubbery to catch the sun. The native growth was thin: a few scrubby willows and birches, some blackberry bushes, several types of spindly shrub I did not recognise. Most of it was head high or less. There was thin grass on ground that was firm, though damp on the surface from yesterday's rain. We covered a surprising area of it with our colourful flotsam.

The sky was clear now, the air fresh. It seemed we had them to ourselves.

From our experience at railway stations, we had concluded that rural Russians are curious people. It was extraordinary that we had attracted no attention here. There were several dwellings visible from hillock vantage points, some with people moving about; yet not a soul came near us. We thought it strange, as our smoke must have been visible for kilometres. It suited us, nonetheless. When we had settled we would make our own reconnaissance.

Towards evening one of the children called. We followed her pointing finger. An elderly woman appeared nervously from the bushes, shuffling a half step forward at a time while looking over a shoulder as if clearing her retreat. She began to shy away when we greeted her. We stopped and made conciliatory noises, staying near the door lest we frighten her off. She approached cautiously, like a wild bird, as if allowing herself to be seen was indiscretion enough.

'Good day!' we called in Russian.

'We won't bite!' someone added in caustic Estonian. 'Russians don't taste all that nice.'

'Oh shut up. Don't scare her.'

Eventually she came close enough to talk, but no closer. Her eyes kept flicking to her exits. She was Caucasian. Beyond that, we could not tell. A cotton scarf over her head came right down to her eyebrows. It was folded on either side to cover her cheeks, ending in a knot under the chin. Her eyes and skin were dark, her teeth stained and broken. No hair showed.

'Where do you come from?' she asked. She was easier to understand than the Ostiaks.

'Estonia,' I said. 'We came up the river last night.'

She nodded noncommittally. In fact the whole ensuing conversation was desultory. I forget most of it, though she was there an hour or more. All the time we talked her eyes kept wandering, not covering her retreat any more as she gained confidence, but to the clothes drying on the bushes. I, for one, kept close watch while they were within her reach, though to be fair I believe she was curious rather than covetous.

She did give us two valuable hints before she left. Nodding at the smoke from our still damp stove, she told us to make a fire between stones outside and cook on that, in a bucket. Let the old stove burn in before using it, she advised. She also said to light another fire in the evening in front of the open door, to keep mosquitoes away.

'*That's* no good.' She shook her head again at the billowing smoke, screwed her nose up, gave a last somewhat wary look and left, her eyes lingering on the clothes.

Before long we had a good fire burning outside, and water boiling in our biggest pan. We gathered round it excitedly to wait for community soup. Thanks to the provisions sold us by the old Ostiak woman – and to the great cook Hunger working beside Mrs Balter – it tasted heavenly. And there was plenty.

■

The end of the first day in a Siberian collective saw us with a few plus points. Not too many, but the most so far. Our stomachs were full; bedding had dried and was carefully arranged on the floor; the floor neither rattled on wheels nor floated on water; a fire was going; and we had a roof over our heads, nearly all holes stopped.

On the minus side, we had to share beds, because not everybody had blankets. But that had its lighter side. Someone remembered the anecdote about the *kolkhoz* commandant who produced a collective's single super-sized blanket at 'lights out', spread it when everybody had lain ready in a row, and solemnly gathered and locked it up again in the morning. One of the many collective stories. A succession of old ones came out in the dark. They were to become less and less funny.

For me, contentment was short-lived. It was decided that on the following day I would go with one other of the group to look for our train companions and anyone else who might be friendly or useful. We must somehow find more food. That was all right, I was willing and ready. But I had scarcely settled down for the night before severe cramp-like pains hit my stomach and started me on endless trips into the bushes.

Acute diarrhoea is a miserable enough illness, even with all the comforts of modern living and medicine. When you add no bed, no treatment, no toilet and no paper, you have the depths of wretchedness. Add further local touches of Siberia and you have a unique kind of hell.

I spent the next day, between journeys into the scrub, lying on a grubby blanket on the floor, hoping wearily that each just completed run would be the last. Mosquitoes and midges were bad everywhere, but swarmed in trillions in the undergrowth. You hardly had time to bend before whining black droves settled on face, hands, arms, ankles, buttocks.

And in the bushes lurked an unimaginable hazard. Pigs! The collective pigs were like no other beasts I had ever seen, skinny creatures with short bodies and long legs. They were shades of brown and black and white and had stiff hairs sprouting vertically from their backs. Fearsome-looking tusks protruded beyond long, ugly snouts. They snorted excitedly, and shuffled along in quick, nervous runs. I was afraid, until I discovered they were anxious only to get to the excreta. Ugh! Disgusting scavengers, not dangerous at all. Too big and too mean to ignore, for all that. I had to arm myself with a stick and weakly beat the revolting animals off.

■

On the second morning I awoke to a forgotten sound: teeth crunching dried bread. The amazing Mrs Balter had produced some from her magic bag. I felt hollow. She offered me some.

'Do you think I should?' I asked.

'You're still sick, Auntie Ann.' Helju, the same child who had called me to order in the train, spoke up reproachfully. 'You must not eat yet.' Solemnly she took over my management, experience her licence. 'If you're good,' she added, stroking my forehead, 'you can have a whole lump of sugar tomorrow. And now I'll tell you a fairy story if you like.'

I hid my tears under the blanket.

■

Three boys came in, our first callers. They were runny-nosed, barefooted, and dressed in rags. Behind them stalked the same old woman who had spoken to us the first day. I remember nothing about the boys but their unforgettable entrance. As they stepped inside, their eyes switched in turn, as though jerked by strings, to a sight behind me. The four froze in the doorway. Small eyes bulged huge. Mouths fell open.

I turned in my bed not to miss the spectacle and my eyes also

82

popped. Across the room, from wall to wall, a length of cotton jigged merrily under its load. Neatly threaded along it from one end to the other was a waving row of paper currency. It took a couple of deep breaths to realise this was Mrs Balter's money hanging out to dry. Three thousand roubles in all, in hundred, thirty, and ten rouble notes, the result of a morning's work taking them out of her waterlogged case, carefully peeling them apart, and sewing them together. The astonishment of the four boys was so comical we could not help bursting into laughter: slightly hysterical perhaps, but genuine nonetheless, and as good as a dose of tonic.

Mrs Balter had been in business. She had had a general store in a country town. Three months earlier, when Estonian money had been declared non-currency, she had already been accepting – had *had* to accept – Russian notes, and of course had since traded in nothing else. She must have been clever to hoard some, and fortunate as well in that she had dealt in cash. Salary-earners and professional people had nothing except what could be saved from recent – Russian – wages or fees. Bank accounts had been rendered non-existent, property confiscated, pre-Russian money valued at nil. Such wealth as Mrs Balter's was rare.

The 'old' woman turned out to be the mother of one of the boys. She was forty-five. I would have put her as sixty. Apart from its benefit to us, the laughter worked wonders with her. The ice had been broken. She became talkative, full of advice and helpful suggestions. Most importantly for the moment, she promised us milk, and a large, old iron cauldron which we could pick up any time. Mrs Sein, the other 'communicator', decided to go with her right away, taking Enn to do the carrying. Such an offer must not be let slip. The two discussed their operation, deciding to make an exploration of it.

I desperately wanted to join Mrs Sein and Enn. They wouldn't hear of it – naturally enough, as I could scarcely stand – and that made me peevish and sulky. I behaved badly, turning my back to them. I think perhaps I resented Enn so easily switching teams. He had been my offsider for so long, I had come to count on him as mine alone. Now, although the pains had eased and my last call to the bushes had been a couple of hours ago, it was silly to even think of going, childish to argue, and rude to snub them.

They left with relations between us somewhat strained. I

decided it must not happen again. Such behaviour was unlike me, and not good enough. I was better off than most of our company, and should not complain. We had more than enough to contend with without petty squabbles.

■

'Soup? What sort of soup, Mrs Balter?'

'This one will be different.'

'How different?'

'We'll make it first and name it later.'

She sent us off to bring in all the food bags. A few handfuls of rice went into the new cauldron, then some flour, semolina, a dried crust, a potato, peel and all. With a cheer, Mrs Balter poured in a packet of macaroni she had unearthed from somewhere. Enn arrived back with several bottles of milk and some of that went in, too, followed, after serious consultation, by one of the salted fish. The result was thick, virtually odourless, and milk white.

'Well, what do we call it?'

'Let's just call it soup.'

I determined to eat some, come what may. I knew it was taking a risk, but two days of complete – after weeks of partial – starvation had left me jelly-legged, and if I said no now I feared I might miss out altogether. Helju gave permission. I enjoyed the feast with her. I even spent a good night; only one trip to the bushes, no protest from bowel or stomach.

Enn saw me in the morning getting about without assistance. I was feeling stronger all the time. He grinned, which was the best medicine I'd had. I was glad he held no grudge. He was still a boy.

'Ha,' he said, 'I've found it at last, the cure for gastroenteritis! All you need is mixed cereals, milk, water and one salted fish. Boil in an iron pot over an open fire. Take greedily in a single large dose.'

'And three witches to stir the brew, I suppose,' said the cook.

'You said it, Mother, not I!'

■

'Aipalova is in the opposite direction. There won't be anybody to see us.' Aipalova was the name of the settlement. 'So let's.'

'Count me in.'

'Why not? There's no more to be done here.'

Our third morning. I was talking with Mrs Sein and Elvi Lohvard. We had done everything possible, which wasn't much with seven housekeepers to one room. The children were quiet and reasonably happy. There was no further news.

We literally itched to do one thing more. The very thought set skin prickling afresh, as we slipped quietly away from the group.

Resolutely we marched through the scrub, hesitated no more than a fraction of a second, peeled off and slithered down the sloping muddy bank into the Vasjugan. The water was cold, slow moving and murky. We were down to the last piece of soap between us, and had just enough for a good lather each. Hair and all. Delicious! We squealed and played like children. First bath, first time clean for over a month – though in water where a hand could not be seen five centimetres under the surface. We had the river to ourselves, nothing to return to, nothing to hurry for. Despite the cold, it was hard to leave.

The mosquitoes decided for us, just in time. We had barely thrown on clothes, about to start back, when a young couple appeared, walking parallel to the river. Our own path crossed theirs.

'Of all times!' muttered Mrs Sein.

'Could have been worse,' Elvi giggled. 'Could have been two minutes earlier!'

The couple stopped, staring in open astonishment at our dripping hair, wet skin, and muddy feet; and at the underclothes and shoes we carried in our hands. We had no option but to wait, smiling self-consciously, trying not to look as sheepish as we felt.

'You've been swimming?' the man asked.

The accent, I thought, was Ukrainian. A good-looking young couple; married, presumably. They seemed very serious-minded, not the sort to be put off with a shrug and a sarcastic comment.

'Well – yes,' I answered for us.

'But why do you go today when the river's so muddy?'

Cautiously, I said we had not bathed in a long time, which may or may not have been an adequate answer. They did not look like fellow deportees, train- and boat-travellers. If they were, they may have understood.

The woman shook her head. 'You are a funny lot. Swimming! And such nice clothes you have, yet you go round bare-legged.'

Unabashedly she inspected us in turn. 'And some of you even wear men's pants!' News had travelled: there were no slacks here. 'Scared of pigs,' she said seriously, 'but not of the river.'

The grapevine *had* been busy! Lord, I felt myself blushing, was it I who'd been seen with the pigs?

They put their heads together and talked earnestly in whispers. About us. The occasional gesture and glance made that plain. We were left to look at each other, uncertain whether to be amused or cross.

Finally they reached a decision. The woman nodded. The husband turned to us. 'Would you like to come to our house for supper this evening?'

A doubtful enough invitation after such deliberation, unquestionably warranting polite refusal in civilised circles.

'Thank you very much,' I accepted immediately. A meal! It could solve a day's problem. A week's! Then I told my friends, who agreed without question.

The couple gave brief directions, said courteous *au revoirs*, linked arms and left us staring after them. The thought passed through my mind that we must look something like the Ostiak woman who had run after me with the pair of wet stockings I had left behind. Her stunned expression, as I had rather off-handedly told her to keep them for her trouble, was comical. She couldn't believe it. Nor could we believe this.

'Are you sure that's what they said?'

'Positive.'

'Who are they?'

'Who are we to look a gift horse in the mouth?'

Hesitantly, we stood on the path, hair still dripping, river slime caking our feet. Mosquitoes whined, otherwise there was silence. Our initial excitement was invaded by doubts. Who were they? What were they? All we had was a Russian name, directions, and an invitation to eat. Incredible.

'Why would they ask us?'

'Why indeed?'

'It may not be safe.' The stories of people simply disappearing in Siberia were legion. 'It'll be after dark.'

'What about the others?'

'We can't include them.'

'Can we leave them?'

'What else can we do?'

■

In the afternoon we went to look for the schoolhouse in the settlement centre. Mrs Sein and Enn and I went, the other two having some idea of local geography after their morning excursion. During that exploratory walk they had heard of the 'village' and the whereabouts of other deportees, presumably from our barge, said to be at the schoolhouse.

We soon found it, only two or three kilometres away. While other buildings of the *kolkhoz* centre were scattered about on the higher banks and hillocks, the schoolhouse was on low, soggy ground and in very poor repair. Built of logs, like all Siberian buildings so far, it was a single room, standing in a patch cleared of growth other than weeds. Single file tracks entered the small earth yard from every direction, whether made by pigs or people I could not tell.

The whole centre groaned from lack of care. The tiny cabins squatting between patches of potatoes, vegetables and tobacco were uniformly untidy. The schoolhouse was the worst, from rotted foundation to weather-torn thatch. Even the vegetables were badly kept. Mud, slush and water lay about everywhere and our hands waved continuously, brushing off mosquitoes. The water and insects could be blamed on unseasonal rains, the reigning air of poverty and disrepair could not. Even the animals were part of it. The cows, some with horns, some without, were small and bony, long-haired and caked in filth. The one skinny horse we saw was sway-backed and dull-eyed. Only the mangy pigs showed any energy, grunting, snorting, and dashing about at a brisk run. Some lean, cunning-eyed, roaming dogs had us thinking of hungry wolves. I shivered at the sight of them.

We saw a few small grubby children, but no adults. The children scuttled out of sight as soon as we looked their way. No chance of questioning them.

Incredibly, among all this destitution, several complete and valuable implements lay disintegrating. A plough lay out in the open, rusting under its original coat of paint. Weeds grew through a set of cogs. Some wagon parts – heaps of wheels and trays – were scattered about, weathering way, with enough paint still showing to indicate that they had never been used.

We stopped a couple of women. I asked in my best and humblest Russian if they knew somewhere we could buy milk or potatoes. They grunted and turned away. 'And the same to you,' muttered Enn.

Near the middle of the settlement a loosely concentrated cluster of buildings included the schoolhouse, which doubled as meeting-place, hall and clubroom. They were spread well apart by ordinary town standards, the ground between cropped bare. We passed close to several cabins from whose windows and doors inquisitive eyes followed us. We must have been a sight picking our way down the 'street' in our good shoes and clothes, with our once-permed hair, a handbag and an umbrella between us, and I in my navy wool wide-legged slacks.

Near the schoolhouse we found a number of our companions from the train. If our quarters were miserable, theirs were shocking. They had no heat or water, and were dreadfully overcrowded. We soon heard their tale. All these poor people had spent hours standing on the river bank after we had moved to the Ostiak cabin, the local management having no idea where to put such numbers. Eventually a few with very sick children had been billeted with residents, while the rest had been brought here. They had been told there was a nurse in the settlement, but no medicines – and they had not seen the nurse yet. So the many sick, numbering nearly all the children and half the adults, had had no relief at all. The locals had kept a wary distance. Even those who had been billeted said they had been treated like lepers. Two babies had died since landing. Several others were close.

I came across Mrs Toome from Narva. Her ten-month-old daughter was lying limply on a pillow on the floor, eyes closed. Mrs Toome didn't seem to recognise me. She was holding a tiny, transparent hand in hers, trying to warm it with her breath. 'Feel her hands, please?' she begged. 'Feel them. They're not cold, are they?' They were icy. 'Listen. She is breathing all right, isn't she?'

Another voice stopped me as I moved on. 'Ann, it is good that you are here. Silvia needs attention. Are your children still well? Be so good and go quickly for a doctor. Silvia is breathing irregularly, I think perhaps she is dying.' So matter-of-fact. 'She needs the doctor immediately.' Then a sudden flare of temper. 'Why don't you go then?' It was an old school friend. We had

had long consoling talks on the barge. She knew my children were not with me and that there was no doctor. Once, as a prefect at school, she had rescued me from some scrape I had got into. I had admired her. Now, more than anything in the world I wanted to really help her and I could do nothing but mumble hollow words of hope and pass on.

Half-blinded by tears, I left the room. I wanted to hide somewhere under ground, or a million kilometres away. I walked out with Enn. Tears were rolling from his eyes too. Just seeing him reminded me my children were still at home. I didn't know whether that made it better or worse.

'It's terrible,' Enn whispered.

We went to the centre of the settlement, trying to buy food from huts along the way. Everywhere came the same answer: 'Netu – have not' – or a grunt and a turned shoulder. We kept going, if only to quieten conscience, and found the main street. It was unsurfaced, as muddy as the tracks we had traversed. The cabins were in neat rows on either side; a couple of them, bigger than the rest, displayed carved wood decorations over doors and windows. There was also a director's office, with a sign to say so on the door right alongside one of the better cabins; we assumed these to go together. We found a shop and a child-minding centre, both empty.

There was probably accommodation for a hundred people in the immediate area. That number must have been at least trebled in the influx. And we were stuck here without friends or provision. Might as well be on the moon.

The transport barge had gone back. Was this the end of the line? If so, how could they possibly house us, feed us, keep us alive? Perhaps our dinner hosts could tell us. Though my appetite was as depressed as the rest of me, I could hardly wait.

■

The others were sitting like gypsies around a campfire when we returned from the settlement. Three of the women had become suddenly ill, the worst of them Inge, who rocked and wailed. They needed medical aid. Since Mrs Sein was the better nurse, I was elected, as the other Russian speaker, to hurry back to the village to seek it. Neither Enn nor I could muster the courage to tell of the situation there, the utter uselessness of going. It was easier to nod and walk. 'I'll try.'

I went straight to the director's office. If anything was to be achieved, it was the only place. A harassed-looking man in a black uniform came to the door. The uniform was familiar – NKVD.

I told him our position, knowing the futility. Who here didn't need medical attention? Who was to give it? With what? But I had to try.

'The nurse will come and have a look at them,' he barked.

'Where is she?'

'I don't know. I'll send her.'

'Do you know when – ?'

'Today.'

'Can I take back some medicines?' I asked, surprised. He had looked mean enough to have shut the door in my face. So far he had been civil, if a bit short.

'There are none.'

'Well – '

'Well what?'

'What can we do then?'

'You can go to the devil!'

I left quickly, on the point of telling him I had been doing just that. One of these days my tongue would get away from me and land us all in trouble. The man in black had suddenly seemed very angry. Nothing could be achieved by irritating him further.

I reported back, parrying the inevitable questions. The patients were quiet, resigned now, even Inge.

We three with the dinner invitation fluttered around most of the afternoon, trying to make up for our good fortune. We could offer little, and hanging about was nerve-racking. The nurse had not arrived, and I didn't have the heart to say she never would. We hesitated, protesting that we could not leave, hoping to be persuaded.

'Do go, there's nothing more you can do. Somebody might as well have a good meal. Besides, it leaves three more rations for us here.' Good boy, Enn!

'Well – '

'Off you go then.'

'If you're sure – '

'Of course.'

We left them huddled around the stove, with another fire outside to keep mosquitoes away, as the old woman had taught us. Out of sight, we broke into excited chatter like teenagers on a spree.

■

The cabin was better kept than any we had seen. It had a porch, glass windows and wood carvings over both. The entry was clean and neat, as was the kitchen garden around it and the one room within. There was a table, some stools, and a wide bed covered with a mosquito net. In the bed a child was sleeping in clean clothes and clean blankets.

It was the table that caught our eyes, though. Salt fish, potatoes, bread, butter, milk! Plenty of them all, a spread fit for – whom?

'Do please start. Help yourselves.'

Polite demurrals came hard.

'Thank you, we're in no hurry.'

'Please.'

We gradually lost our reserve. Our hosts asked questions, showing genuine interest, while encouraging us to tuck in. I found myself between mouthfuls telling of life at home, my family, and the journeys on train and barge. But I didn't dwell on the arrests or the tribulations: it would have been silly to risk saying anything to which our meal ticket might take exception. The woman cried as she listened, which I took as encouraging. She brought out more food, even sugar to have with our tea. Her husband was not obviously stirred, but he nodded approval as she went to the larder.

At first I was reluctant to ask questions in return. We did not know who they were; though sympathetic, they apparently were high in local ranking. We were in the land of the enemy, I had to keep reminding myself. During the course of the evening, the man told us they were an 'agriculturalist team'. Just what training that entailed, I did not find out. His wife was an agronomist – which explained the garden and the wealth of food, and, I supposed, the mosquito net and other small signs of provincial prosperity – and he an expert in animal husbandry. They had both lived their lives in the vicinity, he said. I gathered that was unusual. His parents

91

had been deported to Narymm from the Ukraine in 1918 when he was a baby; he was candid about it, but showed no malice and volunteered no opinions. We did not ask about hers.

We were told about local conditions. As a specialist, he was one of the few healthy men from the district not to be drafted into the war. I noted this away in my mind, as it meant other men we ran across were also likely to be officials, or at least to have some political consequence. We would need to be careful of any we encountered.

We learned that on top of the reduction in work force this had been a bad year for the farms – the scattered corn fields had been sown in spring as usual, but heavy rains had washed out the crop in many places. So the *kolkhozniks* had been ordered to re-seed using the corn set aside for food. 'Quotas first' was the order from the top. The crop must go in with no outside help and no replacements for food stocks. This seemed to be accepted as a contribution to the war effort. Because of the washaways there was little pasture grass for the animals. The farmers were in trouble.

Aipalova, they told us, was also one of the best areas of Narymm for fishing and hunting, and the exceptionally wet season had prevented the depleted population from meeting quotas in these fields, too. Things were bad all round: people could not get to the rivers to fish; grazing animals – domestic and wild – had roamed out of reach where there was food. And, of course, the men were gone. And the experience. And the guns.

The people remaining had been left entirely dependent on their own produce, so it was understandable we were unwelcome. We certainly did not look like productive workers, and there was real fear that the food would not last if it had to be further shared. The word had been spread among established settlers (by whom, we did not ask) that we were to be treated as unwelcome aliens, as enemies of the State. We were warmongers, criminals, outsiders, undesirables. The locals had been warned not to help us, not even to communicate or sell or exchange anything with us. Hence the indifference and the slammed doors. Even the compulsory billets' community standing was jeopardised, which explained their aloofness.

'Only a few of you – and they will be the young, strong ones – will be kept here,' our host told us. 'There are nearly six hundred in your batch, you know, far too many for this collective. It can't support them. The majority will have to move soon.'

'Where?' I asked.

'Oh, all over the place.' He shrugged. 'Depends on the commandant. He's in charge of the area. But I'm sure he'll keep only workers here. No non-producers.'

This was bad news. Our carriage-load from Rakvere had become a family and they were breaking us up.

'If you can,' the Ukrainian advised, 'go to Maisk. It's a bit easier up there, further from the district commandant's office.'

'What is Maisk?'

'Another collective. Like this one.'

'How far?'

'About two hundred and fifty kilometres.'

As we were leaving, our hostess gave us a whole fish, a handful of aspirin tablets and a bottle of milk. We accepted with token protest.

'Come over every evening,' she promised, 'and we'll sell you a bottle of milk. We have a whole cow!'

At the gate we were given further advice. Don't ask questions. Don't tell much about yourselves. Don't argue. Don't trust anybody. Don't believe promises.

We were deeply moved. It was plain that they were putting themselves at risk in trusting us, although we were only vaguely aware just what the risk was. I felt guilty about our earlier suspicions until I realised we had merely anticipated their own counsel.

'What about the war?' I ventured to ask.

'It will end soon,' the man whispered. 'You'll be home before long.'

'Do be sure to bring the bottle back,' his wife reminded us. Bottles were rarer than milk.

■

By morning our newfound security was obsolete. The order came for everybody to report to the office, where a clerk who must surely have been an army reject – he was pale and emaciated – told us we would be moving out soon. Our destinations had been assigned.

I went to see the man in black again, this time accompanied by Mrs Balter and Enn. He looked no less malevolent than yesterday.

'Our group would like to stay together,' I said.

'The placements have been made already,' was the curt answer. 'Alphabetically.'

'We would like to go to Maisk.'

He stared at us. What do you know about Maisk? was on the tip of his tongue. I thought for one panicky moment he might ask, Why would you want to go to Maisk?

To get as far from here as possible.

Oh Lord, stop him!

'We're related,' I said quickly.

'All of you?'

'We three.' I pointed to Enn and his mother. The others had not been so enthusiastic about Maisk. Being close to medical attention for the children meant more to some than distance from authority. On the other hand, they had seen none of the promised attention, so they were vacillating.

'I'll see about it,' he said. 'But don't think I'm going to start changing the whole list.'

'Of course not.'

I felt sure he was angling for an argument, in case he could stamp on us. Our indifference made up his mind for him.

'Better get your things ready. The lot of you. The boat for Maisk will be coming in soon.'

'All of us?'

'That's what you wanted, isn't it? You're the leader of a group, aren't you? Well, get your batch ready. You'll start off together in any case.'

What had we done, committing our whole 'family'?

■

We had been in Aipalova four days, and already four people had died, little Silvia among them. I had no love for the place. And I would have hated to go back and ask the man in black to change anything again.

We made ready for the two-hundred-and-fifty-kilometre journey to Maisk. First stage: Aipalova to Novo-Vasjugan.

8

THE 'FAMILY' DISSOLVES

No river steamer, this one, nor a towed barge. An open rowboat: a round-bottomed tub with several rows of seats and two sets of oars. The man who had brought us to the river from Aipalova turned his horse and cart for home and left us to climb in.

There were twenty-two from the Rakvere carriage; Mrs Sein and Mrs Toome had stayed in Aipalova. There was also Mrs Nigol, from Narva, with her daughter, Lehte, who was eighteen and very ill. A man from the collective farm had been sent with us to steer. Twenty-five people in all, and their luggage. The boat sat low in the water, wavelets lapping over the sides at every movement. There was water in the bottom and it was taking in more.

We took it in turns to row, four at a time, while the children and resting rowers bailed with mugs, dishes, saucepans, whatever they could find. Lehte had a high fever, and suffered bouts of shivering followed by drenching sweats. At times she was delirious and whenever she coughed, which was often, she cried with pain. We thought she had pneumonia and could only help Mrs Nigol nurse her, by shading her, keeping her quiet and drying her face.

It took us all afternoon and until eleven o'clock at night to get to Novo-Vasjugan, twenty-five kilometres away. Hands blistered, faces swollen and sore from mosquito bites, we climbed from the boat to look for the horses we had been told would take us on. There were none. There was nothing except a plank landing and a couple of posts to tie the boat to, and a rough sloping track leading to the pale sky. High on the river bank some young people were dancing to an accordion, one of the old

95

type with buttons instead of a keyboard. I asked them the way to the hospital. They pointed into the fading twilight towards the middle of the settlement, a sizeable town compared with Aipalova. We asked for directions to the office where we would report, but here we had no help.

Enn came with me to the hospital, which neither looked nor smelt like one, perched on the highest point in the town. It was a log building like all the others, though bigger. A nurse at the door told us nobody could be admitted without the commandant's written authority.

'But how can we get that at this time of the night?'

She shrugged.

'We've looked,' I said. 'We can't find anybody, and the girl is terribly sick, lying on the river bank.'

'I don't know,' she said. 'I'm sorry.' She sounded almost genuine. 'I am only allowed to stick to my orders.'

I repeated Lehte's symptoms, and the nurse looked worried. 'She may be dying there,' I insisted.

'Perhaps you should go back and see if she's any better. If not – '

'No.'

'Eh?'

'No.'

'What then?'

'We are not leaving here until we know what to do.'

She was vacillating. She had some professional conscience, enough to prod at. I stood my ground while Enn fidgeted.

'But – '

'Going to look at her is a waste of time. You know that. We'll only have to come straight back. She won't be better. That girl should be in hospital.'

'It's not your decision.'

'If it's not yours either, whose is it? We'll go. But only to bring her back here. We'll leave her with you, then we'll find the commandant.'

She was plainly relieved that she could now pass on the responsibility. 'Just hang on a minute and I'll call the doctor.'

He was young, I guessed in his early thirties. He listened, though he was cross with the nurse for calling him. Part way through my explanation he interrupted. 'Yes, she is obviously ill.

Never mind the commandant. Bring her right away. Nurse, can you get these people a stretcher?'

Lehte was unconscious when she went through the door.

■

Another school-cum-community hall. Much bigger, it was again one large room with a podium at one end. Seats were stacked along the walls and it seemed that every square centimetre of floor was occupied. Groups of people, mostly from our barge, had been gathering here for days before our arrival. Estonians, Latvians, Bulgarians for certain, probably others also; but we were concerned with where, not who. Every possible place seemed taken. Only after pleas in the name of the children, and threats of violence to persons and baggage, did we get a small corner of the podium to rest the sick and the young. They were tired and fretful, their mothers exhausted. Enn quietly used his muscles on their behalf while I did the tongue-bullying. My God, what were we coming to? There were still restraints, but we were steadily going back down the evolutionary ladder in the fight for personal and tribal survival.

I went for a look around. Since there was no way of relaxing inside, being on the move was second best. Soon I tired of prowling and spoke to a Latvian woman who seemed glad to talk. Exchanging pleasant words gave me an eerie sense of relief that we still had the ability to rise above dumb-herd level, and I was sure she felt the same. She told me that many more people had been here, but they had been packed off again in small groups, she did not know where. She had been here several days now – all the time we had been at Aipalova – and still had no idea what was to happen to her, or to those with her. I learned that the building was normally a school by day and a 'clubroom' by night. I think she had been a teacher. She wished me a bewildered goodnight and blinked vaguely at the chaos.

Most of the night, between walks, I spent leaning against the wall or propped semi-sitting on the baggage. In this position, some time early in the morning, Enn shook me awake.

'Come out,' he whispered. He seemed excited. 'I've been walking about the town,' he said when we were out of all earshot. 'There's a queue forming by a shop. They say they've got cigarettes and sweets.'

It was barely daylight. We waited a long time in the surreptitious queue, eventually coming away with two kilograms of candied sweets, ten packs of cigarettes – the new austerity kind: long tubes of paper and short ends of tobacco – two litres of cranberry drink and a kilogram of honey cakes. We couldn't buy bread. That was for ration-card holders only. But we did get two kilograms of real coffee, for which we paid seventy-five roubles a kilogram. At least, Enn paid for it. My hundred roubles were almost gone. Enn rushed back to our group in time for them to do some buying before everything sold out.

The schoolroom had taken on the look of a field hospital. An orderly and a nurse had arrived. They were good people doing their sympathetic best, moving among the sick, handing out white powders and the ubiquitous ointment for lice. These seemed the only medicaments. The bad cases among recent arrivals were sent off to hospital, including Mrs Toome's little girl and one of the Lohvard children.

Mrs Holm could venture no further with Inge, and Ella Falk could not afford any risk with Mai, who was all she had left. They decided to try for the list to stay in Novo-Vasjugan. I went with them, wondering if this meant our family was splitting up. Mrs Toome and Elvi Lohvard were eager to stay: their anxieties were immediate and went only as far as the children. Would there be beds for them? You said there's a doctor. Were there medicines? I was still determined to go on to Maisk, as were most of the others. But with Mrs Sein, our only other Russian speaker, already left behind in Aipalova, who could help those in hospital or on the list? Who interpret? How could they manage?

As it happened, the sick were the lucky ones. We did split up, and those left behind had the better of the division.

Chaos reigned in the hospital too. Some of the patients had been shifted into the long corridor, some to the bathhouse next door. The main building was crammed with beds, patients, relatives, visitors, baggage: everything except nursing staff and equipment. A small one-roomed hut in the backyard served as an infectious ward, filled with children, two and three to a rough iron bed, mainly suffering from gastroenteritis. The light was dim, the air foul, the noise indescribable. People rushed about the main building calling, complaining, crying, cursing in a dozen languages. Children fretted and screamed. New cases were coming in all the time, and there was no-one to deal with them.

Lehte was 'as well as could be expected', looking awful, tossing restlessly in the hubbub, her bed pushed into a neutral corner. The youngsters we had just brought in looked as though they would be all right, with reasonable care. We could only hope they would get it. At least they shared a bed, commandeered by their mothers, I suspected. We heard there were new boatloads arriving every few hours and that it had been going on like that for a week or two. Other boatloads were leaving. All the new Estonian arrivals were from county Virumaa: from Narva, Tapa, Vaike-Maarja, Porkuni and other towns I knew well. I did not feel like looking them up. There was no longer comfort in sharing adversity, only further depression. It was better not to know.

With the sick off our hands, and a stomachful of crowds, I took a deep breath and wrinkled my nose. Enn said, 'There's fresh air outside. For God's sake let's go somewhere we can breathe.'

■

We got back in time for a meeting taking place in the hall. They had just come to the main item, the inevitable NKVD speech from the man in black, warming up to one of their extraordinary harangues. In one breath he was vilifying us all as blood-sucking hostile imperialists; in the next, exhorting us to the greatest of efforts to defend the common glorious birthland which we all loved with all our hearts.

There was not one Russian among us. Our husbands had been taken God alone knew where; also our children, friends, relatives and neighbours. Our countries had been overrun and our people deprived of every human comfort and dignity, many of life itself. We stood as expressionless as we could, backs straight, eyes and mouths shut, while he spouted his obscenities, and could only wonder. Did he believe any of this? Did he possibly think he'd get support from us? Presumably he did, otherwise why do it? They must be completely programmed for such ridiculous garbage to flow so freely: so pat, so rehearsed, so earnest.

At least, our thoughts were still our own. I made another promise to myself: to do as little for them as possible, and whatever I could in a positive way to avenge our personal and national injustices. Nothing was said aloud. We were fully aware of the power of the NKVD.

The director took over from the man in black. He told us to prepare for a three day journey. We would be supplied with bread at the rate of one kilogram an adult, nine hundred grams a child. He read out a list of names, of about two hundred people, who, with their families, were to be on the next transport. He did not say where. Of all the people from our carriage, only Mrs Balter and Enn and myself were on the list.

■

It was a minor heartbreak, dissolving the group. Back in the schoolroom we spent a good part of the night going back over our hardships, and further back to the good times. Just over a month ago we had been strangers, but in a few weeks we had become closer than close. We had shared adversities, pooled our last scraps of food, seen death together. We knew each other as few families do. And in the morning three of us would leave, perhaps never to meet the rest again. So we talked of the day the war would end and a clean white ship would come to take us all home, together, our whole group, to our loved ones. Then we would never be sad again.

■

We had gathered at the river bank early in the morning, about two hundred and fifty of us all told, unconscious of the warm sun and clear sky. This time our barge was smaller than the first and towed by a tiny primitive river tug-boat. The barge looked a hundred years old; I felt sure in its heyday it had been pulled by horses, possibly by men. There were two hatches on the flat deck and a small central cabin for the 'overseer' and a nurse. The overseer was a big fellow who looked as though he only needed a whip. By midmorning we were aboard, having slept little since our tearful parting.

If the Ob trip was bad, I thought to myself as we poured onto the deck, this must be the very end. We'll never make anywhere but the bottom in this wreck. We pushed through, over scarred decking, looking for a place to settle, finally finding one below. Once again we were near the steps under the forward hatch. 'Like home,' Enn said.

The barge moved off in silence except for the puffing of the tug, and, though we tried to make ourselves comfortable on the baggage, sleep was a thing of the past. As the day warmed, the reek of pitch lining the rotting planks mingled with the stink of spilt kerosene, slopping gently with the garbage floating on scummy green bilge. We abandoned rest and went upstairs; it was impossible to stay below.

I stood among listless people lining the deck and wondered, How could we get this way? Each buried in his own thoughts, no eye for surroundings, no tongue for neighbours? Was it just fear that made us so docile?

Why doesn't someone scream? Why don't I? Why don't I jump overboard . . .

I didn't jump. Nobody screamed or did anything. What *could* we do?

If we jumped, where would we go? How could we survive in this awful country? And if we did, even if we got out of Russia, we knew that our people back home would probably be the ones to suffer. We had already seen babies die, mothers go mad. What would they do – and to whom – if one of us crossed them?

We had to accept that we were prisoners, but must we resign ourselves to be slaves? I decided again that I would *not* die. They wanted me to, so I would not. I would live, perhaps to tell.

■

For three days we travelled upstream from Novo-Vasjugan. At night, sand bars and sunken tree stumps frequently forced us to stop. Once or twice each day we tied up to the bank and were allowed to land to cook food. We three did not take advantage of this, as Mrs Balter and I were afraid of wild animals. The banks were muddy, the undergrowth threatening, so we stayed where we were. Besides, we had nothing to cook and no utensils.

On one of those nights I talked with the overseer – the 'Boatman from Vasjugan' we called him, from a popular Estonian song, *The Boatman from Viljandi* – asking about Maisk. He told me it was the centre of four *kolkhozes*. Well-to-do ones, he said. A good collective. He said there would be transport waiting for us: they had horses. It seemed a superior place, I was glad we had applied for it. But I would believe the horse-drawn transport when I saw it.

Once, on the second day, when I stood by the tugboat cabin dressed in my slacks, smoking a cigarette, the nurse spoke to me. She was plainly puzzled. 'Do women really wear trousers where you come from?' she asked. 'Or are you half man?'

She was serious. I hoped I would not need nursing.

On the third evening, we stopped. The vessel was clambering over logs and sandbanks in shallow water. It bumped and rolled until it could go no farther.

'Those who can walk, get off and walk. We're practically there.'

The nurse showed the way. 'Not far.' It turned out to be all of four or five kilometres. We formed a silent line on the soggy, narrow path following the course of the river and walked. For well over an hour we were fully occupied keeping on our slippery feet while fighting off insects. 'Transport waiting.' I consigned the boatman to the devil and concentrated my thoughts on one thing: rest.

'Look,' said the nurse. 'Maisk!'

All we could see was the barge moored at the bank. It had arrived before us, and the remaining passengers were off-loading luggage, piling it haphazardly in a field. There was no horse, village, or even cabin in sight, just a bare, muddy landing. I saw an Estonian man I knew, Captain Kesa, a soldier and socialite. Once the life of a party, he looked morose. We nodded good day.

'Will there be transport for us?' I asked. Walking any farther, carrying luggage, suddenly seemed too much.

He shrugged. He was not interested.

'Is your family with you?' I asked.

'Yes.'

'What sort of spirit are they in?'

'Spirit?' he muttered. 'What spirit? We are dead. All of us. Dead. Our corpses have just been thrown on the banks here. This is where we'll rot.'

I remembered the Latvian man's bitter remark to me on the Ob. 'You ought to pickle that optimism of yours, Ann, and put it away,' he had said. 'There's no use for it here.' But if I am to live, I told myself, I must not become defeatist.

I turned my back on Juhan Kesa, not foreseeing the important part he and his wife, mother and daughter were to play in my life in Siberia.

■

We reached the top of a low hill and finally encountered Maisk. Log cabins were scattered along the roadside, a few further back, more dotted along the edge of the woods. Some small, some smaller. A few in the middle, fair-sized. Some were leaning over; a few had props supporting them, but most didn't. Moss roofs; rough timber roofs; thatch roofs; some of birch-bark. In the half-light one sight gave my heart a rare thump of encouragement. Around each cabin was a patch of garden. Some even had flowers.

The 'waiting transport' eventually came, two long wagons with sides like horizontal ladders, two horses per wagon. A bearded old farmer drove one, greeting us *en masse*, waving cheerfully, talking to nobody in particular. 'See, our new *kolkhozniks* have arrived!' Lack of response did not discourage him. 'Hello, citizens, hello!' he called merrily. 'Hop on the wagons now. Sick people first. That's it. Bags and children up. You too, *baba*.'

Russians use this as a term of endearment for older women. He pointed a thick finger at Mrs Balter and Captain Kesa's mother. As ladies of the old school, they forgave him the familiar 'you' and the cheeky 'old women' just as they forgave the pointing finger. He was an old man, he could be tolerated. Mrs Kesa inclined her head graciously, Mrs Balter thanked him sincerely. They were weary and grateful.

As we picked our way up the rutted road behind his squeaking, lumbering cart, I decided that he was not a party member. He couldn't be, he was human. As he prattled on I conceded that I might have to add old men to my reluctant list of Russians I could not hate: peasant women along the rail line, Ostiaks, starving children, descendants of deportees (Estonian particularly, but including Ukrainian). Who, Ann Lehtmets, are the real Russians? A curly question. Who is the enemy? Some time when you are less tired you must try to answer that one.

We passed through a cluster of cabins. The garden patches that had taken my eye were fenced and neat, mostly growing potatoes. There was also tobacco, cabbage, carrot, and beetroot. The fences were made of sturdy vertical logs. Probably to keep out my friends, the pigs, I thought. A few had hinged gates, others a plank either side to form an angled ramp for climbing over the top. Among the potato patches were yet another luxury: open box-like toilets. What next?

We passed by a small log office, and stables, sheds and fowl houses. These were ill-kept, dung-covered and dirty. Again there was disorder and waste, as in Aipalova. Neglect of implements and public amenities was evident on all sides.

'Where are the people?' asked Enn.

We had seen none.

'Perhaps there aren't any.' I was tired, hungry and ill-tempered. 'Perhaps this luxury is for us alone.'

Our reception committee waited on a grassy patch in front of a rambling single-storeyed building in the centre of the settlement. The commandant – our new man in black – was there, also the *milits* [policeman], recognisable by his dowdy uniform, and two civilians, who proved to be the schoolmaster and the director of collective farms. There was also an audience, which preferred to listen from windows and around corners. Barefooted children dashed out and back again, gawking at our clothes and shoes as though they had never seen the like before.

The director cleared his throat. 'Now then.' He seemed a reasonable man. Our instructions, given without flourish, were to unload the carts – except for the sick, who would go to hospital – and to await further orders.

Then the commandant began the nonsense again about pulling together against the 'imperialist foe'. I toyed briefly with the idea of putting my hand up and inquiring: who was this beastly incorporeal adversary we'd been dragged so far to conquer? But more NKVD invective and pep talk would surely follow. More waste of time.

I caught Enn's eye. Shopping? Ready! Experienced, we left our bundles under Mrs Balter's wing and slipped away in the warm-up phase. First come, first served; any after first would probably get nothing.

I asked several small boys before one pointed, and, having pointed, ran. The rest just stared. They looked healthy enough, though on the scrawny side, and, judging by their clothes, they all had big brothers. Most, after a lengthy look, scuttled off. Not one spoke.

The door was open. The shopkeeper stood outside, gazing in the direction of the schoolhouse. We had come in a wide circuit. He turned to look at us interestedly.

'What have you to sell?' I asked politely.

'Whatever you want. We have smokes, biscuits, sweets, sugar. Everything!'

He followed us in. The shop was much like the one in Novo-Vasjugan, a long counter in front of a shelf-lined wall. On the counter were scales and a knife. The shelves were more empty than full, holding cigarettes, boxes of nails, a few packets of sweets, some leather straps, and a couple of rolls of coloured cotton print. There were a few iron cooking pots, matches, and odds and ends.

He let each of us have twenty packets of cheap cigarettes – ten kopeks a pack – and, between us, a kilogram of sugar, two of barley sugars and one of pink, watery-looking biscuits. I asked for more, but the shop was filling with our fellow travellers and he would not oblige. Undoubtedly, prices would soon rise.

Back at our belongings, we found we had visitors. One came running to me. 'Ann,' she cried. 'I knew I'd find someone from home!'

Selma had travelled the whole way with us, starting on the same train at Rakvere, though neither of us had known it. She was an old friend. We traded a few names, avoided others.

'Here, I've brought something with me.' She had a bottle of milk and a piece of bread. 'Just in case.'

'Thank you!' I took them awkwardly.

'Any Rakvere people here with you?' she asked.

I shook my head. 'We did have, but we left them at Novo-Vasjugan.'

'I came up two days ago. There were quite a few in our lot. Some are on my farm.'

She told us we would be billeted with *kolkhoz* families spread around the district. There were several collective villages, several kilometres apart, in the complex. 'See if you can be sent to mine,' she said. 'The Sjemljedelets, in Maisk itself.'

I tried immediately, going straight to the director. He was shocked at the suggestion. 'Choose your own destination?' It seemed this was just not done. 'No, no! You have already been placed.' However, I did find that the Balters and I had been allotted a *kolkhoz* named Udarnik, which was at the far end of the settlement, two kilometres distant. We were to move off immediately.

'I'm sorry,' I told Selma.

'We'll try and keep in touch. Be brave.'

'Till we go home together.'

We gathered our bundles. One of my parcels was missing. Some clothes, I thought. Stolen, or mixed up with others? I thought it was nothing important, but I could not be sure. I would have to be more careful now we were no longer among our own.

'*Davai, davai!*'

Two hundred people were staying behind in the schoolhouse, awaiting allocation deeper in the country. For us, the six-week journey was ending.

'Nearly home.' Mrs Balter was unusually cynical.

Home. Udarnik, Maisk.

Ann (on left) as Commissioner of Girl Guides,
attending World Jamboree in Hungary, 1939

SIBERIA

*Ann in doorway of Novo-Vasjugan sewing and shoe-making 'factory',
which became her home in 1952.*

Ann (seated) with four friends: Novo-Vasjugan 1956, main street.

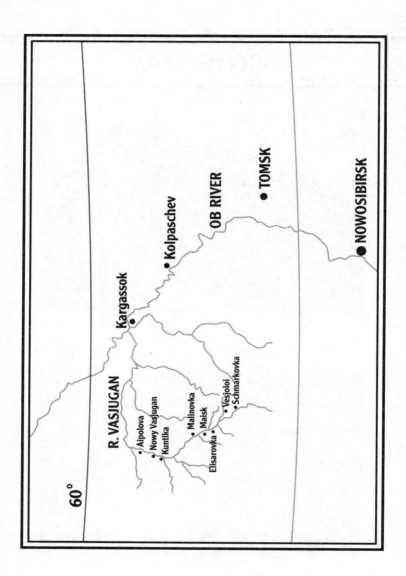

9

FOREMEN AND LANDLADIES

It was a piatistenka, or five-walled house, the fifth being a wall across the middle to make two rooms. We were fortunate, as our driver told us.

'Whoa. This is it. A piatistenka for you, heh? Lucky! And your landlady all ready to receive you.'

The horse plodded to a stop.

We inspected our new home silently. The front came out to 'street' level. There was no kerb to the bare earth track; but there was a fence, which extended several metres either side from the front corners. The neighbouring cabin was thirty metres away, built in the same manner, fronting the street, fenced from the corners, precisely in line. Across the way was a similar row; short vertical logs for the fences, seven or eight long thick straight horizontals for the houses, with plenty of space between. All were trimmed fairly neatly, ours better than most. It should have been a good omen.

There was a hinged gate in the fence, and behind it a grim-faced woman. In her thirties, I judged, and not pleased to see us. She had a dark cotton kerchief tied tightly down to her eyebrows, making her look even grimmer. She wore the usual long, dark, cotton skirt. Over her blouse she had a *fufaika* – a three-quarter-length quilted jacket – again of cotton, and patched with pieces of unmatching cheap cotton material. Perhaps she didn't know it was the middle of summer.

'Good evening,' I ventured.

She shot me a venomous glance and turned her back, leading us through the gate around to the rear of the cabin. We made resigned faces at each other and followed. A small, open porch had two doors leading off it, one to each room. She indicated that the bigger room was hers and that Mrs Balter and Enn were to move in. She literally threw their luggage in, then put a hand to my shoulder, pushed open the other door and shoved me through. She had not yet uttered a word.

Her final act brought an explicit and unrefined response from me. Until now, her malice had shocked us into silence too. It must have registered, because she mumbled, 'Natasha will be here soon. Wait!' before slamming the door.

There were only two doors in the building, both off the back porch. The rooms did not connect. The four windows were small; two in front, one to each side; and one at each end.

From inside, the windows looked tiny. They were fixed, and made of bits of glass puttied together. The area of clear glass was less than half the window space, which left the room – about four by five metres – darker than it might have been. A clay cooking stove, white-washed over, was set into the connecting wall. Against the end was a narrow wooden bed, quite tidily made, and covered with a patched cotton eiderdown and a pillow with a cotton print slip. Tidy, but none too clean, I saw on closer inspection. There was a wooden box under the bed, and a cross-legged table and two cross-legged stools beneath the front window. Near the door was a large wooden chest with a heavy lid, like an old-style glory box. That was all. No wardrobe, dresser, or mirror. The floor was bare boards, unpolished and unswept, with a roughly cut square hole that could only be for a cellar.

I went outside to find the toilet. There was none. Right under the window, just inside the fence, was a heap of cow manure, the ground around it littered with foreign calling cards, revolt-ingly and unquestionably human. I thought I was getting used to the primitive. But this, here, directly under the window? My urge evaporated. I could wait until dark.

■

Natasha was a surprise. Small, dark, and black-eyed, she was young, probably not much more than twenty, and good-looking.

'I am the cow woman,' she said, and seemed proud of it.

'Hello, Natasha. I am Ann.'

'You know me?'

She was delighted, and began chattering. She liked cows, did not like forests, liked pretty things, thought summer was nicer than winter, there was plenty of room here, I could make my bed on the big box and use her stove at any time for cooking. She said much more, mostly of little consequence, while I listened, trying to keep up with her prattle; among the chaff there might be some grain. All the time, her bright eyes darted between me and my suitcase.

I was still sitting on the case, Natasha still talking, when the door was thrown open. It was our morose neighbour. 'What are you sitting around for?' she demanded. She ignored Natasha, planting herself in front of me with a lot of gesturing. 'Go to the stables and get some straw for your mattress. You won't find servants here to order around!'

For Heaven's sake, who was giving orders!

'I haven't a bag to put straw in,' I retorted. Even the camel's back could stand only so much. 'And anyhow, what in the devil's name are you so angry about?'

'*Oi batjuschki*! – Oh dear father!'

It was like switching on the sun; hostility evaporated in a flash. She threw up her arms and smiled delightedly. 'This one can speak our language!' She glanced at Natasha, to whom it had never occurred that anyone should do otherwise. 'Mine are dumb things.'

I would have to remember to tell Mrs Balter.

'Yet they've got such clothes,' she went on, the warmth going out of the smile. 'And all that luggage!'

I avoided looking at my own case and grubby bundles, quickly assuring her that the Balters were nice people. 'They are really very friendly. And no trouble. They just don't speak Russian.'

'What is your name?' she demanded, brushing the Balters aside.

'Ann.'

'Anja.'

'Ann.'

'Mine is Marusja.'

'How do you do?'

'Where do you come from?'

I told her, also telling her that we had been deported because of the war, that we had no wish to be here billeted with them,

111

that we would prefer to be in our own small homes not disturbing hers, that we were sorry about it, it was not our doing, and we did not know what had happened to our husbands.

'That's of no importance,' she said. I gathered nothing outside here and now had importance. I wondered why she had asked. 'Come, I'll give you a bag to carry the straw. You can sew up the sides of a sheet to make a mattress.'

I got the straw. Marusja lent me a large needle and some linen thread. The mattress, soon completed, was longer than the bed, which was just as well, because the box was not long enough for me.

'Take bedding' had been one of the last orders given in the flat at Rakvere. In ignorance and fluster, I had packed sheets. I had also put in my almost new, feather-filled, winter cover. Though I had cursed the bedding many times as an impediment, I had managed not to part with any of it. I had had no heart to use it in the bedchambers provided on tour, so it had remained packed.

Now it emerged. I had base, palliasse, sheets, blanket, and all I could do was fret. The sight of a made bed with its yellow silk quilt was too close to home. I was provided for, but what did Elmar have?

■

Outside once more, I could face the world. A strange world.

Ours was the last but one house. The 'street' was semi-cleared earth with tracks through the weeds. Beyond were bushes, small alders, with heavy timber behind. Natasha had gone, the sun shone, all was quiet; it should have been a beautiful day. Along the edge of the forest, surrounded by scrubby growth, I could see several large barn-type buildings that seemed to be in very bad repair. In every other direction were potato fields, even back along our street toward the village centre. There were more elaborate buildings down there. The biggest, with a few balustraded steps leading up to the door, was the kolkhoz office. I had been there already for permission to get the straw. The storehouse itself was next door. The settlement of Udarnik comprised about thirty cabins in all, and a few sheds and stables. The cabins were spread along this one road that ran between the wilderness at this end, and Maisk, two kilometres or more away, at the other. There were no people and little else to be seen.

112

I stood by the gate, wrapped in misery, when I sensed some-one approaching. Raising my eyes, I saw a tall, strange-looking man loping in long, quick steps towards me. A quilted coat hung from his big, bony shoulders, and a thick winter cap, with ear covers flapping to the rhythm of his stride, stuck fast to the back of his head. Rough moccasins on his feet made them look like hoofs and muffled his step; he was close before I noticed him. He had a stringy beard, weathered face, and a wild look in his eyes.

I decided to get out of his way and turned towards the house, trying to hurry without being obvious. I was much too late. I heard the gate creak behind me, then his footfall and whistling breath. Before I could quicken my step two big hands came round and closed on my breasts. My own hands moved faster than my brain. I heard him gasp, then hiss, 'The devil's cat! She's ploughed up my mug!' as I fled. I had registered nothing more. I had simply struck and run.

The door slammed behind me. I was alone. There was no lock. Any moment now . . .

I was sitting on my suitcase when Enn rushed in. I gasped in relief to see him, not the Russian.

'Ann, what happened?'

I couldn't stop laughing, though I was shivering at the same time. Soon I thought I would scream.

'A man just came into our room with his face all bleeding. He's hopping mad! He and Marusja are having a shouting match. Then I heard you laugh. Stop it, Ann. Stop it!'

I stopped. I could hear them next door now, going hammer and tongs.

'I've just made a start at ploughing.' I held out my hand. 'See, I've still got the dirty skin of a Russian under my nails!'

'He must be Marusja's husband.' It seemed a fair guess. 'But that isn't all, I'm afraid. I think he's the camp brigadier. Our boss.'

■

Through the wall I heard laughter. They had made up. Not that that meant any joy for me. Those two would laugh as they gouged my eyes out, which they probably would do, given half a chance, I thought. My God, what a start! It had cost me a lot of sleep, even though I felt no small satisfaction in having drawn Russian blood. The bed was a cloud. What a pity I could not fully enjoy it. Now I could only wait and see what would happen next.

Natasha was not in. I hoped that Enn would come soon with news. I got up, made my bed and dressed, but did not venture outside.

Enn came eventually, and Natasha with him, followed closely by the brigadier. A brigade was a work unit, the brigadier the foreman. The fresh scratches showed like paint marks down his face.

Now I'd catch it!

Enn and I held our breaths.

I stood ready to absorb the onslaught. I would surely be blasted. But I was a stranger to Russian nature. A wide smile split his face as he offered his hand. 'We're not used to visitors,' he said amiably. 'I came home just to see what you was like.'

He had been making hay twenty-five kilometres away, and walked all the way back for no other purpose, Marusja told me later.

'We knew you was coming,' he went on genially. He had the same wild look, same whiskers, same clothes and rough voice. But now a smile, which looked genuine. 'Couldn't sleep in peace till I'd found out whether you was black or yellow, men or women, spoke a proper language or gibbered like monkeys.'

His speech was as crude as the rest of him. But yesterday seemed forgotten. Perhaps he was not a compulsive breast-grabber. Perhaps he was sorry, though I could not expect an apology.

'Glad to see you're white,' he said cheerfully. 'And can speak. That's good. Civilised. Just like us!'

They had not heard the name Ann before.

'Anna?'

'No. Ann.'

'Ann-ya.'

I became Njura.

'How did you manage those heavy things, Njura?'

I was obliged to open my case, unwrap bundles and display the contents: frocks, coats, shoes, under and outer clothing. One bright red and white polka-dotted summer dress surfaced. Natasha squealed. Her eyes lit up so brightly as I shook it out that I offered it to her. She said she would take it for rent. It

114

fitted her well. She looked radiant – firm-bodied and slim. She pirouetted, laughing, in her home-made slippers soiled with fresh cow manure, guileless as a five-year-old.

I was glad to be rid of the red dress. I knew the second I saw it that I could never wear it again. My recently acquired dislike for the colour would only increase, I was certain.

■

'Look, some lephoshka!'

Indeed, it was worth looking. Marusja came at midday with a bowl of thick potato soup for me. She also had a wheat cake – *lephoshka* – made from flour and water, baked on top of the stove.

We had parted amicably a little earlier, after an hour or two's idle talk. She had actually seemed interested in exchanging information. The others had half-listened, Marusja's husband wearing a wolf's grin, Natasha smoothing the dress with admiring fingers. There was no mirror.

I had been careful with my questions and even more so with answers, remembering the warning from the young couple at Aipalova. I learned little, told little. Marusja and her husband had lived here most of their lives. My husband and I had lived in Rakvere, Estonia, thousands of kilometres away. They had never been far, did not want to. We had lived in a small apartment. Yes, something like this one. We had been deported. We did not know why.

'Plucky girl!' Marusja said, giggling as she put the food down. 'You sure taught my old man a lesson. He's always trying to get his hands on the women. Don't worry, eat this. And if you need anything, come to me. But only when he's not here. Understand?'

I nodded. I felt I could trust her. As long as she could trust me not to encourage her husband. She was making it clear enough. She had no illusions about him.

■

We began 'shopping' early because, of the two days allowed to settle in, one was gone. Food reserves were practically nil, Mrs Balter's money was dwindling, and we did not know when – or if – we would get another opportunity. We decided that the three of

115

us would stick together.

The huts in the immediate neighbourhood yielded a small bucket of potatoes, ten eggs and a litre of milk. Not bad, especially the eggs. Not good, as it represented only a few days' sustenance. Few souls were prepared to do business; most, including nearly all the farmers' cabins scattered farther out, where we had hoped for more, had only a terse 'Netu' for us. We were no more popular in Udarnik than we had been in Aipalova.

We walked the two or three kilometres into Maisk, but the shop had nothing. Resigning ourselves to returning empty-handed, we did a tour of the parts of town we had not seen. Behind the shop, near the river, was a street with a large grain store, a cooper's shop, a slaughterhouse, milk depot, two school houses, and a post office with a few simple gadgets for weather information. There was also a sprinkling of superior residences, with two rooms and separate kitchen. Last along the row was a hospital, about fifteen-bed size, with a notice saying 'Doctor's consulting rooms'. No hours.

Some of the houses had a small cowshed on their land. In fact, each of these 'higher rentals', as we called them, was allotted five hundred square metres – about twenty-two or twenty-three metres square – and a few even had a primitive boxlike toilet. Enough for a degree of privacy, if not comfort.

'The bigwigs,' I said. 'Their tails won't freeze in winter.'

They would be for the NKVD and the police chiefs, the director of farms, perhaps the shopkeeper and schoolteachers.

'Thought they didn't have an elite,' Enn observed.

'Communism,' said Mrs Balter, and used a word I had not heard from her before.

■

In the evening I walked alone. Tomorrow was the first of August and we had to report for work. It was also my birthday.

If I were at home, tomorrow morning Elmar would get up early and leave the bedroom, quietly, in order not to disturb me. But I would be awake, as he would know, feigning sleep. Soon he would be back with the children, on tiptoe, shushing each other. I would stir in surprise when they sang 'Happy Birthday'. Then they would kiss me. Tiiu, Tiit, Elmar. Then the presents . . .

'Good evening.' An old woman – pointed out to me earlier as

the nightwatchwoman of the village – greeted me near the sheds. I replied curtly. Company was not on my program.

'You speak Russian?' she asked sharply. She had stopped. I was obliged to do likewise. She looked about like a bird, studied me shrewdly, and beckoned me to follow. I could not refuse without being pointedly rude, as she already had her back to me. I was intrigued, anyway. Perhaps, I reflected, a diversion was a godsend; I was beginning to feel sorry for myself. She led me behind an untidy stack of straw alongside the stables, halted, and motioned me to sit down. She checked back along the path we had come by. We were well hidden, no doubt of that. She seemed to want it that way. I didn't care.

'You're one of the new ones.'

She looked like any other old woman in Siberia in her long skirt, blouse, patched jacket, homemade boots and kerchief to the eye-brows. Except for one quite remarkable thing. She wanted to talk.

'Yes,' I said warily, although she had not really put it as a question.

'Ah!' She had knowing, bright eyes and a conspiratorial look. I thought she might be crazy. 'I'm sorry for you.'

I was feeling sorry enough for myself. Tomorrow I would be thirty-seven years old. I felt perhaps I did not want to stay with her any longer.

'Don't go,' she said, though I had barely stirred. 'We've plenty of time to talk. As long as we stay out of sight.'

She was right, of course. Time was one thing we had plenty of.

'Yes, I'm sorry for you. Where do you come from?'

I told her. She had a good ear, even if she were a little mad, and soon I was pouring my heart out. She nodded repeatedly, this old stranger behind the cowshed, and didn't interrupt once.

'Yes,' she said, when I'd finished. 'It was much the same with us, the first ones.'

She talked then, telling me how those 'first ones' had been brought to Narymm from the Ukraine and the German settlements of the Volga in 1917 and '18. The men and older boys had been separated, sent elsewhere and never heard from again. Only the women, children and older ones had been brought up the Vasjugan.

'They just dumped us on the banks,' she said, 'at different spots along here, along three hundred kilometres of river. Nothing else. No food. No boat. No arms. No tools. No cover. Nothing at all. Only what we managed to carry with us from home. Left us – women, children, old people – to fend for ourselves.'

She told me in a trembling voice how they had gone about felling trees and building huts. Winter had begun. There was no question of moving: anywhere else was too far to go. Immediate shelter was imperative. The stronger ones with the better tools could cut bigger logs, so they had the better huts. The next strongest had the next best, and those with no tools had to wait to borrow them. They learned to plaster the insides and seal roofs to keep out the weather, and build their own ovens and stoves from sticks and clay. They lived off the earth. Or died.

'I had my mother with me, and two children,' she said. 'I'm alone now.'

She put the death toll of those first settlers at eight out of ten. Mostly they had died from starvation, some from sickness, a few from snakebite. Many had been killed by bears. Others had simply lost themselves in the forest and perished from exposure, or been overcome by swarms of mosquitoes.

'It's easy for you,' she said. Without ill feeling. 'You've got roofs over your heads, no matter how poor or crowded. And there are established fields now. Crops, hay, and farm animals. You shouldn't starve.'

She meant it literally. I wondered how her children had died, and my heart went out to her poor shrivelled soul. She had not mentioned them again.

'But you'll have to work for it! You're city folk, most of you, and you're not used to work. You've got good clothes. You'll have to exchange some with us, get working clothes. But don't rely on that, don't trade everything too quickly or you'll finish up in trouble. Work for your lives. Keep everything you can. Above all, you mustn't be afraid of work.'

She told me how collective farms were heavily burdened with quotas of produce to be handed over to the State. And how each individual had a personal quota to fill – a milk quota of a hundred and thirty litres a year payable by every household regardless of whether they had a cow or not; a butter quota; meat, twenty kilograms a year per adult; wool, the amount she

118

could not remember; grain also – and how each item of output was recorded and tallied.

'Watch them, too. Watch those bookkeepers. You'll earn it right enough, make sure they give you credit for everything you do.' If you were unable to fill the personal quota then it was added to next year's. Alternatively, the value of it was reckoned in penalty work days and added to those that had to be put in on the collective farm. There was no dodging it, the quota was everything.

There was land tax to be paid, and now also war tax and contributions to compulsory state loan tickets.

'If you kill even one of your own animals, there's a percentage has to go – '

'You can have an animal? Something you can call your own?'

'Oh yes. If you can pay for it.' She did not read the cynicism in my interruption. 'But a percentage goes to the State. If you kill a pig, for example, they take the skin. Sometimes it's complicated. You pay an extra meat quota on a piglet bought in spring to be killed in autumn, but if you buy in autumn you're exempt from the surcharge.'

I was too tired to puzzle it out. It was not going to affect me anyway; I could not see myself as a pig owner after my acquaintance with them so far.

'That's what most of us do,' she said, getting to her feet. 'Buy before winter. But they can't be kept in the farm sheds, those private ones. That's the catch. You're lucky, Natasha doesn't keep a pig or hens so you won't have to share your bed with them.' She cackled and left.

I remained sitting on the straw heap, stunned. Was this real? She might be a little crazy – dear God, who had more right to be? – but there was a lot of sanity about her, too. Twenty-five years! She looked almost seventy. Her mind was rocky, inconsistent. Some parts had been dead for years. They had to be, for the rest of her to stay alive.

Tomorrow I would be thirty-seven years old. Elmar had found something special for me, to compensate for what had been happening. He had been hinting for weeks.

■

Something was shaking me by the shoulder. I mumbled 'Go away' but it would not stop.

119

I saw a big, rough hand and a man standing by my bed. He had two or three days' growth of beard. I had never seen him before.

'What do you want?' I stammered. He didn't look dangerous, but I pulled the quilt to my chin automatically.

'*A vot!* – Why! – to work, citizen!'

'Work? Today?'

I was still sleepy. I had been dreaming. I knew it had been a terrible dream, except that the moment it ended something beautiful was going to happen, as long as I did not slip back into it. 'But it's my birthday!' I burst into tears.

The man was taken aback. He shifted from one foot to the other, waving defeated hands about. '*Ladna* – well – you can stay home today. But stay put. Keep out of the way. Don't let yourself be seen by the office. *Ladna*, don't cry!' Muttering, shaking his head, he escaped.

Later, the same man, another of the original Ukrainians, was to spend several years in prison for his sympathetic actions. Section 58 of Stalin's Criminal Code covered such anti-Soviet behaviour. That day I was ignorant of the risk he was taking. Perhaps he was, too.

I stood at the window to peer out, and put my ear to the dividing wall. Nothing. No movement outside, no sound in. The Balters had gone, which made me feel guilty. But I would not know what to do or where to go if I left now. Presently, I saw several Russian women going to work, carrying axes, saws, hoes, each with a small bundle in the free hand. They were all in patched, quilted jackets, mostly wearing homemade tscherkis, or moccasins; a few wore rubber overboots.

I spotted a group of our own. Marju Kadaja was one, an operetta prima donna from Narva, in a pair of slacks and a silk blouse with matching scarf. The wives of two businessmen from Kivioli were with her, wearing silk dresses and carrying little parcels. Lunch, I supposed. Their hair was combed and they were talking. They did not look unhappy heading across the open fields. It was a lovely day. Now I wished I were going with them, even if it were only working a potato patch. It would be better than being cooped up here.

Later, I saw them coming back. Their shoes were muddy, clothes torn. They were silent, dishevelled, their arms covered in mosquito bites. They walked slowly, heads hanging. It had not been a lovely day.

The Balters were too tired to talk. I had cooked some potatoes with their last few strips of salt pork, sneaking in during the day, hoping Marusja would not catch me. Her husband, the brigadier Skakalkin, had gone; back to the forest, I assumed.

They could scarcely raise the energy to eat before falling asleep on their makeshift bed of planks, mother and nineteen-year-old son together. There was not enough room for separate beds, as Marusja had two children; newcomers had to take what was going. Mrs Balter and Enn were beyond complaining. I went back to my lonely room without even finding out what they had been doing.

My birthday was over.

10

THE MAN IN BLACK

'You'll have to work for it!'
the nightwatchwoman had told me. 'Work's the answer.'

Older women and those with children went to the fields.
The younger ones and older boys were sent to clear the forest. I
joined the three I had seen yesterday to make a tree-felling gang
of four: one opera singer and the wives of two businessmen and
a lawyer.

There were not enough saws, axes or hoes to go round. By the
time we had found out our allotted task, there were none left. We
were told to borrow from neighbours, which meant another door-
to-door canvas of the established kolkhozniks, some of whom I
had seen before in my search for food.

'Lice!' one of them spat at us. 'Come to live on our backs, and
now they want our axe as well.'

I had been warned while sitting on the straw heap. 'They'll
be unfriendly to you,' she had told me. 'They've been expecting
you for weeks – you parasites and profiteers – we've all known
you were coming, and only those with the longest memories will
have any sympathy for you. And not many of them, either.'

By late morning we had managed an axe and a saw – a big
two-man crosscut such as none of us had ever seen before – and
we headed, weary before we had begun, for the forest.

The axe refused to strike in the right place. The saw dug in its
teeth, kicking and bucking like a live thing. Weak from hunger,
ignorant of technique, we fought them both. By evening we had
felled and mauled one large aspen, trimming branches, and burning
smaller limbs as my co-workers had been shown yesterday. Tired

123

and disgruntled before we had started, we were exhausted by the time we were half-done with the tree. Now it was finished, yet the stump remained. We had no idea how to deal with it, which didn't matter, because we couldn't have done it anyway.

Marusja's husband came to inspect our work. It was the end of the day, time to take tally. He had decided to stay a while in Maisk, now that he was here. He was the Boss. He could go where he liked, do much as he liked. Apparently this was it.

'Shirkers!' he yelled. 'Agitators! Come to sponge off us, then expect us to do all the work for you!' Filth poured off his tongue in a stream that ran unbroken for a full two minutes. It was an impressive production. We waited apprehensively. 'Tomorrow you'll go with the real workers. You can't be trusted on your own. Bloody female loafers. See how they do it while you trim and burn the branches.' Even he could see the futility of today's toil. But he had to impose his own terms on commonsense.

For the day's work I was entitled to line up with the others at the kolkhoz store for my ration of bread. Five hundred grams for every worker, plus three hundred for each dependent child. My face was bitten, dress torn, legs and arms scratched and sore. I limped back to the cabin, clutching the precious bread, ate it and fell, fully clothed, on my bed, as Natasha had already done on hers.

'But you shouldn't starve . . .'

■

'Immediately,' she said.

'What? What for?'

Sleep must be rationed here. Like food. It was the middle of the night and the cleaning woman from the office was shaking me violently.

'Up!'

'What time is it?'

'To the office. Time? Who cares? Straight away now. How should I know what for?'

I heard her go next door to start on Mrs Balter and Enn. The wild idea occurred to me that maybe they were sending us home: it had all been a mistake. I hurried, as I had been told.

The room was filled with people. As far as I could tell, all were from the last barge. The only others present were the two men at the desk: the black-uniformed NKVD man and the director of the kolkhoz. On the desk in front of them were piles of papers. Conveniently and ostentatiously placed on top of the papers was a revolver. The director had seemed all right at our first meeting. I didn't know the other, but the uniform was enough.

The man in black rapped on the desk with the gun, and suitable silence fell. The director said, to nobody in particular, 'Everybody here?' and nodded to his colleague.

The man in black raised cold, expressionless eyes. 'You have been called here to sign some documents. Those who speak Russian – translate for the others.' He allowed time for the two or three among us to do so.

Signing documents? At this hour of night? The silence was complete except for the shuffling of papers. Any optimistic fancies had vanished by this time. We waited fearfully.

The man in black deliberately picked out one sheet. 'First,' he said, and read directly from it. He read coldly, clearly, without looking up. It was short and stated simply that the signer sought to join a collective farm, specified as this particular one. He finished reading. We translated. It seemed harmless enough. Most of us thought: Well, if it pleased them . . .

'Second,' he rapped, 'I the undersigned accept the award of twenty-five years' settlement in – '

My ears rang. I looked at my co-translators. They were as stunned as I. We had heard right. Twenty-five years! Coolly. Like registering for a social club. No crime, or trial. First mention. Sentence: twenty-five years! Sign here: I accept.

There were gasps, cries, then shouting and hysteria, with the two men at the desk banging and outshouting us all, finally waving the revolver for a quavering quiet.

'Third.' He picked up one more document. The director looked over and, I thought, shook his head slightly at it. This committed the signer to paying a special war tax as an alien. The rate was three hundred roubles per household per year.

More crying as we translated. More hysteria. But it hardly mattered: three hundred roubles or three thousand. The twenty-five years still rang through the air, and, for all their shouting, banging, cursing and revolver-waving, the two made no impression. We were beyond control. A third man, whom we had not noticed before, quietly locked the only door behind us. The uproar went on.

'Come and sign. Come up and sign!' the man in black thundered.

Nobody moved forward. He was furious. He called individual names and nobody answered. He was almost apoplectic.

The director looked worried rather than angry, whether for us or for himself I could not tell. They ranted and cajoled in turns, the NKVD man threatening us spasmodically with his revolver. Worn out as we were, the pandemonium on the floor subsided at last. We settled to a resigned hush while they kept it up, but there was no movement towards the pen.

'Everybody has to sign. You can't be kolkhozniks without being on the books, who do you think you are?' The man in black thumped the gun on the table, the barrel pointed our way. 'I'll tell you what you are. Parasites!' I was afraid he would fire; so was the director. 'It will go easier for you. You'll find out what happens if you don't!'

No paper was signed. Finally, the doors were opened to the first tints of morning and we left to a parting threat. 'We'll see about this! By the great father, we'll see!'

What would they see about? I wondered in the cold fresh air. What else could they do? I had no energy for company, even shunning the Balters; I had barely enough to drag myself back to bed.

A man stopped me before I had cleared the village. My brain was as spent as my body, too fatigued to protest. Though alone and defenceless, I felt no fear. I felt nothing.

'Wait. You speak Russian.' He sounded old. There was not yet enough light to see clearly, but the hand he put on my arm was firm.

'I am not one of them,' he said, and pulled me round a corner. We were behind some sort of shed. The only lights I could see were a few fading stars. 'I know what was going on in there. I am with you.'

I made no resistance. I did not care much one way or the other.

'Trust me,' he said. His voice was low and urgent, the accent faintly familiar. 'Don't sign that you want to enter the kolkhoz. Don't pay the war tax. They're not compulsory. They can't force

126

you. But you must sign that you've been sent here for twenty-five years or you won't be registered for anything.' He shook me roughly with the hand still on my arm; I don't know whether to waken me properly or to stop argument before it began. His voice was barely above a whisper. 'You'll get no work, no bread, no place to live. Believe me, I know their laws. I was sent here like you. From the Ukraine. I know. Just sign the one, not the rest. I'll talk to you again on Sunday.' He disappeared, a shadow into the darkness.

Who was he? A spy? Was this a trick to get us to sign the most infamous of all their documents? Perhaps. If so, it was certainly more subtle an approach than tonight's performance.

Suddenly I felt lighter in my heart. He must be genuine. They weren't that clever.

Sunday. I wondered where? how? who? Did we really have a friend?

∎

Saturday. One day to Sunday, and my appointment.

I still had things I could trade for food, but there simply had not been time. Tomorrow I could do that. And rest. Food for my famished body, rest for my battered limbs. The day's work was no easier than any other but – what could the Ukrainian do for us? – there was something to keep going for.

Each new work day had added torture to the last. Roused early, each morning we stumbled into the forest. Stiff, aching muscles struggled with saw and axe. A losing struggle. It seemed we would die of weakness before we mastered their use.

'Come on, Marju. Pull when I push.'

'I can't. These damned blisters on my hands – '

'Tear off a sleeve and wrap them up like mine.'

'I don't want to ruin any more clothes. I might need them for trading. And besides, I've got enough mosquito bites already.'

'I'd swap your hands for my face. Ugh. I can hardly open my eyes. And my legs!'

'I know. And the flies at the blood where you've been scratching!'

We had no food through the day; we could never save enough from the night's ration. For water, we had to walk to the edge of the forest to drink from puddles. On all fours, like animals.

Mrs Balter, home from the fields a little earlier than Enn or I from the forest, had potato soup ready to supplement the bread ration. The store of eggs and milk was gone, potatoes nearly. It was little more than hot water, our soup, but it was wonderful.

'Enjoying it, Ann?'

'As always, Mrs Balter. Thanks.'

'Not too late for your bread tonight?'

'What do you – ?' I began, and checked myself at Mrs Balter's enigmatic smile.

Last night our team had been late out of the forest. The store-room had been closed. Enn had slipped me a few bits of dried bread, slyly, without his mother's knowledge; she would have worried; about me perhaps, about her son certainly: he could not afford short rations. I had felt guilty accepting. We both hated the stealth involved but, to avoid worrying her, it would obviously be better not to tell. How demeaning! Deceiving a friend, conniving with her son outside her door over a few miserable crusts of stale bread! I had looked at Enn, giggled embarrassedly, and sneaked them into my room to eat alone. Now I could only blush and mumble, 'No.'

Tomorrow I hoped to see the Ukrainian again, as we needed advice. The night after the meeting there had been another, this time arranged by the *kolkhoz* chairman. He had put us through another performance. The threats this time had been interspersed, for a little variety, with more convincing periods of coaxing. Again, we were there for a long time. Again, we talked it over among ourselves. The chairman, in an expansive mood, encouraged us. I told several people of my adviser and his counsel. Most were sceptical. In the end, three women, each with small children, decided to enter the collective. Risking even a day's ration of bread was, for them, too great a hazard. To my intense surprise, Mrs Balter elected to do the same. That was all, however. Nobody signed the other documents. The fear of signing was greater than the fear of not signing.

■

Saturday night. Sauna night. A real occasion. There was one sauna for the settlement, fired once a week. We had heard about it at the storeroom. We also heard that it was compulsory. We raised a cackle or two of dry laughter – Saturday night bath night, children, like it or not! – as we were told, in all seriousness, that any female who did not turn up in time for the women's session was driven – driven, we were assured – in with the men. At the right time, in the right place, the possibilities were obvious. This time, this place? We decided we'd be very early.

I took some clean silk underwear with me. I would have to 'eat' it soon – silk underwear should have good trading potential – so I would get some pleasure out of it first. Clean silk on a clean body seemed a distant heaven. I hid it carefully, together with my shoes, in the sleeve of my overcoat and let the heat soak into me, dreaming of luxury. Others around were lost in the steamy distance. The Russian women talked. The Estonians, like me, shut themselves off in private worlds of their own. Clean body, clean clothes, a day's rest to come . . .

I went home barefooted, wrapped only in the coat. Everything else had been stolen while I baked.

■

'A vot, *citizen*. To work.'

'But this is Sunday!'

'Our country is at war, citizen.' Was there a note of irony in the Ukrainian accent? 'There will be no waste of our labours. There will be no day of rest now until winter.'

And there would be no keeping my appointment.

■

Night after night I was at the office. From the time of the second meeting, the group of four who could speak Russian was tacitly appointed a kind of representative committee for all Estonians in the settlement. Whenever there was some business in the office about work, pay, living quarters, and so on, one or all of us were called there. Requests, pleas, complaints. A child was sick. The work was too hard. Tools were blunt, the vermin intolerable, there was nothing to eat. Landladies were uncooperative, or they thieved.

One group of twelve, all Estonians, lived in a derelict office building. The windows had been broken and there was no new glass to be had. The stove was crumbling. The door fell off. They were impractical people, incapable of mending things. They, alone, needed a full-time interpreter. I was called in frequently because I was 'single' and because I did not mind. The fact was,

I would rather be with people at the office than alone at home. I heard others' news and worries, most of it depressing; but at least I heard about life outside my own narrow compass.

Marusja helped me, although not too actively. She was careful, mindful of her position as the wife of the brigadier. Yet she liked company. Sympathy for deportees had nothing to do with her openness with me; I believe she gave us no more thought than a barbarian empress gave her captive slaves. But I was different. I had rebuffed her husband. Though she never said so, I gathered he now thought of me as a she-cat rather than as a woman. Which gave me a distinct advantage with Marusja.

She had a man. She had a man who was a philanderer. And women here outnumbered men by more than twenty to one, long odds in any language. Even foreign women were still women. I was a proven non-rival, probably the only one she knew, friend or foe. She could relax with me, her natural humour had an outlet. She came in to see me often to exchange a few words and questions, though I doubt if she was interested in answers, occasionally confiding a useful hint. In the main, although she was talkative, she avoided direct reference to work and conditions. There was no real rapport. For my part, I was glad of the company; I did little asking, less talking, in the main agreeing noncommittally. Guarded self-concern was becoming part of Siberian survival.

I scarcely saw Natasha, the pretty cowgirl, my sub-landlady and room-mate. Early morning and late evening she was busy with her cows. I occasionally saw her at night, sleeping, usually fully clothed. These were the times I was going to, or coming from, meetings. She never woke at my movements. I presume she ate and rested again during the day, while I was in the forest.

One night, after a frustrating session at the office, Marusja came in, friendly but troubled. I waited warily, a defensive chameleon ready to adapt to its environment. 'Why don't you sign the papers, Njura?' she said after a while. 'And join the kolkhoz?'

'Why should I?' I asked coolly.

Marusja was intelligent. But it would be as pointless arguing a matter of this nature with her as it would be trying to convince a desert Arab there was a God other than Allah. As I was tired, I had no such intention.

'Why not? You're here. You're in it anyway.'

She was right, of course, but there was one colour this chameleon could not – would not! – assume.

'We all should. So we can all work better together. Life would be much easier.'

'Easier? For whom?' Though I could not turn red, I was beginning to see it.

'A vot, for you, of course!'

'Oh rubbish!' All my good intentions were forgotten. 'You are a Russian, Marusja, you don't understand. You belong here. You sing the songs they give you, you dance their tune. We are Estonians, wives of Estonians, mothers of Estonians.' I was rapidly losing control. 'You know what Siberia is to us? Criminals are sent there! Murderers! For ten or maybe fifteen years! And we? You say we should sign for twenty-five! What for? What have we done?' The caution of days went in a few wild seconds. 'You're mad. You're all mad! Go on, run to the office now and tell on me!'

'Njura, I was about to tell you to hold your tongue.' Marusja was hurt more than offended. She was also impatient. Looking back, I could hardly blame her. 'I heard it said in the office today that you are one of the provocateurs, a real troublemaker, always there demanding something. Be more careful, Njura!'

I decided I would, as she slammed out of my room into her own.

The next Saturday night we were called out again. It was the war tax this time. After the usual treatment we were called, one at a time, before one of the foremen. Apart from our own brigadier, Skakalkin, there were two or three others who appeared at irregular intervals. This one looked as mean as any of them. He had the papers in front of him.

My turn came. I prepared to refuse, as everyone had before me. But politely. Marusja's warning was still fresh. I must not draw attention.

I fronted the desk as my name was called.

'You're not needed,' the foreman grunted. 'Next.'

I looked at him in surprise.

'Go and get some sleep,' he yelled. 'Tomorrow you go to voskresnik.'

I left quickly. I knew that one. Voluntary work without pay.

∎

131

In the morning I looked for the Balters, and found only Marusja.

I had had a sleepless night. Why voskresnik for me? What would it be like? Why was I not needed with the others?

Natasha had snored. Mosquitoes had whined. Another Sunday lost, no chance to look for food. Would there be bread after voskresnik? Where is Elmar now? Tiiu? Tiit? I had prayed for strength until the night was over.

'They didn't come back from the meeting,' Marusja told me. 'Better get yourself ready, we're leaving soon. Forget them. They'll be back some time. You're coming with me.'

She was going on voskresnik too. After my outburst of the other night, I did not like to ask questions. Perhaps she was an overseer. Perhaps she had actually volunteered! Not likely, I decided, as I went with her to the office. There, I found that most of those who had been called out last night had been taken to the commandant's office at the other end of the village, and locked in. They were still there. The few left free were angry and afraid.

'Why?' I asked.

Mrs Meret, the wife of a notary from Narva, was my informant.

'We all had to pay some money for the war fund,' she told me. 'Or if we didn't have money, then we had to make it up with clothing. Men's clothing.' It was fairly well known that a lot of the women had some of their men's stuff with them, brought all the way from home when we had not known we were to be separated. 'The ones who decided to pay were escorted to their quarters immediately and brought back here again to hand over the money or the goods. The ones who refused were taken away and locked up.'

'But surely they all refused!'

'Some changed their minds.'

'What about you?'

'I was going to pay. I had enough money. But they saw my husband's suit in my case and took it.' She was terribly upset. 'I tried to stop them. I offered them the money but they took the suit.'

'The Balters?'

'They refused.'

A Mrs Estam was making a lot of noise in the office. She had

132

two children with her, one a boy who was almost adult. They had taken men's clothes from her, too. She was voicing her opinion on Russia, Russians and all things Russian loudly and clearly, while her friends tried to quiet her. She said aloud everything we had ever said under our breaths. She did it beautifully, in a continuous lucid stream that any drill instructor would have envied.

'What is she saying?' one of the officials demanded. He turned to me, snarling. 'You can translate. What is she saying?'

'I don't know,' I said.

'You've done it before, devil take you!'

'I couldn't catch it all.'

'She's Estonian, isn't she?' he shouted. 'Tell me what she says!'

'It's a dialect.' I cocked my ear to Mrs Estam and shook my head. 'I don't understand most of the words.'

He didn't believe me. I frowned in concentration and he turned away, muttering.

I began to think that Marusja might have marked my name down for voskresnik. She knew I would refuse to sign any war tax papers, and that I had neither money nor men's clothing. By anticipating the list, she could save me from the black mark of refusal, the lock-up overnight, and the punishment of extra work for not paying the tax. This way, I had also had the chance to sleep before work.

If she had done this for me I should be grateful, which made me determined not to find out. My native cussedness. I was not going to thank her, nor would I be beholden to her. She was still a Russian; I preferred not to know if she had done me a good turn.

As it happened, all the younger single people had had to 'volunteer', as well as one member of every household belonging to the kolkhoz. We were sent on a six-kilometre walk to a remote part of the forest, where we were to clear a wide path. Assuming that there was reason for such work, it could only have been to make a firebreak. Nobody seemed to know.

Many large cedars had already been felled, their trunks and broken branches lying among the stumps. Other trees had been brought down by the big ones as they crashed. More again had been torn up by storms howling through the bared strip now

133

that the protection of the giants had gone; they lay strewn along the area with new growth sprouting up between them. We had to saw the large trunks into short logs and roll them to the side of the clearing, then remove and burn the smaller growth.

Work, says the old proverb, is not a hare; it does not run away at your approach. I started my day by sitting on a big log to rest my swollen feet. I was joined by Mrs Murak, the wife of an engineer from the brown coalmines at Kohtla-Jarve, and then by the old man who had promised 'more on Sunday'.

He sat on a log next to me to roll a plotski from home-grown tobacco. He offered it to me. I refused politely, though I hungered for one.

'Listen. And tell the others.' He was not in a hurry, nor was he wasting time. 'When they tell you to saw, saw. When they tell you to carry, carry. Never say you can't or you don't know how. But don't let the work kill you. Just keep on moving and groan now and again. You're all pretty frail, but you'll toughen if you live. I've been through it all; deportation, imprisonment, this . . .' He waved his calloused hand at the vastness around us. 'Eat your bread ration all at once, don't pick at it. Picking ruins your stomach and plays hell with your nerves, then you won't be able to sleep and you'll suffer from decay. Don't eat potato peels.' And his final gem: 'Don't pinch from your landlords. But the *kolkhoz* belongs to everybody. Understand?'

We did.

All day, Mrs Murak and I worked hard at appearing busy. We rolled logs, tugged at shrubs, grunting loudly at appropriate times. Minimum achievement, maximum effect. The most difficult part was keeping straight faces, especially at the end of the day when the foreman stood us up as an example.

'Put your backs into it like these two, you lot, and we'll be getting somewhere!'

It was not hard to look embarrassed. Reproachful silence from fellow Estonians was our only other reward. We did not care. We had learned something. We could pass it on later.

11

SHOPPING IN SCHMARKOVKA

It would get worse. Groaning, alone, was not going to be enough. For voskresnik it served its purpose, but ordinary day-by-day work from now on was to be paid by results. In future, the director told us emphatically, food and pay would not be given for nothing. We had finished our apprenticeship.

A number of our women tried to work harder than their strength permitted to get extra bread for their families. It was summer, and for a time it was possible. For most, there was still a little money left, and a few clothes to trade for food. Inevitably, however, resources ran dry. Equally inevitably, as output of effort exceeded intake of nourishment, debility and wasting resulted: privation, exhaustion, sickness, death. A first law of nature. Young mothers perished from starvation – officially 'failure of the organism to thrive' – and their orphans disappeared into distant children's homes. Of these, few ever returned. And no more will. As citizens of the nations they were born into, they are gone. Without identity or kin they are truly the children of communism. Thousands and thousands of them. Not Estonians any more, nor Latvians, Lithuanians, Ukrainians, Romanians, not even Siberians. Just communist Russians, state-produced, state-taught.

The sixteen and seventeen-year-old youths were in just as difficult a position. Sent to work as men, few could sustain their norms, the units of output required by the state to qualify for subsistence allowance. Their organisms also failed to thrive. Of those who did not die of starvation, many contracted tuberculosis and died anyway within a few years. Young girls seemed better able to cope. Their work, at first, was not so heavy, the norms within reach. They managed to ward off extreme malnutrition long enough to acclimatise.

Life the Siberian way was just beginning. It was to become a grim struggle with just two possible outcomes. Success: survival. Failure: death. Each of us would be occupied increasingly with his or her own personal contest. There would be progressively less concern with others'.

There was no succour from outside, no sympathy from within. The rest of the world was busy with its war; our own people back home – those who were left – were kept ignorant of our condition and whereabouts and, in any event, were powerless; and the bulk of Russians were completely uninterested. Most Russians would claim, rightly or wrongly, as they have done for fifty years now, that they did not know about deportees to Siberia – voluntary migrants and criminals, yes; but *deportees*? If there were any such people, they must be national liabilities, and therefore it was all right.

The Kremlin was interested, as was its executive arm, the NKVD. They were both very interested. The Kremlin, in its wisdom – whether by considered opinion, or the whim of one man – had passed sentence; the function of the NKVD was to carry it out. The Kremlin sentence was national annihilation. The program? Simple. Execution or slavery for refractory adults, mass kidnap and brainwashing for their young, threat and persuasion – direct or indirect – for the rest. As long as the overall result was attained, method did not matter, but the simpler and more profitable the better.

■

Enn and I found time for a shopping trip after *voskresnik*. This voluntary labour was truly a picnic, I could inform him.

Our partnership still held. The Balters had money; I spoke Russian. The hundred-and-thirty roubles passed to me in the carriage by my friend at Rakvere had long since gone, Mrs Balter's dried-out notes had not. She and a few others with money or spare clothing had not yet really felt the pinch.

I talked. Enn paid. The results were meagre, and expensive.

'It's the war.' The effects had reached Maisk at the same time we had. Coincidence? A capitalist might have called it the law of supply and demand. 'You know things are scarce now. How much have you got?'

One bucket of potatoes: twenty-five roubles. Five eggs: five roubles. We could not hold out long at this rate.

■

'Put your raincoat up on the load,' said Marusja. 'It will get heavy on your back.'

'Make ready,' I had been told yesterday. 'You leave tomorrow for Schmarkovka.' I had been working near the forest for several days, clearing the land of small growth, raking, and tying harvested oats into bundles. Now, I had to prepare for a journey of thirty kilometres and, what was more, to stay for several weeks; which presented no difficulty as there was so little to pack. The one bright spot was Schmarkovka's reputation as a 'good' kolkhoz.

As far as I could tell, I was the only Estonian making the trip, and spending weeks with no company but Russians was not my idea of a holiday. Even more depressing, on that same night all men of eighteen years and over were called to the commandant's office, and told to get ready at once, as they were being drafted into the army. Of three Estonians who qualified, Enn was one. He was preparing to leave.

Mrs Balter had left early for work. She was stupefied, poor woman. We felt she was better out there than in the village, after this last crushing shock. Could any horror possibly be worse? Her son in the Russian army!

It was almost time for me to go, too. I turned back to Enn to help him with his final packing, ignoring Marusja. We shook hands. My heart was heavy. He put a wad of money in my hand and said: 'For you, Ann. Mother doesn't know about this. Will you look after her for me?' I took only twenty-five roubles. They had done so much for me already that I had to refuse more.

There was no more time for goodbyes. The cart bound for Schmarkovka was waiting in front of the cabin, my bundle of belongings on it. I was ready.

'Go on, throw it up,' urged Marusja. 'Even a pin gets heavy on a trip like this.'

I tossed the coat on the cart.

The driver turned on me. He was short, stocky, blond, about twenty-five. He had two or three days' dark golden stubble on his face – Sunday was two or three days past – and bright eyes and black fingers. He looked healthy. I never discovered why he was not in the army.

'Damned fascist!' He swore at the top of his voice to catch every possible ear. 'Exploiter! The horse has a heavy load as it is. Then you – ' he used the familiar form of 'you', sweetly, as an insult – 'come along with your coat.'

Marusja laughed.

What with Mrs Balter going off like an automaton, Enn likely never to be seen again, and my transfer to Schmarkovka, I had had enough. Now it was 'fascist' and 'you'. It was too much. I had lost my temper before, and got away with it. I knew I could not expect the same again. But I was beyond caring.

'Who do you think you're talking to?' I exploded. 'If there's an exploiter or a fascist around here, it's you! You there, sitting on your lazy bum up on that cart while women walk!' I spat and sent him to the devil's grandmother, all in my best newly acquired Russian. I had picked up a lot this past month.

His mouth dropped open. Recovering, he laughed delightedly and slapped his leg. I thought he might fall from his perch in his mirth. I hoped in vain.

'Hey, you shouldn't get so angry over such a little thing. You speak our language, eh? Come on, climb up yourself, if you're tired.'

I did not climb on. I swore I would not if I were on my last legs, and the devil himself was after me. Which made me like him even less, because I would have dearly loved to ride.

I consoled myself that I was richer by one more experience. In dealing with a Russian, the louder you yell and the harder you swear, the more he will reckon with you. It seemed to apply to peasant and boss alike. I followed the cart along the road, still fuming. Sergei, the driver, flicked at his horse, still laughing.

The rest of the party, five solid-looking Russian women, plodded behind phlegmatically. Sergei and I might not have existed. Schmarkovka was a long way and they were not wasting energy.

Kamenoi. Six kilometres. I had heard there were Estonians there. We passed the buildings of the village but I did not see a soul.

The road wound on. It was a fair surface, graded by hand-wielded spades and tamped firm, taking the easiest course over gently undulating ground. Trees were always close, either natural forest or clumps and copses left in cleared land. We saw few animals, no people. I marched alone, not too uncomfortable in my walking shoes, slacks and jumper. The Russian women, silent as the forest, stayed together to make it clear who was the outsider. They all wore tscherkis, home-made shoes of thick leather base sewn to leather uppers with the seams outside, the uppers gathered and tied behind the ankle by a thong. They made feet look like hoofs, and walking a silent progress. Two of them also had on their 'extension' uppers, a cotton legging worn from shoe to knee as protection against scratches and insect bites, but the others were bare-legged under calf-length, dull cotton frocks. It was warm. Now and again, a bird twittered. It could have been pleasant.

There were no fences and little indication of the track. Occasionally, in a gully, big logs were laid tightly together crosswise, to give a firm base in the thaw. There was no water flowing now, little lying anywhere. My feet soon began to tire, so I took my shoes off for a short while where the going was soft.

Elisarovka. Twelve kilometres. A pitiful group of poor buildings between swamp and river. A few pale children's faces appeared at windows but none came out. We rested for over an hour on the bridge of the water mill while the Russians ate bread, with butter and potatoes, and drank milk. All I had was my five hundred grams of bread, of which I had eaten nearly half on the way. I sat away from the group, so I would not see their spread.

'Sergei,' Marusja called, 'why don't you offer Njura a smoke?'

I glared at her. She knew I was craving for one, had been for hours, and that I was trying not to see or smell the beastly driver puffing his. She winked back at me.

'Do you smoke, too?' He used the polite 'you' this time and threw a tobacco bag made from a pig's bladder in my lap, following it with a piece of newspaper. 'Here, have a plotski.'

'Might as well put it in my cheek and chew it,' I muttered.

'This you'll have to learn,' said Sergei, and dropped himself down next to me.

He rolled the cigarette deftly, demonstrating the steps.

'Main thing is to lick it – so – else it'll come to bits.' He licked it carefully all over and handed the wet product to me, showing his green teeth in a grin. It had gone too far now for backing out.

I could only fake a smile and accept it. At least it was a smoke and, as 'need made the ox plunge into the well', I put the repulsive thing in my mouth. Sergei's grin widened. He clapped me on the shoulder, and grinned at everyone. They scowled back. Far from my intention, he was now my champion.

∎

The haymakers' camp was three tents. Each would comfortably sleep six, perhaps eight people. There were already at least ten in each tent, all asleep as we pulled in at midnight. In front of every one a small fire was smouldering, grass thrown on top to smoke the mosquitoes away. The others quickly found places – the women by pushing into spaces between cursing sleepers, Marusja with her husband, who was the boss of this work brigade – while I stayed standing in the smoke of the main fire between the tents, not knowing what to do.

Sergei peered through the darkness and recognised me. 'Come on.' He led me to a tent. 'There is a bunch of Estonians in this one.' He woke a young Russian girl and told her to move next door.

'Why?' she complained. 'I was here first.'

'You can sleep next to me,' Sergei said.

She took up her bedding with a will.

∎

The Estonians turned out to be three boys: Robert, Ants and Edgar. Edgar Randin, the youngest of them, was a year or so younger than my son, who would be fourteen next month. A child, alone in a place like this and scarcely out of prep school. The others were a little older and bigger and stronger. I knew Edgar, who had been in our carriage, but not Robert or Ants. Edgar's family, and the Nommiks, had followed us up the river, and were the Estonians we had heard of at Kamenoi.

Early in the morning work began; for the Russians, after breakfast; for us, on empty stomachs. They ate the food they had brought with them; we had to wait for our daily five hundred grams of bread and half-litre of watery potato soup to come up from the nearest kolkhoz.

The experienced hands cut hay with scythes. We could not use them, so we were to follow with rakes, but not until the sun

140

was well up and drying out the dew. We were shown how, and began. By that time, the cutters were well ahead, now stooped and sweeping, now stretching up to rest or to sharpen their wicked-looking blades.

Haymaking went on for nine, ten, eleven hours a day, day after day. It was not as difficult as wielding an axe or saw had been, but it was tiring, none the less. The ground was hilly, the mosquitoes and marsh-flies troublesome, and hunger was with us all the time. Back and stomach muscles complained constantly, legs and arms cramped at effort that should have been easy. For compensation, we could keep together and speak our own language.

'Auntie Ann, look!'

After a couple of lucky finds we had learned to watch for wild strawberries and blackcurrants under the grass and on the slopes, the finders sharing. These were a tremendous lift to morale. Much more importantly, they helped to combat the scurvy that was never far away on a bread and potato diet, although we knew nothing of that then.

We had a pleasant surprise at the end of the week: Enn arrived. The three conscripted lads had been kept in the commandant's office for several days of interrogation and indecision, and finally sent home. They were not considered loyal or trustworthy enough for 'the world's greatest army'.

'They almost apologised to us,' Enn said. 'We can't become heroes!'

Our food ration improved. Enn had brought with him some potatoes, butter, dried bread and a little salt meat, which he insisted on sharing. Our protests were not persistent. He also took over the management of sleeping arrangements and, with his love of order, he had us much more comfortable. Until now, we had each slept wrapped in our own bedding, occupying one corner of a tent shared with a half-dozen Russian women. Enn decided it would be warmer, and the ground softer, by spreading his large quilt as a common mattress and having three blankets for cover instead of only the one thickness each, top and bottom, as we had before. Edgar had no blanket at all – the Russian who had arrested his family must have had a particularly sadistic streak, telling them they had no need either of bedding or warm clothing – and previously we had had to take turns sharing with him. Now, we were well covered and glad of it, as the nights were cold.

The boys were normal adolescents. No doubt, at home they would have been responding to the stirrings of manhood. But for young men to grow tall and strong like forest trees, they must have roots to sink into the earth, space around, and warmth above. Torn from their native soil, deprived of warmth, once strong young bodies were weakened by hard work and lack of nourishment, their sound minds bewildered forever by the brutal events of recent months. The vital sap of independence no longer ran.

The boys were alone, confused and frightened, though they did their best to hide it. I changed my position nightly, mothering young men who had had little such need for years. Edgar was always next to me. Frequently, after saying prayers together, he would slip his hand in mine so the others would not see, and go to sleep.

Edgar's mother and his nine-year-old brother died of starvation and cold during their second winter in Siberia. Edgar himself died a year or two later. Tuberculosis, it was said. He was not yet eighteen.

Schmarkovka was a prosperous kolkhoz. At the time of the 1917–18 wave of deportations, a hardy group of people had trekked east one winter across the frozen swamp. They were natives of the more habitable Siberian lowlands, genuine volunteers answering the call of their new leaders to open up a virgin land. They were true pioneers, farmers like their fathers' fathers before them. Unlike the deportees who had been thrown on the banks of the Vasjugan, they had come with clothing, utensils, horses, stock, tools, implements and seed. Above all, they had come with generations of knowledge in the farming of similar country.

These Russian settlers had come as a free people, freer than they had been for centuries under the Tsars, and, to a large extent, they had preserved their freedom. Isolation had its advantages. They had no neighbours, no supervisors. They kept to ancient customs, declined social change, practised their ancient religion. It made little difference to them who occupied the Kremlin; 'progress' did not seep that far. All had land, cows, pigs and fowls they could call their own. Industry and hardihood meant that the Schmarkovkans were able not only to survive but advance, pushing into the wilds, clearing and cropping large areas of now productive land, while the forced settlers, ill-equipped in every way, fought an uphill and usually losing battle against the same unforgiving environment. Only a few kilometres apart, Schmarkovka had thrived from the beginning, while Maisk still struggled after twenty-five years.

There were many Estonians in Schmarkovka, nearly all from Virumaa, my own home county. They must have come on a different train, as I had not seen them on ours. Nor did I know any of them.

'Lehtmets? Our member of parliament?'

'Yes.'

'And didn't he have something to do with Virumaa Teataja?'

'He was chief editor.'

'My husband once wrote an article.'

Three times the boys and I were sent into the village to pick up bread for the camp. Each time we gathered in Mrs Ale's room – previously a stranger to me, she was known to one of the boys – and talked. We never asked about husbands, after that introductory meeting. Nobody did now. It was understood.

Mrs Ale and her two small daughters – and occasionally others who knew we were in – brought out potatoes, eggs and milk whenever we came. We talked obliquely of places and acquaintances back home. They told us of their life here, so different from ours in Maisk.

'They call us the "impure ones", you know, because we're not of their religion. We have to be careful not to offend them.'

'Huh!' The boys were not impressed.

'I mean it. They've got lots of funny traditions and customs.'

'But – '

'We have to respect them.'

'Respect their customs? What about ours?'

'You'd be wise to keep on their right side, too.'

'Be careful not to upset a Russian? Pugh!'

'Oh, they're fairly good to us. We don't mind. Every morning you're likely to see them standing before their icons, making the sign of the cross, the father reciting the prayers. And they have different holy days when different cooking utensils have to be used. We're getting used to that, and their other taboos, even gradually finding out the foods that are forbidden on the holy days.'

'No problem to us,' one of the boys remarked. 'As long as they don't forbid bread.'

'There are feast days. And long fasts. We have to observe them too.'

Food was easy to get, as long as one had money or goods for barter, and the prices were far below what we had to pay at Maisk. I regretted travelling so light. But Mrs Ale and her friends looked after us without expecting payment of any kind. I blessed our good fortune.

'My landlady has two cows, two pigs, several sheep and some fowls.'

Such wealth, unheard of in Maisk, was normal in Schmarkovka.

■

Summer. A day of sunshine, with birds singing, and long-drawn twilight, a merry meal-time of delicious food in the meadow, sitting on fresh-smelling new hay; a balmy night for more eating and drinking and laughter and dancing. And heavenly, heavenly sleep . . .

Haymaking on my family's farm, long ago, during summer vacation. It all came back as I lay awake, with Edgar beside me in the dark, manfully stifling his sobs. No music here, no pleasantly tired limbs sinking into heavenly sleep. Sore hands with blisters rubbed raw and oozing through the caked dust. Aching back. Itching skin. The tent filled with the sounds of snoring and mosquitoes, reeking of smoke and unclean bodies. And always hunger.

Mowing nearly finished, the stacking began. The small heaps we had raked had to be dragged to where the men made large stacks. The women showed us how to make a primitive cart of two long branches, pile it high, take up the ends and pull. We were farm hand and horse as well. Even simple tasks took time to learn; like how to gather a bundle of hay in one piece of string, then another and another; how to fix the sheaves to the branches and drag them up hill, down dale, around bushes and over stumps without losing part or all of the load. It took time. We wasted energy. There was no laughter, and no birds sang.

By the end of September we were finished. The brigadier measured the stack by eye and was satisfied. The women watched, and guessed at the payment to come from their toil. I did not know enough about it even to speculate. All I knew was that it was finished and we had been away for a month and a half. Now we were to go back, and I feared the approach of Siberian winter. It would arrive suddenly, I understood, and once here it would last six months. We must get back to prepare.

∎

Mrs Balter had kept some hot soup and potatoes for me. Not another step to go – not another painful pace to lift my weary body – and food! I think I was hungrier than I had ever been. She was a marvel.

'Enn has been back some time,' she said. 'I was worried about you, Ann.'

'I was worried myself,' I said. I had limped the last five kilometres into Udarnik and doubted I could have lasted another one.

We had started out from Schmarkovka at eight. The Siberians were all keen to get home, and thirty kilometres was no great distance to travel in a day. The boys wanted to hurry, too: they had mothers waiting and young legs to carry them. It was a sunny autumn morning, cloudless and bracing, with a fresh breeze coming from the north.

Early on, we went through shallow valleys, and over hills covered in aspen, birch, ash and maple, shining in glorious autumn colours. Briar bushes were covered in yellow blobs, rowan branches bent low under the weight of berries. Other trees I did not recognise had an attractive black cherry-like fruit. 'Poisonous,' said Marusja. I took her word for it. Several times we startled hares into darting across our path. We heard woodpeckers at work far and near. Squirrels hopped excitedly in the branches.

At Elisarovka we rested for the horse's sake. The others were anxious to keep moving. Despite the richness of life and colour around us – or, perhaps, because of it – I was miserable. I must have looked it, because Sergei had stopped the horse just out of the village. 'Hop on if you like.'

He had treated me with protective deference since our first encounter. I wondered about the deference. Although comrades of the plotski, I think he had heard about my skill with the fingernails.

I rode with him until Kamenoi, where Edgar Randin's mother now lived with her other son. Edgar would be coming home later in the day; he had stopped off at Elisarovka with one of the

145

other lads. Refreshed after my ride, I had gone to search, asking two wide-eyed children on the roadway if they knew where there were any Estonians. 'Foreign people?' There was no-one else to ask. 'Yes.' They led me to a small hut.

'The door's open and Babushka's at home,' the bigger one spilled in a rush before the customary flight. What an ogre I must be!

I had knocked and stepped in. To my surprise I met not Mrs Randin, but the mother-in-law of a friend of mine from a neighbouring town, and grandmother to one of my daughter's playmates. All three were here, she told me through tears, the women of three generations. Her daughter-in-law, the only one capable of work, was expecting a baby in winter. 'Oh, that poor girl!' She had then launched into a long tale, which kept me for far too long to consider further calls.

'There are others we know there, too,' I told Mrs Balter. 'A couple of school friends of mine with their children. I didn't have time to see them. And Mrs Nommik.' From the carriage, with her boy of five and girl of seven. 'Poor thing, she has no money or anything to exchange. They've just been kicked out of the room they had, because they can't pay. Two little children! And do you know why? Because the room is needed to bring in chickens for the winter.'

Mrs Nommik had been a washerswoman, her husband a carpenter. Neither had ever expressed, and probably had never held, any serious political opinions. No-one will ever know why they had been arrested; her guess was that her husband had contributed to the exposure of a Russian spy twenty years earlier, in 1918, and had been on their list since. Her only luggage had been what she could cram into the space left in a heavy carpenter's tool box, which she had carried all the way because it was her husband's livelihood. An axe and a saw were, for her, the only useful instruments in it. The tools took up more room in the box than all the clothes she had for herself and the two children together.

Mrs Balter shrugged. 'What can you do about it?' She seemed distinctly unmoved and, for all her goodness to me, I felt cross with her.

'I said I would go back and see them as soon as I can.'

'And Mrs Randin?'

'I didn't see her either.'

Piqued at her lack of interest, I did not tell of my maternal feelings for Edgar.

'The news here is no better. Two babies have died.'

I knew one of the mothers well, and she herself was very ill, the organism failing. Now her landlord was putting her out, as his animals would need shelter soon.

'Three of our boys have gone, too,' Mrs Balter added. 'With a Russian to guide them, sent off into the forest to collect cedar cones. Dear God, out there alone!'

No wonder she had little feeling for the people of Kamenoi. She had no feelings left.

'Oh, Mrs Balter! Who?'

The boys, between sixteen and eighteen, had been given their rations, half in bread, half in flour, and told not to come back for two months. They were to get the seeds – 'cedarnuts' – from the cones. These are edible, really very tasty, and a highly prized export from the area. Each kolkhoz had its quota to send. But the boys had no knowledge of forestcraft, no instruction in survival. They had never had to fend for themselves even in the best circumstances. And, heaven help them, winter was coming.

My own accommodation was in jeopardy too. Natasha, in my absence, had taken in more sub-tenants, a woman from Narva and her daughter. And she had set a rent. 'Ten roubles a month.' She was in one of her sullen moods. These tended to turn on and off with sunny spells between. I was used to them. But there was a mulishness about her now which meant trouble.

'Ten roubles?' I had none. She knew I had none. I had no intention, however, of admitting I had none. She would have to ask for it. I said nothing.

'They're paying it.' She nodded at the new lodgers. 'Each.'

I looked her in the eye and she looked away.

'Everybody else is,' she pouted.

Others were on a good thing collecting rent, why shouldn't she be? She had lived her life here with people who had lived their lives here, unable to read or write, knowing nothing whatever of life outside the kolkhoz. Inside it, she knew as much as anyone. She knew the value of things, and human life rated very low in this market. If I could not pay she would have no compunction about turning me out. Particularly in her present state of mind. Something, or someone, had upset her.

'From now.' She said this grudgingly, as though she had thought about backdating it. If she had, I'd have asked for the dress back. She had probably considered that. I thought I might have to find out what had put her in such evil temper. I did not answer, and Natasha turned away.

The newcomers did not worry me. We found enough room. Maret was quiet and pleasant, her daughter, a nice child, nine years old, Tiiu's age. Maret was from a working-class background with little formal education, but we hit it off well. The rent, however, did worry me. I had no hope of getting it.

Next morning I looked through the case I had packed for myself, and the parcel sent down to the train by my mother. I took out a woollen winter frock and held it to the light. Natasha was watching. I suddenly knew that she had been through my belongings in my absence, and this was a favourite. I showed it to her. Her eyes opened wide and then narrowed.

'It's not much,' she shrugged, but her eyes were glued to it.

It was a pretty frock. It would suit her beautifully. She could be the envy of Maisk. I twirled it round and back, shrugging more elaborately than she. 'I'll sell it,' I said, and folded it again. No response. I patted it into place.

'You can stay for a while.'

'How long?'

'Two months.'

'Huh.'

'Three months.'

'Now, if I took it – '

Natasha got the frock. I won seven months' rent and a roof for the winter. I had got a bargain and felt no remorse whatever.

I decided then to take stock of my belongings, putting aside the clothes that should have good trading value, keeping those more practical and less readily sold. In the trading pile I put a light woollen coat, a camelhair winter coat – I took a long time over that one, it would hurt if I ever had to part with it – three frocks, a couple of knitted blouses and two pairs of summer shoes. For myself, I had left a full-length calf-skin coat, skiboots and slacks, a pair of high rubber overshoes, two pairs of woollen mittens, a woollen swimsuit which I had no recollection of packing, beach slacks and a long, bright lemon, chenille beach coat made in France – why on earth? – a pair of sport shoes and some silk underwear. I kept a few other bits as well. The clothes my mother had sent to the train were a real blessing. I was wealthier than I'd thought. I sent off a prayer for her and an apology for the curses I had aimed several times at the extra load.

Strangely, the items most coveted by locals were sheets, for they could be turned into anything; pants, shirts, blouses, quilted coats. Above all, they made patches. The more fashionable things had little market value and no-one wanted them. Silk had no attraction, at least not for the paying customer, I reminded myself bitterly. Dresses, wool or cotton, preferably coloured, were prized. Unfortunately, I was too slim for most Russian women, and my potential customers were therefore few. Natasha might wake up to that some time. She hadn't, yet.

Things were bad, yet it was possible they could get worse. So I put the most saleable articles aside, keeping the less so, and, though my wardrobe for personal use lacked depth, the trading value was fair.

■

I was out in the forest burning off when the news came that the boys were back. They had been away for a week and returned during the night.

'Are they all right?'

'Poor things, they've had a terrible time.'

The guide had taken them to a hunter's hut far out in the forest where they were to store the nuts, and left them there. They had tried to get at cones high in the trees, for those on the ground had already been thoroughly scavenged by squirrels and chipmunks. They could not get enough to feed themselves, let alone store any in the hut. They soon used most of their bread and did not know what to do with the flour. They became weaker by the day. After four days of useless effort climbing and trying to pick or shake down cones, they decided to find their way back home, walking through the marshy flats along the river by day, huddling together, wet and shivering, to beat the cold by night.

They all had colds, and Ott Ustav had to go to hospital. I was passed the message to get back as soon as possible to go with him to interpret.

■

'What are you doing here? Useless spongers! Always trying to get out of work! All right, what's the complaint this time?'

There was no doctor, despite the sign with consulting hours. The orderly was a member of the party, with a fierce hatred for Estonians. It seemed all party members had learned the same formula: we were vicious parasites, enemies of the people, blood-suckers, and so on *ad nauseam*. We listened through the full recitation. I even agreed with him. Ott shook miserably. The orderly's word at the hospital was law. Nobody was exempt from work through ill health unless his or her temperature was above 37.6°, the only criterion. Then he or she could get a 'blue paper' for two days. Ott was given the blue paper.

'But that's all. Don't waste my time coming back. There won't be any second paper.'

■

There was little time for worrying about others' troubles. Ott and the boys were ill. So were many more. None of us was well. We were kept too busy for gossip or exchange of any but the briefest of news, such as it was, only talking to those working at the same task. When we did occasionally get together, one topic overrode all others. Food. We talked about it, thought about it; alone, we even dreamed about it. We tried the alternative of ignoring it; as far as I was concerned, with notable lack of success. We tried thinking of work, discussing old times, indulging in make-believe of a new life that was always remarkably like the old. There was no news of outside, nothing much of inside. There was only the past to think about as an escape from the present, and fantasy for a future. All on an empty stomach.

■

Neither Ott nor the other two ever completely recovered. Ott was the first, but they were all dead within three years.

12

ACQUISITION, FIRE AND FEAST

I learned the art of acquisition. Acquisition is not stealing. You stole from anyone else, but from the kolkhoz you only 'acquired'.

We were making ensilage. All the Estonians, women and boys, old and young, cut grass at the edge of the swamp to store in the ground for animal fodder. Five holes were dug in the higher ground, each about two and a half by one and a half metres, and two metres deep. For each hole there were six or seven people to cut grass with sickles, carry it and throw it in. The Russians assigned to the hole tamped it down with large wooden clubs, sprinkling salt between layers. Each gang had to fill a pit by nightfall and cover it with straw and earth. New holes would be ready tomorrow. Thus we worked for a week, in a cloud of mosquitoes, to the music of cries of bitten children. In rest periods we did not even have the strength to look for lice, the national pastime which we by now perforce embraced. I would drop on the bare ground with the others and spread myself flat like a sunbather to ease my breaking back, ignoring the insects, crawling up again at the third '*davai*' to find another patch of thin grass and sweep my sickle through it. Tired fingers would then scratch the stricken green blades into a heap to be lugged and dropped into their grave.

The easiest place was in the hole. The Russians did most of that, the tamping and salting, claiming their years' experience was necessary for best results. Incidentally, therefore, best pay.

I took my opportunity, when one of the Russian women was slow to get back from a meal break, and jumped down to help;

despite their claim, I could not believe working upright could be as bad as bending double all day. The bag of coarse salt was in a corner, the tamps lying on the firm, spongy floor of compressed vegetation. I tamped and salted until my fingers burned. I licked them, and licked them again. Soon, some of the precious stuff found its way into my pocket, the first salt I had touched in months. Over the next few days I developed my technique, taking with me small scraps of material the size of a handkerchief sewn up as bags, jumping in to give assistance at every opportunity. I managed to acquire enough to last me months. I considered hoarding for trading, as there was constant demand for it, but decided the risk was too great. The only useful trade was with Russians, and who knew what might happen if I were reported?

Any sense of guilt I had at my first venture into organised stealing – and I believe my upbringing did rebel at first, discriminating between planned robbery and a quick retaliatory snatch – died quietly. This was no crime. Instead of hoarding, I stole systematically for Estonians until the job was finished.

Though daylight was shortening, the workdays seemed longer. There were no holidays, and no hope of any until winter was well established. The fine-weather jobs had not been finished in time. Quotas for the collective were unfilled despite the extra work power we provided, so we had to keep going. How far behind they would have been without us was anybody's guess, yet all but a few of the Russians kept their distance, to the point of open hostility.

We of the 'heavy brigade' – the younger 'single' women and the boys – had been looking forward to potato-picking time. Lately, by tacit agreement, the direct mention of food had been strictly avoided as there was no point in tormenting ourselves, but it must have been in all our minds that potato picking lent itself to the acquisition of a few unofficial calories a day. We should have known better. The locals gave themselves the job, assisted by the 'light brigade' of older women, young boys, and women with children. We were sent, grumbling, to the turnips.

The turnip field was two or three kilometres out of Udarnik. I went barefooted, for my first shoes were already worn out. Boots would be put aside for winter. I had a pair I could have used but I was determined to keep those, together with one dress and a

152

coat, for going home. I had decided early that I would leave in style, not as a backwoods peasant.

Our new job was heaven compared with the previous one. There was a fire going continuously in the middle of the field and someone always ready to dash off into the forest to collect wood for it. The picked turnips were brought near the fire and heaped for collection, later to be taken away by horse-drawn cart. They were not potatoes, but they were food. We ate them fresh, or cooked them in the ashes to be had hot or cold. We even hid some to take home at night for soup.

The turnip diet did not improve my relations with Natasha. It irritated my bladder to the tune of four, five and six times a night. Each time the door opened a fresh blast of cold air came in.

'Do you have to buzz in and out like a blowfly?' She was furious.

'I'm sorry, Natasha, I can't help it. I think I've got an infection.'

'A what?'

'I have to go to pass water.'

'Can't you do it without opening that blasted door?' Silly question.

'I haven't anything to use.' I could hardly blame her for being annoyed. Still, she could be a bit more sympathetic. I smiled into the darkness. 'Perhaps one of your pots – ?'

'What?'

'I have no pot, so – '

'Go to the devil.'

My co-tenant stifled a giggle.

'I thought so.'

'What?'

'Nothing. I'm sorry.' I was, too, though not for her.

A thump and a rustle sounded through the dark, and a terse swear-word. She had turned her back. I made a face at it. Natasha or no Natasha, bladder or no bladder, I was *not* going to stop eating those tubers.

■

It was the end of October. We had night frosts. In the early morning the ground had a crust of ice and the turnip stalks were frozen stiff and sharp. I had to put on my skiboots, although I had wanted to keep them in peak condition for the snow. The boots were warm, but by midmorning the sun had melted the crunching surface, and they picked up great clumps of mud. I found them almost too heavy to drag along.

My fingers became mottled from handling the crackling foliage and beating clinging earth off the roots. They passed from cold to numb to painful, thawed and warmed occasionally by the fire. My fellow pickers and I hardly spoke as we passed. We trudged along like robots, picking in rows, cutting turnip tops with large knives, using the same knives to scrape mud from our boots. We were tongue-lashed repeatedly for not moving as quickly as our overseer expected. Not that it made much difference; we could go no faster.

At night, after work, we were issued our ration of bread. I ate only half of mine now my diet was supplemented, keeping half to pick at during the morning. The bread was thick, heavy and black, with flecks showing where potatoes, skins and all, had been mashed into the bake.

Linda Veike used to say at the fire that you could tell character by the way people ate their bread. There were those who cut it into slices and ate as to the manor born. These were very few after the first weeks. Others tore into it immediately as though afraid of losing some – which could certainly happen if you were not careful. Others again broke bits off to spread the feast over the day. Some even stuck to a rigid schedule of meals. Breakfast. Lunch. Dinner. There were open eaters, and there were secret nibblers who concealed broken-off segments in the palm and chewed slyly with the hand over the mouth, while the main portion never came out of hiding. I was an open eater, taking the whole five hundred grams or whatever part was left of it in my hands and biting off what I needed. I had no suitable knife, even if I had wanted to cut it, and I had discovered that a clean bite wasted less in crumbs than breaking pieces off. As to secret eating, I tried it and saw no point or pleasure in it. This way I could join others or eat alone if the ration held out, as and when I pleased.

For lunch I had turnips and what bread I had managed to save. The others all seemed to have something extra from home. Perhaps they still had money or perhaps they were exchanging with their landlords. I didn't know and didn't ask.

■

'What do you want?'

'You are the bookkeeper?'

'Why?'

'I want to know how much I have earned so far.'

'You've finished the turnips?'

'Today.'

'What do you want to know for?'

Curiosity, mainly. Marusja and Natasha had been discussing their pay for several days. It was handed out annually and based on the percentage achieved of a set norm for each job. Above the norm meant pay, below meant a debit of workdays owed to the State. These would be carried into the next year.

'I would like to know, that's all.'

He flicked pages and became pompous.

'The brigadier has measured,' he said, 'and the office has calculated. At "silo" you made a quarter of a workday per day, on the turnips the same. You will get your bread in advance from the store every night, to be deducted from your salary in January. Tomorrow you go to the potato field.'

'Why – '

'Yes?' His eyes gleamed expectantly.

'Nothing.'

At this rate there would be no salary in January. Only debits. A quarter of a workday a day! Marusja, on the same job at silos, got a day and a quarter. I had heard her saying so. She was a thief! Taking food from our mouths. So was her husband. With the gall to call us exploiters! So was this pencil-wielding . . . I shrugged off indignation. What matter, anyway? The war will surely be over soon. Let them cheat as much as they like. January? We'll be home by then, as long as we get enough to stay alive in the meantime.

'Thank you. Oh yes, quite, thank you.'

He was disappointed at no argument. My share of victory.

■

At home, potatoes were grown in rows. The plants were in heaped up ridges with furrows between. Where picking was not done by machine, the ridges were ploughed open and pickers moved down the furrows gathering the potatoes into baskets.

Here, there were no furrows. The plants grew higgledy-piggledy fifty to sixty centimetres apart, with dirt heaped up about each stem by hand, early in the summer. Now, each pile of earth at the base of a plant had to be broken open with a spade. And behind each worker with a spade two followed to do the picking. I chose to use the spade to give my aching back a change: no rest, since spading was the heavier work.

Again, we had a fire where the children warmed themselves. They had nothing to do, nowhere else to go. We always had some potatoes baking beneath the coals among the ashes, although it was forbidden under pain of vague but fearful retribution. They were good. A little salt, carefully crushed and kept in a scrap of material in my pocket, made them delicious.

Several days went by before the storm broke. I had worked fast, digging open many nests to get well in front of my pickers, and was squatting at the fireside, fishing for potatoes with a stick among the ashes, when I was startled by a burst of terrible swearing right behind me. I jumped, the stick flying out of my hand into the fire.

'Bitch! Whore! Devil's offspring!'

The full flow of Russian abuse poured out at the top of brigadier Skakalkin's voice. He had arrived stealthily, I had no idea from where, and, ignoring others obviously at the same game, directed the whole of his wrath at me. He had never forgotten. 'And no more fires! You hear? You can freeze to bloody death!'

With that he kicked the fire – ashes, coals, potatoes – all over the place and stomped off. We watched him silently. One of the children cried.

We made no fire for the rest of the day, but decided to speak to the kolkhoz head straight away. We gathered in the office, muddy and miserable, most of the Estonian community. The children made a lot of noise. The director looked annoyed. We shushed them and put our case determinedly. We needed warmth, we said, our fingers could not work frozen. The children did not have suitable clothes and were not allowed inside by the landladies. They had to have warmth. The wood we were burning had to be burnt anyway. We were not asking for favours.

He told us we could make a fire, but only near the forest – not permitted near the road. Burning big logs – not permitted; and staying too long near the fire – not permitted either. The director was a fair man. The new rules made it less likely the blaze would be seen by Skakalkin, so he would not lose face, thus satisfying that side.

Only one concern remained now, to us a crucial one. The baking of potatoes was neither permitted nor forbidden: it was not mentioned. Direct consent could not be given, of course, as that would contravene higher rules, and there was always the chance someone would report it to the NKVD. We were getting to know the system.

Next day, a big fire burnt near the forest, and potatoes baked in it while we kept better watch for the brigadier. As it happened, threshing had begun and Skakalkin had gone to supervise it. We had only a few days to enjoy his absence, however, as we, too, were sent off to help with the threshing, leaving the '*Babushka* brigade' to finish the potatoes.

Everybody in the kolkhoz had been looking forward to this time: a tradition had become established that this last gathering before winter, for the last big job of autumn, should be accompanied by a spate of eating. A grande finale culminating in a regular feast. Plenty of good, warm food. We dared not discuss it among ourselves out in the fields for fear of disappointment. The old kolkhozniks did, though, and we heard enough to share their eagerness. Potato soup every day for lunch, with barley, some-times even meat!

It was getting colder, the ground barely thawing out by lunch break. My last couple of days on the potatoes took an age. Hot liquid at lunch-time? Impossible to imagine. I bent to my spade and thought that perhaps I could keep more of my bread to have with it. Pea soup? With crusts to soak in it? In the evening, boiled potatoes, it was whispered, to give it body. With salt! I still had some. I must inspect my hoard to check. It was in a bag in the toe of my shoe, down at the bottom of the suitcase. My stomach trembled. I switched my mind back to the spade. The ground had a hard crust now. Soon, digging would be impossible.

Of all the rumours up to the night before the feast, only two seemed solid and, try as I did not to be too excited, I failed at these two. One was that Marusja had handled an authorisa-tion for the slaughter of an old cow for the threshers. The only meat I had had in months was the odd tiny piece of salted pork

Mrs Balter had so skilfully spun out. The other was that two Estonians, Alma and Helga, had been designated cooks. This might be very good for me, as they had been on my salt list and were grateful.

■

The threshing shed was in the centre of the complex near the rest hut, a real advantage, as the workers were allowed to eat in the hut all during the operation. Even the storeman had special orders: our bread ration was to be brought to the hut every morning. That made us doubly happy as, apart from seeing him grizzling, which gave us malicious pleasure, there was now no more need to search for the cranky quarrelsome old coot to ask for favours if we came in late and exhausted from work. He was practically at our beck and call. Nothing was too good for the threshers!

I got off to a lucky start. The belt on the threshing machine had broken the night before my first day, and work could not begin until nine. Usual starting time was before six, by lantern light. It gave me a couple of hours to take a good look at what we would be doing. The machine was housed under a roof of timber slats supported by high thick poles. It was more or less open sided. The floor was trampled earth. The bundles of wheat sheaves were in a great stack in one corner of the shed, partially protected on the weather side by paling-like vertical planks roughly trimmed and loosely placed against the sheaves. The drum-like machine was nearby, a belt running from it outside some fifteen metres to a rough spindle – the 'motor' – turned by four horses, urged on at the moment in a practice run by an enthusiastic small boy with a whip. The boy yelled and cracked, the horses moved in their slow circle under the belt, and the big wooden blades inside the drum revolved. From where I was, I could see the 'engine', the belt, and the long cylinder inside which the blades whirred. Moving in under the shelter I saw a man at the top of the cylinder receive sheaves from a chute, cut the binding and feed them into a hopper. From one end of the drum poured grain, from the other came a mess of chopped-up straw; from the bottom, finer chaff fanned out into a dusty heap under the crude but effective machine.

The rest hut – *kultiurnoi stanok* (cultural rest home) or

kuljstan for short – was a smallish, one-roomed, one-windowed log hut with a timber floor. The total floor space was about that of a residential cabin. Along the windowless walls were double bunks with straw thrown over them. As in the train, the bunks were a body length deep, allowing sleeping accommodation for about a dozen people each, head to wall. A long bench-type table with a form of the same length on either side for seats was under the window. Otherwise, the room was bare of furniture. When I looked through the wide open doorway I could see loaves of bread on the table. And there were bottles of milk, a few potatoes steaming in their jackets, a handful or two of salt on a chipped enamel plate and a heap of potato skins. The men had just finished their 'cultural' breakfast. Finished, and food left over! They were standing about, they and just about everybody in the whole kolkhoz at a guess, between the kuljstan and the now operational machine. Just inside the door, as I edged up close enough to look in, was another form – a plank on a couple of sawn stumps – and in the corner I caught a glimpse of a whole bag of potatoes. On the wall opposite the bunks hung a large picture of Stalin. I retreated, and joined one of the groups of our people waiting to be told what to do.

The old men of the kolkhoz were quite friendly. They had loosened up, as people do at a party. The sun was well up, it was warm, and they looked us over frankly. We were females. Foreigners, but female. Some asked our names, cracked jokes, gave us tips about the work. The women eyed us with interest too, though more covertly, some of them seeing us at close range for the first time. Not one of them talked to us. If there were any expression other than curiosity, it was malevolence. To the young girls, we simply did not exist. They had eyes only for the boys.

Skakalkin was somewhere about. His name can be literally translated as one who jumps, a jumper. In Estonian, Kargaja. Among other less polite names, we called him 'Kargaja' when talking among ourselves. His loud laughter and raucous crudities could be heard from one building to the other.

'Kargaja is in good form today,' someone murmured.

'Let the jumper jump into hell,' was the response.

As long as his proper name was not mentioned, no favour-seeking Russian could report we were talking about him. It became a game. We got satisfaction out of expressing ourselves openly within earshot. To say pleasantly to him, 'Jumper, why don't you jump into your own mouth?' – or one of many and varied places, mainly anatomical – 'and disappear?' and see him take it as a compliment was childish, and we knew it. But it helped morale.

I was ordered up on top of the stack to throw down the sheaves. The work was not hard, but I had to hurry, bringing bundles forward from the back to toss down to the hungry old engine below. The metal dragon clanked, whirred and rattled; chaff and dust rose thick before drifting out slowly with the slight breeze, a breeze I got no benefit from. It was stiflingly close under the roof, hot, sticky, hard to breathe, as the heat of decomposition, generated and stored in the stack, rose sweet and cloying from each freshly exposed layer. I soon longed for fresh air as my nose, mouth, eyes and ears became clogged with the fine white powder filling the building.

We could rest twice for fifteen minutes, in midmorning and late afternoon. In the middle of the day there was to be a longer break, to give the horses a spell. Cultural hour, they called it.

By the midday rest period, I was dead tired from climbing over the soft, uneven surface. My hands and arms were a mass of scratches, and I was sweating freely. Face, bleeding limbs and damp clothes were all covered in dust. Even so, my lot was child's work compared with that of Meeri and Leeni. Their duty was to use big wooden scrapes to sweep chaff from under the machine and push it into a heap some distance away. They looked like a pair of ghosts, only eyes and teeth showing through damp slits in their dusty masks. Leeni's eyes, deep down in their holes, blazed. Her slit of a mouth moved. In full-voiced Estonian, she cursed communism and all its works and adherents to the bottom of the pit, as we made our way to the single tub of water for a wash. Some of the Russians laughed. I laughed, too; a real laugh, long and from the heart, as they chortled at their own damnation. Others joined in. Leeni continued, including Kargaja and the mustachioed monster up on the wall in her address. The Russians laughed more. We splashed our faces clean and went cheerfully to eat.

For lunch, every person got a litre of thick potato and barley soup, with bits of meat in it. Meat! The soup looked good, done in a huge iron cauldron outside the *kuljstan* and ladled out to groups or individuals as they filed past. Names were checked off as they were served. The Russians ate like 'civilised people', in groups, a group taking a large common pot to the cauldron, and from there, to a table. Once seated, they fell to, each digging in with his own wooden spoon and slurping up directly from the pot. We ate 'like animals', said the cultured ones, in private, most finding a place to sit, some few standing by the cauldron.

I had with me the saucepan I had found in the carriage, and the wooden spoon I had lifted at Novo-Sibirsk. I took my soup to the edge of the straw stack and ate quickly, wiping out every last bit with the last crust of yesterday's bread kept in my pocket for the purpose. A serious business, a pleasure not shareable. It was warm there, and quiet, and the dust had almost settled. And there was no picture of history's greatest murderer gazing benignly over my head.

■

'So! Your hands are sore, are they?' yelled Kargaja. 'They're lazy, that's what!'

The first week I had worked bare-handed. Though my hands were cut, and terribly painful, I could manage the wheat, then the peas, that had been stored under cover. When these were finished, however, we began on bundles of oats brought straight in from the fields, full of thistles, and half frozen. I had to put on ski gloves. Like the boots, I had wanted to keep my gloves for the winter, but I could hold out no longer. They were pure wool, with a traditional Estonian pattern. One pair was particularly beautiful, nearly elbow length and knitted brightly in five colours. They had been made at the Rakvere School of Handicrafts, and bought at a charity fete.

Two pairs in as many days changed from beautiful things to grimy shreds, and to no avail. The gloves useless, my hands were pin-cushions of prickles, and had started cracking from cold. They became blue and swollen, each crease an agonising open split.

Most of the women bent their heads together to giggle and whisper, nodding secret smirks as I struggled on. A few looked contemptuous. The men laughed aloud; in the main, good-naturedly . . . Pain and discomfort were an ever present part of life. If your own, a bad part that had to be borne. If someone

161

else's, much better; perhaps you could learn from their misfortune. If suffered in a manner a bit out of the ordinary, a diversion, perhaps a joke . . . Compassion was not even a word.

An elderly Ukrainian woman taught me to soak my hands in urine and wrap strips of linen around them. But they got worse, so I had asked the brigadier for different work.

'Lazy, see!'

People turned to look. The Jumper had their attention. He was set to enjoy himself; so was most of his audience. Skakalkin was usually good for a show. Painfully, I peeled the muddy rags off. He looked in awe. 'What devil's kind of fingers have you got?' He kept looking, and shaking his head. Ordinary simple work had never done this before. 'All bloody and blue and frayed.' He shook his head again, and dismissed me. 'Get out with them, then. Go and work on the wind machine.'

■

My partner was Matriona, the old Ukrainian who had advised the urine treatment. She was the poorest of all the *kolkhoz* women, a widow with Lord knew how many children, sick-looking and very thin. She showed me the machine, a series of sieves and fans, that shook the grain from the thresher free of any clinging husks, and blew the remnants away. It was driven by turning a massive iron handle. The faster the handle was turned, the more the sieves shook, and the stronger blew the wind that whisked off the fine chaff. The grain piled shiny and free for storing.

'Not too slow. You've got to put a bit of wind through it.'

I tried.

'Not too fast. We've got to do this all day. Here, like this.'

I copied her.

'You stand up and stretch your back a bit, I can manage on my own for a while. I'll have a spell later when you get used to it.'

I wrapped rag strips round my hands, and soon found the working speed of the machine. The rags had to be dry to slip freely. As soon as one set got damp with sweat or blood, I changed them for another, spreading the first in the sun. Matriona had smooth calluses, sliding over the metal in a dry whisper.

'You'll be all right in a few days.' She was friendly, almost

162

talkative after a time. By the end of the second day, she had shown me some of her tricks. I wondered if she might solve some puzzles for me.

Taking home any food, even a few grains of wheat, was, of course, strictly forbidden. We were not searched often, however, and then they did little more than look in pockets. We made small bags and hid them in pants and blouses, taking home a handful every night. It all went to Matriona's hut, where we kept our separate stores. I did not trust Natasha enough to take mine there.

Walking home late one night, the bags well hidden, I asked Matriona bluntly why the older kolkhozniks hated us so. It was dark, which made it easier. We were tired after a day's work together and I felt we were close. Under an enormous black sky, dotted with a few cold stars, any human contact bordered on the intimate.

'Hate you?' she said after a long silence.

'You are not even Russian. And yet your people are just as bad.' I wondered if I might have overstepped a mark. 'Well, almost.'

'We don't really hate you,' she said. 'But you came here, all at once, only women and children – '

'Do you think we wanted to?'

'No men.'

'No men?'

'Like an invasion on us.'

'Matriona, you know why!'

'With the war, all our younger men have gone and the norms, instead of being eased, have been increased. We have to make up. And then you come in, needing places to live and bread to eat, and you don't even know how to work. All the jobs are unfinished this year. No-one will have enough.'

'Surely you'd have been even further behind if we hadn't come.'

'Perhaps. But not if the men were here.'

'But we can't help that!'

'It's the war.'

'But the war isn't our fault.'

'Isn't it?' She had reservations about that, too. 'Anyway with things as they are, we have very little hope of getting any work pay at all this year: that's why we're unhappy.'

'Matriona, we're like you. We aren't the enemy. We're not even in the war. We're deportees, like you were. We're here because we were sent here. We're not trying to take anything from you.'

She made no attempt to reply. She said nothing the rest of the cold way home, or when I said goodnight, after leaving my little bags. I walked home to bed, miserable.

Next morning, we worked in silence until the first break. When I sat down, Matriona sat beside me. She brought out a larger lunch pack than usual. Opening it, she handed me a bottle of skim milk. 'I'm sorry,' she mumbled, 'I have only half a cow, and there are the children . . .'

I hugged her thin shoulder, tears in my eyes.

■

'Feast time' for the workers. The end of October. The season's final workday. No ceremony, one observance only. 'Feast'. An exciting word in any language. Each worker could eat as much pea porridge and as many boiled potatoes as he or she could hold. There was also a piece of meat and a half-litre of milk for each, all from *kolkhoz* stock and served outside between the two buildings, to be taken and eaten where pleased.

We crowded the kuljstan and overflowed to the now quiet threshing shed. Like everyone, I talked and laughed, but it was a cover. There were two things on my mind: I was grimly determined to scoff as much as possible, and not think about a cigarette.

Meeri told us about Mrs Palgi, a young woman from Rakvere, recently graduated from university and since married. She had died a day or two ago, at Red May kolkhoz. I remembered last seeing her at Aipalova, getting off the barge. She was well then, one of the fittest of all of us, with great hopes of returning home soon, although she had said she was worried 'half to death' about her husband on the other train. How prophetic! A terrible tragedy, we agreed, a dreadful shock. We shook our heads and moved up a fraction in the queue. There was a time that I would have been unable to face food for a day. Now, despite the news, I was thrilled to find myself third in the line.

I ate two half litres of pea porridge in determined succession, with my remnant of yesterday's bread, keeping the crust to scrape out the bowl before sending it after the rest. Such frugality was unnecessary today, but had become a habit as much as licking clean the wooden spoon before tucking it back in my sock. My shrunken stomach cried enough. I ignored it, following up with six or seven steaming potatoes and my ration of meat, resolutely chewing and sucking out every last vestige of flavour before washing the lot down with the measured half-litre of milk.

Meeri and a few others ate less, hovering near the great cauldron, near Alma and Helga, in the hope that some would be left over to take back to the children. They deprived themselves for nothing, despite the cooks' efforts. Skakalkin saw to that.

ESCAPE TO NOWHERE

Winter came suddenly. Already, by November, we had had heavy snow, and the thermometer in the office window showed −7°. The first fall had shaken half a metre out of a dark Siberian sky in a couple of hours.

The kolkhozniks were worried. It had been too sudden. Their winter seed had been sown. They liked to have light falls at first, followed by warmer days for a thaw, then a freeze before the thick snow settled on top. As it was, the snow formed an insulating blanket on comparatively warm ground. The seed underneath, not yet frozen in, would get wet and rot. They would have poor crops with starvation yield next season, or they would have to oversow in the spring, and there was no seed to spare for that.

I was not so worried. I didn't have time, as I had to spend several days' *voskresnik* with Marusja, sawing wood in waist-deep snow in front of the office, digging logs out from the snow-pile and reducing them to burnable lengths for the office fire. Besides, I would not be here next season, I told myself as I hunched over the saw . . . Poor crops, poorer crops, it matters little to me – God, that woman is strong! – it won't be my concern. Whose, then? – Not so fast, Marusja, damn you! – Let them worry, we'll be home before then. 'Put your back into it, Njura, or we'll never get finished.' – Back? Another log like that and I won't have a back, it will be scattered in frozen pieces in the snow here. No crops at all, I won't care. Let the whole blasted kolkhoz starve to death. 'Come on, Njura, why can't you hurry?' – Why can't I hurry? Because I haven't even the breath left to tell you why, that's why, devil take you! . . . Or let them freeze first without firewood, better still. The war *must* end before winter is gone.

Increasing cold put an end to almost all work for the whole collective. We were now facing temperatures of −20° to −30° for the next six months, dropping lower in really cold spells. Women with children were given indoor work to do, in return getting enough pay, supposedly, to keep them alive. They mended fishing nets, now available for leisurely repairs until the river unfroze, and spun flax, twisting the coarse fibres on hand spindles exactly as it had been done for the past thousand years. It seemed the spinning wheel had bypassed Siberia.

The *kolkhoz* had no tasks for the rest of us, so no food. Certainly no pay. For our winter ration we were ordered to the storeroom at the end of November and given five hundred grams of flour.

'Five hundred grams?'

'Plenty,' came the bland reply. 'It'll make twice the weight when made into bread.' A whole kilogram! And that was the end of the flour for the year. No more until January.

Following this announcement, I, at least, could not complain of having nothing to do. The panic gave me plenty of interpreting work at the office. 'Five hundred grams? She says she can't keep her children alive on that.'

'She'll have to try, won't she?'

'But really, it isn't enough.'

'It'll go a lot further if she makes bread. I suppose some of you are capable of making bread?'

'A loaf of bread to last a whole month? It's impossible.'

'Then she'll have to find some more.'

'Where?'

A cynical smile and a lifted shoulder.

'It's murder, I tell you!'

'Make all the fuss you like and see how much extra bread it gets you.'

No amount of arguing, pleading or begging helped. There was no more flour and there would be no bread until the new year.

As the season advanced, collective work went into hibernation, and we were permitted to see to ourselves. A new problem arose: as well as fuel for our bodies we had to think of our external warmth.

It was up to the three of us to provide our own fire wood; and, as Natasha still had her animals to tend, setting off on the path she had trodden into the white desert several times each day, returning only to eat, growl and sleep, it left only us two.

Neither of us carried lunch as we set off: Maret, a thin one hundred and sixty centimetres, and I a few centimetres shorter and lighter. I did not have a midday feed now, rationing myself strictly to two meals a day. Maret had left hers for her daughter Elli. Instead, we carried Natasha's and a borrowed axe and Marusja's saw. No vacuum flask of hot coffee, either. We pulled inadequate clothing across pinched bodies and faces, and started grimly into the forest.

One scrap of satisfaction came to me as we entered the wood; a minor puzzle was answered. I would have shared my moment of pleasure with Maret, but a quick calculation told me it was not worth unwrapping my face. Then the moment passed. I had noticed before winter that, of the thousands of stumps from past years of tree-felling, many stood at eye level and higher. Some, I could barely reach. They must have been cut by supermen. Yet, despite the tremendous height of these remarkable woodcutters – I could look down on the hacked stumps now – they had used ordinary axes and taken as many blows to topple their trees as did we. Puny giants. I had idly wondered about them. Now, I need not.

Several times, I nearly turned back. But our cabin was little warmer than out here, and without fire it would be too cold to support life once winter was really on us.

Maret jerked her axe toward a tree. We changed direction, stopped before it, sized up the trunk. It seemed about right: big enough to warrant the effort, not too big to manage. I raised my eyebrows at Maret. She nodded. Eyes were all we exposed.

The first blow bounced off with a ringing sound and an electric jar up the handle of the axe. So did the next. We inspected the tree, and learned to crack off the icy iron-hard bark at cutting level first. Then, to make a horizontal wedge in the direction of the expected fall. A higher wedge opposite. Then to saw, drop, trim, cut to lengths, stack.

Before exhaustion point, we would tie a couple of logs to our waists and drag them home, leaving the rest for the hoped-for day when we could borrow the *kolkhoz* horse and sled. Walking through the forest, we learned not to stub our feet on humps in the snow. We painfully came to recognise these as the summer-cut tree trunks. We had joined the ranks of the feeble giants.

■

'Tomorrow. Lunchtime. Report for work.'
 'What?'
 'Work. At the schoolhouse.'
I had been dreaming of holidays. Not real holidays, lazing in the sun with my family on the beach at Vosu and swimming, laughing, playing, eating, dancing, though all had flitted through my mind. That was real dreaming, as far out of this world as Alice in Wonderland. I had been simply indulging in practical Siberian half-dreams of the time when there would be no more work for a while. I needed bodily rest. I needed food. And, with time to spare, I could do some trading for winter supplies, visit neighbouring kolkhozes, hear some news. A credible dream, not too far-out.

Leaving the hut at all was a major operation, as the cracks around the door had to be carefully stuffed with pieces of rag to prevent any precious warmth escaping. Every time somebody left, or returned, as Natasha still had to do, the others had to go through a full performance of repairing breaks in insulation. However careful we were, we lost a degree or two of heat every time. Worse, a body returning from outside brought in active cold which leaped off skin and clothing. We spent the days sitting indoors, Maret and Elli and I, reminiscing or making desultory plans for the journey home. The search for head lice was a standard occupation – we had all collected them, there was no longer any point in hiding, or shame in admitting it – as it was with the locals. There was no ointment or other medication available. There was no soap left for washing hair. Elli's scalp was covered in scabs.

We sat in the dark through the increasingly longer evenings, for Natasha possessed neither lamp nor kerosene. She didn't sew, couldn't read, so she had no need for light. Early in the evening and again in the morning, just the twice a day for a short period each time, she lit the stove and let us do our 'cooking' at the same time she did hers, though we seldom had anything to warm. We did not have one of the room-heating types of oven on our side. Fortunately, Marusja's was built against the dividing wall. We benefited from it. Not much, but appreciably.

'Davai. The schoolhouse.'

It was the coldest day we had yet had. My visitor was not welcome. If he had knocked, he would still have been unwelcome. I had been out early in the icy cold for wood, and was alone in the cabin – Maret and Elli had gone two days ago to stay with Mrs Kruus, whose baby was expected any moment – huddling under everything I could pile on my bed. Natasha had gone out early and not returned for breakfast. I suspected she was warming another bed somewhere; the men were not working now, either. Well, good for her, at least it was peaceful here. Or had been.

'Block that door. It's near enough to freezing as it is.'

He obliged, more or less cheerfully. 'Hear? At the schoolhouse. Lunchtime.'

It took time to adjust, after the white glare through the open door. With it shut, there was only just enough light to see by coming through the much-mended glass window and its eight centimetre crust of ice. I did not need eyes to know the Jumper, all the same, or to tell he was in one of his better moods.

'I'm on holiday,' I complained. 'To the devil with work.'

I'd done enough for a lifetime. I had been out again yesterday, the last of the shopping trips I had been unable to do properly before. I was offering my remaining dresses, my good shoes, even my winter coat, for food. No-one was buying. Finally, the wife of the bookkeeper found somebody who was interested in my winter coat, and through her as an agent I got seven buckets of potatoes for it, a litre of milk, nearly half a kilogram of bread and, after a great deal of heated haggling, ten roubles in cash.

'You're crazy if you don't,' he said.

'Do you mean I don't have to?'

'No, but you're crazy if you don't.'

'Then I'm crazy.'

That, I thought, settled that. I had had enough. The only other article I had traded in the past week was a lovely sealskin-trimmed coat, worth a hundred Estonian crowns only a little over a year ago. It was sold for the equivalent of two, plus half a sack of potatoes. Though the coat might have kept my body warm, the potatoes would keep it alive. Now, with my hidden stores of wheat and salt, I was reasonably safe from starvation; for a time, at least, maybe for the winter.

'Knitting socks and gloves for the soldiers. Mending army overcoats,' he persisted. 'It's easy.'

Go out voluntarily in this climate? Just how crazy did he think I was? And all to keep the Soviet Army warm! I refrained from making suggestions that might antagonise the Jumper, although I could think of some.

'Thanks all the same,' I replied. 'My toes would drop off before I got there.'

It was over a kilometre to the schoolhouse, and I meant it. My feet had hardly warmed up from yesterday.

'You'll get bread if you go. You'll regret it if you don't.'

Bread?

'Marusja will give you my old felt boots. They'll be all right for you. And you just go. About two weeks' work. That's all. Simple.'

Bread! I could make some bad socks, I conceded to my conscience, and mess up some overcoats.

'All right, give me the boots.'

Unpredictability is a trait of the Russian character. Perhaps it is a result of protracted revolution, its accompanying uncertainties and violence. Skakalkin surely had it, Marusja to a lesser extent. Natasha too, all of them. It made life interesting. I was never sure whether friendly advice might save my life or send me to the camps.

My hands and feet were stiff when I reached the schoolhouse, and there was a not unpleasant burning sensation in the tip of my nose.

'Your nose is white,' said one of the women. 'Rub it with snow.'

I did so, there on the schoolhouse steps. My fingers started to move. The tingling hurt moved away from my nose. I must be more careful.

There must have been nearly a hundred people in the schoolhouse, knitting, spinning, sewing. In one corner was a large heap of old sheepskin coats, in stages of disrepair from fair to hopeless. The women were cutting pieces out of the worst and using them to patch up the better ones. The reconditioned coats, I was told, were to be personal presents from kolkhozniks and their bosses to the soldiers. Good for morale, both ways. Wool, thread and needles were a gift from the kolkhoz.

There was a lot of activity, little order, people seeming to go from one job to another at will. I followed their example, moving about, keeping warm in the crowd, looking busy. A couple of foremen wandered around, shouting orders with little relevance to the task in hand, which did not matter as no-one was taking the slightest notice. I began to warm towards the job.

I caught one woman, a local, hiding a ball of wool in her bosom. She glared at me. I followed the lead, taking my time, gaining skill. In one week I had acquired two sizeable pieces of sound sheepskin from the backs of coats. This was a tricky operation requiring a high degree of patience, sliding them up the legs of my ski pants and tying them round my shins without being spotted. In that time, I also acquired several balls of wool, some thread and a large needle. All that, and five hundred grams of bread a day from the shop! Now I understood the Jumper: I would have been crazy indeed had I stayed home. As well as the felt boots, Marusja had lent me a large yellow headscarf for the two weeks. I was warmer than I could have been at home in the cabin.

Keeping my ears open, I heard of a man in the next village. I asked no-one directly, spoke to no-one, but sought him out in secrecy the first opportunity I had. He agreed to make me a pair of *tscherkis* – those moccasins tied at the ankle – with double sheepskin soles. They looked like hoofs, and brought me a step closer to native, but they kept the frost out and, I confess, were beautifully warm and comfortable. For payment, he kept the remainders of the skins. From other scraps, and the wool, I fashioned myself a pair of mittens. I also knitted another two pairs, and some socks, on Marusja's needles. She had offered them to me without solicitation, and showed no interest in the source of materials or the results.

When, one day, I met Brigadier Skakalkin on the road, he looked with a sly smile at my hoofs and covered hands.

'See?' he said. 'I told you work is good for you.'

■

We took turns to comfort Mrs Kruus, who spent days on end lying listlessly on her cot. Her only expressed wish was for death for herself and the infant soon to be delivered into an unwelcome world. She and her pathetically under-nourished son were one of four families living in the old kolkhoz office. It was a big room with one window and one door, abandoned when the new office had been built the previous summer, and plundered of anything plunderable.

We were no longer allowed in the main office. It was oven-heated – by wood I had nearly killed myself sawing, I lamented bitterly – and therefore now too good for us non-citizens of the one-class state. We had grown used to gathering there. It had been warm, and we needed a common room in which to meet and talk, or simply to sit together near a fire, to make us feel we were still in touch with the human race. For weeks we had obviously not been welcome. Eventually, we were told to go away. Our foreign chatter had begun to annoy the office people.

There was only one place to go – except cold, lonely 'home', of course – and that was the old office, crowded though it was. Nobody minded. The added numbers did make it easier to look after the life of the poor girl lying-in there, contemplating surrendering it. Not for a minute in those dreary few weeks was she left alone; if she ever guessed why, she never spoke of it, just as her guardians never did between themselves. Her labour, when it began, was long and undramatic, as though nature itself was indifferent to her delivery. The baby was born dead.

'Thank God,' said Mrs Murak.

I was shocked, though sympathetic: Mrs Murak was a devout Christian. The mother said nothing. I went to the office. 'Do what you like.' No questions. No papers. Nothing. The child was never even a statistic.

I took Enn with me to the edge of the forest, where he hacked out a shallow grave with crowbar and axe, put in the little wooden box, set chunks of solid-frozen earth to level it and piled snow back on top. We marked the place with a stick, then Enn faltered through The Lord's Prayer and we hurried home, silent and shivering. Enn, barely nineteen, was now tribal elder, grave-digger, priest. I, reluctant midwife and mother of children, had not even noticed what sex it was.

■

A week before Christmas I was ordered to hurry to the office again. Part way along the road I heard my name called. Enn had received the same message. I waited while he caught up, and we went on together, boots squeaking on the snow, Enn beating his hands together all the way: his mittens were not as good as mine. Robert, Ants, and Edgar were already there, also Helga and Alma, a few Russian girls and four old men. We were the last.

We heard out the routine harangue on our indolence and worthlessness, followed by the routine oration on our good fortune in being privileged to serve the great country and the great father to whom we owed so much. We called it 'the national anthem'.

'Early in January you will form a work force,' – aha! here comes the meat – 'to build new houses for the state. You will be told when to assemble and where. While you are working, you will each be given a pair of cotton and wool socks to wear, and you will each receive eight hundred grams of bread a day as well as hot food morning and night.'

It sounded too good to be true and, were it not for the grudging way the announcement was made, I'd have disbelieved it outright. A glance at the others brought nods. Right. In case we had an option, we agreed to go, unanimously.

Only afterwards did we start wondering. Building cabins at this time of the year? 'Ridiculous.' 'Insane enough with this gang to be true.'

I was prodded into tackling the foreman. 'Why such a rush?' I asked him. 'Why in the middle of winter?'

'That's none of your business.'

'But wouldn't it be too – ?'

'Don't ask questions.'

The Russians on the workforce didn't bother. Either they had completely lost curiosity, or they knew beforehand that there would be no answers. Probably both, I thought. Years of rebuff had conditioned them into indifference. It occurred to me that we were becoming the same: losing interest and individuality as we lost control of our destiny. We were already slaves. It chilled me to think that we were becoming zombies.

'For whom are they being built?'

'Shut up, you fascist slut, or you'll be in trouble.'

I had my own theory. It came as a delicious flash right there in the office, based on nothing except wishful thinking . . . Things were going so badly at the front that the bigwigs were preparing to evacuate to Siberia. They were losing. The Kremlin was being deserted . . . A marvellous notion, too enchanting to share.

I developed the theme over the next few days. Variations were endless: the ramifications and embellishments, occupying hours and hours of thought for a week to come, had high-ranking party members combing the forest floor for cones that were not there, digging bare-handed at the permafrost for non-existent turnips. I had the NKVD terrified we would expose them, show them up, throw them to their vengeance-mad victims. I had Stalin himself, with his moustache shaved clean and a filthy old cap over his eyes for disguise, begging for a crust. I had him on his knees licking boots – Matriona's, Mrs Kruus's, anybody's but mine, for I could not bear to think of him so close – and crying for pity. I was merciless. I was charitable, keeping them all alive to show them misery. I had hours of satisfaction all alone with my theory, never airing it in the certainty that it would be squashed and the disenchantment too great.

∎

Before work on the building was to begin. I wanted to go to Schmarkovka to do some trading. I mentioned this to Selma Piip, who decided to join me. She was young, healthy, and had had the same idea, though she had kept it to herself, which made her a promising companion. Her landlady, she said, had offered her the use of a small toboggan, which she could borrow for the journey. Good. No sooner said than done. News of the plan spread, and before long the toboggan was laden with dresses, shoes, sheets and tablecloths from our Estonian population to be bartered for food. For our trouble, Selma and I would receive a percentage.

We had to seek permission from the office to journey outside the collective. The foreman of the day was in a good humour, and it went more easily than I expected.

'Go by all means,' he said. 'There's no work here until the building starts. But don't forget to come back, don't go over the swamp!'

'Just show us how!'

'Crazy creatures, travelling at this time of year! Just see you get back in time, that's all.'

His jocular remark about going over the swamp really set me thinking seriously of escape for the first time since arrival. Even so, it was a very hazy idea. All I knew was that north and west of Schmarkovka was where the original settlers of this territory were supposed to have come from. They could never have trekked through the swamp in the state we had seen it, but now that everything was frozen hard it must be possible to cross the water just as they and the Ostiaks had done, the latter from the opposite direction centuries ago. What was after that – assuming such a crossing could be made – was pure conjecture. Out there was truly *terra incognita*. Were there trains, rivers, roads, people? Anything other than snow and ice? I decided I would put out feelers, but not here in Maisk. I would wait. Schmarkovka was a much freer place.

We picked a day that was not too cold, −18° by the office thermometer, and started off with the sun nearing its zenith, throwing long shadows behind and to our right. Selma wore thick old felt boots, and I slacks, two pairs of long woollen socks, tscherkis, new mittens and calfskin coat. One went ahead pulling, while the other pushed from behind with a long stick, as our foreman had cheerfully shown us. He thought it a great joke.

The daylight hours of the three days in Schmarkovka were busy, hauling our load from house to house, exchanging, bargaining. By the third night, everything we had taken with us was gone except the shoes and one or two other items. Here, as back at Maisk, the most sought after articles were sheets. We sold two, each for twenty-five roubles. Selma Piip's husband's grey lightweight overcoat went for two kilograms of wheat flour, two kilograms of bread and three kilograms of meat. The meat was *loss*, from a kind of deer with big antlers, coarse and stringy and infinitely better than none. Our hostess for one night was very taken with my floral-patterned silk-crepe dress – she wanted it for a daughter who lived in Omsk – and I got a good price: two kilograms of *loss*, three litres of frozen milk, five buckets of potatoes. A knitted blouse, without buttons, went for two litres of milk, two kilograms of wheat flour and a loaf of bread. The six large red buttons I had cut off and thought of throwing away sold separately for fifteen roubles. Somebody's favourite colour. Not mine.

My beautiful silk-lined camelhair coat remained unsold, although I asked little for it. Its light colouring reduced its value immeasurably. 'Not serviceable.' '*Nyet*.' For which I now thank God.

In the evening, we visited Mrs Ale and others met a few weeks

177

ago, made new contacts and traced mutual acquaintances, looking out for messages to take back with us. This was becoming almost as important a part of trading missions as the trading itself. With communications so limited and nothing of consequence to talk about within our own confines, news of people from the past was our only reminder we still belonged to the world. The pendulum had swung back from not wanting to know.

Any spare time I had was used on a new commercial venture; I had rediscovered a dormant talent. Schmarkovka Russians were as intensely superstitious as their ancestors had been, generations ago. Their religion was truly medieval, a strange mixture of Christianity and paganism. Living in a household was governed by a long list of taboos, rational and otherwise. It was a sin, for instance, to use the same towel to dry the face as was used for the bottom regions. Special cooking utensils were used for different seasons; in particular, those for Lent were put away, not to be touched for the rest of the year. Icons, standing in their own corner of the house, were solemnly worshipped every morning; the head of the household would lead prayers, facing the icons, while the rest recited responses. With much bowing and many signs of the cross he would pray for himself, his family, and guests in the house. There was no hesitation about including us, although strangers must have been a rare excitement before our advent. We were accepted easily, as though we belonged to their way of life. Most of their customs were new to us.

I had remembered, before we started off, how an Estonian woman at Aipalova had made the Russians ooh and ah, goggle-eyed, while she told their fortunes. So I had brought my pack of cards with me, and rehearsed in my mind some of the palmistry and card-reading I had dug out of popular magazines years ago to use for party tricks. It had been fun, then. Now, it was my entree into business.

The cards were made from strips of birch bark, cut and treated by Meeri Kalves. She had painted the spots and court cards red and black with her younger brother's watercolours. She had a real talent. They had been so beautifully done that it was a pity to use them; but their price in salt had to be redeemed.

My very first venture was a success. I promised an arthritic widow a long life, gave her a hint of a mysterious male companion, foretold poor crops and warned her against going to the woods alone. The last bit did the trick: it transpired that only last year she had narrowly escaped a mauling from a bear. Her eyes were like saucers. She thought I was marvellous.

Within a day or two, my fame had spread. I had eager customers queuing to have their fortunes told by the gifted Estonian. I thought it was a shame that, for all my prescience, I had not been able to predict such a response: my fee could have been higher.

■

On my rounds, I had tentatively broached the subject of escape with two or three of my more confidential indigenous customers. I had asked some of the Estonians, too. No-one seemed to mind or was surprised, old citizens or new. They were prepared to talk freely, though usually with the brevity of one word, and I grew bolder with my questions.

'Ridiculous,' said one, with a smile.

'Madness.' The commonest response.

'Impossible.'

'Try if you like.' She said it in the same cheerful tone as if I'd mentioned swimming the Ob.

One of the old residents, however, in a group of Kazakhs, knew of a man in the village who had taken someone across the swamp a year or two ago.

'He succeeded?'

'As far as I know.'

A little later, I steered back to the subject.

'No harm done?'

'How do you mean?'

'Nobody caught? Nobody punished?'

'No trouble at all.'

'He must have been crazy.' One listener shook a solemn head.

'The escapee?'

'No, the other. The one who lives here.'

'To help some poor soul get away?'

'No. To come back himself!'

I laughed with them. All good fun. In the same humour, I asked who the man was. I had many times bitterly regretted not taking the chance we had been offered, on the bridge at Omsk. Perhaps if we had known better what we were heading for, we would have tried harder. Enn and I had spoken of it a

179

few times and we swore we would have. Another opportunity was not going to slip by so tamely. I would follow this one to the limit.'Can you tell me where to find him?'

■

He was tall, bony, strong and good-looking for a man almost seventy. He was also wealthy: he had two cows. His shirt, flopping outside his trousers, was tied at the waist with a tasselled cord in the way of the steppe nomads. His pants, in turn, were tucked into good felt boots. When he talked of trekking, his straggly beard seemed to stick out straighter, and his fine little eyes brightened like buttons in the leather pockets of his face. Mine must have glistened, too. I felt excitement mounting as he talked of distant places. He was willing to guide me across the swamp, he said. It was at least forty kilometres, maybe fifty, maybe many more. I assured him the distance was no problem, though I was a little concerned by his estimate as he was so vague about it. From there, he would show me the way to a railway station. How far that was, or its name, or just where any train might then take me – always providing I could make it in the first place, which he made sound extremely doubtful – was even more obscure. When? We could leave in three or four months, at the end of the winter. And how much? All for three hundred roubles.

'Three hundred roubles?' A hundred fortunes!

'About that.'

'But I – '

'I'd take that coat.'

My calf skin. I shook my head dubiously.

'But I'd have to have it straight away. Now. In advance.'

'That doesn't seem very fair.'

'I have to get things ready. Three hundred roubles or the coat.' He had fallen in love with the coat. But I did not have the money, and I thought I could not survive on the ice without the coat. Not much use getting there a frozen corpse.

Perhaps next winter? Perhaps. If I had the money then, would he still be willing? Yes.

■

The road back was easier. We had eaten well for three days, and sleep on a warm oven had refreshed us. We felt strong, and we were wealthy. The Estonians at Schmarkovka – in better health and altogether more optimistic – had been so much more animated than us that we felt uplifted through contact with them. The load on the toboggan was lighter, too. We were carting only bread and meat, leaving potatoes and flour and frozen milk to be delivered next time the horse came our way. It was not the happiest of arrangements, leaving provisions behind, but we had no choice.

∎

There was excitement in the air. The snow was fine and soft, the short hours of sun bright, the nights cold with an added tingle of expectancy. We had made plans, saved up tidbits. Some of the women went to the foreman to see if they could get extra milk for the occasion. The season of goodwill, they thought, and it was little enough to ask.

The foreman on duty was Lenkov, a cripple in his mid-forties. He was sometimes reasonable. Worth an approach.

'Christmas?' he roared at the top of his voice, for the benefit of all in earshot. 'What's that? Never heard of it! A left-over from capitalist decadence? There is no Christmas.' He was having a great time. 'Children's party? That's a celebration! Don't you know celebrations are a crime against the state? You'll be told when to celebrate!'

Stalin had taken over from Christ. We had forgotten that. Still, it had been worth the attempt, as the odd Russian sometimes forgot too.

∎

By the evening of the twenty-fourth all the saved-up treasures of past weeks were in the old office cum current residence, sneaked in under winter coats, in muffs, tucked into boots and underwear. The goods from Schmarkovka had arrived yesterday, almost intact. We covered the window and prepared by stove light for our first Christmas Eve in Siberia. Mrs Kruus brought out a beautiful hand-tatted cloth to spread over the table of logs and rough sawn timbers. She was recovering well, though lacking colour. Someone else had two candles. The feast – pea soup, hot potatoes and little cakes of flour and water – was put out, the children allowed to turn from their corner. Eyes glistening in the flickering light, they sat before the fire while Mrs Balter read the Christmas Evangelicum. We sang 'Silent Night'. Then we began the banquet.

The children came up, one by one, for their gifts: knitted things, rag dolls, wooden blocks. There was a cup of hot milk for each, and Mrs Balter astonished us again by producing a lump of sugar all round. 'The last,' she said. 'I thought we just might be here this long.'

The children's excitement, the crowd, the carol-singing and the warmth combined to make me feel strangely light-hearted. Perhaps we were closer to the true seasonal spirit than we had ever been, celebrating, despite our own deprivations, Christ's birth; making merry for the sake of the young. We even had 'coffee', roasted by Ott's mother from wheatgrains from my hoard and peas from somebody else's, plus dried bread crusts she had saved herself. For an hour or two we were absorbed, sharing God's goodwill, strangers united in bizarre isolation, almost at peace on earth.

Trudging back through the snow alone, my spiritual elevation collapsed. Now only silence, darkness and the great lonely cold remained. The other was fantasy. Fear for my family overwhelmed me. Were my husband, my children, warm? Did they have shelter, friends, food and a place to sleep?

Dear God, please allow them one Christmas gift. Life.

∎

The day of the building job had arrived. I put on all the warmth I could by the light of Natasha's breakfast stove, feeling rather than seeing the inevitable pair of eyes every time my clothes surfaced. Although used to the scrutiny, I was uncertain of the outcome. Natasha looked suspiciously at my *tscherkis* and my new pink woollen socks. They were not part of the wardrobe last time she had checked. The wheels went round slowly – I thought she would challenge me, and half-prepared a biting explanation – but I left without a word.

I had awaited this day with a curiously exciting mixture of eagerness and fear: eagerness for the victuals, fear of the cold. Here in Udarnik, although I was warm enough to stay alive, I was likely to starve as my meagre stores ran out. Out there, wherever it was, were bread and hot soup, but also a white eternity where even healthy people froze to death. A choice. Warmth or sustenance? The answer was easy. The devil we did not know was preferable. I'd take a chance on freezing.

I had no cap. Instead I wound a silk scarf round and round, over my ears, nose, mouth, chin, everything but eyes, then my woollen swimsuit, finally a strip of 'percentage' tablecloth, commission from the Schmarkovka trip, wrapped tight to keep the rest in place.

We were to be in the office by seven. It was over three hundred metres away, but the moment I stepped outside my nostrils picked up the aroma of hot pea soup and cooking meat. I ran; I might be too late. The smell grew stronger as I passed the thermometer just outside the office door. I looked automatically: –35°. I pushed my way through, and stopped to take in the full bouquet. Pea soup and meat, no doubt about it. I looked around in surprise at the dingy office that had magically become a restaurant. People chattering, plates clanking. And food! I could even see it. One of the boys waved. Not a first-class restaurant, the chatter not really idle, the dress hardly la mode. No glistening white tablecloths, or thick piled carpet. No head waiter to lead me to my plush chair. No neat smiling waitress. The clatter was not the silvery tinkle of cutlery on fine china, but the solid clunk of wood on wood.

Was there any left? I spotted Helga standing at the stove beside a steaming pot. She caught my eye and ladled a serve of soup up and back into the pot. Good. I was in time. I went straight to her, standing close. She measured the regulation half litre into the bowl I carried and dropped a sizeable chunk of meat in with it. She had scooped from the bottom, the thickest part. At the head of the table nearest us sat the brigadier, handing out bread with one hand according to the list he held in the other. Eight hundred grams. Wheat bread! I found room next to Alma, put down my plate and took my spoon from my sock.

No conversation at this table. Today we eat, tomorrow we work.

■

Heaps of raw lumber had been scattered on the river bank two kilometres downstream. The job of us women, occasionally with the boys' aid, was to strip bark and trim the logs before the men shaped them with axes. Alma and I were supplied with a 'steer-plane', a two-handled instrument like a great spoke-shave. We straddled the logs – trunks of small pines and cedars about thirty centimetres thick – first carefully placing a bundle of straw under our seats to prevent us freezing to the timbers. It was less tiring this way than standing and leaning down, though still hard on the arms and shoulders. Either way, feet, hands and face hurt constantly with cold. A fire burnt near by, fed by the trimmings, and we stamped to it time and again to warm ourselves and keep the blood circulating. One task we performed with extreme diligence was keeping it going.

It all seemed senseless. No-one seemed to know what or who the houses were being built for. Why here, of all places, was quite unanswerable. This was no site for good cabins; they might as well be at the North Pole. The order had come from Novo-Vasjugan, however, and that was that. I told nobody of my own thoughts on the matter, nursing my dream with quiet delight . . . The defeat of communism. Total collapse. Soviet leaders banished, cowed, fleeing to the wilds. Hurrah . . . Careful now, I had to remind myself. No daydreaming in banner headlines. It might show.

On the third day, we had a visitor. We could see at a glance that he was some important official, brought in on a smart sleigh pulled by the *kolkhoz* stallion. He wore high felt boots, and a fur hat, long sheepskin coat and a pair of dog's-fur gloves; and he carried a *nagahn* – an army revolver – on his belt. At this stage, the walls of three huts had been erected, windows cut, roof timbers put in position. Work was going on at a good pace. We came in for routine abuse all the same. Alma and I, probably because our clothes proclaimed us as foreigners, were singled out for a special blast.

'You two there! Sitting like a pair of cows on that log all day. You've hardly moved. Get to it!' As if he would know.

'Careful, Ann.' Alma's word of restraint was well timed. She was a highly intelligent girl, younger than I, usually quiet and thoughtful. She was good for me, with her ability to smooth peaks of mood and divert crises.

'How interesting,' I muttered. My chilled body could still raise a flush of anger, as Alma had known. 'We're a whole zoo! Work horses. Leeches. Running dogs. Parasites. Now cows. And all the time I thought I was just a goat for being here in the first place.'

The man said nothing. He had the same pinched look and

bottomless cold eyes they all had. He stared steadily, long enough for both of us to know he would not forget. I stared back, hoping to conceal my revulsion. He said goodbye to the foreman, and drove off quickly.

'I've never pulled the wings off a marsh-fly,' I said to Alma. 'I've never killed a snake. I even hate to squash a spider. But I could have clubbed that little beast to death without batting an eyelid.'

I was perfectly serious. It was almost frightening.

'Siberia is the playground of the worst thieves, the biggest rogues, the toughest criminals in the whole of Russia,' Alma said earnestly. 'And that's saying something.' She had the knack of keeping a straight face. 'We are the declared enemies of a great and noble nation. Indeed we are, that's our qualification for entry. We have on occasion shirked. We have refused to sign papers. We've stolen turnips from the fields, shame upon us, and vilified our hosts. All very weighty crimes, you will no doubt admit, worthy of severest retribution. But if you had beaten that man into the turf, Ann, you would have made it: you would really belong!' She laughed, making me laugh with her, and changed the subject to warm food and the coming night's sleep.

In the weeks of building we worked hard. We commuted, which meant a long and tiring day, and rested when we could in front of the fire. Occasionally the whole working party gathered at the blaze and we foreigners found ourselves for the first time almost accepted as *kolkhozniks*. They talked normally in front of us, even with us. They asked once – just once – why we were here, shaking heads in polite disbelief when we said a few words about our previous life and deportation, then asking no more. We left well alone. They did offer advice on work and a few hints on kolkhoz survival. We listened and learned. Mostly, they simply talked as they would have without us. We were neither invited in nor pointedly ignored. The one subject not touched – whether through ignorance, lack of interest or intention, we did not know – was the war. They probably knew no more than we, yet we expected some gossip or conjecture. Not a word. Despite this we felt, perhaps guardedly, that they were friendly. That was awkward, in a way, as I, for one, was committed never to allow friendship.

Up to now, we had heard crude language in plenty – or

thought we had – and had been able to turn our blushes aside. Here, we were included in conversation and had no option but to listen. Their speech was uncouth, usually crude, occasionally downright filthy. To them it was as natural as salt to soup: just normal peasant talk, often colourful with, every now and then, a pearl dropping.

Nikon, the wag of the group, came trotting up one day when everyone was huddled for warmth. 'Comrades, have you still got all your precious possessions, all your delicate things, or did the cold get them?'

It was a particularly cold morning, with the temperature at –48° by the thermometer inside the first cabin door. My only precious possession was half a day's food ration, three parts frozen in my calf coat pocket. The men said nothing. I could sense them watching expectantly.

'Delicate things!' I muttered, scowling.

'My old woman, see,' he went on, 'made me a little sheepskin bag to keep mine warm.' He displayed a neatly sewn bag, big enough for my fist, enough to keep a small meal warm, close to the body, with string from the top long enough to tie around the waist. I inspected it minutely. It could be a good idea. 'I've got one on now,' he went on. 'This is a spare.'

'What do you keep in it?'

'My most valuable possessions, of course.'

I had to ask, though the answer might kill me. 'Your bread?'

He probably had meat. My stomach contracted at the thought.

'Oh no,' he laughed delightedly.

'What then?'

'Guess again.'

'To the devil with you. Meat?'

'Close.'

'All right, I give up.'

'Eggs!'

'Eggs?' I had a ringing in my ears. When had I last seen one?

'For my eggs, vot*!*'

Nikon led the concerted roar as he patted the front of his pants.

∎

Freeze and laziness notwithstanding, six little houses were completed. They stayed untouched for the rest of winter. In spring they were dismantled in sections, and floated back downstream.

The full story came to us later. From the combined exertions of four kolkhozes, components for twenty huts reached Novo-Vasjugan in the thaw, to furnish twenty officials with cowsheds. So much for the sharing of reward for effort in the classless society.

Well before that time, Alma and I were listening to everyday crudities without turning a hair. No longer did we lay them in the aisles as we did over Nikon's eggs. We laughed at jokes without discomfort, instead of pretending ignorance and giggling like schoolgirls later. So much for social distinctions.

14

EVICTION

It would be nearly three months before any work in the fields would begin again; three months before regular rations would come our way. I had my reserve of six buckets of potatoes, a little flour, what was left of my wheat, a couple of slices of frozen milk and about two kilograms of peas. I counted out the potatoes and measured the flour and peas with my spoon. I thought that if I had no more than four small, or two bigger, potatoes a day, and a spoonful of flour or peas every second or third, I could almost spin it out, depending on windfalls for the rest.

I was unemployed again. Our promised three hundred grams of bread a workday, due in January, was never seen. The kolkhozniks got theirs. Newcomers were told we had eaten in advance. Those quarter-day's and half-day's pay were having effect. We owed the rest. Most of us, in fact, would never catch up.

It was not much, my winter larder, but many had less. Some of the children went from house to house, begging for something to eat. It was hard to turn them away. But I did. We all did, time after time, every time feeling dreadful. The little twin Kolk girls from Johvi came. I knew them and could not refuse. Some came from Kamenoi, some from Berjosova. These I could. Berjosova was a German kolkhoz some sixty years old where, until recently, the workers had been better off than most, because they were more skilled than the Russians at farming and at making and selling handicraft. Since war had begun, however, conditions had been made impossible for them, with more work, tougher quotas, increasingly crowded quarters, bans on personal sales,

189

less fuel and food. Of those who survived this winter, nearly all were to succumb to the next, when they were squeezed even harder. If we were the enemy, Germans were the arch-enemy, despite the fact that they had been settled on the Volga for generations, and had never seen Germany.

One of our *kolkhoz* women came to the cabin one day with a message for me. She had been on a two hundred and fifty kilometre trek, taking food for a working-party cutting lumber deep in the forest. She told me she had been to *kolkhoz* Medvetka – 'The Bear' – a long way away and had seen some Estonians there, dressed in rags and literally starving. One of them – she knew no names – had asked about me. A small woman, she said, dark and soft-voiced, speaking good Russian, and with a young son. Aina Matas, I recognised, an old school friend from Kunda. The Russian woman said that she had given her her own last bread and potatoes on leaving. She had tears in her eyes as she told me about it. I shed tears too, and thanked her. There was nothing either of us could do but weep. Aina had been a dear friend and I was sure that I would never see her again. I was wrong.

■

'Natasha is going to throw us out.' Maret was worried.

We waited – Maret, little Elli and I – day after short day from first light onward. We waited, curled up or stamping about, for the evening, so we could light a fire and cook our watery soup. Maret and I had grown very close in our confinement, of necessity sharing everything.

'Oh, she has her moods.' But the cowgirl had told me, back in summertime, that her sister Frosja was coming to live with her. So Maret was probably right. 'Anyway, we've paid our rent in advance, so she can't do it yet.'

'It's all right for you,' Maret said peevishly. 'There's still room for you; even if that sister does come, she'll probably want you to stay, now you're her private secretary.' Her petulance was directed more at Natasha than at me.

She was right again. Natasha had had me writing letters to Sergei, the horse man, letters he would pick up at the office should he come and go without seeing her. They could be either loving or threatening, happy or miserable, according to her mood. I did not mind: it occupied blank time and could prove useful. I would read them back to her while she listened, like the child she was – a rather beautiful and ignorant child. She had found a weapon of power, but, as yet, was uncertain in its use. Sergei was her slave. The letters were her whip. I copied as she dictated, gaily or sullenly, as the mood took her, avoiding expression or inflection of my own, thankful to be handling the pencil and paper she brought for me. Whether or not Sergei read for himself at the other end, I did not know.

'We're both useful to her,' I pointed out. 'Apart from the letters and the rent – and she is pretty greedy for that, remember – we keep the place clean. Then there's the wood, and the vegetables outside, when it thaws. She's better off with us here.'

'I know that. But you know how unpredictable she is. Her moods. She always seems to be annoyed at us.'

'Probably at Sergei.'

'He'll throw her over and she'll take it out on us.'

Maret did not know that Natasha had had a child by Sergei, now being looked after by his or her parents somewhere. I was not supposed to know, either. You would never have guessed from her body, and Natasha never directly mentioned it, but Matriona had told me, and some things I had had to say in the letters confirmed it.

'I think she has him hooked,' I said.

'What difference? We're the ones who will suffer.'

Things, however, took a different turn. One very dark night, Natasha came bursting into the hut. 'What are you squatting on your bums for?' she screamed. 'Don't you know what's going on?' She had a wild pitch to her voice, like a terrified animal. 'Get out and have a look. At least do that before you die!' I had never thought to hear her so frightened; she was not a fanciful girl.

We ran out, and were startled, too. Half the sky was covered in blood-red flames racing from the horizon back and forth across the firmament, flicking from the edges of the white earth, right up to heaven itself. A huge column in the shape of a cross stood out from the flames. It was eerie; the fiery cross standing bold, while the tongues of hell licked up and around, all without sound, in a windless world. I could feel the exaltation of a medieval priest, the fear of primal man.

People gathered near us. The silence was broken by women crying, some of them praying. A few drew on long-neglected disciplines and crossed themselves. Whispers were exchanged.

'It means death.' 'The end for us all.' 'A dry season.' 'There will be a long and bloody war.' This was finally agreed as the likeliest interpretation, Maret and I adding maliciously: 'Christians winning.'

Natasha was hysterical, running about in the weird glow, shouting and crying in turn, not making the slightest sense.

'It's nothing.' I tried to calm her. 'You must have seen the northern lights before. Haven't you?' I thought a rational explanation might help the poor girl. 'It's the Aurora Borealis. It's only – '

Her hysteria was cured. Gone in a flash. My role of psychiatrist with it, and my roof. 'You and your superior wisdom,' she snarled in my face. 'Go to the devil and take it with you. I've had enough of it. The first day of summer, you find another place to live.'

So now I had one more worry, Maret one less.

■

Enough light to see by pushed through the fragmented glass-and-ice window, so it was time to get up. Natasha would be back soon, after her early chores with the cows. She would light the fire and cook herself some breakfast. The wood was hers, so we were not to light it without her. Once lit, if we had anything to cook, we could use it. Until then, we could only wait.

I pulled on the clothes I'd spread over the bed as an extra blanket, taking off my nightdress in the way that ensured least loss of heat in the change. As a gesture to civilisation I still stuck to wearing night-clothes, and was determined to do so as long as they lasted. Sometimes I wore my coat over the top. But last night was not so bad, I had just thrown it across the blanket over the day clothes. Maret was getting up now too, carefully, trying not to disturb Elli, who had curled into her for warmth. The child was thin and lethargic, and slept a lot. I pulled my rubber overboots over the thick new socks, shivered, and put on a heavy dress and the calf-skin coat.

'I'll take it out,' I said to Maret, and unsealed the door.

There had been twenty centimetres of snow overnight. Natasha had ploughed through it along our path, leaving her footprints. 'Devil take her,' I muttered. She had left the snow for me to clear, as usual. Clear the snow, get in the wood, tidy the room. And the moment she felt like it – out! 'Bitch.'

192

I shovelled the path clear, tossing the fresh snow up and out. We had little more than a tunnel left now, open on top. The ceiling was an icy clear sky, high above. I sloped it up ten metres or so, tamping down a walkway, then went back for the pot Elli had used through the night. I emptied it in the clean snow, where the contents promptly disappeared, picked up some wood and went back inside.

For my own toilet needs, I was privileged to be allowed to use the brigadier's latrine. This was a hole in the ground under a lean-to against the cowshed. Not a deep hole. When the heap under the single log seat rose too high, he would knock some of the frozen mass off with an iron bar left against the wall for the purpose and leave it in the snow. Not unhygienic, I came to realise. But in the spring? Would he really spread it over the vegetable patch when it thawed, as someone said? His own vegetables? And was it true that he invited others to use his latrine to have more for the purpose? The answers were yes, and yes, but by the time I knew them I was less fastidious.

Natasha came back, steaming cold, and lit the fire, our fire, except we could only use what she did not want. She cooked some breakfast; I did not see what. I usually found something else to do when she was cooking, and kept clear. Today, I would prepare for a wash. I collected my cooking-pot full of snow, ready to put on the stove as soon as it was free. Natasha said nothing, as usual, except the occasional swear word as something went wrong, or one of us was in her way. Finished, she stomped out again. Maret resealed the door. Her turn. I put my water on to warm. Maret had some thin soup to heat up for Elli.

'Bitch,' Maret said quietly. Again, her turn.

We had no watch between us, but it was about 9.30. There were six hours of daylight left and I thought I would do some visiting, as the day was not impossibly cold. I had my wash, even using a little of our soap, which was made by pouring boiling water over ashes in a bucket and allowing the mess to stand overnight. The shiny, caustic liquid left after the ash had settled was used for both bodies and clothes. I used some now and rinsed clean with the warm water on the stove. A towel would have been nice.

The road was passable, packed down by Sergei's horse and sled and the few people who moved from one place to another. I went to the Estonian 'community' hut where we sat and talked – no cards, no books, there was nothing else to do but talk – before I decided to go home, calling at Mrs Balter's on the way. Mrs Balter and Enn, with Brigadier Skakalkin and Marusja and their two children, lived well, all in the same room, Mrs Balter and her adult son sleeping on the same bed. They had an oven going most of the day for warmth, and a real kerosene lamp to see by. Luxury. My writing was done by tattnina – a 'junior' – a small bottle covered by a tin cap with a hole, a linen wick, and what kerosene Natasha brought home. I sat with my two friends on their bed, while the Skakalkin family went about its own business three metres away. Our only privacy was language, as there were no curtains or divisions in the room. We sat talking desultorily, until it was time for me to catch the end of Natasha's evening fire and warm up my soup .

It had been a fair day. Bad ones were awful, huddling frozen in the half dark in the daylight and in the pitch dark all night. No visiting, no callers, no alternative to thinking. And what pleasure in that? Six months without word from outside, without change here. The Red Army was apparently not yet defeated. Maybe it wouldn't be? It didn't bear thinking about.

I knocked at the door, stamping to keep my feet alive while I waited for Maret to unseal it. She would be cross, though she usually displayed only weariness; she was a nice person, with the extra worry of a daughter. Two unnecessary openings for the day, costing heat each time. She didn't even grunt.

I went in to wait with her for Natasha, and food. We were companions, close now to being firm friends. Dinner? Three potatoes and a few peas, positively the closest to a cheerful thought for the day. I wiped out my iron pot, put in a mug of water from the drinking bucket – Natasha refilled this every second day or so, bringing it back from the river where a hole had been cut through the ice – and the vegetables, and waited. I had set the fire earlier. My turn. Maret sat on her bed, waiting silently, while Elli lay dozing.

Natasha came in, lit the fire, cooked, ate, swore, took off her boots, and climbed into bed. Maret and Elli watched listlessly. Our landlady was in a black mood. Not unusual, not important; just maybe worth noting. Nothing to do but have my own meal, go to bed. It was already dark. With no letter to write, there was no point lighting the borrowed tattnina.

Another day gone, another night to come.

15

SPRING, SEEDS AND SAUNAS

Spring came early in 1942.
Already, towards the end of April, the snow had begun to melt,
which meant there was work to be done.

The *kolkhozniks* knew what was what. They set about the
various tasks, getting in early, ensuring pay. We exploiters knew
nothing, discovering jobs only when they were filled. Day after
day, despite emaciation and loosened teeth through winter
tsonga, we reported at the office, clamouring for work. Work
was bread: bread was nourishment and vitamins, lack of which
caused *tsonga*.

Most of us had 'eaten' all tradeable clothes and had no edible
reserves. We were told nothing, fed nothing. All approaches
were met with indifference. Daily, and more loudly, we made
our demands. Daily we went home empty-handed.

'No work, no bread.'

'Well, give us work. That's what we're here for.'

'There is none.'

'What about those Russian women?'

'Nothing left. They were here first.'

'How were we to know! Without bread we'll starve. And
what about the children? You want us all to die?'

'I don't make the orders. Just get to the devil out of here.'

'We did that yesterday.'

'Do it again, then, and stay out. You're a pack of fascist trouble-
makers.'

'We're not going before you give us work.'

Eventually, in exasperation, they created new jobs. The boys were sent to the forest to burn dead branches, several families were set to work making bricks from sand and clay; most of the single women and girls were despatched ten kilometres away into the marshes to gather cranberries. Cranberries! we said scornfully. They must be morons. Who ever heard of cranberries at this time? You were lucky if they hadn't all gone *before* the snow came, let alone now! But the quota of wild berries for Udarnik had not been filled, and an order was an order. To go on orders meant bread, irrespective of whether berries were found or not, even though the bread was only an advance on the allowance. I was an exception. I was 'in luck', and assigned to the 'heavy brigade'.

The boys and brick makers had impossible norms. They were eating in advance, too. But it didn't matter: it was *now* that counted. They ate and stayed alive. The word 'future' had lost meaning.

The berry quota remained unfilled. The pickers were back in a few days, buckets full of air, hearts full of lead. The marsh was still frozen, with a thin wet daytime film on top, icy cold, slippery, treacherous. They had made themselves a shelter of branches and spent the nights around a big fire, afraid of the bears they had heard stirring in the wood. The days had been futile. They had seen patches over water that, to their surprise and frustration, were red with berry-laden bushes, but unreachable.

Seasons later, with years of acquired local knowledge behind us, we were to search out cranberries at this time of year: they were sweeter than in season, after their full natural ripening and thorough deep freeze. By then, we could manage those swamps.

■

The larch oil factory was ten kilometres away. We lucky ones of the heavy brigade were sent to replace five Russian boys, who were to begin ploughing in the fields. We walked the distance, and found our living quarters: a single-roomed hut, with shelf-like bunks lining the walls. The air was thick with smoke limping from a poorly designed stove. All ten workers on the site lived here: the five of us, three Russian women and two older men. The Russians, with the boys who had left for the fields, had been in occupation since March. Five weeks. For us, it was the first work for spring.

Next to the hut was a giant wooden keg with a sort of iron stove at the bottom. The keg was to be filled with larch branches, packed down hard, and the lid fitted on top and weighted with logs and stones. Then a fire would be lit in the stove and fed, day and night, until oil dripped from a tap at the bottom of the keg. Presumably, the heat and pressure drove out the precious oil, which we were told went to help the nation at war. Meanwhile, the factory poured thick smoke over everything in its vicinity, in particular the hut where we were to live.

Our job, the Russian girls told us, was to break off larch branches and carry them to the scales. There, our individual tallies would be recorded and the branches fed into the wooden tank.

Easy enough, I thought. Better than doing nothing, and there was food at the end of it. I was in for a shock.

I began work alone, as we had agreed would probably be best, making my separate way into the forest. To my increasing dismay, I found the lower branches of all nearby trees already broken or cut off. For my harvest quota I either had to climb, or go deeper into the forest, through melting snow and ice-cold puddles whose depth could only be judged too late. By nightfall, I was wet through, chilled to the bone and tired to dropping point. I had brought in two hundred kilograms of branches. The norm was seven hundred and fifty. My friends fared much the same, which was small compensation. There seemed no way we could improve.

At night, we received five hundred grams of bread and some boiling water. It was called tea, but it was boiling water. We, the exploiters, as our fellow workers referred to us with monotonous predictability and venomous pleasure, seldom found room near the fire to dry out our bodies or wet clothes in the evenings. The others were in before us, refusing to budge, and we were in no condition to push. In the same way, our beds were nearest the door, from where a constant chilly draught, smelling strongly of oil and thick with smoke from the factory, came in. I did manage to bake my three potatoes – all, or perhaps more, than I could afford each night – either sliced on top of the stove or buried in the ashes. There was no sharing now: the struggle for survival was strictly a personal affair. If you had more than the next person, it was a matter of good luck – and guard it. The Russians seemed to have food in plenty. Fortunately, we usually came in after they had finished and did not have to watch.

The Russians openly scorned us for our small tallies, though I suspect, from the regular amounts they brought in, they must have had secret stores to draw on, from the easy times. We knew we could expect no leniency from higher up. If we complained, we would be given higher quotas, or sent back. Others would then replace us, and the farce would be repeated with a change of cast.

By the second week both Ott and Edgar were coughing badly. I had a cough too, which I tried to suppress because it hurt, and there were times when breathing was difficult and painful. After one of these bouts I left early from the forest, afraid that if I left later I would not get out at all. A night in the open, I thought, would be the end of me. Part way out I had another attack of shivering and coughing, each convulsive bark sending a knife-like pain through my chest, doubling me up. I crouched in the slushy snow, close to tears, unable to straighten. Propping myself against a tree until the spasm passed, I dreamed of a soft bed in a warm room, a hot-water bottle at my feet and a hot sweet drink at my lips. The pain subsided, and I nearly stayed. I was at peace there. It took a tremendous effort to get up and make my way back to the cabin.

I would have liked to have gone home, back to Udarnik, though it meant losing the ration. At least I would have the comfort of my own bed, clean clothes, and air I could breathe. Maret and Mrs Balter would look after me, but I did not know the way and did not want to ask.

The leading hand finally put the three of us to sawing and chopping firewood. 'Children's work – for babies,' sneered the Russians as they went past, and we had difficulty managing even that. The boys were little stronger than I, equally lethargic, equally racked by coughs.

At the end of the second week the *kolkhoz* foreman came to let us know it was our turn to visit the sauna. Everyone else went. The two boys and I decided we would go too, following the others' tracks through the snow until we knew where we were. By this time I was swollen all over, my feet hardly fitting into my boots. Ott and Edgar, though they each had a fever and were very sick boys, supported me for most of the ten kilometres.

It took us five hours to cover the distance, and I knew that without their help and encouragement I would have sat on the road and closed my eyes.

∎

The boys and I went to the hospital the day after 'sauna'. We each received a blue paper, a few powders, and advice to rest and eat well. Eat well! I could not resist respectfully asking what the nurse-orderly would suggest. Eggs, meat, butter, cream and white bread. Seriously. We thanked him, in tones that nearly lost us our blue papers.

On sick days there was no bread ration. For two weeks I lay on my cot, looked after by Maret and Mrs Balter, and ate all my reserves. Every second day I had to get up and go to the hospital to renew the certificate. The boys, I heard, recovered more quickly. I was glad, as they had been very good to me.

∎

'A job?'

'Yes.'

'You're serious?'

'Quite.'

'You want me to find you a job?' He grinned. 'After the last one?'

'I do.' That had been three weeks ago.

'What sort of a job?'

'An easy one.'

I meant it. I was still very weak, and my cough was troublesome. It was all I could do to drag my bony frame to the office. My reserves were gone. I couldn't work hard, and I could not afford another illness. The organism wouldn't stand either.

'You're lucky,' he said grudgingly. 'They want a fire-watcher at the *tokat* factory.'

The larch oil episode, my first stroke of 'luck', had nearly killed me.

This time, my good fortune brought me to the *tokat* factory, a large shed, roofed and roughly walled by straight thin logs, standing apart from the 'houses' at the edge of the wood. In it were two huge ovens with grates and, along the walls, piles of birch bark and stacks of sawn timber. The birch bark was the source of *tokat*, the timber the fuel. I had to spread the bark in even layers onto large trays – like outsize oven slides – crudely flanged and grooved to run fluid off from one corner. These slides had to be stacked ten deep in the oven, with the open corner correctly positioned. The whole lot was closed in by building up the front opening with clay bricks and sealing it with clay. The director of the factory showed me how, then how to start the fire.

Then came fire-watching, the tedious part, the job I had been assigned. Heat had to be raised steadily, until juice began dribbling from the tap draining a small reservoir positioned under the run-off corners. Once right, it had to be kept fairly constant until drainage ceased. A day and night of fierce burning started it running, another two or three completed the operation. All for eight or nine litres of *tokat*, a thick, shiny, pitch-black mass, like axle-grease, and for just that purpose, from each oven.

The job itself was easy and the place dry and warm. The pay was the same as on the last assignment. No wonder that miserable man had been so reluctant. I was indeed lucky: it was too good for a foreigner. The only problem was getting rest, as the furnace had to be restoked every couple of hours. And even this could be made up as, after each three-day stint, I had a day off while the ovens were cleaned and repaired. That was the job of the factory director, a thin yellow-eyed, yellow-toothed old man with a perpetually running nose and a straggly beard. He was also the village storekeeper, which was anything but a full-time occupation.

The first night I spent squatting in front of the oven, with my home-made poker close at hand. I had begun with a plain iron bar until reminded sharply of the laws of heat conduction. A few layers of birch bark glued on with resin did the trick. I was afraid to sleep because the fire might go out, in which case so would I – and my last source of bread. That was the primary use of the poker: a fire-stirrer. Apart from that, the shed door could not be closed from within, and the director had suggested he might come in the night and help. Alone, and far from the nearest neighbour, I felt I had better show I could do without him; I was not sure what sort of helping I might be in for.

Next day, I told Ott about the door. He was very good. He acquired an iron hook from one of the unused machines lying out in the open, and looped it between the timbers of wall and door in such a way as to make it impossible for anyone to enter without assistance from inside. Armed with that and the poker and Mrs Balter's alarm clock, the job was child's play.

So smoothly and quickly was it finished, in fact, that at the end of my stint the *kolkhoz* head was so surprised, and in such good humour, that he promised to make me director of the factory the following year. Already? he said. Only fifteen days, and all that birch bark turned into *tokat*! I was fully aware of how difficult it would have been without the alarm, and of how previous firewatchers must have lost days every season by letting fires go out and having to restart them. I accepted his praise gracefully, however, shrugging modestly, saying nothing. You never knew.

The next compliment came from the director-storekeeper, who offered to reward my efficiency by making me his housekeeper. I nearly accepted, for he had a warm hut, a big reserve of potatoes and, of course, the store. I gave up the idea after a talk with Mrs Renni. She told me that she had been his tenant, and had been thrown out in the middle of the night the previous summer when she had refused to share his bed. Although my accommodation situation was still critical, I told him he was too generous. I was a restless sleeper, I said, with a tendency to violent nightmares. I had the poker in my hand at the time, twirling it casually, and he did not press the offer.

■

Fortune was smiling on me. Within two days of finishing the *tokat*, and right on Natasha's deadline, I had my double wish: a change of house; and employment. I could have thought up a few far superior wishes if I had let my mind loose, but there was no Aladdin's lamp.

My new bed was the top of the calf's pen. Quite acceptable. Up to now, I had been sleeping on a box in Natasha's house. The pen was no harder and I was assured that the calf was a sound sleeper. The house belonged to Ustinja, a one-time Ukrainian, with a schoolgirl daughter. I say 'one-time' advisedly. She was now a Russian.

The transfer had come about through a chance meeting with Mrs Mikael one evening. She was a comparatively new acquaintance, fiftyish, kind and reliable. We talked of the usual things before I asked her, as I asked any Estonians whose living quarters I did not know to be full, if she knew of a place for me.

'There would be room with us,' she said hesitantly. 'My son and me.'

I was delighted. She lived in Red May *kolkhoz*, only a few kilometres away.

'I shall have to ask the landlady first.'

'Of course.'

'And my son.'

'Naturally.'

'Principally the landlady.'

'Yes.' Sensing a degree of uncertainty, I waited. Nothing was to be gained by pressing her.

'The thing is that she's a party candidate. And she hates Estonians – I mean really *hates* – I don't know why.'

'I'd be quite at home, then.'

'She might just be greedy enough to take in one more,' Mrs Mikael mused.

'Will you let me know?'

'She has a twelve-year-old daughter, too. Needs watching. She's light-fingered. And a real troublemaker. A spoilt brat.' Charming. It sounded as though my friend was having second thoughts, maybe regretting her offer. Or perhaps she was simply weighing up personalities. Mine and theirs. Compatible or not? 'Really, she can be quite vicious. You would have to be careful.'

'It still sounds better than where I am.' Nowhere. And a Ukrainian would have to be better than a Russian, I reasoned.

'All right. I'll talk to her.'

'Tomorrow?'

∎

My rent was soon decided, and paid up for five months, until September. The price was a woollen dress – too small for Ustinja, near enough to a fit for her daughter – for sharing a room with Mrs Mikael, her thirty-year-old son, a dozen hens who customarily spent the whole winter on the oven, and a calf. Calves, from the time they were born in early spring, remained inside until summer. This one's box – my bed – was just inside the door; the Mikaels were under the tiny window; the landlady and her daughter slept in the enclosed entry porch. Mrs Mikael was

202

right: Ustinja was greedy.

What was to happen beyond September I did not know, and there was no sense worrying about it. I would manage somehow. For the moment I was a citizen of Red May, with a roof over my head, new room-mates, and a landlady I was to learn to loathe.

.

Flax and hemp were harvested at the end of summer. The hand-cut stalks had been stooked in the fields to dry out, then soaked for a couple of weeks in shallow dams at the river bank during autumn to start the strong stems rotting. The tied bundles were gathered again and allowed to dry before winter set in, and were put away, eventually to be brought out from storage for final processing. This was the time.

Beating the bundles was cnsidered one of the lighter jobs – for the *babushka* brigade, to which I had been assigned after my illness. We were allotted the hemp, Russian women the flax. No need to guess which was easier.

Each armed with a short wooden club, smooth from years of beating, we would take a bundle of the strong finger-thick stalks and whack the top until the seeds fell out. Then we would lay the stalks on wooden blocks and beat them till they were thoroughly crushed, soft and pliable. Some of the rotted pithy wood fell out on the floors, some rose in a fine yellow cloud. Yet more remained bound in the stringy hemp fibres. The resultant limp light bundle was thrown to the other end of the shed where the heap would later be gathered and taken for scutching. The seeds – oh, those seeds!

As it happened, all the other members of my team were city born and bred. My own country experience had begun when I was sixteen, just after the Great War, when my parents had begun farming. Holidays were spent on the farm, although I had stayed with my sister in Rakvere for schooling. I recalled gathering hempseeds back in those dreamy days, collecting them in handfuls, picking them one by one and eating them. I even remembered encouragement from the elders – 'Go on, eat up, they're good for you' – so I surreptitiously rubbed the husks off a few. I put my teeth into them gingerly at first, then with relish. The taste came back from out of the past, nutty and pleasant. And my empty stomach made no complaint.

203

'What are you doing?' Mrs Kesa was the oldest of my work-mates. She had once been almost obese; I suspect that eating had been her ruling passion. Her clothes hung on her now like sheets over a pole.

'Try some,' I said. 'I think they're edible.'

Soon all of us were at it. In the breathing spaces between thumping bunches of stems into fibre, we would gather a handful of the heads to rub between palms and heels of hands, loosening seeds from husks. Then, carefully blowing off the light chaff, we picked seeds one by one from the open hand and popped them between willing teeth, like squirrels. The seeds were tiny, flat, triangular, smaller than an apple pip – a thousand would hardly constitute a meal – and delicious. As something for nothing, a total triumph.

By Saturday, we were nearly half way through the stack. Our arms and shoulders ached from unaccustomed exercise, hands grew tough under blisters from the clubs. We thought we had done fairly well, which was a relief, as it was the brigadier's inspecting day. We might have anticipated what would happen.

'Haven't you finished yet?' he roared from the doorway.

It had to be Skakalkin. He pointed at the two piles, one done, one not. We were used to him; his approach did not vary much. He did not expect an answer; we did not expect him to be satisfied. It was all very predictable.

His angry little eyes flashed about. 'Where are the seeds, then?'

I translated for the women. We looked, innocently, one to the other – shrugging shoulders, spreading hands, shaking heads. The elaborate pantomime went on for quite a while before I turned back to him. '*Njema* – Not any.'

'The seeds, the seeds!'

'*Njema*.'

'Satan's pigs!' yelled the Jumper, waving his arms wildly. 'In the morning you get to the sauna and beat the flax. You can eat the dust there.'

He spat in my direction – 'Slut!' – and stormed out cursing, great-coat flying in jerks behind his bony frame. I had been blamed again. I did not mind this time, as I suppose I was responsible. Anyway, we had had a victory: he could not get back the seeds. Someone had omitted to tell us that their collection for oil was part of the operation.

We did eat dust. Scutching, or combing out the flax fibres, was a dirty job, with no rewards, as the linseeds had already been removed. The partly rotted straw had been beaten as we had done the hemp; we carried out the next step with big iron brushes, dragging bundles through the bristles to send up clouds of dust from the dried-out pulped stems. It might not have been bad if we had had an open shed, or a ventilated room to work in. But no. Of all places, we had the dirty sauna.

Siberian saunas come in two categories: 'clean' and 'dirty'. In the clean ones, the fire is completely outside the sauna room, the large stones forming the back of the big, enclosed fireplace-cum-chimney doubling as part of the wall of the sauna. Heat is transmitted into the closed room by radiation from the almost red-hot stones. In the dirty saunas, the back of the grate opens directly into the room to be heated. No dividing wall or chimney. The sauna is thus warmed both by the fire stones and by hot smoky air straight off the fire itself. In our collective, we had one of each. The Ustavs, Ott and his mother and two young sisters, lived in the dirty one.

Since Mrs Ustav was the only one of us who knew how to manage a hand spinning 'wheel', she had been put in charge, not only of spinning, but of the whole operation. Logical enough, we conceded, though she knew little of the previous processes.

She lived in the sauna, hence the spinning wheel had been duly installed there. This, we agreed, was eminently reasonable.

She had to supervise the scutching personally – for what reason this was essential was beyond us, but essential we were assured it was – therefore the whole works were also sent to the sauna. This included the masses of partly treated fibre, the brushes, and the entire operating personnel. Logical to a point, we admitted. But in the sauna of all places! To argue that a more suitable venue – with room and ventilation – could easily be found would be wasting breath, risking a tongue-lashing, and perhaps costing the arguer a job. And bread.

So Mrs Ustav sat and spun, at the same time directing us in the use of the brushes, in her private residence that was more like a coal-cellar than a factory. She soon had us covered in fine, yellowish powder that had once bonded and swelled strong flax fibres in healthy growth. I pondered the fate of those once firm and beautiful plants: uprooted, starved, thrown to the elements, beaten into dust, combed into thin limp fibres. Hm . . .

We worked industriously, standing or sitting on the sauna's hard stepped benches, the Jumper's threat of the Ustavs' expulsion from their home providing the incentive. 'Get them moving or out they go. You with 'em.' By the end of the day, only teeth and eyes showed through yellow crust. Clothes, hair and skin were coated. So were mouth and throat, probably lungs and stomach as well.

Saturday night, as always, was bath night. During the day Mrs Ustav and Ott had the alternative of shifting belongings out, or piling them into a corner in the anteroom while the fire was lit. They always shifted out. It was safer.

Smoke was already pouring into the main room as we cleared it, settling on many years' accumulation of soot and dirt, and now on the fresh flax pith. The temperature climbed as the stones took in heat. Such a busy little building! The factory had been closed; the home had been evacuated; now the public bath was almost ready.

With the fire dwindling to glowing coals, the old sauna man washed the steps and floor free of surface grit and ordered that two big tubs of clean water be carried in. I helped with the carrying without much complaint, as we knew women were first in Red May *kolkhoz*. But strictly Russian women or regulars, as I discovered only after doing the work. Then men. Then us, the non-regulars, unless we wanted to go in with the men.

■

We found ourselves spending the greater part of Saturday evenings in or around the anteroom, awaiting our turn. That first night, I was incensed. Those a bit longer in Red May were used to it.

Russians were never in a hurry, particularly men. At the sauna they took their time, not in the least mindful of those following. It is a national characteristic not to alter established ways; to resist, if necessary to ignore, change. It simply did not occur to anyone to vary the custom of years: Russian women went in first, men next; it had been so from the dawn of memory. That there was now an extra category did not enter consideration. There was no malice, no deliberate penalisation, merely no thought. But certainly no change. Rarely was there water left by the time we got in, and the stones had lost most of their heat.

Soap had long since gone, including my home-made ash-soap from Natasha's, and my new landlady would not have anyone 'messing around making that stuff in *my* house'. Necessity the teacher, I washed by rubbing fresh ashes over my body, my face, into wet hair, flicking up circulation with birch bundles picked specially for the purpose. I brought in my own pan of clean rinsing water, cold. A matter of pride. My hair was growing dull; hands and nails were hard and grimy; I dreaded to think what was happening to my complexion. Nevertheless, once a week, I could feel clean.

Drying was a snag. I was not yet accustomed to the Siberian way of donning rough clothing over wet skin. However, there was no alternative but to learn. Who would ever have thought of the humble bath towel as one of life's real refinements?

16

OMENS

As the thaw advanced, it was back to the forest for us. All building timbers, paper-mill logs, lengths trimmed for the kegmaker – everything, in fact, that had been cut and prepared last summer and was lying waiting in the forest – now had to be carted to the river bank. Soon, the snow and ice would be gone, and the stream would flow fast. The wood had to be ready. Once into the river here, it would be floating in great islands down the Ob in a few days.

For several months we had been, to varying degrees, isolated by the terrible cold: individual from individual, *kolkhoz* from *kolkhoz*. In midwinter, confinement had been complete, often to the house, certainly to the village. As spring had neared, neighbouring villages had come within reach; we set out on tiring marches on crisp, blue days, and silent walks home through endless snow on glittering black nights. By winter's end those dreary, lonely nights were mercifully shortening. As the short spring progressed, so did the hours of daylight, and our possibilities both for social contact and for collective work. Thus I met Tiia Laane.

Men carried the bigger logs, beams and props. Kegboards – *klopkas* – were left to the women and boys. Seven hundred *klopkas* a head was the daily quota; to be picked up in the forest, carted a kilometre or more and stacked at the riverside. We tied the boards into bundles with rope and hauled them on our backs through the snow, slush, and icy puddles to the bank, guided by a beacon fire. Then, feet wet to the knees, hands freezing, bodies aching, we tramped back for the next load, goaded by the promise of a bonus of extra bread for exceeding the seven hundred boards a day. We never made a bonus.

Tiia came from Narva. Her husband had been a journalist acquaintance of Elmar's. We met by the fire, and instantly teamed up.

A good nature and cheerful outlook are rare enough attributes at the best of times. To find them in the mother of a five-year-old son, here in exile, would fairly arouse suspicion of collaboration, deception or mental defect. Yet Tiia had such a nature, plus honesty, integrity and intelligence. My early reservations evaporated in minutes. How she managed it – for she had brought virtually nothing with her from home – I shall never know. She saw brightness in the future, despite looking facts squarely in the face. She had a child today and tomorrow and for an indefinite period thereafter, and was fully aware that his life depended on her own physical well-being. So she worked hard, as hard as possible without risk. I tried to match her attitude, as she seemed stronger for her buoyant approach.

'Devil take these things, Tiia. You'll break my back.'

'You took twenty last time and managed that all right. Think of it! Twenty-two *klopkas* this time and the next ten times and you've saved yourself one trip.'

'Uh.'

'Or is it nine?'

'If I get there at all.'

'You'll manage. Remember the Jumper – '

'If I could only forget!'

'"Behinds sticking out like working oxen", eh? All right, let's work like his blasted oxen.'

'If I could feel my fingers! Then perhaps I could tie this rope.'

'Come on, now. Lift this hundred-crown pack onto my fur-covered shoulders – careful of my new gown! – and let's ski down to the village. The drinks are poured. The party's waiting. I don't want to be late for the ball.'

We hoisted loads of *klopkas* onto each other's backs, carried, dumped, trudged back for more, stopping work once in the day, for an hour at lunchtime. We sat on logs by the fire then, eating bread, warming hands, drying footrags. Even though I still had boots, some of the others did not, so I preferred to keep mine at home. They would have been ruined in no time here anyway. We managed by wrapping our feet in scrap materials.

210

The brigadier and the Russians went home for lunch. The breaks became semi-private gatherings, like club meetings, for us. We saved food for them, seeing people we had not seen sometimes for months, meeting others, hearing news. Bad news. All bad. We met nevertheless, for the sake of company.

Tiia and I tried to view all reports dispassionately. If we happened to know the subjects of tragedy, we eschewed discussion, detachedly, as though they were strangers.

One item caught my ear. 'Did you hear? In Kamenoi, a whole family of Estonians.'

My heart contracted. I broke our rule. 'Did you know them? Their name?'

'Nommik.'

My carriage companions. The poor confused washerwoman with her little boy and girl. No clothes, just a carpenter's box.

'They couldn't pay any rent – had to live in a deserted hut – '

Perhaps I could have helped them. I had been close. I had even gone there once, missed them, and promised I'd go back.

'First the mother, then the children. They kept together until the mother went, then the children were put into the "kidpool". They only lasted a couple of months – died within a week of each other.'

I could not bear to hear more and signalled to Tiia. We took our footrags down from the green twigs stuck out over the coals, and put them back on; not quite dry, just warm enough for a minute or two's comfort.

'Did they get a burial?' someone asked.

'In rags. No coffins.'

'You couldn't have altered anything, Ann,' Tiia said, as we went back to work. I was terribly depressed, though I knew she was right.

Next day, it was the mother of the twin girls who had been begging in Maisk: the Kalks from Johvi. 'Failure of the organism.' And Mrs Pihlakas' baby, unborn when I had come back from haymaking in autumn, had lived and died. Others, too. Some I had known, many I had not. Tiia the same.

We had had no further deaths at Maisk, but the *kolkhoz* had not escaped the cold touch of officialdom. From Red May, a young mother with a nine-month-old baby had been arrested for theft. No-one knew what she was supposed to have stolen, except

211

that it was a small amount of food. From Kombain, Mrs Kelch, the German-born wife of the director of Narva's textile factory, had been charged with refusal to work and agitation of the people. They had both been sent somewhere 'up the snow road'.

Then there were the boys from the cedar-cone expedition. None of them had recovered. They were feverish and thin, all coughing constantly, particularly young Oidermaa, who was now unable to get out of bed. They were off the ration roll, all three, so their land-ladies had chased them from their quarters, and the commandant had put them, boys and mothers, into a dilapidated, deserted hut. The Ustavs had relieved pressure there by taking the dirty sauna. The male nurse at the hospital had diagnosed galloping consumption, and jauntily recommended plenty of good food, with fresh fruit, lots of sun, fresh air and rest.

Pleasure in our 'club' was short-lived. We could seldom enjoy bread at lunch hour, as there were new crises daily. We began to wonder who would be next. She? Me? What would it be? Sickness? Arrest?

Sickness meant starvation, that we knew. Arrest, we did not know, as those who had gone had not come back. The prospects did not bear contemplation. We had all, at some time, pilfered food; we had all, at some time, publicly cursed the *kolkhoz*, the bosses, the landladies, the whole leprous system. All had thus committed crimes against the Soviet state. Not one of us was safe, now or at any time. It appeared that both of those latest cases had stemmed from incidents months earlier, suddenly brought to light.

■

The vast Vasjugan area was populated, though thinly, with depor-tees. Deportees do not fit into the 'free' communist state. Obviously, you cannot be part of a team and not be in it. Thus if newcomers refuse to join the system, they must be ignored or annihilated, either course having much the same result. If, on the way to obliteration, they can be made productive for the state , so much the better for the state. But this is incidental. As individuals, as *people*, we no longer existed. We could suffer, slave and starve. As far as the Kremlin was concerned, what we did in these respects was immate-rial as long as we were meanwhile useful and created no nuisance.

■

I still had a few dresses and two pairs of shoes, almost the last of my non-essential baggage, and decided to exchange them, trying hard to console myself with the knowledge that they would fit me only where they touched now, anyway. My home-going clothes. Hardly the right wear for Siberia, I thought, but somebody might like some pretty things. I must have food. I was weak, my feet were swelling again, and several teeth were loose.

Mother Mikael told me of an old man who lived some distance away. 'He's probably over seventy,' she said. 'They call him "The old man of the white cow".'

'Sounds harmless enough.'

'I wouldn't know.'

'Where does he live?'

'On the edge of the forest.' She told me where.

'Do you think it's any use?'

She eyed me dispassionately. 'How would I know? He's sold milk and potatoes before, I can tell you that much.'

I went one evening, taking a silk scarf and a pair of shoes. Dresses would not be much use. I found his cabin, knocked, and stepped in more boldly than I felt.

The old man was on his bed, fully dressed even to his worn felt boots. The bed had not been made in months. I could see the filth even by the weak light of his sputtering lantern. Crumpled blankets sprawled over the foot end of a flattened straw mattress. He lay on top. Probably, as it became colder in the night, he simply pulled the grubby things over him, clothes and all, and got out the reverse way in the morning. He sat up as I came in, wafting his stench toward me.

He patted the edge of the bed beside him. 'Come right in,' he said. 'Sit down.'

I moved back a few centimetres, resisting wholesale retreat. I was after favours. The smell of stale tobacco was in the air and, after months without, I was suddenly hungry for a smoke. I decided to ask for that, too, after the food.

'You'll get some.' I was beginning to see better. A couple of crusts curled on the earth floor beside the bed. He was grinning toothlessly. 'You're still a fairly young *baba*. And without a man, I guess. Just stay a while.'

This was not unexpected. I thought I could handle him. I shook my head and offered the shoes.

213

'Stay the night,' he cackled. 'I don't need women's shoes. You'll get your food.'

'Take the silk scarf then. It will look fine on a man. For a piece of bread and a litre of milk.'

'What the devil do I want with a silk scarf?'

'You can sell it.'

'What for?' He leered.

'Whatever you want.'

'All right, I'll take it. And sell it back to you!'

'I just want bread and milk.'

'Come to bed or get out,' he grunted. With surprising speed he reached for the hand with the scarf, grabbed it, and pulled before I could jump out of his way. I tugged back. He was not going to get something for nothing.

'Let go or I'll scream!'

Understandably, my panted threat had no effect. Not even a bird would hear. I struggled for the scarf. He jerked me close to his foul breath and body. He was strong. Suddenly, I was more afraid than angry, and took a wild swipe at his face with the shoes. I missed, but succeeded in freeing myself.

I ran outside and, to my chagrin, burst into tears. A useless, stupid thing to do, I thought between sniffs. Self-pity is not nourishing. Nor is anger. My stomach was a knot, my head dizzy, my legs trembling. Afraid now for more than honour, I made straight for Mrs Balters's place to ask for a meal. It had come to that. I was going to beg.

Enn let me in and my resolve melted immediately. In the three weeks since I had last seen her, our dear, good-looking, straight-standing first lady, our proud 'carriage mother', had changed into an old woman. She lay listless on her bed, pale and sunken-eyed. She made no attempt to get up, displayed none of the usual courtesies at seeing me. Of all tribulations, this was the most pathetic and the most frightening.

'Where have you been, Ann?' Enn's voice had an edge. He was worried, perhaps had been looking for me. He pointed at the shoes and scarf I still carried. 'What have you been doing?'

I told them about the old man of the white cow. Mrs Balter nodded absently now and again, scarcely interested. Marusja and her family heard, too, while they ate their bread and soup, which didn't matter, as they couldn't understand. I could hear

214

them at their food, smell it; try as I might not to look, my eyes kept straying to the table. My stomach crept into my throat. My story rambled. I felt near collapse.

'Good night,' I wished Mrs Balter. I could bear it no longer. Nor could I ask for anything. 'Get well soon.'

Enn saw me out. In the porch he pressed ten roubles into my hand. I took it gratefully. He reached into a bag in the corner, put a finger to his lips and took out a handful of dried bread and a few potatoes. 'She would have offered if she'd been well enough,' he whispered. 'If you're in trouble again, let me know.'

■

Mrs Mikael looked cynically at my shoes. 'You've still got them?'

'You knew what he was after!'

'I didn't know how hungry you were.'

I was angry at Mrs Mikael and glad I had hidden Enn's food. She would have arrived at – for her – the only conclusion.

I cooked the potatoes, and ate the lot when nobody was home to embarrass me in my wealth. 'Never tease your stomach!' my grand-father used to say. Enn would also have approved. Mrs Balter would not; she kept things for rainy days. She had failed to notice that, for her, it was now pouring.

■

'Out to the forest now. Quick. There's work. Davai, up you get!' Still dark, and my goad was the *kolkhoz* bookkeeper, with a work order. 'Put your shoes on,' he added with a sly chuckle. 'It's wet in the forest these mornings. Carrying them around today won't do you any good. Not necessary, anyway. You'll get your bread from the store tonight.' And, in case I had not yet twigged: 'You won't even need a scarf for it!'

Barely dawn, and yesterday's abortive business deal was common knowledge already. It had to be Marusja. Mrs Mikael wouldn't have had the chance. I must warn Enn and Mrs Balter. We would have to be careful if she – or perhaps the children – could understand Estonian as well as that.

The bookkeeper exited in a gale of laughter. One of these days . . .

By seven everybody seemed to be at the office except Mrs

Balter. We were to go and burn branches. Women, children, some of the Russian girls as well. Some had lost so much weight during winter that they were swaying on their feet. Those with children were the worst, having exchanged their last clothes and forgone their last mouthfuls. But at least the youngsters were alive. Meeri and Mrs Ustav had big gaps between remaining teeth. The latter said that Ott and his friends were still running slight temperatures. They were here all the same, or there would be no rations. The lack of vitamins had loosened teeth, peeling gums away, as well as causing skin troubles and general weakness. We were a pitiful bunch, with no smiles.

We collected the foliage shaved from building logs, shaking snow out of the branches, standing in puddles around heaps where the snow had already melted. Warming frozen feet and hands by the fires was allowed twice a day: ten minutes in the morning and an hour at midday.

Soon it would be potato-planting time. The *kolkhozniks* had said it would be an early season, with a warm spring, but the time was not ripe yet. It was something to talk about, though, something to think about. The sooner the seed potatoes went in, the sooner the new ones would come out, and we remembered baking them in the fields last autumn. A treat to look back on and forward to.

A week finished the burning, then we had to fill in time back in the forest preparing logs for building. I was again teamed with Alma. The *babushka* brigade stayed near the edges of the field, collecting and burning smaller growth cut down by the boys and some of the younger women. The purpose was eventually to clear the land for farming. Alma and I were sent with the Russian girls deeper into the forest. We were the chosen ones, the fit, selected to do the heavy lumbering. Or that was the story. Skakalkin did the choosing, and he liked Alma no better than he liked me. We were handed a kolkhoz saw and axe and told we were a team. Perhaps we were, but we lacked something besides spirit; by the end of the first day, our sweat and labour had levelled two whole trees – not very big ones – and sawn them into logs. We knew that at such a rate we would surely starve. We also knew that with our rusted saw and axe we were unlikely to improve to subsistence standard.

Next morning we took the tools to the office. The bookkeeper sent us to the brigadier. We found the Jumper and showed him. He roared, ranted and waved his arms. He declared that he had no time to coddle us and sent us to the storekeeper, who was not at home.

'Let's try next door.' The *kolkhoz* head, Kalesnikov.

'Why not?' Even the cautious Alma had had enough.

It was scarcely his responsibility but we thought that he would surely head us in the right direction. He came to the door himself, tallish, slightly built, grey-eyed. He had curly brown hair, straight features and, usually, a mild manner. Even allowing for the Russian ability to about-face, we had found him reliable and reasonable on previous occasions. This time, he was anything but cooperative.

'Saws? Why come pestering me with them?'

'As I said, we've tried everyone else. We only want – '

'You want too damned much.'

'But – '

'But nothing. If you ever come here annoying me again, I'll cut out your ration altogether. Off to the devil with you!'

'The devil? Now, at last, we're getting to the top,' muttered Alma.

'What did she say?'

'Nothing. Just "thank you for seeing us".'

'Huh.'

Alma was too direct to be popular with our hosts, though she usually had the self-restraint to avoid confrontation.

I knew that the Mikaels between them had a saw and an axe not in use at the moment. I knew also that they would be in good order, as 'young' Mikael worked in the smithy of another *kolkhoz*, and he was a conscientious man. We found both him and his mother at home and, after a lot of talking, persuaded them to lend us the implements just for the day. He even promised to sharpen ours in the evening, a grudging but nonetheless firm promise. The man had a right to grumble, we admitted, as he was not supposed to work for another *kolkhoz* – which was why I had not asked him in the first place. As we lived and starved under the same roof, however, he had found it difficult to say no.

We thanked him hurriedly, and rushed toward the office to report for work. We had wasted a lot of time running around with our blunt saw, and it had been said that being late three times meant losing five days' pay at the end of the year. We were not sure about that, and had no intention of finding out the hard way. In either case, we were losing time, and time was bread. Last year, we had eaten our pay in advance. 'Looks as though we won't do any better this year,' Alma said, as we hurried, she with the axe, I with the saw, to fell our quota of forest giants. But first, the office.

We had not yet reached it when Dusja, the bookkeeper's wife, came flying out with a wild look in her eye. 'Oh, oh, what am I to do?' she cried. She was quite distraught, wailing like a wounded pig, beating her forehead with both hands. 'Oh, oh, oh.'

We stopped. Dusja didn't.

'What is it?' I called after her, hoping to show more concern than I felt. Aside from sympathy for Dusja, which was minimal, we were much concerned with the bookkeeper. A good mark from her might earn one from her husband, whom we did not yet know as well as we would come to. It was he who could report us as late. In any case, the cause of such panic might be interesting, as Russian grief could well be our joy.

'Oh, a terrible, terrible thing!'

'What's the matter? For goodness' sake! What's happened?'

She spoke without stopping. Courtesy was never one of Dusja's strong points. We had to move along with her, ears bent to catch her lamentations. 'How can you not be crying, when the order has arrived that our men must go to the war? Oh, my Pavel! And the dear director! Oh God, what will become of me now!'

We looked at each other, and let Dusja go her tortured way. She had not even registered who we were. I felt my heart give a jump. The Russians must be in trouble at the front, else surely they wouldn't be sending their reserves into the army in spring. The bookkeeper was hardly a front-line fighter. This was really scraping the barrel! And no wonder Kalesnikov was grumpy.

Alma was strangely quiet. I was to discover why later.

The office was crowded with crying women, consoling the new warriors and each other. The men, in turn, were abusing all fascists, the cause of their troubles and the root of all evil. They were worried and, above all, furious. That was understandable, too, as they were royalty here; they would never have it so soft anywhere in the army. As we approached the desk I suddenly realised that we were the only non-Russians in the room. All the others were out in the fields and forest, hard at work.

'What are you looking for?' Skakalkin, the Jumper, was behind the desk, yelling as usual. 'Get back to work!'

We disappeared quickly. We had been called fascists too often to risk it again now. One shout from some hothead would be enough.

'Did you hear that? The director, too!'

'Well,' Alma said on our way to the forest, 'if nothing else, it might keep them occupied enough to forget about us being late.'

'They might just forget to sign us on!'

'We'd better get some results, then. For proof.'

'We've won a sharp enough axe!'

We set to, and lowered several good trees, piling our logs to best advantage for the count. Measuring was done by eye, based on the size of the log-pile. Judicious stacking could give a good solid appearance with a lot of air in the middle. And who had shown us this? None other than brigadier Skakalkin, who came to do the measuring. Altogether, a very good morning's work.

On our third day, we had a failure. It had to happen. So far fortune had been with us, with all our trees felled according to plan. Towards evening, we chose a tall, straight pine, a beautiful tree with a good clear fall-path. We planned to chop off the main boughs and trim the branches that night, so that in the morning we could saw it into logs. It would make many.

I started the cut on the side it was to fall, and Alma finished it. A good, deep notch. We took the crosscut, and sawed until the great pine swayed and groaned. We stood back breathlessly. Then, with a tremendous roar, it began to fall exactly the wrong way. Branches caught at the shrubbery around and we screamed and jumped clear. Just in time. The huge trunk hit the ground with a terrific thump, bounced and came to rest with its butt end back up on the edge of the stump. Twigs stopped quivering. The dust settled. Alma and I looked at each other in dismay. The borrowed axe had been dropped and it now lay under the tree, with its handle splintered like a twisted match.

We inspected and conferred. It would be difficult and dangerous to do any sawing with the tree as it was, balanced on the stump, so we made a lever to ease it off. Together, we heaved and shoved, but all for nothing. The trunk would not budge. We sat down to rest, panting.

'What on earth do we do next?'

As if on cue, the Jumper came bursting through the bushes. He was carrying a gun. 'What devil's hell are you raising here, you lazy blank cows? I could hear the blank crackling and blank blank screaming kilometres away.' He had an enviable vocabulary. 'What have you done? You don't know how to saw, you blanks. You go about it like blank blanks.' He outdid himself. 'And you've broken the blank axe. For that you – you, Njura! – will go without blank bread. You blank blank. You were in charge of it!'

I had heard curses and obscenity before, from him and other experts, but never had anything like this been directed at me. We had stood automatically as he approached. I still had the end of the lever in my hands and, tightening my grip, I swung the timber missile at his feet, with the most malicious intent.

'Hey – ' He jumped, not a moment too soon.

'I'm going to the commandant,' I whispered. Alma moved beside me. 'You can't talk to us like that.'

'Help me get this blank tree off the blank stump. Then you can take yourselves to the devil himself,' he growled. He picked up the lever and, single-handed, easily shifted the trunk. It settled fussily on the ground. Then, without another word, the Jumper snatched up his gun and loped off into the forest.

ı

I made no complaint. I went as usual to the office to claim my bread and I was not given any; he had stuck to his threat and cancelled my ration. I wouldn't have gone, would have stayed away rather than risk being refused, except that pride comes a sad second to hunger. Even so, I decided not to say anything.

It was an interesting situation. Normally, Skakalkin would have jeered at the threat of being reported. He knew very well – and knew I knew – that far more harm would come to me than to him. Today, however, there was a marked air of insecurity among Russian males fit for army service. Perhaps he had that in mind when he went off so meekly into the forest. It was a much more likely explanation than penitence for his language. Perhaps everything would be easier now that the threat of call-up was in their minds. It was a good thought. The Jumper might now be a little wary of overstepping the mark. On the other hand we could not afford to bait him: he did, after all, still hold the whip. Stalemate.

As it happened, this was almost our last day on the saw and axe – *kolkhoz* ones, with a new handle supplied without question by the new storekeeper, blades kept in perfect order by Mikael – as potato-planting time had come. No more searching for fill-in jobs now: the real collective farming season was here.

A few fields had been sown with the winter crop just before the first snows. It would germinate soon. The ground was softening in the warm sunshine, soaking up water as the last snow melted, and early weeding had to be done. Half the women were assigned to this.

The rest of us had to sort and cut seed potatoes for the other fields, now ploughed and crudely harrowed ready for planting. The shoots were trimmed for seeding, the rest put aside for eating. Nothing was wasted; on the personal front, my little pockets were coming in handy again.

I found myself teamed once more with Matriona, again for a menial job. Skakalkin, I thought; he rarely missed an opportunity. We had to wash the potato bags, which was done by carting the dirty things in wheelbarrows down to the river – heavy mud-caked sacks in big wooden barrows with wobbly wheels, over the roughest of rough tracks – and washing them and hanging them out to dry. The water was cold. Each bag absorbed kilos of it, making them terribly heavy to slosh about and lift clear again. One by one, we carried the sodden weights to nearby bushes or fences to drape over and let drip. We had finished by nightfall and hoped they would dry by tomorrow.

'My poor back,' I groaned. 'I can't wait to crawl into bed.' It would be as welcome as a feather mattress.

'No chance.'

'What?'

'Well,' Matriona said hesitantly, 'someone has to guard the potatoes for the night.'

'They're not our concern.'

'I suppose not, but then there's the bags.'

'Who'd want to pinch them?'

'I don't know.'

Four calculating eyes turned to the bags in a new light. Who indeed?

'Who said they have to be guarded?' I asked thoughtfully.

'The foreman.'

'Well, if he's not here soon – '

'There's nobody else. One of us has to.'

She went on quickly, beating my protest. 'My husband is at home now, and the children. Would you do it, Njura? I can give you some milk. The cow has calved.'

Why not? If I could make something out of it. 'How many bags are there?' I asked.

'I don't know. About a hundred and fifty, there should be. I think.'

'Weren't they counted?'

'I don't think so.'

'No record?'

'I shouldn't think so.'

'What happens tomorrow?'

'When they're dry, we take them back and stack them in the storeroom.'

She studied the dripping sacks scattered around us. We understood each other well. 'Two or three shouldn't be missed,' she said. 'Bring them to my house in the night. Leave them under the porch. I'll dye them with willow bark. Pick out a good one for me.'

Two for me, one for Matriona. A few seed potatoes; one half litre of milk; later, two brown skirts with two large pockets on each. A few more dirty jobs please, Jumper.

■

The days stretched out. Rain clouds alternated with clear skies as the sun looped higher. The snow had gone. Planting began early in the morning, and we were not allowed to leave the fields until gathering darkness made it impossible to do more. Digging, planting, lugging bags of shoots. It was dark by the time we could get to the store to pick up our daily bread. Then, all of us at once, every worker from the four *kolkhozes*, converged on the central distribution point. I had to queue for up to an hour and a half, milling about in the cold and dark, waiting for names to be called; the replacement storekeeper was hopeless. Soon the complaints reached the temporary director, our former lumber foreman, Petkov. He was a quiet and sensible man.

'You.' He pointed at me. 'You're a quick walker, you speak Russian, and your handwriting is clear. You will be the bread collector for your work brigade.' He appointed others for other brigades, leaving the Russians to collect their own in the customary way. This was an unusual display of wisdom which suited me well. It necessitated my leaving the field an hour before the rest, with a list of names from our brigade duly signed by the foreman; I then presented it at the store. There, I was given bread already cut and weighed – five hundred grams a worker, three hundred a child – to take to the much roomier office nearby, where individual workers picked it up on their way home, ready sorted. It was certainly quicker for us, and relieved the storeman of the paperwork that did not come easily to him.

One evening, early in my bread-carting career, I was left with five hundred grams over, as Mrs Oidermaa had become sick with influenza overnight. I could not get to see her that evening, but kept her bread and left her name on the next day's list. The foreman crossed it off when he checked the list the following day. The next night I took her two days' ration, and found the poor woman was almost covered in rough brown spots; some were open sores. I remembered her as having thick, dark curls, and now her scalp was showing white in patches; she still tried, but she could not hide the patches with her pitifully thin grey-brown thatch. She was very unhappy about her hair. 'The spots don't worry me much,' she said. 'They must be caused by a lack of something.'

When I left the bread with her she burst into tears. She had been giving half her ration to her son, one of the cedar-nut boys.

There is an old saying that tells us that courage is the first half of victory. I tried my luck by leaving a blank space at the bottom of my bread list above the place for the foreman's signature, and adding a name after he had signed. The storeman never seemed to check numbers, and none knew our names. It worked. For the next ten days I left two or three spaces and profited by one to one and a half kilos of extra bread at each distribution. I lived well, and Mrs Oidermaa improved.

The blessing lasted only ten days, then they began issuing bread from the *kolkhoz* storeroom again. I never discovered why.

■

It rained lightly almost every day now, causing new problems. The few shoes left were falling to pieces. Most newcomers, like myself, had rags wrapped around feet. Top clothes were torn and soaked. There was no such thing as a waterproof. The ground was slimy and stuck to our feet, hands and knees. Planting was in full swing. The potatoes themselves, although in bags, were wet and freezing to the touch early in the morning. The bags were ingrained with last year's dirt despite our washing; the resultant cold, slippery mud was transferred to backs, shoulders and thighs as we lifted and dragged the dead weights along the rows. Our feet were really no worse than the rest of us: muddy heaps of rags. None of which, of course, was allowed to hinder the work. The Jumper saw to that.

I was a 'spade man' this time with the boys and the Russian girls. Digging was hard, with the ground just thawing out, and we had to move fast to get the crop in. But we didn't have to crouch, so I preferred it to planting.

When the sun came out, work seemed lighter and my own outlook correspondingly bright. When it failed to break through, I was as miserable as the weather, my eyes constantly drifting to the fire at the edge of the field, where the younger children of working mothers were allowed to huddle. With the Jumper about, I did not dare breach regulations. We were not allowed at the fire and, of course, not allowed to eat the potatoes or to take any home with us. Fortunately, even with Skakalkin, rules were not strictly policed at Maisk. At the neighbouring *kolkhoz*, all workers were regularly searched on leaving the fields. Here, it was possible to get away with a little surreptitious acquisition. We had been well advised; Maisk was a 'good' *kolkhoz*.

By the time planting was finished, I had a bucketful of seed potatoes and I didn't need more help from Enn, who had been covertly boosting my ration. All good shoots, too. I had been through them thoroughly several times, and cut off and eaten the *jopkas* – the bottoms.

Nothing but good news! Our director was back – he came right out to the fields to tell us – with his call-up deferred. Everybody was glad about his return, even the deportees – possibly especially the deportees – because he was a moderate man, despite our occasional disagreements. He had been away only two weeks, and we had missed him already. We knew he was better than most, and feared we might get one of the tough ones – a truly chilling prospect – in his place. He was pleased to be back, understandably enough given the alternative, and told us so.

To cap off a memorable week, on the Friday evening, with little left to do, brigadier Skakalkin came out with the news that if we had finished by Saturday, we would have Sunday off. 'And soup for everyone Saturday night,' he beamed. Oh, what a great fellow! In the devil's backside he was. Left to him, we knew where extra rations would have gone. 'With potatoes and barley,' he roared. 'And mutton! The sheep's already killed.' He strutted off. You'd have thought he'd just taken a third curtain call.

'Probably died.'

'Who?'

'The sheep.'

'Starvation?'

'Old age!'

'Not even a sheep could manage *that* here!'

'Failure to thrive, if you please.'

'Who cares? It's meat.'

We were gathered round the cauldron well before dark. Excitement tingled the air. A Russian girl came tentatively to me. 'Look, Njura,' she said. 'I found your spoon today. It is yours, isn't it? In my last dig.'

'Oh my God,' I whispered.

Other days we had had to drag ourselves to work. This Saturday we had been in the field early, working with a will, and anticipation had kept us bright all day. And now this! It was almost too much. There must be a meaning.

The item was indeed the soup spoon my mother had sent to the carriage after me. I had been devastated to lose it while working in the field last autumn. Not only was it useful, but one of the few remaining tangible links with home. The girl would have had no trouble recalling the fuss I had made, the implied accusations; I had run very close to the wind. I now owed the unknown 'thief' – Russian, of course – an apology, and quickly decided on a tacit one.

'It's a good omen.' The girl was viewing me with some awe. I could hardly blame her; I was transported to another world. 'I think you'll go home yet,' she added. I was thinking the same, my heart somersaulting.

225

Trivial triggers can set off sharp recollections. Momentarily I saw beyond the poor tarnished spoon to polished mahogany, gleaming silver, heavy cutlery, glittering gowns. I smelt cigar smoke. I heard Elmar laugh. Then the vision was gone, as quickly as it had come.

The practical gain was that the spoon was useable; I'd no longer have to wait for someone to finish before borrowing one. 'Thank you,' I said.

The girl eyed me again, embracing a blackened spoon at my breast, and slipped away.

Our Helga was cook. She had sent a message via Alma. 'Let the Russians eat first.' This should present no problem. We understood. We would get more, and the thicker soup from the bottom, at that.

The director was in the rest hut. He had personally cut the meat into equal, quite big, pieces. He dished them out with obvious pleasure, all the while telling whoever cared to listen about his trip to Novo-Vasjugan.

17

BERRIES AND BEARS

lma and I had lingered over the last of the soup, making plans for Sunday. I was pleased to be teamed with her as, apart from being a foil for my volatility, we were alike in outlook. She and her husband had had a furniture factory, and her business knowledge was an asset in many of our day-to-day problems. She spoke Russian well, too. Alma had had a lot of clothes when she had arrived, but had sold them off quietly to help struggling families: 'For the children, dear, don't worry about me, I have plenty.' We planned to sleep late, do our few chores, then meet and go to the far edge of the fields to gather herbs and grass for our own soup. Later, we would visit friends at the hospital, talk, and perhaps stop at the Estonian 'club-house' to sit and talk a while longer, as we were doing now, the evening before our day off.

The bookkeeper approached. He had not been wanted at the front, either, and had returned with the director.

'You!'

We ignored him.

'You!' Me. I continued my conversation with Alma. 'You!' He was not a bad fellow, of Ukrainian parentage, here since childhood, and he would probably have been a clerk in any circumstance.

'Me?'

'Yes, you! Report at ten o'clock tomorrow morning. At the shop.'

Why me? I knew. I glanced at Alma. She shook her head sympathetically.

'What for?' I said.

'Cranberry picking.'

'Cranberry picking! Now?'

'A large brigade is going out. To a swamp about five kilometres away. The shopkeeper will be your guide.'

'How nice.'

'What?'

'Whose orders?'

'Brigadier Skakalkin's.'

My fault for asking. So much for our day off. But cranberries were an attraction, and the bookkeeper had said that there would be some bread at the end of it as well. It's an ill wind . . . I smiled resignedly at Alma. She made a thoughtful face.

Enticing though cranberries and wheat bread were, footwear was a worry. My skiboots were still in fair condition, but I had decided to keep them for emergencies; maybe even for next winter, though God forbid the necessity. The potato field had made wrecks of my rubber overboots. Rags or worn-out *tscherkis* were out of the question deep in the wild forest. So what to wear? Out came the pair of shoes I was keeping. I still had socks, slacks, underwear and a sweater put away too, ready for the return home in style. There was also a 'just in case' summer dress.

Now I was ready for the Sunday excursion. My lunch – two hundred grams of dry bread and a cold baked potato – was in my pocket and Mrs Mikael's *konn* was on my back. The *konn* was a knapsack of birch bark, peeled off in thick sheets and resin-glued over a frame of willow sticks bent to an oval shape top and bottom, and fixed with string. It was a comfortable container, fitting the contours of the back very well. Full, it would contain a lot of berries.

I was on time. The shopkeeper was ready, wearing high boots and *fufaika*, the quilted cotton jacket. He had a gun slung over his shoulder. Good, I thought, no need to worry about bears. I had an almost obsessive fear of them.

'Good morning.' I felt quite cheerful. 'Is the berry brigade not here yet?'

'All present.' He pointed at five young girls, two Russian and three Estonian, sitting on the shop counter, sunning their legs. 'I'm taking you there.'

'Are you joking?'

'Joking?'

I had deflated him. A bad move, I realised, to be hastily repaired. 'I mean is this all?'

'How many do you want?'

A large brigade! Six girls, all from neighbouring *kolkhozes*. Blast Skakalkin! I knew only one, Liina Saarde, who went to the same school as my niece. We had discovered this the last time we met, around a fire some weeks ago.

'Fine,' I assured him hastily. 'As long as you're in charge.'

'We may as well get going, then.' Very important man. Holder of the gun, leader of the expedition. He swaggered off, with us in his wake.

We moved quickly. Though it was warm outside where the sun shone brightly, the path still had frost on it, getting thicker the further into the forest we went. We trod a goose row, in silence except for our breathing and the crackling underfoot. The path got narrower and darker. Soon we walked on moss and spent needles, and the air was heavy with the smell of rotted vegetation. On both sides was primeval growth, tall gaunt trees as yet bare of new leaf, closing on us as we penetrated deeper, trapping air and blanketing sound. Gun or no gun, I was afraid. It was quiet as death.

Nearing the swamp, I took off my shoes and parked them under a tree-trunk bridge. No point in ruining them. The ground was getting squelchy. I went on barefooted, directly behind the shopkeeper, stretching my stride to tread his footprints in the cold prickly turf. We had gone some distance like this before I asked, 'Will we soon see the marsh?' It seemed lighter up there, where the path veered, as though the forest had thinned. Perhaps this was it.

'Soon,' he said.

He reached the turn. I nearly collided with him when he stopped stock still in mid-stride. My eyes were level with the back of his neck. Rose-coloured scars of long-dead acne had bobbed over his frayed collar as he strode. The bobbing had ceased abruptly, and I saw the spots pale. He was seized in some powerful shock.

'What is it?' Curiosity overcame caution. 'A bear?' I could not wait for an answer, my heart was so thumping with the thrill. I jumped on a log to see past him. About fifteen paces ahead was a thick broken limb, slanting from its splintered joint seven or eight metres up the parent trunk, right down to the ground. Some climbing fern was trailing up it, seeking sun through the thin winter canopy.

Climbing down, hind legs first, and looking curiously in our direction, was a gigantic brown bear. It must have been two and a half metres high, its shaggy bulk descending slowly, swaying gracefully, hairy feet a scant couple of metres off the forest floor. A mighty, marvellously handsome creature, with a huge head and bright brown eyes.

My native fear deserting me, I went to step higher, for a better look. But the girl behind pulled me away with a jerk of the hand – the shopkeeper had already passed us both – and suddenly we were running pell-mell back along the path. I'd have kept going, charged to frenzy by returning fright, if those in front had not halted. Piled against one another around a corner, the shopkeeper, still pale and shaking, gathered us close. 'Wait,' he said between puffs. He was the man in authority, shaking or not. If a decision to run was to be made, he was the one to make it, not us. 'Wait,' he decided masterfully.

'Be quiet,' he whispered, 'and let's go further back.' Away from the animal; no argument there. 'Quickly and quietly! There's probably a cub in the forest here somewhere, and mother bears are very dangerous.' The girls' eyes were like saucers. We ran thirty or forty paces and grouped again in a small clearing. It seemed safe enough. 'Break off some branches,' the shopkeeper said. 'We have to light a fire, make a lot of smoke.' He seemed to know what he was about, though the uneasy way his eyes darted around did nothing to reassure us. He brought out matches, and started the fire with his cigarette wrapping, a strip of old newspaper. His hands trembled so much it took several tries. 'Now noise,' he said. 'Yell your heads off! As much noise as we can make.'

We screamed and shouted till our throats tingled hoarse.

When, some time later, we went gingerly back to the spot, the bear was gone. The Russian girls – knowing more than we did – were plainly terrified. They wanted nothing more than to return home right away. Our guide pooh-poohed their fears, chin up, chest out, but, from the way his eyes shot over his shoulder, his heart was not in staying here. Oh, no. He would dearly have liked a mass feminine retreat; then he could follow, sounding his scornful trumpet all the way home. What a brave tale he would tell!

Liina, however, upset his applecart. She wanted to go as far as the marsh. The girls argued, but she stood firm, at fifteen the youngest of us all. 'I want cranberries.'

So did I, but this time I was on the side of the majority.

'We've wasted a whole day off – '

'I know, but – '

'And come all this way – '

Mother bears are very dangerous, the man reminded us. Father bears weren't notably friendly either.

'I'm *not* just going to turn around and go back again.'

'Well, go on by yourself.' The Russian girls turned surly.

'Are you sure?' asked the hero. 'You wouldn't rather leave the berries?'

'No.'

'And you, Njura?'

Liina had convinced me now. She was right. On the edge of the marsh and not even to look? 'No!' Bear or no bear, that was just not tolerable. 'How close are we?'

'You can practically see it from here.'

We edged fearfully past the broken bough. From the shore just beyond – if the barely perceptible change from sloppy soil to free water can be called shore – we could see mudbanks in the distance, seemingly covered with bright red berries. I stepped in eagerly. The water covered my bare insteps, and I didn't notice whether it was cold. It rose ankle deep, no more, before I reached the first high ground. Liina was with me. The clumps were dry, the berries real and ripe. We proved it again and again. They were delicious.

'I'll keep watch for you,' called the shopkeeper from the water's edge.

Liina and I picked greedily, one for the mouth, one for the basket. We went laughing from clump to clump, gathering and stuffing ourselves, letting the red juice run down our chins. We forgot about bears and Russians and cold feet. I must have had five litres in the *konn* before pausing to check the shore. The shopkeeper was not to be seen. Liina was near. I called. We stopped to look. Neither man nor girls. We shouted, and had no answer.

'Do you think they've gone home?'

'The girls certainly wanted to.'

231

'Perhaps they saw the bear again?'

'Perhaps. They've gone, anyway.'

'Are you afraid of the bear?' asked Liina. She was a child, thrilling to adventure.

'Not really.' As long as I didn't think about it.

'Are your feet cold?'

'No. Not very.'

'Mine are. But I'm not afraid of the old bear.'

We were fortunate in our ignorance. Cunning, swift, vicious and immensely strong, he – or she – warranted every bit of the Russians' caution. If we had known, we might have had bear in our minds and nothing in our stomachs, instead of berries in both.

By midday, the *konns* were full. 'There'll be at least a bucketful,' I said gleefully, running them through my fingers. 'Even after cleaning.'

'Me too.'

Liina had tied her bright yellow scarf to a branch at the edge of the marsh. It served as a marker to the path back. The forest was still and darker than before, now that the sun was going down. We walked steadily, if a little fearfully, as far as the broken tree. Then, imagination being the mother of wisdom, we broke into spontaneous full speed. We continued running, yelling at the tops of our voices, until we reached the clearing where we had had the fire. There we collapsed in hysterical laughter.

■

'There they are!' said the shopkeeper. It must have been five o'clock. We had taken our time, picking up my shoes on the way. Some of the higher ranks, waiting for bread, looked at us as if we were creatures from another planet. Our fame had spread. There was awe in his voice. '*Vot*, what people, these *Estonkas*! They are not afraid of bears' – he should have heard us in that clearing – 'and look, the berries they brought!'

Our innocent bravery paid off, for after selling one bucketful to the shop, we were allowed to keep a half bucket each for ourselves. Added to the commission we had already deducted, this made a respectable supply. We had wheat bread weighed for us without joining the queue and went home with all that food, full stomachs, and two roubles each in money. A good day.

Other conversation that evening concerned the shopkeeper

himself. He had come back only an hour or so before we had, with Ljuba, the prettiest of the Russian girls, some time after the other three. His wife had been suspicious of the two of them for some time, and had gone to the forest in the afternoon to investigate. She had caught them coming out together. The resulting commotion, the gossips averred, had been heard all over the village. Drama and scandal! Our weary existence was livening up.

■

Before he had been called away, the director had proclaimed that every member of the heavy brigade was to be allotted a plot for potato growing this spring. Sure enough, somewhat to our surprise, we were each measured out a strip of unploughed land near the forest.

Reserves of energy appeared from nowhere. Over a period of several days, after the collective day was done, I turned mine over with a spade, making twenty-five soft nests. Into each I carefully worked some horse manure acquired from the stable after dark, and, in all, planted seventy-five cuts of potato, each with a shoot, three a nest.

We all did much the same. None of us were given seed potatoes, yet, miraculously, everybody had enough. And no questions were asked about whence they came. 'God's not the only one who moves in a mysterious way,' Alma muttered.

My patch was at the edge of the road, opposite the *kolkhoz* potato field. I worked there with loving care. When not actually tending it, I thought about it. I walked past it every day, and calculated my autumn yield every time: twenty-five nests of half a bucket a nest – about what the *kolkhozniks* dug from their gardens in a reasonable year – makes at least ten to twelve buckets. Two, three, maybe even four potatoes a day for six months. Safety guaranteed for the winter! I could hardly wait for picking time.

After potato planting there was only lumbering, weeding and brick-making to fill in time before the crops were ready for reaping. Jobs and food were scarce. Paradoxically, winter was beginning to look safer than the present. I was given no opportunity to try the lighter jobs, nor was I ordered out with the heavy brigade to cut timber, though I could have gone if I had wanted. It was up to me. I could work and eat, or I could loaf and starve. Nobody cared. And as I had no hope of achieving the norm at wood-cutting, there was no point in further weakening myself. Any little work I did would be a gift to the enemy. There had to be other ways.

■

Mrs Randin was making her rations out of fish nets, and she started teaching me. I soon found the work needed more than enthusiasm. I would have to become expert quickly, too, as my 'going home' shoes wouldn't feed me forever; they had gone for a kilogram of bread and some mouldy peas – and it had been a wrench to part with them. Knots had to be tied firmly, evenly, without slipping. Mine were loose, and the first net sagged where it didn't pull, pulled where it didn't sag. It was a very poor net.

After several days, it was apparent I was not improving. 'I can do the weaving all right,' I complained, 'but the stitches keep slipping. I think I'll have to go back to the forest.'

'Ah, what of it,' my teacher said. 'Don't worry if it's not the world's best. You're not weaving it for yourself. Just keep on going. I don't think it's for fish, anyway. I think it goes to the front to hide the guns.'

At the end of the week I had just under eleven metres of net. I handed it to the bookkeeper, folded neatly to make it look as regular as possible.

'How much?' he demanded.

I cleared my throat. 'Twelve metres.'

He threw the lot on the scales with no more than a glance. *His* life wouldn't depend on it. 'Huh.' He grunted his contempt. 'Half norm.'

I could hardly contain my joy. I had spent seven days in a warm room, while the rest of the brigade had been in the forest and fields, toiling from dark to dark. My worries had been for nothing, I thought, as he calculated; for net-making you got paid *pro rata*.

Elation was short-lived. I was paid with a reel of net string.

No more, I decided. This was wrong-way traffic. The best I could hope for now was that the quality would fail its purpose.

■

Evening hours with the Mikaels were a comfort, despite having to watch and listen to landlady Ustinja and her daughter eating.

On the fire near the road we made soup from fresh thistles and nettles Mother Mikael had gathered. The peas had gone. We pretended not to notice Ustinja's good, solid food three metres away. As often as not, no sooner had we swallowed our grassy, unsalted mess than we had to rush to the bushes to be rid of it, scouring like sick animals, green and watery and painful. Those quick trips to the nearest cover embarrassed me at first, in the presence of Mikael. But we shared the same trouble, and so got used to it. Our digestive systems never did.

It was our job, as tenants, to tend the fire by the door every night, to keep away mosquitoes. We had an old tin pan on which we heaped hot coals and a few pats of dried cow manure. We blew and coaxed until the manure glowed red, then covered the whole with damp grass. The more it smoked the better the barrier, with mosquitoes forming up just beyond in perpetual armies, biding their time. If the smoke-screen lasted all night, well and good. If not, trouble from both sides, from attackers and attacked.

One night, the fire went out completely. I woke from bites and the humming of a thousand insects. From the front of the house, the door slammed, and curses split the still cold air.

'Now we'll be for it,' whispered Mikael. He stirred, over in the corner where he slept in the same bed as his mother. She kept him between her and the wall. It occurred to me, in the middle of the night, that that was why she had so nearly changed her mind when asking me to share the room: she was protecting him, her son, nearly my age, from me! What a giggle! Now she snored, oblivious to everything – noise, mosquitoes, Ustinja and all – as effective a barrier as the dead fire.

He was right. Ustinja charged in like a madwoman. 'Pigs! Fascists! You can all go to hell! My son away fighting in the war for you, and all you damned Estonians can do is loaf! You cause nothing but trouble. You have the nerve to sleep in my room. You take up most of my house while my own child and I get eaten alive by insects out in the passage!' Fighting for us indeed! Taking over her bedroom! Greedy harpy, it was the only way she could squeeze us in for the extra rouble. 'You, Njura, will pay another twenty-five roubles straight away to keep you here till the end of August. You're the cause of all this. Either that or go to the devil right now!'

235

It would be useless to remind her that she had made the offer and set the rent, or that she had got a dress cheaply. She was mad and meant it, and there was nothing I could do. If she insisted, I would have to pay, or get out: I did not even have *five* roubles. She slammed the door, shaking mud plaster from the walls behind her.

Sleep was finished. My face and arms stung from bites, my brain whirled, my heart was a lump of lead. Twenty-five roubles! I knew the Mikaels had no money. There was no-one else I could borrow from, except perhaps Enn, and I didn't have the heart to ask him for more. There was nowhere to appeal, either, particularly here in this house, where the grasping Ustinja, a party candidate, was the law. I had to remind myself many times in the darkness of my vow not to let them get me down. 'I'll get by some-how' had been my motto so far. 'I'll manage,' I repeated over and over through the restless night. 'They're not going to beat me.'

I went to the office early the next morning to try to get a forest job. I found that the Jumper had already put me, with my old school friend Lia, in the Russian women's and girls' ditch-digging brigade. He still had his knife into me; probably the same with Lia for the same reason. I thought I must ask her.

We had to dig ditches on either side of the road from the office to the rest hut, about three hundred metres. The road could certainly do with drainage. Each trench was to be a metre deep, a metre wide at the bottom and one and a half at the top. Where water would go, if ever they filled, seemed a question best left unasked. Tools were basic: spades, a measuring stick of one and a half metres, with a mark at one metre, and a length of rope.

Lia was morose. She was a city girl, and never, before Siberia, had she put fingers on the handle of a spade, or lifted a sod of earth. 'What do I do with the rope?' she grumbled tearfully. 'Hang myself? It looks strong enough. And the stick would make a nice cross for my grave.'

'We're labourers, Lia,' I said curtly. 'Let's labour.' Humour I could go along with, but not tears. Self-pity was never so far from any of us that we could let it step nearer. 'There's half a kilo of bread waiting at the end of this. Maybe Skakalkin's doing us a favour. Come on, I'll give you a hand.'

The local girls wasted no time on complaint. Without a word they measured lengths and widths, drove marking pegs into the ground and sent clods of earth flying out into the road. I measured two metres only, and began digging steadily, slower than they, expecting to have it finished by midday. The ground ran along the edge of potato fields, and, though still well-grassed, had been trodden down hard.

We discovered very early that the meanest of trades has its tricks. This one was no exception. For an apparently simple task, it proved incredibly difficult. The earth had to be skimmed of grass and roots first. The girls taught us – scornfully. They also pointed out that our spades were blunt, a fact we had already begun to deduce, and that we needed sturdy shoes, which we did not have. *Tscherkis* were not designed for this. The roots were deep, the ground packed solid and still near frozen. By midday I had finished one metre, and my body was aching; by evening, two – and I knew that was my limit. Lia managed less, and was crying openly. The norm was six.

'No bread for ditch-diggers today,' the storeman barked. You're keeping me from my dinner, his cold eyes said. 'Two hundred grams of flour.'

'So little!'

'Little? You call that little!' As if I'd requested fruit cake. 'You can bake five hundred grams of bread with it.'

It was as well that fate took a hand. My landlady – Ustinja – was tall, dark, quite good-looking for her early forties, and notedly greedy both for money and men. Lia's was entirely different. Hers was the *kolkhoz* 'chicken woman', an elderly, quiet soul who owned a whole cow and a human heart. Lia paid eight roubles a month – and I'm sure there were months when no rent was paid and no fuss made of it – and was given a little extra to eat, every now and then, for small favours. This was as well, for she was not tough enough to survive on her own. I could expect no lenience from my landlady, however, and, with only the flour and no roubles in my hand, I was afraid to go home to face her. I had done nothing about the twenty-five roubles, and indeed had no idea where I could begin.

Ustinja had shown no signs of relenting. On the contrary, she had made it clear that she expected full payment immediately, or else.

She had come from the Ukraine, probably in much the same way as we had arrived from Estonia, but ten years or more earlier. I never heard mention of her husband, and can only presume he had been a victim of one of the great purges. Now that was all in the past, and Ustinja was not one for sentiment. She was a survivor. No word of any language other than Russian ever passed her lips; Stalin was God; her son was in the Red Army, and she was proud of it; she herself was a party candidate. It was said that her men included the director and some of the other bigwigs. Which could be true. Men were never slow to take advantage of the laws of supply and demand.

She was waiting for me. 'Did you bring the money?'

I had no prepared defence, but her utter lack of subtlety decided it on the instant, awakening the latent aristocrat. 'I owe you money?' I said loftily.

'Twenty-five roubles. Or out.'

Brushing past her, I walked regally into the single room, Ustinja standing flat-footed in amazement. 'Only twenty-five roubles? I shall have it for you in July, if you would be so good as to wait until then.'

I was as aloof as she had been crude, and was probably no less surprised than she at my haughty performance. I rummaged in what remained of my belongings. 'Here, now, my good woman, take this for waiting.' I handed her my silk scarf, the one I had taken to the white cow man. 'It suits you, you know, you are a beautiful woman.' I tied the scarf under her chin. 'There. So. Oh, the men!' I stood back to admire the effect, hands clasped genteelly.

Ustinja simpered. '*Ladna!* – good! – I'll wait then.' She turned away, preening.

I had bought time, but I was sorry about the scarf, a finely made one from Budapest. Elmar had chosen it himself, an exquisite memento of an elegant city. There it was, adorning my landlady, as she poured pots of cream into her butter urn. To the devil with Ustinja.

I turned my back on the butter-making to go and boil my grass soup. 'Here's some salt,' Ustinja called. She had not taken the scarf off yet, nor even retied my knot. 'Take it for the soup.'

'Well, now!' laughed Mother Mikael. She hadn't seen the scarf exchange. Nor had she heard the nocturnal rampage, I remembered. 'You see, she isn't the hell-dweller we all supposed.'

We'll see, all right, I thought. A pinch of salt! I wouldn't put it past her to call it full payment. If so, she wasn't going to have the scarf for long.

Making butter was a holy ceremony, not to be interrupted on any account by us pagans. They were hard at it. So, after soup – with salt, almost palatable – we crawled to our beds. No talking, just thinking, and trying not to hear the suck, pat and clatter next door.

To the devil with Ustinja, I thought again. But fate does take strange turns. In a matter of minutes I would be pitying her.

I had given up ignoring the noises and was picturing the process as I listened through the wall. The cream; the churning, salting, taking out, patting. They must have a tonne of the stuff, I thought.

A man's voice rasped through the window, 'Hey Ustinja, come over to the office. Your son's death notice has arrived.'

The noises stopped. We three, who hated the woman, stopped breathing too. My God, poor soul! There were long seconds of silence, then the sharp intake of Ustinja's breath before she let it out in a scream. She ran from the cabin, wailing like a wild thing, her daughter following.

I had a vivid picture of my own son – my daughter – my husband – and plunged into Ustinja's nightmare. One of my own, dead! I bit my lip until pain came through, to stop the terror forcing its way up my throat. No, not mine at all. But what if it were? Is that how I would hear of it, shouted through a window by a stranger?

Silence enveloped the hut. No Ustinja. No cream pots clattering . . .

Cream pots!

'Ann?' Mikael's voice came softly from his corner. I was already on one elbow. He sat up on his cot, cup in hand, eyes gleaming. My hand was under the pillow, sweeping for my own, my feet half-way to the floor. My cup was filled before Mikael had climbed over his mother on his way to the landlady's table. No need for words. Just one cup, not enough to be missed, but don't touch the butter. She'd know.

'Children, children, let it be!' Mother Mikael said. She started to cry quietly. 'Death is very painful to a mother. Would you take advantage? Leave her alone.' Her own two daughters had stayed behind. Her husband was with mine.

I poured the cream back, ashamed, close to sobbing with her. How low can a human sink? We are not animals, are we, to scavenge on another's misfortune?

I poured, but the cream was thick. I stopped pouring. Hunger is painful, too – perhaps as much as grief, I reasoned, and the hunger was mine, the grief hers. I cleaned the cup with my finger, licking until both shone. Good. Mikael had finished his. Nothing left for Ustinja to find. Very good. One thing was certain: grief or no grief, she would come back, she would remember her urn had been left untended, and she would look.

■

When I went to work early next morning pots and urn had been washed and stuck inverted on the fence to dry. I had not heard her come home. According to the teaching of Lenin, as we had been obliged to hear at our nocturnal meetings, and from Ustinja herself at home, personal feelings and family sentiment were unnecessary out-moded futile relics of cursed capitalism, quite unacceptable to the forward-looking new order. This all-for-the-State litany was as regular and predictable as the Lord's prayer in church. I did not see Ustinja, nor did I seek her out to extend my sympathies. Bearing in mind the Great One's glorious philosophy, I kept away as much as possible, fearing any such sickening nonsense from her lips would prompt me to do or say something regrettable.

Ditch-digging went smoothly. On the director's recommendation, we sharpened our spades on the grindstone he had put in front of the office. It was thoughtful of him. Lia finished two metres in ten hours, I did three. Still not enough. My peas were finished and edible grasses within reach were almost picked out. Soon, I would have no soup in which to mix my daily two hundred and fifty grams of flour to 'make bread'. (Flour plus air plus water equals bread: Russian male equation . . . If you had time and an oven to bake it!)

On both sides of the road, only a step or two from our ditches, were the potato fields. At midday, we were able to stop work for half an hour; everything in the village closed while the *kolkhoz* officers went home to lunch, and there was nobody to watch while we stole into the fields to dig frantically with our fingers for seed potatoes. They were transparent, tasted bitter, and were probably not very nutritious, but they helped to still the gnawing in our stomachs. We scratched at the heaps and dug the hard ground until our fingertips were bleeding from a hundred points. We ate bloodied potatoes raw, squatting in our own new ditch. We hid more of them in the trench, covered with earth, to be picked up in the evening, concealed in clothing, and taken home for the soup.

Towards the end of July we were packed off to the hayfields; the Russians finished the ditches. By this time we had bored well into both potato fields, and also eaten most of the young pods from the pea patch. The damage to the pea crop could be blamed on any passers-by but if the potato nests should be empty in autumn, the responsibility could be only Lia's and mine. Although we had tried to leave at least one nest for every one plundered, the field near the ditch was bound to look pretty bare. We could only worry and wait.

One evening, after hay-making, I carefully inquired of the director his opinion on this year's potato crop. I had been tending my own patch and wondered what to expect.

'Your personal field has nice healthy tops,' he said, 'but you have planted too much, too closely.' He shook his head, as though puzzling where all the seed had come from. 'I don't think you'll get too much from there.' Of course he knew. He could not help but know.

'Now, the *kolkhoz* field,' he went on, 'should yield a bumper crop. All that thinning out of the old seed potatoes has made room for the rest to grow.'

'Thinning out?'

'You and your friend are to be congratulated.'

'Oh.' Denial would be stupid. I tried to look interested, if slightly puzzled.

'You think mine should be thinned?' I ventured.

'Oh, I wouldn't bother. Too much work.'

'Work never hurt anybody, they tell us.'

'Yes, I often saw your backs moving about among the plants there. I don't always go home to lunch!' Grey eyes twinkled under big bushy eyebrows. He really was quite a good-looking man. 'Your perseverance and devotion to the common good have been a constant marvel to me. And especially your digestion.'

I did not ask about the pea crop.

■

I was ordered out with the first batch of haymakers to a nearby marsh. I was the only Estonian, and the only beginner. But Marusja had promised to teach me to use a scythe, and there was barley soup with milk for lunch and a daily bread ration at five am, just before starting time, so I decided not to protest. Bread *and soup! Anything for that.*

Either haymaking is an art to which you must be born, or I am simply not meant to handle a scythe. I was hopeless. After twelve hours of hard trying my scythe edge looked more like a battered saw. Stones, stumps and shrubs kept getting in its way. Even the hour's rest in the heat of the day, and the soup that went with it, did not ease my frustration. There seemed no hope of ever learning, as Marusja reminded me every few minutes. It was impossible to ignore her taunts; my instructress – she was becoming my tormentress – would not let the matter rest even on the way home. She walked behind me, talking 'confidentially' to the woman alongside.

'There's no sense trying,' she stage-whispered. 'Njura could never be taught. She doesn't even know how to sharpen a scythe, let alone keep it sharp or cut grass with it. All she does is waste my time.'

'You can cut your own damned hay,' I turned and snapped at her. 'Don't let me hold you up.'

■

At lunch next day I buffeted the scythe on a tree stump until it was bent almost double. Scythe, sickle – bang! Communism, Russians – whack! My workmates, astonished but enthralled with the performance, watched in silence. Finally, panting, I threw the wreck to the ground.

Marusja was the first to recover. After a slow beginning she had plenty to say. Then the foreman began. Then the others, all together, in outrage. I had to go without soup, which did not suit me at all. I was ordered home, which did.

'Devil of a wench,' one old-timer sent me off with a growl, 'she handles a scythe like she's killing a snake. Now it's buggered!' I felt suddenly penitent for having violated his respect for his instrument.

My career as a hay-cutter was over. So, it dawned on me, was my first year in Siberia.

18

THE WELL-KNOWN GERDA

In this great expanse of lowland, one season occupies six months of the twelve. Winter hurtles in on a series of violent storms; winds roar from the Arctic Circle a mere thousand flat kilometres away; great drifts of snow pile over the country; marshes and waterways freeze. Winds then drop; cold creeps slyly from the north; temperatures go down, and stay down. The country is frozen solid, the days are short, bright and icy. This is 'failure of organism' time, the time the rest of the year must make up for. Six grim months with nothing to do except survive.

Spring touches the temperate zones first, a thousand equally level kilometres in the opposite direction, the sun not yet high, the northern earth still frozen. The south warms; and rivers run, flooding the flats in the massive thaw that advances with the climbing sun. Snow melts; the frozen earth softens, becomes mud, and dries, all in a quick spring of barely two months.

Summer follows closely, the lack of modifying mountains allowing southerly winds to sweep up over the steppes, usually hot and dry, occasionally moisture-laden and bringing rains in sudden deluge. Brief summer, shorter autumn. All too soon, the first night frosts, the first snows, return; and a couple of months after summer's peak it's back to winter.

I must hurry. Having endured one winter, I must make the most of summer to prepare for the next.

My two remaining warm coats – the calfskin-fur and the camel-hair – had attracted attention before. In particular, the wives of two neighbouring *kolkhoz* heads had inquired guardedly about them, but my price had been too high. In fact I had not yet been quite desperate enough to bargain, even to consider offers; nor had I quite lost the satisfaction of knowing that I, the despised foreigner, could still arouse envy in the top brass of the classless society. I had lost curls, colour, figure, but I still had some spite left. I reduced the camelhair to a hundred roubles – and I would have liked to sell it for that. It would be risking my life to part with the fur, as it was my only remaining really warm piece of clothing. With a hundred roubles – if I could get it – I could pay Ustinja and, in autumn, when the *kolkhozniks* were short of money and flush with vegetables, lay in a winter stock of potatoes and peas.

I had done the rounds of our own *kolkhoz* and the nearer villages of others, but found no-one at home who had money to buy. That had taken two days of unemployment. Today, my luck was better. I had traded a fifteen-centimetre strip from the bottom of the calfskin, together with wool inner and silk linings, for two kilograms of wheat flour and a bucket of potatoes; the mother-in-law of the head of the Maisk *kolkhoz* 'Fulfilment Committee' could now make a hat for her husband. My coat, instead of being seven or eight centimetres below the knee, was now seven or eight centimetres above. I still had the camelhair, still had no money, and still had no firm arrangement with Ustinja.

■

The night of the sale, I had a message from the office. Be ready early tomorrow, it said, to leave with a berrying brigade for Malinovka, eleven kilometres away. The messenger also told me that Kargaja (the Jumper) and a few other men from the area had been called up for army service.

Both notices were good. The long tiring workdays did not allow much contact with others around us, so I did not mind going farther afield for berries. Maybe I would meet someone. And berries, after all, were food. As for the second item, the new mobilisation could well mean worsening of the Russian position at the front. And I certainly would not fret for the Jumper!

In the morning I presented myself at the office. It was bare except for the same fellow who had led the last berry brigade. He was behind the desk, showing all his metal teeth in a supercilious grin. The call-up had not gone that far, obviously.

'Ready?' he smirked.

'Where are the others?'

He made a great scene of scanning the empty room. 'What others?'

I had a vision of going under his protection again.

'The brigade.' My good mood was evaporating. 'Moron,' I added in Estonian.

'You *are* the brigade.'

'And you?'

'No.'

'That's a relief.'

'Eh?'

'Me? By myself?'

'You need help to pick berries?'

'Maybe not to – '

'Then what?'

'Why to Malinovka?'

'That's the order.'

'How can I go alone?' I protested aggressively. 'I don't know the place, I don't know where to go, and there are bears in the forest.'

'But you're not afraid of bears!' He had been leading up to this all along, I saw: revenge for the imagined slight on his manhood. 'And you're a first-class berry picker. We all know that, don't we?' He went on with his childish taunt. 'Better than you are a haymaker, anyhow.'

'But I don't even know the way.'

'All right,' he snapped. 'The boy Saarde is off to Malinovka at lunchtime.' He tired of his cat and mouse game. 'You can walk with him or go alone. Take your pick. And one more thing: see the director first.'

'In that case, your honour, I'll consider going.'

He gave me a sour look and bent to his counter.

■

The sky was clear, the sun as near as it would get to overhead when we set out. It was hot in the open, stifling when we reached the forest. Endel Saarde, aged thirteen – brother of Liina, my last berry-picking partner – was my companion and guide. Endel had grown tall in the past year, though thin with it. He was good

245

company, uncomplaining, with a mature sense of humour; a fine boy who should have been studying maths and playing basketball. Instead, he carried messages from village to village through forest many a healthy man would never dare enter alone, and was forgetting how to read.

Little light filtered through the branches of tall and ancient firs, as Endel picked our path. They were giants, with trunks a metre or more thick, top growth exuberant and almost out of sight. The air below was cool, heavy with their breath, smelling damply of the centuries of rotting cones and needles on the ground. The path was easy, though knowledge was needed of its few forks and turns. Sometimes we had to step over or around logs, fresh-fallen or green-mossed with age. We made fair time and must have been over halfway before Endel pointed up. 'Look.'

The forest shadows had deepened, and rounds of light no longer danced on the floor. I had lost all sense of direction long ago, relying implicitly on my guide. I looked up with him. Treetops, a few minutes ago swaying gently, were convulsed in agitated movement against a rapidly darkening sky. The soft whisper of wind had risen unnoticed, and even as I listened built to a steady roar, broken only by the snap of breaking boughs and the groan of straining timber.

We stepped suddenly out of forest to a patch of marshy lowland. Only a few stunted pines grew in boggy turf, yet there was no relief from the gloom. Where there should have been light was dark. A great heaving black cloud was rolling over us at a terrifying rate, with lightning flickering, thunder booming. In no time at all, it seemed, the great wave engulfed us, black as pitch, and we could scarcely tell forest from clearing. The flickers became flashes, the flashes great explosions of light ripping through the mass. With each flash a rending crack rocked the air between earth and low heaven before it racketed off into the distance. Jagged swords tore the sombre skies apart. The first raindrops fell, singly, as large as fingertips.

'Quickly!' I pulled at Endel to get to the shelter of the great trees, and ran.

'No, this way!' Endel yelled, grabbing my arm. 'Under a small tree,' he screamed between thunderclaps, 'not – big trees in a thunderstorm.'

We pressed close together in the open against a shrivelled

pine, Endel's coat over our heads. Within seconds all hell gathered above us, and the drops became a barrage. Flashes ran together, one blinding burst on another lighting the tumult in brilliant fire, showing trees bending beyond a bubbling lake, all the while accompanied by the howl of sudden wind and an irregular cannonade of thunder. Above the uproar we heard the pistol-cracks of great boughs breaking and trees splitting down the middle. We were quickly soaked, and standing in water nearly to our ankles.

Endel's eyes were huge, excitement suppressing his fear. Wonderful youth! Impulsively, I tightened my arm across his shoulder and smiled. God had not preserved us through a year of purgatory to kill us off out here. Endel felt my pressure and returned the smile. Despite the splendid eruption God was good.

In half an hour it was all over. We stepped out faster than before, as we had time to make up and our cold, cramped limbs welcomed the exercise. If we had had shoes they would have squelched. As it was, I took off my rags. Endel had none to preserve. Muddy water squeezed pleasantly through our toes.

Growth varied as we traversed the wide spaces; groups of immense needle trees; great areas of leaf varieties; tracts of shrubbery in different colours and shapes; new grass; mosses in a range of greens; flowers singly and in clumps. No two places were the same.

'Auntie Ann, you're steaming!' Endel laughed from behind. He dodged around me on the single-file path and skipped in front. His clothes steamed in the sun too, as did the earth itself. I laughed with him, delighting in the warmth, for the moment as young as he.

We walked many kilometres, up and down hillocks ten metres high, and in all that time saw no sign of human occupation. The occasional tracks we crossed – and the one we used – were probably made by wild animals, maybe even bears.

All around, in bright sunshine, wild flowers flashed blue, yellow and red through the green and purple growth. Birds sang, grass shone, bees hummed; drops fell from leaves, sparkled on the grass, and our feet sucked softly on sodden turf. We rested on the bank of a slow-running stream to dry out clothes and eat our meagre lunch.

'Oh, Endel, isn't it beautiful?'

'Not long now, Auntie Ann,' Endel consoled. 'We'll soon be there. Over the next hill we'll see buildings. Maybe people.'

What terrible comfort. It was people that had spoiled it all.

■

Endel had been almost right. Over the crest was a wide track going roughly in our direction. It had soon divided into two, however, still with no buildings in sight. We could not tell which to take. The boy spat in his palm, slapped his finger in it and grinned in the direction the spittle flew. 'That's the way,' he said. 'Never fails.' Nor did it this time. The trees soon thinned and through the gaps we saw our destination, on a clearing by the river.

Malinovka consisted of miserable huts spread wide apart, some with sods of weedy earth on the roofs. They had dilapidated fences and broken windows, mended where there was enough good glass left, boarded over where there was not.

The shop was bigger than Maisk's. We recognised it by its central position, the size of the building, and its open door. Otherwise, it was just another log hut in the loose-packed collection. It was clean, which was encouraging, and the keeper was there.

'Hello,' I said companionably. He was a human being. We had made a long journey since seeing one. 'We are from Maisk. Endel here has a letter for the director.' I spoke for us both, although Endel spoke fluent Russian.

'And you?'

I stood to my full one hundred and fifty five centimetres. 'I am the berrying brigade.'

I should have known better. There was no place for flippancy in this humourless country.

'Where are the others?' He took time out for a good swear. 'There are supposed to be ten of you – or twelve. I've even got the bread ready!'

The magic word. I was immediately polite.

'The letter is here,' I smiled. He still looked cross. 'And I have one specially for you, from our director.' He had given me a note requesting quarters and sustenance. 'Please read it. And I'm sorry I'm alone. It isn't my doing.' Bread for twelve!

He read the letter, mellowed, weighed us each a piece of bread – not half a gram over the ration – and directed Endel to the office. Wasted politeness. Endel took his share and went his way.

248

'Any friends here?' the shopkeeper barked. He was so much like the one in Maisk.

'No.'

'Try Gerda. The big house with all the children. Maybe you can stay with her.'

'How do I find her?'

'Everybody knows Gerda. Be in the shop at eight in the morning, and I'll take you out for the berries myself.' I hoped he knew more about forestcraft than the other one. 'I'll give you your bread then, too.'

The magic word again. I refrained from asking what would be done with all the spare bread – as if I didn't know – and sought the well-known Gerda.

■

An hour later I was at home. In this tumbledown little hut, built many years ago by a reluctant pioneer, I met friendliness I had forgotten existed. Standing alone, in the middle of the flowering potato field, it had indeed been easy to find: one incurious local finger pointing across the field was enough. A girl of four and a boy four or five years older had met me on the doorstep. They were bright and talkative children, and before their mother came home I had a fair picture of the people of Malinovka. I remembered them from the barge trip – though not of our 'family', they were noticeably attractive – and I found myself hoping anxiously that their mother would accept me.

There was never any question of it. Gerda Arula arrived with a smile, as if she had known me all her life. The grapevine had been busy. She sent Peet with me to get a bag of straw for a bed, arranged a site, and quickly had potatoes on the boil.

'Bread we do not have, we've already eaten a month's quota in advance. But we've got potatoes.' She wagged a mysterious finger and counted out some for me, already one of her family, keeping a careful half for breakfast. 'We have salt with them here. I won some telling fortunes – from cards, you know – and found a bit when they were unloading at the store.'

I had not had such a sense of belonging since before the world went mad. Earth floor, mud-plastered log walls, grass-roots showing through the ceiling, clay stove, crude table with bench seat, wide bunk with wobbly legs: yet this was a real home, with warmth and mettle, attributes that sprang from Gerda, shone through her children, and infected me.

'Do you have your own potatoes in?' I asked. These were delicious. It worried me – though not too much, she was so genuinely carefree – that I must be eating special rations. 'What sort are they? In Maisk, we burrowed through the best part of two fields, but the new ones are only the size of fingertips yet.'

'Our own?' she laughed. She had probably been plump. Her skin was still good despite lines of wasting, and she had a way of tossing her straggling fair hair back over her shoulders that suggested she must once have had fine soft curls. Her eyes were a lively grey, shining with merriment now. 'We don't starve in this land of plenty. Everything belongs to everybody, remember?'

We finished our meal. It did not take long.

'Come on now, we'd better hurry,' said Gerda. 'Peet, give me a hand.' You would have thought we were going to a party, she was so cheerfully brisk. 'Ann, you go out and bury the potato peels please. And bring in the night toilet. Put it in the hall. Then we'll get tomorrow's dinner.'

The toilet was a hole in the ground covered by an old sack. I threw in the peels. It seemed rather odd to be wasting good compost; Gerda was so sensible. Or was it not being wasted? She seemed to know what she was doing. Cover them, she had instructed, so I covered. The night toilet was an ancient bucket. I covered it too, and brought it into the 'hall'. Which, in such weather, seemed unnecessary.

'Now,' Gerda ordered, 'off you go. Peet will show the way. I'll stand guard and fetch the drinking water.'

I was beginning to cotton on. Plenty of potatoes, cryptic comments, hiding peels, standing guard . . .

It was no longer light, not yet dark. Care would still be needed. How I would like to live with a woman like that, I thought, as I crawled behind Peet in the furrows: she makes life worth living. I kept my bottom down, as instructed, and held it down until we reached a stick poked into the ground.

'Here,' whispered Peet. The soil was sandy, making burrowing with the fingers a pleasure compared with the clay at Maisk. We dug, taking a few tubers only from each plant, smoothing back the disturbed earth before passing on to the next, quickly filling a bucket.

'That'll do for today. I hear Mother whistling already.' The boy is so like her, I smiled to myself. Competent. Bright. 'Put the stick in the ground to mark where we got up to, and off we go. Quick now. Keep down.'

The timing was faultless. We had crawled back at full speed, hidden the bucket inside, washed our hands, and been sitting on the doorstep looking innocent for no longer than a minute before the nightwatchman appeared. He was a scrawny, bearded man, about sixty, with a stiff leg. Gerda and the children waved him a cheery good evening as he limped up, shaking his head at the futility of the effort. He had heard about the arrival of the new one, he said, and asked a few questions about Maisk; about the crops, the weather, one or two people whose names I knew. He was not very interested in the answers, just the conversation. We got up from the step. He followed us inside. It seemed the custom. He offered his 'Mahorka', the cheapest pipe tobacco of all. I declined, much as I would have loved a cigarette. Most smokers grew their own tobacco, curing the leaves by hammering a nail through the stalks into a south-facing log wall for the remainder of summer. I was used to that now, but wasn't desperate enough to roll the compressed mass of rank-smelling Mahorka into old newspaper. He lit up, and shuffled out again, around to the single window of the hut, its broken glass patched and filled until more light was stopped than could ever get through. He picked up a plank, obviously there for the purpose, and nailed it firmly across the opening. It was now impossible to get out that way without removing it; if we did push it off, which would be simple enough, there was no replacing the bar once back inside. He worked with the bored air of a man who had performed the same chore the same way a hundred times over.

'Should be fine again tomorrow,' he grunted. 'Could do with rain.'

'That's good,' Gerda replied cheerfully. 'I suppose we could.'

I looked in amazement at my hostess, who was not in the least upset by being gaoled. 'There was some trouble last year in the crop,' she said carefully, in Russian, for his benefit. The gleam in her eye said that this was a game. 'They suspected the children of stealing potatoes at night.'

The old man outside muttered. 'Waste of a man's bloody time.'

251

'Oh, I see.' I clucked sympathetically. 'Yes, I see that must have posed a problem. I suppose the authorities do have to be careful.'

The man looked through the doorway – 'Everybody in?' – nodding as he checked.

'Yes. They take the precaution of shutting us in at night.'

'*These* children?' I asked, scandalised.

'We don't mind. Potatoes are precious, after all. Community property. They belong to everybody, so they must be guarded well, to ensure proper and fair distribution.'

'That's what I like about collectives.'

'An order is an order,' said the bearded one. Our noble dialogue didn't move him one way or the other. He picked up a solid birch log resting against the wall and closed the outward-swinging door. 'Goodnight.'

'Goodnight,' chorused Gerda and the children as the log slid crosswise into place.

'The wolf is fed, the sheep unharmed.' I think the proverb is Russian.

■

'Come on, hurry up! I don't have all day. Your bread's there, in the *konn*.' The shopkeeper shoved one at me impatiently, flapping it open just enough for confirmation. 'Now let's get going.'

The berry country was only a kilometre or two from the *kolkhoz*. The man kept up a steady stream of advice as we walked. Don't go too far into the forest (Don't worry, I thought, I don't fancy getting lost.) Keep your eyes open (I dared not ask what for.) Watch where you step (He's telling me there are snakes!) Yell loudly if you sight a bear (Oh my God! . . .)

'Home is over that way.' He pointed vaguely back through the woods. We'd been going in deeper for at least twenty minutes. 'I'll fire a shot towards evening to give you direction.'

He fished a few matches and a strip of striking material out of his pocket – my survival kit, I assumed – and went. I stood on the mossy path, peering fearfully into the dark growth whispering ahead. Back in Maisk, I had wished for nothing more than a free assignment picking berries or mushrooms. Now that the day was here, I wished I was anywhere else.

Luckily, I came on bushes laden with blackcurrants, my

favourite berries, near the path only a short distance in. I picked a few to taste, looking up and about nervously, like a squirrel. Delicious! My fears gradually dissolved. I moved eagerly from bush to bush, and by the time the sun found its way down through the trees, my stomach was satisfied, the *konn* half full. I thought I must have about six litres of big, juicy purple berries. I cleared a round place beside the spongy path, made a fire on the moss, threw grass on top to make it smoke, and lay down to rest. I was tired, but had quite forgotten snakes and bears.

The sun was still high when I woke. I moved quickly, and had almost topped up the *konn* before I heard the gunshot signal. As a directional aid it was useless, but at least he hadn't forgotten me. I found him easily enough, and he beamed when he peeped into the basket.

'Good girl. I didn't think you'd bring back any!'

'Why did you send me, then?'

'Not my idea.'

'What will I be paid?'

'About eight hundred grams.'

'Rye or wheat?'

'Wheat.'

'Money?'

'You can't expect everything.'

'A full workday?'

He pursed his lips. 'Appropriate time to be credited.'

I didn't pursue it. I was pleased with myself; I had conquered the forest.

■

Gerda's hut was in isolation, by order. I could only wander the forest daily, and hope to see others at the sauna on Saturday night. I particularly wanted to see two families from Rakvere I'd heard about on the grapevine, although I didn't know them well.

As days went by, I became less sure whether or not I wanted to see them. In fact, I was uncertain about many things. People. Myself. 'Home'. An odd thing was happening to me. Only a day or two ago, I had thought I had found relative contentment with Gerda and her family. It had been a long time since I had lived with love. Yet, I was restless. And I had *not* conquered the forest.

■

One morning I walked for a long time, my mind on other things. I had left the path far behind in a haphazard search for berries, flitting from one group of blue spots in the distance to the next. They were few and far apart; I must have struck it very lucky the first time.

The sun seemed to dip abruptly. I hurried to find my homeward track, but nothing looked familiar. I realised, too late, that I had taken no note of direction. Anxiety swelled to panic, and I ran. Why had I been so stupid? Could I really be lost? My heart pounded as I zigzagged to and fro. The shopkeeper! Would he miss me? I kept stopping to listen, but heard no shot. 'I must control myself,' I said aloud, but there was no sun, shadow or sound to indicate which way to turn. I set off anew, calmly at first, then with a burst of frantic energy, guided only by instinct, control already forgotten. I could not last long at that rate, and stopped again.

When you are lost in the forest, stay put. Conserve your energy. Light a fire if you can do so safely. I remembered all sorts of advice. If you run, you may be going farther in. Make smoke, it gives a chance for searchers to find you.

I started looking for sticks. Was I wasting time? Would anybody come looking? Gerda perhaps; she was the only one, but would she know where to start?

Make lots of smoke. A fire keeps off the wild animals, and smoke attracts searchers. Oh Lord, let there be smoke! And searchers!

Smoke? No sooner was the thought in my mind than the smell was in my nostrils. Was I dreaming? I sniffed again. No, to be sure. Incredibly, not only smoke: tobacco smoke! Ridiculous. But true. Or was it? The smell was in the air. Yes. Faint, but unmistakable. I dropped my sticks and sniffed like a forest creature, darting off in the direction that I thought it stronger. And there was the path; I had been only a few metres from it. Which way? I stopped, sniffed again, and ran. It was undoubtedly stronger. I tossed my *konn* under a tree for more speed. It toppled and the berries spilled back over the path. *Kurat!* – Damn!

At the next bend, I saw him. He turned, startled, whipping the gun from his back as he did, pipe still clenched in bared,

254

blackened teeth. It was Matriona's husband. Clark Gable would have been less welcome.

'*A vot!* Njura!'

'I was berrying.' The words came pouring out in relief. 'Got lost. Oh, am I glad to see you! Thought I'd never get back, I smelt the smoke. Do you have one for me? Let's sit down, my legs are shivering. Won't hold me up.'

'*Vot*, Njura! I didn't expect you here.' He did not look particularly surprised. He never looked particularly anything. 'I thought maybe it was a bear gone crazy, running to attack an innocent walker.' We sat. 'But no, it's only Njura.'

'Yes, it's me.'

'Njura.'

That was now satisfactorily established. I could only nod agreement.

'Lost, at that.'

'Yes. Do you – '

'*Vot!* You live like this in the wilds for long, you become like a wild creature. You smell things a long way away. But you?' He shook his head, and puffed slowly. 'Lucky for you. There aren't always smoking men in the forest.'

'Yes.' I didn't need to be told that.

'Very lucky.'

'Yes indeed.'

He had been quick with the gun. All his speed must be concentrated there.

'You should be more careful.'

'I will.'

'People get lost in here and never seen again.'

'I've heard.'

At last, he passed the tobacco bag.

'Much more careful.'

He had been on a hunting assignment for some time. I puffed contentedly on my *plotski*, half listening. He had been living alone in one of the huts built for the purpose. He told me about shooting hares and birds, stalking deer, and sighting bear tracks.

'Now I've filled my quota. I'm going home.'

I supposed Matriona would be glad to see him. As long as it didn't mean another baby.

'I've handed everything over to the Malinovka storeman and

had all my workdays recorded.' He was pleased with himself. He was in front. 'I'll be home in a few hours.'

Home . . . Maisk . . . There was a ridiculous pang in my chest. He gave me a small handful of tobacco, and meticulously measured off some paper. We stood and stretched our legs. It was time to go. I retrieved the *konn*, packing the spilt berries in. We were on a path strange to me. I was surprised, going back that short distance, how they all looked the same. It would be so easy to stay lost. He pointed my way, politely said goodbye, told me to be careful, and disappeared in the opposite direction, walking fast. His gun was slung over his shoulder, his pipe in his teeth. He was singing.

Lucky man.

I had the most absurd longing to go with him.

19

NEW SIBERIAN PHILOSOPHY

Next morning it began raining as we left the village, the workers for hay-making, Gerda and I for mushrooms. The Russian women turned back – 'too wet for gathering hay' – and I began to do the same, annoyed with myself for having left my coat at Maisk.

'You're not made of sugar, are you? That you'll dissolve? Come on, I'll come with you. You'll get a plus working day.'

Gerda led me deeper into the forest than I had been before. Hardly a ray of light penetrated the matt of tall birch and aspen: fallen trunks, rotted stumps and treacherous moss were hazards in the gloom. Although I felt I could manage the forest, I spent more time looking for her, dashing ahead like a hare, than I did for mushrooms.

The rain dripped steadily through the trees. We were wet to our teeth, and cold. My arms and legs were soon badly scratched, and my potato-bag skirt, tight and heavy when wet, rubbed painfully against bare skin.

But the return was worth it: a full extra work-day, a personal *konn*-ful of mushrooms, and five roubles.

The work was probably harder in Maisk, the reward undoubtedly poorer. A plus work-day and roubles! For all that, and despite the sense of belonging with Gerda, I was surprised to again feel a pull to Maisk, and family – even if only acquired family. Perhaps one needs a place to return to, whatever its disadvantages.

■

'Here's your five roubles.' For the third time. I was getting rich. The storeman must have read my thoughts. 'Tomorrow you go back to Maisk. Your job is finished.' Whatever my job might have been ... And whoever gives these orders? ... 'If going alone bothers you, you can wait a couple of days. The postman goes then.'

'I think I'll go tomorrow,' I said promptly.

'Sure? You'd have an escort.' The storeman was not altogether a bad fellow.

'Now, thank you.'

'Always in a hurry, you *Estonkas*. Except for work.'

I was already planning my return. 'I would like to wash my feet and hands.' I demonstrated in the air. 'Do you have soap?' ... Why not? While the luck was running. Champagne! Caviar! ... 'And tobacco?'

'There's none for sale.' He reached under the counter. 'But your legs look terrible, at that.'

'Thank you,' I said dryly.

He came up with a small chunk of strong-smelling grey-looking soap and a half handful of Mahorka.

I looked at both, the irregularly cut square that could get me cleaner than I had been in months and the chopped tobacco stalks that served as pipe weed. My eyes must have glistened.

'Off with you now. There's no more where that came from.'

'How much?' I fingered my five roubles.

'Take it.' He tore a couple of pages from an exercise book. Cigarette papers. 'Perhaps some day you can afford it.'

My stars must have been in the right places.

I had planned a meal for Gerda and her family. Now it would be a farewell dinner.

The nightwatchman's wife had promised milk. I went to her, money in hand, stepping gingerly.

'Dear Lord,' she exclaimed. 'How can you walk on those?' She clapped compassionate hands under her chin. 'My little dove, come in! I'll bathe them and put cream on them. It'll sting a bit at first, but I'll soon make them better.' The good Christian soul fetched water, warm from the oven, sour cream in a tin mug, and set about tending my legs.

'There, my little pigeon, all finished. Better? Walk stronger on them now. And dress them again in the morning.' She put some of the cream on a strip of birch bark and went to break off a piece of soap. I stopped her, showing my prize from the shop.

'Ah, so our storeman gave you some. Little pigeon.' I did not know whether she meant him or me. 'Yes, we know what it's about here in this *kolkhoz*. We all came from the Ukraine a long time ago. We've been through it, what's left of us. The director, too.'

She went to her cellar for a bottle of milk and a big basin of old potatoes. I asked the price, fearful I would not have enough.

'God will pay me.' She crossed herself and sighed. 'Oh dear. What have we all come to?'

Clearing the lump in my throat, I muttered a promise that I'd never forget her kindness.

'Ah, off with you!'

The dinner was easy, spoilt for me only because the two children were a constant reminder of my own. I chided myself for letting sentiment intrude. Nice children, kindly neighbour, considerate storekeeper notwithstanding, I still hankered for Maisk. Gerda, observant and ever practical, put the children to bed early and told me she had arranged visits to Asta and Eda, my two acquaintances. The nightwatchman would leave the door-bar loose, but he would 'keep an eye on the kids'.

■

Asta's husband had been a high-ranking army officer. She lived with her two sons in a worn cabin on the edge of the next *kolkhoz*, two kilometres away.

'Here we are,' called Gerda. She had declined to discuss either of the two households on the way, keeping me in suspense. 'Now we'll see how she's making out.'

I was pleasantly surprised. Asta and her boys were neatly dressed – almost Sunday best – and the small room was more than clean. There were curtains, drapes, silk covers on the beds; the boys' beds were even screened by hanging sheets. The stove front was whitewashed, a good-sized enamelled soup pot simmering on top. Everything was spotless, everything in place.

We had mutual friends, though I had scarcely known Asta, and the greeting was warm. My main difficulty, at first, was in hiding amazement and envy at her style of living. We had not much time for chatter, though. Indeed, conversation after the initial burst of name-swapping was not easy, as she had a way of letting a sentence drift off into the air. I recollected Asta as a statuesque young woman, straight, confident, well-dressed. Certainly she was still extraordinarily well-dressed; but her assurance had gone. She sat us down for soup and hovered over us, nervously apologising for the poverty of her fare. She had little concern for word of others, no ear for news, no interest outside her own place. Conversation ground to platitudes. The boys – Leo, aged ten, whom I remembered as an energetic cub scout, and Eric, fourteen, a zestful school friend of my son – were thin, pale and listless. The meal was an embarrassing affair, fortunately brief.

'Such a shame there was so little.'

'Plenty, my dear,' I said heartily. And there was.

'If I'd known earlier you were coming – '

'Not to worry.'

'Still, one likes – '

'The main thing was to see you, Asta. And the boys.'

'I'm sorry I couldn't – '

'We understand.'

'But – oh, you know how difficult things are in this dreadful place.'

'Goodbye, Asta.' Mercifully, Gerda cut it short. 'See you soon.'

Out of earshot, Gerda talked with an edge to her voice new to me. 'And soon will be soon enough. "You know how difficult things are!" As if we don't! Who does she think she is? As if weÕd never known better! "I'm sorry there's no turkey!"' She mimicked Asta's plaintive voice very well. I laughed uneasily. Asta really was on a cloud. 'As if she alone – and what makes *her* so special I don't know – should have the right to be able to put on a banquet!'

'Oh don't mind her.' I felt I had to defend Asta, who was firstly an acquaintance of mine, not Gerda's. 'She was trying her best.'

'Her best indeed! See those boys' clothes? And wailing about chipped plates! Does she imagine we've never eaten from a decent table?'

'She looks sick. The boys, too.' The life had gone out of their eyes, reminding me of Peter's. I shuddered. 'Asta certainly keeps them looking their best, but they're not well.'

'Looking their best! I'd rather mine had flesh over their bones than a tailored suit. But you can't afford to worry about them. It is a pity, though: they're nice boys. Maybe they'd all look better if she flogged off some of those silk covers and silver spoons for a solid meal or two. I tell you, the way she carries on, they won't make it.'

'Oh, don't say that!'

'Let's go and see Eda.' Gerda could not remain annoyed for long. 'That place will buck you up.'

It looked like a collapsed haystack silhouetted in the moonlight, the gaunt trees behind the cabin black and still. We knocked, opened the rickety door, and entered. Just as you can't judge a book by its cover, you can't judge a hut by its shape. The inside was dominated by the father of all Russian ovens. There was a table and a couple of stools, a shelf next to the single uncurtained window and one wide cot, all dwarfed by the massive oven. Eda was climbing down the ladder propped against its side.

'Hello darlings! So nice of you to come.' She, too, was thin and pale, almost shockingly so, but her eyes had the sparkle of Gerda's. 'Just lit the snot-nose as a welcome sign.' The candle flickered bravely, grease starting to run. 'So come on. Step up into the drawing room for coffee and cakes, we'll be more comfortable there.'

We climbed. All Eda's possessions were on the oven top: a tattered suitcase, a straw-filled sleeping bag, a baby's pillow and a wool quilt. Neat and tidy; but, unlike Asta's, this place had warmth. The flame of the 'snot-nose' danced merrily in the corner while we ate potato cakes and drank milk from a tin. The landlady, we were told, owned half a cow.

Eda had been a teacher. She had been picked up on the morning of June 14, and loaded into her carriage in sandals and summer dress. All she had with her was her baby, a single suitcase with baby clothes and food, and what loose change she could find in the house. Her husband had been gone some months, one of the early ones arrested. In the train, Eda told us, a woman from Narva, a stranger, had pressed her to take a valuable ring 'for the sake of the baby'. She had sold the ring in Novo-Sibirsk to a woman from Romania. Eda thought it had saved her life, though it failed its purpose; the baby had died in Aipalova.

'Things are not too bad. I've been lucky with the landlady, she's a good woman.' She nodded into the smoky shadows below. 'I teach her son and do a bit of knitting for the *kolkhoz* Russians. She won't let me starve. When I'm better, the director says he'll give me a job in the office. I know Russian, and the collective bookkeeper has been mobilised. They're in a bit of a mess. I rather suspect there's no-one else in the place who can handle figures.'

∎

'I hardly recognised her,' I said, on the way home. 'Only a year ago, she was so beautiful.'

'That'll come back once she gets down off that oven, and gets some decent clothes on. She's got what it takes. I don't believe she'll be in real trouble.' Her cough, bright eyes and flushed cheeks seemed trouble enough to me. Gerda had noticed them, too. 'If only she can hold her health a while longer.' Amen to that, I thought.

'I must find a warmer place for next winter too,' Gerda said. It seemed the problem was general. 'I don't want to freeze to death. Or the children. If we lose any more condition we won't last another winter.' She was serious, not despondent. 'But there's no sense worrying too far into the future. Not in this hell.'

∎

When Gerda shook me, the sun was rising into a clear blue-ing sky. The nightwatchman's wife improved the early hour by coming with a litre of buttermilk. 'Be careful with those legs, and God go with you.'

I left half her gift, with a piece of bread, for the children. This was less an act of generosity to them than a gesture at tending my own. We didn't disturb their sleep. Gerda came a short distance with me, on her way to the hayfield, where our wordless farewell stopped short of tears. In a few days we had found empathy rare in a lifelong friendship. There was no knowing if we would see each other again.

I knew the way, and decided not to waste a beautiful day by hurrying. Evening would be time enough to get to Maisk, where all I had to look forward to was hard work, an empty stomach and Ustinja, the landlady, waiting to pounce with her perpetual demand. I wondered again at the strange pull that drew me back.

When there is little to look back on that does not bring pain, and even less to look forward to, there is nothing left but the present. The present – as defined in my new Siberian philosophy – is a slot in time between past and future, neither in one nor the other, thus free of the agonies of either. One can learn to live in successive slots: a good trick, developed in the solitude of an endless winter. I intended to do so today, to live minute by minute, in this day only. I planned carefully, aiming for the halfway point to Maisk in the best walking hours. Maisk and its miseries would keep.

Still before noon, I lit a fire on the bank of a creek and put the potatoes on to bake. I chose my spot carefully, stripped, and waded into the running water, taking pleasure in kneading age-old stones beneath my feet. I washed myself, body, hair, underclothes too, with the grey soap, taking my time, finally climbing out to firm springy grass. The air was morning cold. I put on outer clothes and patted myself dry, Russian fashion, hung the underclothes toward the sun over a bush, and sat down to roll a *plotski*. My stock of tobacco had been carefully eked out by adding sawdust and dried black currant leaves, an art I had picked up from the men of the lumber brigades. There was plenty and there was time. I closed my eyes. The smoke tasted coarse, but satisfying. I lay back to enjoy the peace of a tiny slot in time.

■

'Hi there!'

I jumped in fright. Two men in black uniforms stood by my dying fire. They had guns across their backs. One kicked impatiently at the ground.

'So, citizen, what are you doing sleeping here?'

How do you answer that? I'm tired? No, not wise. Busy? Hardly. I looked flustered, which I was not, and helpless, which I was. Remembering my underclothes strung over the bush, I avoided glancing that way. They didn't seem to notice.

'Where do you come from?' The speaker stirred the ashes with his toe. My potatoes! 'And where are you going?'

263

'I was sent to Malinovka to pick berries.' They had the confidence that denoted rank. Though I was not sure who or what they were, I tried to match it, hampered as I was by being conscious of my attire – or lack of it. Nor did I want to offend or provoke them. 'I am now on my way back to Maisk.'

'*Ladna.*' He waved at the fire with his foot before turning away. 'Make sure it's out properly before you leave.'

Silently, I cursed the destruction of an idyll. But I was forced to concede that everything was still going my way.

■

Perhaps the tide had turned. The sun was well down as I hurried through the forest, knowing I could afford no more wallowing in the present; the next move had to be considered, as it got dark quickly here and I still had a stop to make before Maisk. On the way with Endel I had noticed a bush of young raspberries in a clearing. They should be ripe by now. I had scoffed my potatoes and was no longer hungry, but a patch of raspberries could not be left to rot or be picked by anyone else.

I became apprehensive as I approached. Everything was too good to be true. I was clean, dry, fed and rested; I was approaching home. Nearing the marshy land I rejoiced, as I knew I was on the right track. High grass, thick scrub, few trees, a track winding along the spongy edge, that big clump of cedars just before the berry country. I recognised it all.

The thicket cleared. I was in the raspberry patch. And, to my unreasonable anger, all my fears were confirmed. Most of the bushes had been trampled down. There were plenty of lovely berries. But who – or what – would do that to the bushes?

I tasted a few. They were delicious. Too bad about the bushes, I told myself, forget them. Though my appetite was soon satisfied, I filled the buttermilk bottle the nightwatchman and his wife had insisted I keep as a gift. I picked more, choosing only the best. Though I do not entirely deny gluttony, there was more to it; it was a matter of packing in the vitamins. Instinct, and old-timers' warnings, advised saturation when the opportunity arose.

The distant crackle of breaking branches reminded me of the damaged bushes. I listened. There was no doubt. Someone – or something – was near. The direction eluded me.

'Who's there?' I called tentatively in Russian.

The crackling stopped.

'Who is it?' I tried in Estonian.

No response.

I ran back to the path and its dubious safety, stopping to listen. The noise started again, just as before. It seemed to come from where I had been.

'Are you working in the forest?' I tried Russian again.

Silence once more. The air was still, the sun almost to the horizon. Why no answer? Not a twig snapped, not a leaf breathed. The world was closing on me. A bear! What else would behave like that – running amok in a raspberry patch, trampling bushes down – it has to be a bear!

I knew that I should make a lot of noise. I tried, but I had no voice. I should run. I had no legs.

The crackling started again, and suddenly my legs took over, stopping only when I burst onto the Maisk hay-field two kilometres from the patch. I collapsed on a tree stump while my muscles recovered. Perhaps it had been a cow, or a Russian who did not want to be heard – not a bear at all, I told myself. But I would never take such a risk again.

I dragged my weary limbs over the fence. Ustinja poked her head out. For the first time, I was almost glad to see her.

'You're back,' she said. 'Did you bring my money?'

20

DEATH AND STARVATION

'May I go to Vesjoloi on Sunday?'

'Vesjoloi?' The director was terse. He did not like being put on the spot, and he knew that I had been waiting in front of his office all evening. Finally, he had to come out and face me. 'What for?'

'A friend of mine lives there. I have to pay my rent and I know I can get money from her.'

'Why come to me?' he growled suspiciously.

Marusja had been responsible for that. I had spoken to her about going, sounding her about asking her husband's permission.

'Why ask him?' she had said. 'Go, by all means, but don't speak to him, ask your friend the director.'

'What do you mean "my friend"?'

She had given me a sly look and a shrug. 'You'd have more chance. He won't say no to *you*.'

I had left the matter there. She had insinuated that he might do for me what he wouldn't for others. I had to face it, there was only one implication, and the director was an important frog in this little pond.

So! Well? Now, don't pretend ... If that's so ... He's not too old. Not bad looking. We've always got on pretty well. You must admit the idea doesn't exactly outrage ...

I had cut short *that* stream of thought.

'It's the busy time, you know that. I can't allow you to go.' He was as surly as I'd ever known him. 'Anyway, it's a long way

267

off, and there are bears in the forest.'

I needed no reminding, but I was furious with Marusja. She'd either taken in stupid gossip, or was deliberately giving me the run-around. The director looked positively hostile. I'd have done better with Kargaja.

'Enn would come with me,' I said curtly. 'Please let us go!'

I had spoken to Enn and suggested the visit without mentioning the seriousness of my problem. He was eager, as long as we had the director's permission.

'*Ladna*,' the director said abruptly. I think he sensed that I was determined to go, with or without sanction, and going without meant going alone. He was a man with a conscience, even if he was not bestowing special favours on a somewhat deflated me. 'But be back at work Tuesday morning.'

■

It had been Mrs Mikael's idea. While I was away, she had visited a friend in the hospital. The friend had told of an Estonian woman in the Vesjoloi – 'Merry' (good God) – *kolkhoz*, who reputedly had brought with her a case containing thirty thousand roubles. Routinely, I had asked who. 'A Mrs Vellmer.'

'Vellmer? My sister had a friend of that name.'

'Perhaps it's the same one. She must have plenty. All the *kolkhoz* bosses are in debt to her.' Mrs Mikael knew my position with Ustinja well. 'You should go over, particularly if you know her. She'd be bound to help you.'

'If it's the same one.'

'If not, what's there to lose?'

We began at first light, hoping to see Mrs Randin and the boys in Kamenoi. I still felt guilty about the Nommiks. Perhaps, too, we could buy some milk; Enn had a little money. We also had with us the primus stove we had found in the carriage; it was a valuable item, considered jointly owned. But, although it was Sunday, and still early when we arrived at our neighbouring *kolkhoz*, everyone was at work. The village was dead. Kamenoi was a terrible place.

We passed through Elisarovka. All the Estonians there were working, too. We could not linger. We stopped for a rest on the bridge where Sergei had rolled my first *plotski*, before plunging off through the forest, reaching Vesjoloi – the 'merry' *kolkhoz*, whose popular name was 'Death and Starvation' – by lunchtime.

No excitement. No hold-ups. No bears.

It was like the others: lifeless, with dusty unmade roads, and bare of human habitation except for a few unkempt, dull-eyed children. More than the usual number of unpleasant-looking dogs and pigs were scratching at the dirt. The roofs of stables were falling in, the thatches hanging in wisps. Farm implements, old cart wheels and disintegrating trays lay rusting near the forest. Every cabin looked grim and untended.

'It's worse than any of them,' Enn muttered.

I stopped a dirty-nosed boy. His brown eyes roved from me, to Enn, to his getaway route. I smiled. He hitched up baggy pants and stepped back a pace.

'Do you know where citizen Vellmer lives?'

'Course I know. Everybody knows.' As if I must be crazy. 'She's rich.' That would surely make her unique. 'She lives near the office.' He pointed and disappeared.

We happened at the right house, first off. The woman was at home. I introduced myself, reminding her that I had met her through my sister. She was not enthusiastic. I introduced Enn, and she invited us inside, eyeing us both, I thought, a little warily, especially Enn.

She lived alone in a single, large, clean room. The mud plastering seemed intact, and the roof in good condition. There were lace curtains at the windows, and a Kelim rug on the floor. A soft settee against the wall had new-looking cushions and the painted wooden bed was covered with a lace quilt, a scattering of feather pillows at the head. I took in the grandeur at a glance and, ridiculously, felt gauche.

'Oh, yes, I remember,' she said. 'Salme's sister.'

Annoyed at the cool reception, and my own unaccustomed awkwardness, I almost found a biting retort . . . Whose sister was she, then, that she could condescend to me? . . . Diplomacy stifled it.

'Yes, we last met at Ell's.'

We ploughed on hesitantly, until Enn intervened. Picking a gap, he thrust the burner at her.

'Thirty roubles,' he said bluntly.

She shook her head. 'I have one of those.' At least it made for less forced conversation. 'But there's no spirit for it. It's a good stove, but no use to me.' It was not much good to us either, for the same reason. 'Try the *kolkhoz* director, he might buy it.'

'Where would I find him?'

Mrs Vellmer became much more friendly. I guessed that she had people coming to beg from all over the country. Enn, with his burner, was easily dealt with; she could lower her guard. Well, I thought, I need roubles more than she needs sympathy. Salme's sister indeed! I'm not going to leave like a lamb. Nor am I risking starvation to save her – and me – embarrassment.

'Just a few doors down. You can't miss it.'

'Do you think thirty roubles – '

'I don't know. But don't mention money, ask for food. There's no money in this *kolkhoz*.'

Was that so? 'In this *kolkhoz*' implied inclusion of herself. Deliberately? Hm. It was not what we had been led to believe.

I signalled Enn to leave. Obediently, he shuffled out with the primus. The moment the door closed, I forthrightly told Mrs Vellmer my situation. I had no money, no way of getting money – short of selling my few remaining clothes, with the risk of perishing from cold – and was likely soon to have no roof. Now I was begging.

Without a word, she went to her mattress, took something from under it, and handed it to me. In those few seconds, I realised just how dependent I was. My receiving hand shook. Thirty roubles.

I promptly burst into tears. From relief, self-pity and shame. Mainly relief.

By the time Enn came back, we were sitting at the table, with steam rising from hot porridge. Mrs Vellmer waved her palm. We set to willingly, unembarrassed. Anyone who could eat like this could afford to share.

Enn went off to spend the night with a school friend named Talts, living here with his mother, the wife of a Narva hotel owner. I roomed with Mrs Uus, from Rakvere, and her seventeen-year-old son Jaan. We stayed up late with two other Rakvere people. Jaan offered me his cot, after some prodding from his mother. He had been one of my sturdier cub scouts. Now, he was sickly pale except for fever spots on his cheeks. He had a carbuncle on the back of his neck and stoically endured his mother expressing pus from it, then dressing the angry-looking crater with clean rags, as we talked. I refused the cot, shooing him off to bed early.

Mrs Russ, also from Rakvere, was in prison for stealing potatoes; the child she had stolen for was dead. The mother of another of Tiit's friends, with two other Estonians, had killed the *kolkhoz* calf; she had foolishly allowed meat to be found in her hut, and had been taken to Novo-Vasjugan and sentenced to two years in Tomsk, a bad prison, leaving a daughter of seventeen and a fifteen-year-old son to fend for themselves. Mrs Linse, Mrs Arumae and Mrs Argen had 'failed to thrive'. I had known Mrs Argen, and had had a message for Mrs Arumae. The three Linse children and the others' two each had all been packed off to a State home.

A young woman ex-Sunday-school teacher had been arrested as an agitator and whisked away. Mrs Kreening was living with her two small children in a cold, dirty hut, near starving, as she had run out of saleable goods during the winter; I suspected Mrs Vellmer was supplying quiet aid.

Only later did I discover that the Lohvards were also at 'Death and Starvation'.

■

I delivered greetings from a woman in Udarnik, told the news of Red May, and took messages for other people around Maisk. Finally, I lay down to sleep on Mrs Uus' floor.

Enn and I left for home richer by thirty roubles, four kilograms of flour and a bucket of potatoes. The goods were the proceeds of the shiny stove; the director had been delighted with it. His only stipulation had been that the victuals be delivered to Mrs Vellmer's after dark and that we have them out of the village before light.

■

I met Mrs Talts again in 1955. She was working in Novo-Vasjugan as a maid to the *kolkhoz* bookkeeper. Her son, Enn's friend, had died long before. Her nerves were in a pitiful state and, only a few months later, she broke down completely and died insane in Novo-Vasjugan hospital. Mrs Kreening and her two children perished together before the next winter began. Jaan Uus never saw eighteen. The orphaned Estonians probably became exemplary Russians, lost to the civilised world forever.

■

I would have liked to pass quickly through Kamenoi on our way back, it was such a depressing place, although I still half hoped to see the Randins. But our Elisarovka contact had been very insistent that we make this one stop, to see a friend.

'You must look Helga Kaljuste up,' she had said. 'She'll be so pleased to see you.'

Helga Kaljuste was only a name to us then. She was to become much more.

The weather had been kind, and we had made good time in order to make our calls. We had decided to ask directions from the first person we met. This happened to be a bearded man, a Russian. Normally, we would have waited for another passer-by. He must have been something grand in the village, for his beard was well trimmed and he wore a natty suit. I wondered whose husband's it once had been.

He had shrugged blankly at the name Randin. And Kaljuste.

'Helga Kaljuste?'

'Ah, Helga!'

He leered. I gave him my stony stare.

'*Vot*, there she stands, on her doorstep. I've just come away.' He looked back and waved coyly. 'She's been giving me a little rejuvenation.'

He tugged his whiskers and strutted off with a chuckle. Odious man, too pleased with himself. Rejuvenation indeed! From an Estonian? Perhaps nothing had been taken for the suit, after all! Who was this Helga, rejuvenator of smart officials?

The woman on the steps had a seven-year-old boy with her. She fitted the local picture like a diamond in a dungheap. She was about thirty, pretty, with blue eyes and honey-blonde hair, in a bright floral silk dress and white shoes. She filled the dress well, and her hair was freshly curled. She even wore make-up, to me the last straw.

'*Kurat!*'' I exploded. Patriotic indignation rose in a flood. Who was this Christmas cake?

It was too late to go another way. She was watching us, bright-eyed, ready with a greeting. In any event, Enn had none of my reservations, and it would have taken more than me to stop his advance. My first anger past, I kept pace with him. Who was I to criticise? She had a right to live – and a son to feed – how she did it was no concern of mine. She was far from the only one. I controlled a flash of jealousy that she could look so young, so fresh, that she could put a gleam in a man's eye. I even had time to think that it might all turn out for the best. Enn was no longer a boy.

Introductions. Enn's eager, mine cool. Men! No perception . . .

'Come in. Sit down. Have something to eat. You must be tired after your trip.'

I accepted, with little grace. To be patronised by a – whatever she was – was a bit much. Where did she get food to give away so casually? I'd have refused, if it could have been done civilly.

'We had word you'd be coming. Glad you made it. The boy has been watching for you from the doorstep while I trimmed that old goat's hair.'

Suddenly, the food looked delicious.

■

We had no sooner left Helga's than Enn began. 'Did you notice those legs?'

'They're very good.'

'Good! They're beautiful! And her eyes – '

I agreed they were blue. And her hair fair, smile sensational, heart kind, cooking first class. It was not difficult, because he was right every time. From the moment that I remembered she had been a hairdresser – it had been mentioned at Elisarovka – I had warmed to her myself. Shame on my suspicions, and just as well I'd kept them quiet! I think Helga had read my guilt and, amused, informed us that the man was one of her 'regulars'. For the rest of our stay she had baited me with double-meaninged digs, all over Enn's head.

We had finished firm friends. She even suggested I live with her, rent free, if I could not find a place in Maisk. She had arrived with her tools of trade and very shortly had been named official barber of the area. Paid mainly in food, she spent a good part of her time hair-dressing, only working in the *kolkhoz* four days a week. I resolved that if I had to begin over again, I would take up the scissors.

Enn's interest in her was good, I decided. He had not shown much enthusiasm for the girls of Maisk, although there were a few eligible ones. On further thought, I felt a degree of relief with his infatuation, as there had been a couple of occasions when his attentions to me had threatened embarrassment. Now, we were back to easy comradeship, and I could laugh with him over his attraction to Helga. He made no secret of it. Anything but. Later, after Mrs Balter's death, it was to blossom into a relationship, the envy of many, lasting for three years.

Mrs Balter was ill when we arrived home, and obviously upset. It was already dark. She showed no pleasure at the bottle of milk Helga had sent with Enn, and scarcely even greeted us. Instead, she burst into tears. Enn was immediately contrite, but she shook her head: it wasn't his neglect. She was short of breath and coughing a lot, wheezily, which worried me more than I dared show.

While we had been away, Mrs Balter said, a close friend and one-time neighbour of hers, the wife of an attorney from Narva, had suddenly become sick. This was a surprise, as she had seemed so healthy. Sick enough to be taken to hospital, Mrs Balter whispered. It must be serious then, I agreed. To me, it was much more distressing to see solid Mrs Balter reduced to tears. There seemed nothing we could do. Enn's good humour evaporated and I, suddenly tired, continued on my way.

Ustinja did not help matters. I went straight to her to pay my debt, and she was reluctant to accept it. Whether she was in a fresh bad mood or still the same one I did not know. I felt like asking, acidly, but decided only to remind her that a deal was a deal.

I pushed the money at her – payment to the end of the month – and all she registered was disappointment.

'What we agreed,' I said tersely.

I was suddenly sure that she had been thwarted. She had been expecting me to come begging, and had looked forward to a scene; perhaps a dramatic refusal to allow me inside. Now, instead, she grunted and turned away, her frustrated scowl my only receipt.

Mikael had better news. Mrs Mirt and her two sons, sixteen and eighteen, had built a hut for themselves from timber off-cuts, discarded rounds, sticks and birch bark. They boasted a home-made brick oven, mud-plastered, even a chimney standing bravely on the roof. All winter, they said, they had been warm, with the house completely covered in snow, like an igloo. They had cleared only the door and tiny window. Mrs Mirt, I was told, had offered to share it with me.

Two offers in one day. How considerate were our own people, how inhumane the others. Had their hearts withered in Siberia? Would ours do the same?

21

ANNUAL HYSTERIA

Greed will push you down a hole, they say. Was I going to my punishment?

Alma came with me to the office. It was good of her because she did not have to, even though the *kateljok* – tin cooking dish – they would produce as evidence was hers.

'Why you again?' she said. 'We were both in it.'

I agreed that it was unfair. The episode belonged to both of us.

We had been ordered to the pea fields, just the two of us, which should have made us careful, or at least suspicious. Kargaja would have been behind it.

On our third day we had gone well prepared, Alma with her tin cooking dish, and I with my handful of hoarded flour. It was a fine fresh morning. We wasted no time getting a fire going and picking a panful of peas. Add the flour, a little water and, hey presto, porridge for breakfast.

Then came the Jumper, bursting out of the forest like a wild man. It had happened once or twice before and we should have been accustomed to it. 'What, you again?' he yelled. The surprise had not been well rehearsed. Triumph glittered in his slitted eyes. Swearing fearsomely, he grabbed the *kateljok*, most of the green mess still sticking to it, and shook it at my head. Alma and I winced as our precious meal plopped to the ground. 'Report tonight! Slut! You won't get away with it this time. This will cost you five days!'

We went on with our picking, carefully – very carefully – hiding a good-sized bucket of peas under the moss at the side of the road, late in the day. So we were going to be punished. Let there be a suitable crime.

I was not so much fearful, as resentful. These summonses were irritating beyond reason. I pushed open the door in front of my partner.

'Don't be reckless,' Alma murmured. 'Be humble. That man picks on you.' I could agree there, and I'd had enough of it. 'I'll go halves with you in any deductions they make, but don't make it worse.'

The director sat at the desk, slowly waving the *kateljok* in his hand. I could not interpret his expression. Several other men were present, *kolkhozniks*, all watching with interest. He made a point of showing it to me. 'Yours?'

I nodded. So did Alma. He did not even glance at her.

'What's all this about cooking?'

I had expected Skakalkin, and his customary histrionics. I had anticipated a verbal battle, some real fire. But there was hardly a glow. There was no Jumper, no noise, no fight. My vexation had nowhere to go; I sputtered like a damp fuse.

The director did not even swear. He said, '*A vot?*' – 'Well?'

'We were hungry.' I ignored Alma's warning glances. 'We wanted to finish the job before evening, so we decided to eat before we began, to give us strength and save time. If we'd been stopping on and off through the day to chew raw peas, we'd never have got it done.' One or two of the men laughed, and the director gave me an inscrutable look from under his eyebrows. Perhaps he was going to lecture us on our duties to the motherland, on the evils of capitalism, on the virtues of equality for all. 'Take off five days if you like, but just do it without any fuss and don't curse at me, I'm tired,' I said quickly.

The director said nothing. Alma took a deep breath. Someone laughed expectantly. Otherwise, you could have heard a pin drop.

I picked up the pan, still with burnt flour stuck to its bottom, and left. Alma was beside me, head up, eyes flashing, the most loyal of reluctant companions. I had a strange, elated feeling that we had blundered into a victory.

■

The road home took me past the herdsman's hut. Alma had gone her way, cautiously exultant, and now my own euphoria was ebbing. I passed the hut once, retraced steps – it couldn't be! – and passed it again. Undoubtedly, yes, lilac. Siberia is brown and grey, with a ground season for white, and one for green. Colours are rare. Lilac is the rarest of rare.

There had been laundry hanging under the roof earlier, I recalled, but this particular washing I would surely have noticed. It must have just been hung out. I walked brazenly past the window of the hut to the open shed, gaining boldness with every stride, for there, without question, were my stolen silk scanties and vest, no doubt taken by 'mistake' from the bathhouse last summer by the wife – or the herdsman himself, if he was that way inclined. Let them claim them back if they dared. I knew my own pants!

I snatched them off the line, standing tall with indignation, almost disappointed that the act went unseen. Home I went with Alma's *kateljok* in one hand, my undies in the other. It had been a good day.

■

'Tenants of hell, what have you got to laugh about?' Ott's mother was perturbed. 'It's no laughing matter.' We stopped, as she looked so upset. 'Lia is heading for misfortune. Maybe others, too. Mark my words. Water and white clothes mean nothing but trouble and sorrow.'

We were not too concerned. Although we indulged in fortune-telling in various forms, none of us was superstitious: none of the younger ones, at any rate; particularly not Lia and I, the two most active in the game.

The days were terribly long. Night lasted three or four hours, and most of the remaining twenty were for work. There was little time for the dream- and card-interpreting we were becoming quite famous for. We were likely to be approached in work-breaks, or when there was no-one about. 'Have you got your cards?' 'Can you read my palm?' 'What does it mean if . . .' and it was always worth a crust of bread or a potato or two; no true believer would think of not paying. It was unfortunate that we had too little time to make the most of it, and a pity that some – such as Mrs Ustav – took it seriously.

Lia had told us her dream while we were in the office one morning, waiting for work orders. It had not disturbed her. She had been on her way home from somewhere, she said, wearing a big, white shawl over her shoulders. She thought that she had been going to meet someone. Then, instead of the road in front of her, there was suddenly only water, deep and dark. The rest was lost. We each made our different readings – from romantic to ribald to gruesome – until Mrs Ustav could stand it no longer.

'You be careful!' she warned. 'Don't take it lightly!'

It was too late for care. Lia had hidden a bag of peas wrapped in her jumper under a bush two or three days earlier. The brigadier had found them. He made a tremendous fuss, and Lia lost both peas and jumper. The same day we were spreading new-mown hay on wooden trestles to dry. Each trestle was like a pair of wide ladders hinged at the top, or a long, clumsy clotheshorse, standing stiff-straddled in the sun. Alma and I were working there with a few Russian women. Lia was in the next field. One of the Russians was the herdsman's wife, the one partial to silk underwear, who complained loudly about 'such a woman, who walks around with her nose in the air, all dressed up' – Lia had mainly bright summer clothes which, perforce, she wore summer and winter – 'when she doesn't know how to speak our language, but does know how to steal.' The washing taken from her line was not mentioned in front of us, naturally enough; that ground had apparently been covered before by Mrs Herdsman to her cronies. She obviously did not know whose it originally was, or she might have been quieter, but she was guessing it was Lia who had taken it. For prudence's sake, I also forbore, which was unfortunate for Lia, who now had not only lost peas and jumper, but had gained an entirely unwarranted reputation as the *kolkhoz* thief.

Next, Mrs Meret died, which surprised even the knowledgeable. Four of us were immediately given a half day off to dig her grave and bury her, which was no concession as it was 'leave without credit'. The Russian custom was to bury their dead before sundown, hence the hurry. Why us? There was never cheaper labour. They even gained four rations of unclaimed bread out of it! We used the time well, managing to send her on her last journey in a box, which cost most of the clothing she had left. Rare, if belated, luxury.

Immediately after the funeral – conducted in the semi-dark, as no-one was allowed time off to attend – Mrs Balter became ill.

278

She had been fading perceptibly, rising from her sick-bed, ankles swollen, pale as death, and panting, uncomplaining, off to work. Only her will was left, the incredible spirit that had quietly produced miracles – money, sugar, clothes, salted meat – and that had kept her frail body upright for so long, a beacon to us all. It was no longer enough. Now Marusja had decided that she could not have a sick, old woman so close to her own family: Mrs Balter, having to stay home more and more, was exposing the children to the devil knew what. She had to go if she couldn't get out to work.

The Randins at Kamenoi had already been evicted, and joined Mrs Ustav with Ott and her two younger children, who were about to leave the 'dirty sauna' they now occupied. An ancient hut was to be restored for them all. It hadn't been established who was to restore it. Whether it would help much was doubtful, for it was apparent that Ott and Edgar had tuberculosis. The question of who was to care for them was pure rhetoric. From the Russian viewpoint, they were sick dogs, to be shovelled to the periphery of the community; no question of proper diagnosis, no thought of treatment or provision for elementary welfare. Compassion and communism, it seems, do not co-exist. Whoever has no value to the State has no value at all.

There was little, indeed, to laugh about. Unsuperstitious as I was, I began to hope not to dream of white and water.

■

Sauna night. Tomorrow was Sunday, the first one off for weeks. I decided to go to the sauna early and keep my ears open, perhaps prepare a trip to a neighbouring *kolkhoz*, maybe one I had not visited before. I still had to see about a new abode, and I might be able to do some trading on commission.

Instead, I overheard some Russian girls planning an excursion of their own. They were going to gather *kalbaa*. 'Gathering' was an ear-catching word; it meant something for nothing. I was immediately interested.

'*Kalbaa?*' I interrupted. 'What is that?'

They were not disconcerted by my lack of manners. 'You don't know?'

'Some kind of berry?' I thought I had heard the word 'pick' as well as 'gather'.

'Silly! Leaves!'

'What sort of leaves?'

'They are green' – that was worth a giggle – 'and smell and taste like garlic. They're medicine against *tsonga* – scurvy.'

I really sharpened my ears. My teeth were loose in swollen gums, and I had wondered why the locals' were so good.

'We collect and dry them for winter.'

'Can I go with you?'

'*Ladna*, come along then. As long as you're not afraid of bears, or a twelve kilometre walk there and back.'

'Where shall I meet you?'

By the time we reached the forest, I felt like resting. It was nearly thirty-five degrees already; I was panting, and the shade was heavenly. But the girls hared along the shadowy path, looking fearfully both ways as they went.

We reached the place, my guides' instinct for direction unerring. The ground under the trees was thickly covered with *kalbaa*, its dense green leaves, spread in profusion over a wide area, reminding me of lily-of-the-valley. Just as thick were the mosquitoes rising in angry black clouds at each step into the growth. The girls were quickly on their knees, shovelling leaves into bags with both hands. I was much slower, using one hand to swipe at the murderous hordes while I picked with the other, with the result that both were ineffectual. I was still pulling, swatting, and swearing, my bag less than half full, when the others were ready to go.

'Come on there, hurry it up!'

'Just a bit more.'

'How can you stand those mosquitoes?'

How indeed!

'Look, we'll go back the way we came. You know where the big pines and firs are?'

'I think so.'

'We'll get some resin.'

'Wait for me there, then.'

I was quicker alone. The forest pressed in, pricking uneasily at my back and scalp. With the nearly full bag tied across my nervous shoulders, I set off at a trot, passed through a clearing I had not seen before, and stopped, breathless. On each side of the path, pink and white peonies were in full bloom, crowds

of them. They were incredibly beautiful. I turned back to pick
an armful, calling to the girls to come and see. There was no
answer. Disappointed for them, I went on picking, calling again.
Still no answer, only me in a small clearing, lovely though it was,
in the middle of the taiga. Only me! My God! I was still on the
path, safe; but fear of being lost and the ever-present horror of
bears pumped adrenalin to my heart and gave wheels to my feet.
And there were the girls. Waiting, giggling.

'Oh, you – '

'We heard you but we thought we'd teach you what it's like.
Were you scared?'

I confessed, and they clapped their hands in delight.

'Did you see any bears? Are you frightened of them? Did we
teach you?'

I nodded. As if I needed teaching.

'Here you are then, Njura. We got some of the sap for you.'

I took a hard lump of the sticky stuff, and put it in with the
kalbaa. Two or three of the girls were already chewing. Likeable,
generous teenagers, as ingenuous as ten-year-olds. Why on God's
earth must they grow up?

'Would you like some flowers?'

'What for?'

'They're so beautiful!'

'They're only *bujengs*! Throw them into the bush,' one said
scornfully. 'That's all they're good for.'

'Or give them to Natasha's cow,' said another.

I suddenly felt depressed. She was not joking.

The flowers were wilting by the time I got to the gate. I
dropped them in the shade of the fence, before sharing the
kalbaa with the Mikaels and Enn. Whether or not it would be
worth the trouble, only time would tell.

■

The next Saturday I had my annual bout of hysteria.

We had been working like beavers all week and, although
the previous Sunday had been free, we were allowed the next
as well, on the condition that all *kolkhoz* hay was properly
stacked, and a few other stipulated collective jobs done first. So,
day and night, we worked for the Sunday, which happened to be
my birthday. Children, old people – Enn's mother, despite our

protest, came out to the fields – everybody worked. To encourage us further, the bread, even a plate of meatless soup one day, was brought out to us.

All work was done by lunchtime Saturday. I decided I would ask for two days' bread in the evening, boil some pea porridge, and go out mushrooming as a birthday treat. I was still planning it when I pulled the gate open. Lia was there waiting, looking grim. With her was the old woman from next door, planted solid.

'There's a patch of hay near the marsh that hasn't been stooked yet,' Lia said in Estonian. 'This old witch says she'll report us if we don't go with her.'

'Tell her to go jump in it.'

'I did.'

'In Russian?'

'Estonian.'

'Try it in Russian.'

'You do it. I've got to live with her.'

I decided against it. Ustinja might hear about it, although the two were barely on speaking terms.

'Half a day's work,' grunted the old woman, and stuck a piece of bread and a rake in my hands.

Half a day! We worked solidly, ignoring the swarms of mosquitoes, but well into evening the end was nowhere near. Bitterly, I told Lia of my birthday plan.

'Well, why not knock off now, then? I'll stay till it's all done.'

'I couldn't do that.' Half-heartedly.

'I haven't anything else to do,' Lia shrugged. 'Let's give it a try.'

The old hag wouldn't hear of it. 'Who do you think you are? Loafing all the time.'

'But just for her birthday. I can finish this.'

'*Nyet*. Back to work.' She turned her broad rear to show us how.

I threw down the rake. Perhaps, as they say, the devil took hold of me. I burst into sobs of rage, rising to shrieks. I stamped, beat my fists on the air, and finally took off and ran. Anywhere. To get away from the place. And, of course, there was nowhere to go. So I ran in a circle, and shrieked and beat and stamped again.

I remember the old woman's look of astonishment, changing into fright. She grabbed me by the arm.

'Don't worry about it,' she said hastily. 'About the work. We'll leave it for now.'

I realised I had taken off in the direction of the river, and what she must have been thinking. She probably had no more than a superstitious fear of lunacy, a reasonable fear in the circumstances, I grant. If I had simply shown rage, and yelled at her, she would not have turned a hair.

'Just put it down,' she soothed. 'Off you go. Both of you. I'll come back and finish it myself in the morning.' She muttered off, shaking her head.

Lia led me to the store. She looked at me oddly, too. I pretended not to notice. We were late. *Kurat!* The store was closed.

The hysterics had passed but I was in a cranky mood. A day wasted. To go home like this was too much. I left Lia without telling her my purpose, and strode direct to the foreman, Lenkov. He lived across the road from the store. I was too late here, as well. His wife told me he was back from the sauna and asleep.

'Come back in the morning if you must see him,' she said. 'About nine o'clock.'

■

I was there at nine. Lenkov was not.

I waited.

He appeared shortly before ten. Perhaps he had not been told. Or perhaps he thought I would not stick it out. Obviously annoyed to see me, he gestured me aside. I stood my ground, and made my request.

'Double ration? No.'

'It's due to me.'

'Go to the storekeeper and ask for it,' he said tersely.

'The storekeeper won't give it without authority.' Of course, he knew this full well.

'Then tell him Lenkov sent you.'

'It will need a written order.'

'You'll have to wait for it. I'm busy. I've got a meeting to attend.'

'I'll wait.'

I sat on a bag of wood shavings. It was too late for mushrooming, too late for anything. It rained lightly, but the weather was warm. I felt rather like a Buddhist, sitting patiently awaiting the handouts of fate. My shadow contracted before me, and began lengthening on the other side, before the foreman reappeared.

'Didn't you get wet?' he smirked.

'I did. But the sun has dried me out again.'

'You wait like the devil for a soul! *Ladna,* come in. I'll make out the paper.'

■

I had been lucky on my birthdays.

On the first one, due to floods of tears, the brigadier had allowed me the day off work. This time, I would have a full belly. They should happen every day.

On second thought, God forbid even one more here!

The luck was short-lived. I had forgotten that the first of August was not only my birthday: a night or two later, coming home from flax-picking, I found all my belongings in an untidy heap outside. Ustinja had shifted back in. If I had shown her money, she might have moved out again. On the other hand, I had had more than enough of Ustinja; if I had had money to show, I would have concealed it. Business is business, a roof is a roof; but pride is pride.

I had no roubles for her, only what was left from 'Death and Starvation', so there was no decision to make. I moved into the home of the homeless, the sauna across the road, by the marsh.

The 'apartment' had some good points. There was no rent to pay, we were all Estonians and, after Saturday's use, it was warm for a day, useful should we be here into winter. I found a spot on the top step, next to the Randin family: Mrs Randin, Edgar, and his younger brother. The Ustavs – Ott, his two sisters and their mother – occupied the middle. The ground floor was vacant.

On the bad side was the fact that it was a 'black' sauna, without a chimney. Smoke poured through it every firing, leaving a greasy, sooty film that could only be partly scrubbed off. With no window, hence no ventilation, it was perpetually dark and damp. Every Saturday morning, of course, we had to clear the place out; possessions would be piled outside and left in the care of the youngest Ustav, eight years old, until we returned from work. Otherwise, we had it to ourselves. We slept in our clothes, cooked in the fireplace, and ate communally. We had wood for our fire, though we were warned mortally against using it, stacked against the outer wall.

Ustinja looked in, feigning the innocence of a passer-by. I was shaking out bedding.

'Oh, dear Father!' She opened her eyes wide and clasped her hands in classic surprise. Blasphemy, I thought sourly, the father would undoubtedly be Stalin. 'You, Njura?'

I had already wiped my shelf clean, which was as important as the storage of bedclothes and palliasse in these quarters; Mrs Ustav had been threshing again, the dust was everywhere, and sharp little 'linen-bones' bit worse than fleas. I laid my bed gently on the cleaned space, taking my time. Ustinja followed, peeking and clucking in delighted distaste.

'Yes, me.'

'But here? In this place?'

'What's wrong with it?'

'It's – *a vot* – not very clean, is it?'

'You bathe in it.' Obscure innuendo was water off a duck's back. I poured a bit more. 'I can't help it if it's soiled.'

'With these people?'

'I've been with worse,' I said pointedly.

'You're not allowed to stay here, you know.'

'Did you come on business?' Mrs Randin called from her corner. 'If not, close the door as you go.'

'You might be sorry you're not more cooperative!' came Ustinja's parting shot.

Very likely.

22

ROMANCE

Autumn was warm and dry, following a mild summer. Harvesting and threshing were well up to schedule, Udarnik in fact promising to be the first of the four in the collective to finish. I at least, with sharp memories of the frozen thistles and bleeding hands of last year, found the thought a spur. To work hard, and finish before the freeze, was good for the fingers, and gave a head start to proper preparation for winter, with always the chance of picking up some extra vitamins in the spare time. I had learned to care for my health. It was the one key to a future.

The sauna was to be evacuated, Ustinja having speeded things up. The Ustavs and Randins were to move into their renovated hut, where the cracks between logs had been stopped with tow, the walls plastered with yellow clay, the stove rebuilt. The roof had been reinforced and freshly turfed over, most of the work done by Enn and the younger boys. There were even curtains at the crazy window. Ott was full of plans for Christmas, inviting all who had lodged with them last year to see the new apartment. He hoped to be completely well by then.

Vilma Akker approached me one evening. She had been talking to Mikael, Ustinja's remaining tenant. 'My landlady has offered to put you up,' she said.

I had heard that the same landlady had been very good to Vilma and her young son, Paul. I had known Vilma vaguely in Rakvere, but had seen little of her here. Tonight she had made a special visit. She belonged to Red May and lived part way between the two *kolkhozes*.

'It's very kind of her,' I said cautiously.

'She is a very kind person.'

'But – you know – '

'No rent required,' Vilma anticipated.

'None?'

'I told you. She's kind-hearted. She heard about you and offered.'

'A Russian?'

'Ukrainian.'

I could not stay where I was. And when the Ustavs and the Randins moved, their tiny new place would be crowded enough.

'All right, then. Thank her.'

'Do it yourself, if you like. Why not come back with me? I have a barrow here.'

Indeed she had: a wheel, a shallow box and a pair of shafts. More than adequate for my worldly goods.

■

The hut was in the lee of the forest. We entered through a neat miniature porch, sides made of birch bark, floor of well-scrubbed planks. There was a large wooden cot along the right hand wall of the single room. A boy of about thirteen was asleep on it. A mild-looking woman my own age, dark, careworn, slim and serious-looking, got up from the foot end. Vilma quietly introduced us: 'Njura, Karpovna.' The boy was Ivan, Karpovna's son. She would be sleeping with him, I presumed, as there was no other bed, only the neat pile of Vilma's bedding stacked in a corner. Little Paul's cot was against the same wall. He, too, was asleep. The far wall had a large oven and tiny stove. Along the left was a window, a table, and two wooden seats. Introductions hardly completed, to my surprise I was briskly ushered outside.

Behind the hut was a cowshed of birch planks and bark and straw, fixed to a stout log frame scarcely big enough for an animal to turn around in. Karpovna's pride in it was touching. It was empty at the moment, but the landlady was an owner, Vilma informed me respectfully, of half a cow. We never did hear in Siberia of part ownership, always ownership of a part.

'I tend and feed and milk her for two days,' Karpovna told me gravely, 'then my neighbour takes her for two.' It was now the neighbour's turn. 'She's a very good milker.'

288

I took Vilma's cue, and expressed astonishment and admiration.

'At last,' my new landlady said with some warmth, as we returned inside, 'I can talk like with another human, *vot*. Vilma talks Russian funny, all mixed up with her own strange tongue.'

She was sorry to be in such a hurry, she said: she worked as a nightwatchwoman. She had stayed to meet me. Her hospitality became effusive, a rush of words tumbling over each other, from pure, nervous generosity. She was not, I decided thankfully, garrulous by nature, simply a nice person released from the restraints of language.

'Make yourself at home, Njura. Plenty of room. It will be warmer for both of you if you sleep on the floor. Vanja won't wake up. No room for more beds, anyway. I'm off to work now. It's a nuisance. Every second night. Vilma will get you something to eat. See you in the morning, we'll have a good talk.'

Paul was reserved in the beginning, but it was not long before he would sit on my lap. Ivan – Karpovna's 'Vanja' – was sullen. The children had been warned about us *Estonkas* at school and, despite his mother's friendliness, he was not going to accept another imperialist enemy easily; Vilma was embarrassment enough for him.

It was the stories that eventually won him round. At first he pretended not to listen, sitting as far away as possible from his mother and me – which was not far. When the chores were finished, we would talk about the usual topics: home, families, memories, even hopes. Karpovna was fascinated by this improbable world, truthfully translated. We got around to films, I don't quite know how, and soon I had to recall and recount the plots of Jackie Coogan and Shirley Temple movies.

Ivan had never seen a movie and his mother had only hazy recollections of travelling 'flickers'. She had been one of the people dumped on the bank many years ago; how many years one did not ask: it would be too many to account for Ivan if, as I gathered, her husband had not come this far. Only women, children, and a few older men had made it here, none of their own men. Karpovna made no mention of this period, I had to go by what other Ukrainians had told me. There were questions that were never asked in these places. Ivan was her child, hers alone.

He listened, unwillingly at first. In the end I had to repeat stories, in particular *The Secret Garden* and *Steel Boy* over and over again. A piece of bread, a potato or a mug of milk stimulated my memory to better tales, maybe an occasional new one. Karpovna was as enthralled as the boy. My mind was kept active during the day preparing the night's story, knowing they would both be waiting, eyes popping, mouths open. She promised a bed on the oven in winter, and I volunteered to pick her potatoes after work. Survival seemed assured until February when workdays were to be paid up, fairly safe even beyond that. And Ivan and I went many times *Around the World in Eighty Days*. If I stopped to pick up a loose thread, checking the story with Vilma in Estonian, I was told to hurry and get on with it, so we could finish before getting off to sleep. Then, if it was Karpovna's night off, I might have to go through a movie, just for her. Some of their directors would have been surprised.

■

Potato-picking time was around again. I had tried the first nest of my private patch several days ago. I could hardly believe it. Nothing! A handful of pigeon's eggs. This was a dreadful blow, almost my worst yet, I had so built up hopes on a good yield.

I had to find a way to improve the harvest.

By the third day the new system was smooth. Just before finishing time I would empty my bucket into the communal bag, then begin to pick another at the moment everyone else was taking in their last load ... Good worker, that Njura, hates coming in empty, but a bit of a slowcoach. She should watch us, use her head a bit, learn better planning! ... By the time I had filled my bucket I was alone in the field, the old hands well on their way home. I then hurriedly 'emptied' it into the unattended communal one as I ran to catch up ... Silly Njura, she should take it more slowly ... Without quite reaching them I would call that I was stopping off at my private patch to gather a few for myself.

I was bending over the second freshly dug nest one evening, complacently dropping my tiny tubers into the half-full bucket, when I heard steps behind me. It was too late to do anything but continue.

'Strength to you!' The greeting of a passer-by to one who is working. 'How is your harvest?'

Fear gripped me. It was Kalesnikov, the director himself. He already had his hand in the bucket. I was finished. How many years? Five? Ten? I sat back on my heels and kept my eyes down, sure he could hear the hammering of my heart.

'Middling, is it?' He was in fine humour, so far. 'Some little ones, some big ones. Strange. None in between. And all the big ones are on the bottom!'

I said nothing, kneeling at his feet, trembling hands in the earth.

'All from only two little nests, too!'

He straightened up. Here it comes . . .

'*Ladna*, keep on picking. You have a long way to go home.'

He went on his way humming. From my position of prayer I looked after him, speculating.

■

Perhaps there was something in what they had been saying: Alma, Marju, Sergei – and Marusja, of course. I wondered coolly, for a minute, if I should take the sly advice of some of them.

One evening, I recalled, on our way home, he had asked me if my legs were tired from digging all day. I recalled his raised eyebrows and the teasing of Alma and the others. 'Rubbish,' I'd said. 'He looks like that at everyone,' and I almost believed it.

Then there was the time I'd asked Marusja if she thought I dare ask her husband's permission for my trip to Vesjoloi. 'Why not try the director? He might *like* to do you a favour.' After my deflation – some time after! – I had asked her what she had meant by it. 'Oh, just some of the men drinking at our place one night. They were talking about women as usual. Some of the younger ones. You Estonians. Like Erika Purre. Someone said she was on with the storekeeper.' We had heard the same story. 'The storekeeper's wife dragged her out of the shop by the hair' – an embellishment on our version – 'and made her nose bleed.'

'So what does that have to do with me?'

'I'm coming to that. Then the director said he wasn't interested in Erika, but "*Vot*, Njura," he said, "That's more my style. The trouble with her, though, is she goes round with young Enn and scratches anybody else like a wildcat!" '

I had been angry and sent Marusja by the quickest route to the pit. Not with any special thought for the director's sentiments – if he was that easily put off, he wasn't too serious – more the 'going round with Enn' and its implications. Perhaps a grain of truth in the last bit had sharpened my reaction, too.

I had not given Kalesnikov a second thought then. I did now, remembering other small incidents. There was the office girl who told me, with a malicious smirk, that Skakalkin would have had me starved for the pea porridge episode, had it not been for the director; the Jumper had gone off swearing when he heard I had got off scot free, but Kalesnikov had refused to be browbeaten. Now the potatoes. And the bookkeeper in the rest hut, as far back as last year: 'Look, in the springtime even a wood-shaving falls on top of another. Aren't you a woman at all, Njura? Are you made of wood? Or even stone? Why are your claws always out?'

'Really,' I had said, quite cheerfully, 'I don't think about it.' I'd have been annoyed if it weren't for his expressive speech.

'Well then, do think about it. There's a man here who has liked you from the start. He just doesn't want to be scratched, like the brigadier. And now you've got so thin. You can't have much to live on. And this man could help you. He could even get you a job in the office.'

'Thank you very much,' I had said stiffly. The memory of my family and home was not that far away, and in any case life was too hard to think of anything but living. 'And besides, there's your wife Dusja.'

The bookkeeper had laughed. 'You silly little one! Not me! This man's wife is in hospital, if that's all you're worried about. She won't be coming out, either.'

The director's wife had tuberculosis.

■

Lia laughed when I told her, which I did only after thinking about it for a day or two. Though I told her as a funny story, I watched closely for a reaction. Lia was shrewd, worldly, rarely despondent – except when confronted with such practical impossibilities as ditch-digging: her leanings were artistic rather than physical – and I preferred to tell her rather than Vilma, or even Alma. I felt a need to tell someone. I was very unsure of myself,

292

and her opinion might easily sway a decision that was desperately important, however airily I presented the details.

I gained nothing. She laughed, but she was preoccupied, her attention straying under my scrutiny.

'What, not you too?' I exclaimed. Something in her attitude showed I had struck a nerve.

'Well – '

'Come on, you'd better tell me.'

She hesitated. 'I haven't told anyone before.' Lia was a shy girl, despite her outgoing manner. Apart from that, there was always the possibility of repercussion from tale-telling. 'It was last autumn, about the end of threshing. Wet snow was falling.'

'The director?' I think I might have been a little jealous.

'Oh, no. No, it was the stableman.'

'Ugh!' He was about sixty-five, seldom shaven, always grubby, and had a smell of horses stronger than the animals themselves.

'Yes, ugh! Rather than get wet I decided to sleep in the shed, on one of the bunks there.' I knew them. On really wet nights, quite a few people did not go home if other shelter was available. The stables had bunks and straw. 'I didn't know he was there. He woke me up in the middle of the night, and promised me bread, meat, milk – just about the world – if I'd come and live in his hut and be his housekeeper.'

I nodded. This was not so unusual.

'He didn't waste any time. He said I'd have to let him sleep with me first. As you know, my Russian isn't too fluent and I was still only half awake. Before I'd really worked out what he was talking about, he'd climbed into my bunk and was tugging at my slacks.'

'The dirty old – '

'I was on the top bunk. It wasn't very dark and I could see his stumpy teeth, and hear him grunting as he pulled at my clothes. And then I looked down. He didn't have any pants on and – well, he was ready! You know, all ready to go!'

I giggled.

'It wasn't very funny at the time.'

'I know. I'm sorry – '

'No, that's all right. Really, thinking of it now, it *was* funny.' Lia chuckled. 'Talking about it makes it funnier. Just thinking about it by myself, I only remember how scared I was.'

'What happened?'

'Well, this is where it really does get funny. Can you see me jumping off the bunk? I must have just about jumped right over him, and started running. And he came after me.'

She giggled again, finally breaking into bursts of laughter, talking in gasps between peals. 'Me in my socks, holding my pants up . . . and his dirty old shirt tails flapping . . . and still at the ready. Twice round the hut we went . . . like Hector and Ajax . . . in the slush . . . and I knew I couldn't keep it up much longer. I grabbed a plank off the wall and turned around . . . like a club . . . I threatened I'd hit him with it, you know where . . . and his enthusiasm . . . sort of . . . dropped.'

By this time we were both convulsed.

'He sent me to the devil then – he really looked so disappointed I almost felt sorry for him – and I grabbed my boots and ran home.' She thought about it again for a few seconds and added, most uncharacteristically, 'Bloody Russian *orikas*!'

That started me off again. Worse than before. Now it was I who could not talk.

'What's so funny now?' Lia demanded.

'*Orikas*! Oh Lia! You're not a country girl!'

'Well, he is an *orikas*!'

'Call him a pig if you like,' I said through my tears. 'But you know what an *orikas* is? It's one that's been castrated!'

■

'What was all that mirth about?'

The others could hardly wait till lunch break for Lia to go through it again. As one story begets another, we heard a few more over the midday crusts.

Alma had been offered a job as clerk, to begin next week. She knew what her duties would include. She was making him wait for her decision, but she would have to be politic. The book-keeper had a mean streak; he would be a nasty enemy.

Aino Kask had gone to an elderly man to trade a pair of her husband's shoes. The man was blind, but he had a reputation. Aino had had her plan ready. He was home alone when she went to make her sale. He felt the shoes, tried one on, put them on the table behind him, and said he was prepared to buy. But first he must know more about the seller, and since he was a poor, blind man, the only way he could get to know her better was by feel; he must do this to know if the merchandise was worth the price. I suspect that he knew something of Aino as, despite having two children to feed, she was young and remained almost plump. She agreed, and allowed him to touch her face, her neck and start on her bosom. Here, she said it was time to pay. He eagerly gave her three roubles. She whispered close to him, 'Is that all?' He felt on, and added a few potatoes; some game meat when she made rustling noises with her clothes; then a half piece of soap and a box of matches as his hands reached for more. Aino sidestepped, put the goods in her bag, picked up the shoes from the table and left. 'I don't think I'll hear any more from him,' she said, 'but I'd like to hear the earful his wife gives him when she takes stock.'

Lia looked at me. I shook my head. My story was not for circulation.

I would have to make my own decision about Kalesnikov. He had certainly treated me well – I could have been destroyed by the potato business – and he was presentable enough . . .

I'm sure mine was far from the only story not told.

■

'Did you hear? Ott had a haemorrhage last night.'
    'Will he last till Christmas? His party?'
    'He won't last the day.'

■

The boys dug his grave under a birch tree. Ott had been a popular boy, even with the Russians. His mother was equally well respected. The foreman ordered a coffin be built and allowed a cross to be made; he even promised the horse and the best dray after work, as long as there was no other use made of it. One of the boys could drive.

Enn's mother, though very ill, conducted the service; she had done many another. She rode on the dray with the wet-eyed driver and the new square coffin. Every Estonian in Udarnik followed, and most from the whole of Maisk.

We lowered the box to find that the grave was too short. It remained tilted, as further digging encountered a sticky yellow substance oozing from below. Perhaps another grave, I thought wildly. Enn covered it quickly with a grimace and, in the gathering dark, nobody else noticed. By the time the cross was erected and the last hymn – the Estonian National Anthem – sung, it was as black as pitch. The singing of the anthem was in defiance of an order regularly made and ignored.

Of all the service, one incident remained supremely clear in my mind, and still does. Kalesnikov had watched our procession go by. He had kept his hat on, even smoked, displaying no more feeling than for a dog trotting past.

Kalesnikov may like Njura. Njura may have begun to like Kalesnikov. Ann Lehtmets would never let Kalesnikov touch her. Or so she thought.

■

The weather remained fine. Colder, but no snow yet. Harvested potatoes could be left overnight in the field, covered with their own tops to keep the frost out. Different from last year, when they had had to be bagged and taken straight in by horse and cart. Now, men and horses were released to get on with the threshing. We might be finished early this year, which meant a bonus for Udarnik.

Good for us, too. One irresistible heap lay near my path home. Lord, lead me now into temptation! I mentioned it to Vilma – off-handedly, as I was not yet sure of her.

'Might be worth looking over,' I said casually.

'Let's.' She was unashamedly enthusiastic. 'And it had better be tonight. I've got bags. Karpovna's taken Ivan to the bathhouse. She's going from there to a school meeting.' My respect for her increased.

We took down the bags, prised weeks ago from the tight fist of the *kolkhoz* and hidden in the ceiling. It was a good night, dark enough to see without being seen. We had ten buckets bagged and hidden in the forest behind the hut by the time our landlady and son returned.

In the morning, Vilma spoke to Karpovna in her improving Russian. It was no longer practicable to refuse to speak it. 'I sold some of my baby's clothes for potatoes,' she said. I had forgotten she had started out with a baby. 'For food. I don't know where – '

'Never mind, my dear.' Karpovna asked no more. 'Store them in the cellar. I'll clear a corner for you.'

296

At lunchtime next day we brought our haul to the porch. Karpovna's eyes widened. What baby's clothes they must have been!

In the evening, Ivan helped stow it. No worry now about our landlady or her son; they were accomplices.

■

Perhaps it was a cold coming. Perhaps it was nerve strain. I thought I had a slight fever, and felt unwell.

'I would like a certificate for two days off.'

Luckily, the Russian nurse who took my temperature was one whose fortune I had told some time ago. I must have been right, or at least have impressed her. She left me with the thermometer long enough to be rubbed with the wool rag in my pocket, flicked it the right way, checked it, and took it to Dr Janovna.

Dr Janovna was Latvian. To us, she was Dr Ausma, her Christian name. She was 'one of us,' despite the patronymic; the Russian version was a mark of respect few deportees had been accorded as yet. We had all sorts of hybrid names. It would be some time before somebody would ask my father's name – Tonis – and I would become Anna Denisovna. It was a signal honour to be accepted as an equal!

Dr Ausma looked at the thermometer, at the nurse, at me, and wrote out the blue slip.

Though certainly not feeling up to potato digging, time could not be wasted. I had earlier made tentative plans to go cranberrying with Mrs Lageda; she had been before, with some local girls, to the same marsh I had picked with the storekeeper in spring, and had promised me some footwear. Now it was muddy, and I took a child's delight in splashing about in my borrowed wading boots. So much more fun than last time, virtually barefoot on ice.

Left to myself, I cried off and on. It was peaceful here. The earth smelled fresh, the growth sweet, berries easy to find. Small birds chased around the low growth and from high in a scraggy pine came a call: 'Tiiu, Tiiu.' And, from a little distance, the reply: 'Tiit, Tiit, Tiit.'

The sun was high when our *konns* were filled. We had been greedy as well as preoccupied, giving no thought to the way home. It was physically tiring, too. Straps cut in. I tried easing my thumbs under them, but found I needed both hands to fend off mosquitoes. We rested often. Once, I stumbled badly and caught my boot on a stump, tearing it. Lucky we're nearly out of the water, I thought. Luckier I didn't sprain an ankle. The one could be unpleasant, the other disastrous.

A bucketful went up into the loft for the winter. They froze hard up there, and would come down, a few at a time, to be sucked like candy. It would be good to have some left at Christmas to bring out for the children.

A half litre went to the mother of the boy whose boots I had borrowed. He grumbled at the hole. 'Stop complaining,' she said. 'Put a patch over it.' And to me: 'Any time – ' as she stored the precious fruit. She was Estonian, and knew her priorities. The boots, I discovered when I asked for them again, belonged to a Russian, for whom he was mending them. The lad was capitalising on his treasured bicycle repair kit. Good business!

I had thought at first that I would spend my remaining day picking potatoes for a woman whose husband was in the army but, when the time came, I did not feel up to it.

'Why not?' asked my landlady.

'I just don't feel well enough.'

'It might be worth it,' Karpovna advised.

'Besides, her place is right next to the highway. It would be risky. I might be seen. I'm supposed to be sick.'

'But listen,' Karpovna persisted. 'She has kerosene. I know she had plenty, and there's not too much around. And she's a good payer.' It looked like goodbye to my sick day. 'While you're at it, get some matches and a strip of phosphorus.'

'Phosphorus?'

'Or sulphur – whatever it is. Matches aren't much use without something to strike them on.'

You must never let up, never forgo an opportunity, especially where the rarer items were concerned.

She lent me her *fufaika* and a kerchief – 'Wrap it round so only your nose and eyes show' – to reduce the risk of recognition. I worked as though they were my own potatoes, and made two buckets for myself as well as three roubles and the kerosene, matches and striker I asked for. She was indeed a good employer.

I had a sense of achievement. Sickness in Siberia very rarely paid.

23

GOLDEN GRAIN

Vilma had a brilliant idea. She was still working with the grain, and almost every day she brought home one or two small bags of wheat. This we chewed uncooked, thus wasting none of its value.

'Instead of these little handfuls, what we need is a decent-sized haul. You know, a whole bag. That would see us pretty safe for the winter.'

'There's no harm in dreaming.'

'You'd like some?'

'What do you think?'

'It can be done,' she said dramatically.

'By whom?'

'Me, with your help.'

I waited while she unfolded her plan, the two of us sitting cross-legged on the floor, Karpovna and Ivan only a metre or two away, in another world of language.

'You know how my machine is placed at the back of the *tat-schok*, right next to the cemetery? Now, I could get a bag out through the back wall there, into the cemetery. There's a big birch in just the right spot. But that's as much as I could do. From the shed to the cemetery, understand? I couldn't get it out of the cemetery.'

I was beginning to get the idea, and I wasn't liking it. Vilma would be taking a great risk. It was conceivable that she could get away with pushing the bag through, then, on some pretext, going round behind the *tatschok* and concealing it. Obviously, she couldn't take the chance of picking it up after work and lumping it home. Somebody else, perhaps. Guess who?

I knew the birch. Ott was under one like it. Vilma's hand was on my arm, persuading, while we tried to look unexcited. 'If you could bring it back, we could go halves.'

She was right. It was a well conceived plan. We had had the first light snow, ideal for the purpose, as it was cold enough for people not to want to hang about, not yet impossibly so. The cemetery, a desolate place at any time, was thoroughly deserted now. Vilma was well situated inside, handling grain. I was out of work, outside.

'And the fuss about the cow has just about fizzled,' Vilma concluded.

A fat cow in the neighbouring *kolkhoz* had died mysteriously. The commune's vet, with a little prompting, had said he thought it might be the Siberian plague, which was rife on the other side of the marsh. It was reported that some local Estonians had smiled at the diagnosis, though they had been the ones to suggest it. The animal, he'd said, had to be buried without delay, not butchered for the bosses, as usual. The next morning, there was only a hole in the ground with head, skin, leg bones, hoofs and entrails left. People from this side – Estonians: who else would risk the plague? – were suspected. Nothing was found, however, and nobody, before or after the freeze, caught the Siberian plague. But there had, as Vilma remarked, been a fuss.

'Maybe,' I said. 'But I wouldn't want to cause the next one.'

■

I shuffled to the tree, heart beating fast, deciding that I was not cut out for a life of organised crime. The pine log was propped against the birch, Vilma's signal that the bag was buried, the coast clear. If something had happened to raise an alarm, she would have found an excuse to dash outside, behind the tree – sudden nausea, or phobic panic, depending on the circumstance – knocking the branch down in her hurry. I half hoped that it would be down. It was there, though, and I was on stage, alone. I thought of walking straight on. Then I thought of the wheat, and of Vilma's reaction to the wasted risk and effort.

I lowered my *konn*, fiddled with the few birch bark pieces poking from the top to make it look full, carefully checking every direction, and knelt over the spot where the bag should be.

No-one in sight. What if there were? . . . Just a crazy Estonian, praying over someone's grave – in the middle of the day, did you ever see anything like it? – on her way home with a load. Funny people! . . . I thought briefly of Ott, under just such a tree, offered a brief genuine prayer, and wondered who was here. Some other poor deportee perhaps – may her spirit give me strength. No hitch. I pushed aside the surface snow. It was there. God give me strength. I looked up in supplication, eyes roving. No-one. Trembling hands swiftly lifted the treasure, shoved it into the *konn*, rearranged the birch bark. Then the snow, and Vilma's tracks from the *tatschok*. Fifteen kilograms of wheat! Easy! Excitement tingled from my fingers all the way up to my throat. I got up, checked the impulse to dash away, hammed it with a sign of the cross, and plodded off, trying hard to make the load look light.

I had to go back along the road, the same way I had come. Footprints in the forest snow could give us away if the loss were discovered. No voice called me back, no hand grasped my shoulder. Near home, I turned into the woods to wait for the landlady to emerge. I knew she would come: it was near milking time, and it was her turn at the cow waiting in its stall. I slipped out the moment she reached for the teat, scurried for the hut, slid the bag of grain under my bed, and dropped the *konn* carelessly in front of the stove. By the time Karpovna returned I was sitting on the edge of the cot, knitting. Nothing would budge me till she went off to her nightwatching.

■

Now for the milling. We had nearly twenty kilograms of wheat all told, with Vilma's small bags. Karpovna had grinding stones, but we decided against asking for them; they made such a noise, when in use, that neighbours might hear. And our nearest neighbour was a man not to be trusted. He had just returned from a ten year sentence for repeatedly raping his thirteen-year-old daughter. He knew we detested him and we suspected that he would not hesitate to report us. If caught, we would be in serious trouble. So would Karpovna, who would, at best, have her grinding stones smashed.

The only alternative seemed to be the commune mill, where the dangers were obvious. Then, to our surprise, we realised that neither Vilma nor I had ever seen one in Maisk. Was there one anywhere near? We had to find out quickly; even if it meant a risk. The subject was brought up in conversation with Karpovna.

We got our answers . . . No mill here. The other side of Red May. Not in operation all the time. Yes, working now, it would be flat out for a few weeks. The miller, just out of gaol. Probably for pinching; nothing much. A nice man. Busy at the moment, milling for the *kolkhoz* bakery.

In the morning I set out with twenty kilograms of wheat on my back and the thrill of fear pounding away in my heart.

Our neighbour had done ten years for his crime. Not such a stiff sentence really, remembering that a crime against the State was more serious than one against the person, even for so disgusting an offence; my reward, as a deportee stealing from the *kolkhoz*, would be more severe. He had been to gaol, and he had come back. God knows where I would go. The camps, probably. And we had not heard of anyone coming back from there.

Such reflections were hardly conducive to a pleasant stroll. I trudged on, my load seeming more and more a great lead-weighted beacon, flashing '*thief*'.

Sleigh bells! I froze, the hair on my neck rising. I was through the village, out in the clear, safely past the last cabin, with only the stables on the corner between me and the road to the mill. Only two kilometres to go, the easiest two, all danger past. Now this!

I stood, petrified. Nothing in sight yet. But it was only a matter of seconds. Sleigh bells meant one thing – authority – and the only blind spot in my field of vision was the bare side wall of the stable. Still, I stood immobile. They must be just around that corner, and every jingle a horse-pace nearer.

Don't panic, don't arouse suspicion. But how?

Be natural . . . With a *konn* of stolen wheat on my back? . . . You must not run. Steady! Now do it . . .

Heart pounding, I made for the building, barely five steps away. No hope of avoiding being seen. The bells were nearer. I could hear solid hoof-beats; now the horse's belly noises; now its breathing. Dropping my pants, I squatted, feet apart, baggy dress up over my knees, *konn* pressed between the wall and my shoulders, face to the road. The horse clopped into view. The sleigh swished around the corner, the near runner so close I could see nail heads. Two men were in it, one the director of Red May, notoriously hard. I turned my head, all modesty and confusion, pulling hastily at the rough skirt as if to hide bare flesh and pants, in truth to ensure them seen. The men laughed raucously, one of them shouting a crudity. My heart kept thumping, but the sleigh did not stop.

I sat limp on the snow for a long time, shaking. Ten years or more behind barbed wire – God knew what else – had passed me by at touching distance. Slowly, I gathered courage, picked up the *konn*, walked on unsteadily. One thing seemed certain: the mill must be working, else why was the director here? The road led nowhere else. Now, it depended on the miller.

The waiting bay was empty and the loading platform bare. There was no doubt it was operating, the noise had been getting steadily louder from a kilometre away. Out on the river side, a man stood in a doorway. I went up to him, dropping my *konn* on the way. He was small, hairy, and, judging by the flour cling-ing in his whiskers, had to be my man.

'Good day, citizen.' My greeting was mild. Until I knew more about him, I decided it was best to be politely naive. He had jovial eyes and a steady stare. It was impossible to gauge any-thing else through the snowy-tipped facial growth. His clothes were ragged, as floury as himself. 'Can you tell me where I can have my wheat ground, please?'

'You can't.' The quick eyes looked for my wares. 'The *kolkhoz* grain is in the works now.' The wheel clunked its rhythm, and the big stones squealed their protest. 'And it's rye.'

'Oh.'

'What kind of wheat have you got, anyway?' Speech as direct as his eye. 'And where did you get it from? Workdays grain hasn't been dished out yet.'

I explained in involved ambiguous detail how I had bought the grain from various individuals, how hard I'd saved for it, how much I had paid at each transaction. If he were half as confused as I, the story should pass.

During my speech I offered him some *samagon* for a *plotski*. He rolled a courteous thin one, my eyes jealously patrolling every movement. It was the first supply for many weeks, the result of my recent wealth, and I could ill afford wastage. Since our first few days in Maisk, there had been no smokers' supplies in the shop; in fact, for the past six months the only item on the

303

shelves had been an Exit sign, a mystery nobody felt like unravelling. And, since tobacco was not grown by the *kolkhoz*, only privately, there was no way of obtaining it except by private sale, and it was rarely available even to the 'wealthy'.

He let me go on. Whether the story, the *plotski*, my charm or plain boredom finally got around him, I don't know, but eventually he nodded. 'Soon as the rye's finished. Shouldn't be long. Perhaps you'd better not hang about here. Where is it, *vot*? I'll get it. You can go over to my house and wait.' I think he had been on my side all along.

Even if there were a clean place to sit, I could not have sat still, so I began moving things, cleaning, tidying. The place was a mess, covered in sawdust, shavings, and fine white dust from the mill. He did his woodwork in the cabin. The bench he used for planing and sawing also served as a table. Even the bed was coated. A couple of spots at the bench had been cleared for eating, the remains of past meals showing as irregular lumps under the drifting deposit.

A broom turned up in a corner, so I swept. A stinking cloth that could not have been used in months emerged somewhere else, with a bucket, and the stream was just outside the door. It was somehow reassuring to create order out of chaos, soothing to be occupied, satisfying to see a result. I had just decided I had had enough, when I heard his cheerful nag.

'Where the devil are you? Come on, the grain's finished. Good stuff, too; where'd you get it? I can't stop the mill to wait for you.'

He stopped short at the door and broke into a grin. I had dropped on a stool at his bench. '*Ladna*, you've done a good job here.' His bird's eyes took it all in. 'I thought perhaps you were asleep.'

'Not far off it.' Indeed I was suddenly weary.

'Come into the mill.' He slapped my behind as I went past. 'Here you are. If you want any more done, just bring it to me. But come at the right time. You've been lucky today.'

He didn't know the half of it. I could still hear sleigh bells. 'What do you call the right time?' I asked, automatically. I doubted I would ever do this again.

'Oh, depends. Come and check first.'

'I have no money.' I felt mean. I should have warned him. 'You'll have to take shares.' A percentage of the finished product was fairly normal procedure.

'What would I do with extra?' he said. The merry glint hardened. He scooped a couple of handfuls of *kolkhoz* flour out of a bin. I saw his point, suddenly remembering his unexplained criminal record, wondering what would come next. A criminal record in this perverse place was more likely in his favour than against; but he was a lively fellow, and there was obviously no woman around. I looked for a weapon.

He dumped the flour with mine. 'Keep it,' he barked. 'And don't worry, I was deported myself.' He mixed the new lot in with a stick, scowling, talking staccato all the while.'I've been to prison, too. I don't owe them anything. Not a thing. Other way round. No matter.' His good humour returned. 'Have the first loaf to my health. Hear me? Now, for the devil's sake go quickly and don't let your tongue wag to anyone. Hear? To anyone.'

■

Karpovna was home when I arrived. We had resolved not to conceal it from her, as flour forever hidden was not much use to anyone. Her eyes widened at the size of the load. I launched into my lengthy explanation – what I had traded for it, how much paid, where, why, when – all over again. No need to consult Vilma, she would approve. I was getting better at the fiction with experience, beginning to believe in it.

Wasted. She was interested only in the goods, not how we came by them.

'Beautiful flour! And so much of it! We'll bake bread tomorrow. Really first class. Lucky you! Where did you get – Never mind. Come on, let's cook some *lebjuschkas* now. So much!'

My legs were still unsteady, but watching the heap of little cakes vanish in front of us, seeing Vilma's surprise, Ivan's glee, Paul's look of contentment as he licked his fingers, had me telling Vilma the story of the day as a huge joke. I thought that her relief would match mine until, when Karpovna and Ivan were out at the cowshed, she showed the calibre of her nerves.

'Ann, look at this!' Her bra and pants disgorged three more little packets.

'My God, girl, you'll get us shot!'

'We may as well get fat first.'

■

Vilma accumulated another ten kilograms. 'And there's more where that came from.' One of our boys had to go to the Elisarovka mill. He offered to take the grain, for a share. Vilma demurred – 'Why? When a little effort saves us the percentage?' – but I delivered it to him gladly. 'Don't look at me for that "little effort"!'

Next day, I was alone in the cabin when the lad's sister came running. She had a note from their mother. 'Our house is being searched. Vilma's grain found. Had to tell whose. Hide everything, they're coming to you. Hurry!'

The boy had left his job in the forest without permission, the girl said breathlessly. Which was not so bad, except that he had been issued with a *kolkhoz* gun for hunting. Someone had noticed, reported him missing, and they were looking for the gun. Damn! What bad luck! I thanked the girl, who disappeared into the forest.

We had nothing left in the small bags, only the bulk grain, and I could not do much about that in the time. I knew Lia, only fifty metres away, did have some acquired small bags. Although I was in charge of Paul for the day, I decided to run over and warn Lia in case they called on her. I had barely got back to pick up Paul, when I saw them across the fields. Two men. There was nothing to do but sit inside and wait.

They burst in without knocking: one a policeman in uniform, the other a foreman from my *kolkhoz*, one of the less popular ones. The door banged back with a tremendous crash. I was on the cot, Paul on my lap, looking suitably surprised and frightened.

'Is there any grain here?' the *milits* demanded.

'No.' I looked bewildered. 'I don't think so.'

'You don't have any? We'll find it if there is!'

'No. Not here, that is. I bought some for Vilma – '

'Who's Vilma?'

'My room-mate.' I looked at the foreman. The policeman also looked at him. The foreman nodded. 'She's given it to someone to be milled.'

'Who?'

'One of the boys, I think.'

The *milits* was stamping through the small building, throwing things about. 'Hey, look!' he yelled, pulling a half *konn* of wheat from behind the landlady's cot. I had not known what to do with it, deciding to leave it where it was, covered by her sheepskin coat.

'So you don't have any!'

'It's not mine.'

'What's this here, eh?'

'It belongs to our landlady.' She did get a legitimate ration. I hoped they wouldn't check with her. 'There's more spread out to dry on the oven, too.' They would see it anyway.

The two picked up grain from both places, studied it on the palms of their hands, crushed and smelled it. I hoped Karpovna would not be cross with me.

'This isn't it!' the *milits* exclaimed.

The foreman agreed. 'Nothing like.'

This was a puzzle. That on the oven was ours; Karpovna's was a mixture, mostly her own stock.

'Where is it?' the *milits* demanded. 'The golden stuff.'

'I told you. All we had has been taken to be milled.'

'Come on now, the rest of it!'

'There is no more.'

'Where did you get it?'

'It isn't mine. It's my landlady's.'

'Not this, stupid. The other!'

'I bought it.' My standard story would not do here, but I could think of no other. I went through it, padding here and there with a bit of extra confusion, thankful for the practice, until they told me to shut up.

'We'll see about that!'

They were intent on finding more grain, seemingly too much so to waste time on questions. Yet, there was something sly about that last retort, as though the *milits* had a card up his sleeve. They searched the room, the cellar, the cowshed, the edge of the forest. They shifted my legs to look under Paul's cot, they shifted the cot itself, but, with the child crying loudly on my knee, they did not disturb us further. Nor did I try to stop his wailing, merely bouncing him harder whenever one of them came near for, sewn into the mattress I sat on, were flattened flour bags. It was their daytime hiding place. At night we took them out from the straw, in case Paul wet his bed.

'If I knew what you were looking for – '

'We'll find it.'

'Sorry I can't help.'

'You may be more sorry, yet.'

'Shush, Paul.'

'Nine o'clock tonight, you report to *militsia*. That Vilma too.'

∎

Lia came, crying. All the small bags she had brought from Udarnik had been put into bigger ones. All these, except one, had been hidden in the woods. That one, she had rushed out and put under the manure heap in the yard when I had given her the warning. And though the warning had prepared her, the result was the same. Fresh footprints in the snow had made finding the bag a certainty.

'Oh, oh! What am I to do?'

'Think yourself lucky they didn't get the others.'

'What will they do to me?'

It was not a time for reproach, but Lia's lamenting got under my skin. 'What are you wailing for? You've been naive enough to get caught before, silly enough not to have learnt. This time it's not the *kolkhoz* office, it's the *militsia*. You know what that means! Oh, go on home, Lia. We'll let you know if we think of something.'

∎

What on earth had he meant by 'not it'? And the 'golden stuff'?

Someone must know, and it worried me, but whom to ask? In the meantime, the meeting at nine o'clock . . .

Ivan came home from school. Tentatively, I told him of my visit. He just laughed. It had happened before. 'Not to worry. They do that at the drop of a hat.'

Vilma arrived later. She, too, was laughing, explaining why before I could close my astonished mouth.

'They searched everybody as we were leaving the *tatschok*,' she said merrily. 'We'd had plenty of warning' – the grapevine had been working overtime today – 'so no-one had anything on them. You should have heard the squeals! It finished up like a circus. I've even had a man's hand on my breast – right here, like this – first time in a couple of years!'

Everybody seemed to be laughing or crying. I was in no mood

308

to tolerate either. Tersely, I told Vilma of the day's events on the home front, and felt instant guilt to see her levity plummet to depression. In the discussion that followed, she had half an answer to one puzzle. She knew Red May was the only local kolkhoz to grow '*Golden Wheat*', and our milled spoils had come from Red May. Clearly the grain they had examined was 'not it'. Was it our big bag they were tracking? The flour in Paul's cot? Otherwise, we had only the worry of the nine o'clock summons.

Only!

■

Mrs Ivanovna, a Russian-born Estonian from Narva, had had a reputation in Estonia as a shrewd businesswoman. She was the fount of wisdom, always managing to know a little more, a little earlier, than anyone else, which disturbed me in this place, instead of simply irritating me, as it had done at home. With anyone who collected and distributed intelligence as she did, there could well be a catch. I wanted neither a positive nor a negative balance in her book.

Now, I was desperate enough not to mind being beholden. In my heart, I believed she was trustworthy, so I decided to take others' advice and consult her.

She offered a cup of syrup – she knew how to run her affairs, all right! – and listened attentively. Sharp-faced, steady-eyed, intelligent, she had me concentrating on telling a coherent story, and heard it through.

'You were unlucky the boy was caught with that stuff on him.'

'It was the gun.'

'Now you must keep calm,' she said. 'And listen.'

Her confidence worked wonders. It was what I needed.

'Tell the *milits* you bought the grain from a young Ostiak.' I listened as I was told. Her self-assurance was remarkable, if not endearing. I could never like her, and had no trouble holding my tongue. She clearly expected no interruptions. 'On the road, near the hospital. He is quite young, about twenty-five. You paid a hundred roubles, and you received a loaf of bread, five eggs and a piece of meat, as well as ten kilograms of wheat. Remember that. Ten kilos, one loaf, five eggs and a hunk of meat. That is

309

the black market price. You see, it was golden wheat you were trying to mill. There's precious little of it, and they knew that at least a bag was missing. Now, there are only two places anywhere near here that it's grown. One is Red May, where yours came from – '

'But they said it wasn't!'

'Don't believe them.'

'They're trying to trap us?'

' – and the other is Uvaal, where some of the Ostiaks are allowed to grow it. Well-established *kolkhoz*. Not too far away. They do sometimes sell it around here. I know, I've had some myself.'

My heart was lighter already. The enemy was not the jump in front he thought he was.

'All right so far?'

'I bought our wheat from an Ostiak.'

'Right.'

'I've never seen an Ostiak,' I said. Not a young one, anyway. 'What does he look like?'

'Well, if you're questioned, say he's young. About twenty-five. Fairly tall and slim. Sunburnt. Very dark hair and eyes. Wearing knee high deerskin boots, fur outside, tied under the knees with *lunts*, and a fur hat.' *Lunts* are strips of hide.

'Good.' I was thinking clearly again. 'Does he wear a *fufaika*?'

'A *fufaika* and quilted trousers. He actually lives in Uvaal. Don't forget that. Uvaal. It's an Ostiak *kolkhoz*, and it's about twenty-five kilometres from here. He has promised to bring you some deer meat, next time.'

'Thank you.' I could have said more.

'No need. Don't come back here. I'll hear how you get on. And don't let them find that flour; they'd know you had more than ten kilograms, and you'd be in trouble. You'd better hurry now to drill your friend. There's not much time.'

I had Vilma repeat the story on the way to the office. 'For God's sake, whatever the pressure, we must not differ. You can afford to be a bit vague, you only heard about him, remember. I did the buying. You were working. I met him when I went to the hospital that day.'

■

'Would you know him if you saw him?' asked the commandant.

I felt that I had told my story with conviction. The Ostiak from Uvaal had impressed him. He could see no possibility of my inventing a story to cover the secret of Golden Wheat.

'From any distance.' I was firm about it, even enthusiastic. 'He is the first Ostiak I've ever seen. I couldn't mistake him. He was – '

'Never mind.'

Vilma had been in the other room with the milits. We came out at the same time.

Without further word, we were handed back our little bags, empty. I looked, swore, felt unreasonably indignant, but finally decided not to press our luck.

Lia also, interrogated in the same session, came out well. Her landlady had told the inquisitors she had given Lia a bag of wheat in exchange for her tenant's red printed silk scarf, which came as a complete surprise to Lia. Everybody knew the scarf. It had been the envy of all the Russian women since we had arrived. The landlady now flashed it unashamedly. Lia's grain was of the ordinary kind, so no further questions were asked, not even why she had pushed it under the manure. The scarf was almost certainly unnecessary.

■

The wolves were sated once more, albeit with our grain and scarf; and the lambs – though shaken – still breathing.

24

DESJATIDVORNIKS

Threshing had finished so early this year in Udarnik that we had won the *kolkhoz* competition. Little changed, except that the end-of-season celebration was more elaborate than usual; there was more meat in the pea soup, possibly milk to go with it. To commandant, director, and foreman, it meant commendation from somewhere above. To the Russians it meant 'holiday'. To us it meant we had been pushed harder, and were more tired, and with no work we received no daily rations.

The early snow had given us a welcome break, nevertheless. Now, with the thaw, there was a rush of cleaning-up to do before real winter gripped. We were sent to the turnip fields to rake tops for winter feed; into the forest to burn twigs and gather briar berries for the State quota; and out in the marsh to pull up moss, a source of winter vitamins for sheep and cows. All for three hundred grams of flour a day, plus the odd few berries and stray turnip we could stuff into mouth or clothing.

Vilma and I even looked forward to the cold change. The strain of preparing for it had been wearing, but as a result of our labours and good luck, there were potatoes in the cellar, cranberries in the loft, and a big bag of flour under a loose floor-board beneath Paul's cot. We had changed its hiding place, not telling the landlady, raiding it in secret and sharing like true Christians.

I had helped pick Karpovna's potatoes, as pledged. Now, for my supper, I had to help sort them in the outside cellar by the light of a *peer*, a burning sliver of wood. They were the seed potatoes. The eating potatoes went under the hut, into the inside cellar, where they were within reach.

The outside storage had been dug out of the earth many years ago, roughly lined, and ceiled with timbers except for a crude trapdoor in the middle. It was dry and relatively clean, its previously exposed roof now covered with twenty centimetres of manure and turf for insulation. It was hidden from passing view except for the trapdoor – which, though covered, stayed propped open a few centimetres – and a length of piping, which stuck out at an angle from one corner. Karpovna called this the breathing tube. When the frosts came, she would close and cover the door, and stuff the end of the tube with hemp, sealing it with clay. When the weather was warmer, she would scratch the end of the tube out from beneath the snow, and unseal it. Her marvellous industry would be rewarded. We had seen the trouble some households had in the spring last year; the top layers were frozen but the bottom ones had gone sweet.

■

The temperature dropped and the ground froze. A thick layer of snow fell, and the thermometer showed a steady $-15°$ to $-25°$. The frost cracked. Karpovna crossed herself. '*Vot*, winter won't stay in the sky this year,' she said cheerfully. There was no fear of the seed rotting by spring. Even I knew that much now. It would have been a different story if the surface hadn't frozen before heavy snows.

Vilma's job was 'winding' the grain. She was not sorry that Red May was late this year; she brought home her last bosomful of grains 'for Paul to strengthen his teeth on' almost a week after Udarnik's feast. We enjoyed our first few days in the warm hut, washing, delousing, cleaning and taking stock of depleted wardrobes. A lot of clothes had gone the bread road. Acquired threads of wool and cotton, strips of fur and hide, pieces of *kolkhoz* materials, bits of soap, fish-bone needles, put-away scraps and worn-out garments came to light. Summer had seen us prepare for winter. By the end of winter, we should be ready for summer.

I must stop myself from thinking along such negative lines. I must think more of going home – and believe in it.

■

'Come to the office.'

A runner from the office, a Russian girl. She looked friendly enough.

'All of us?'

'Just Njura.'

'Why?'

'Do you know the Lageda family?'

'Not well.' They were some distance out of Udarnik. 'What's happened?'

'Come to the office. You'll hear.'

'I'd better go, I suppose.' I certainly did not want to.

The *milits* was behind the desk. I'd been seeing too much of him lately. The bookkeeper and one of the foremen were with him, looking unpleasant, perhaps more than usually so. There were nine or ten Estonians as well, not the Russian-speakers this time. Puzzling: I could not make out a unifying factor.

The questioning centred on Malle Lageda, her son Endel, and friends of hers, Olga Groskova and her daughter Ljuba, none of whom were present. That was a relief, as it quickly became apparent that their absence was the point of the meeting and, knowing little about them, there was no possibility of trouble for me. I felt almost light-hearted when it came to my turn.

'When did you last see them?'

'I've never met them. The Groskovas, anyway.'

'You've seen them?'

'Why?'

'I ask the questions.'

'What do you want to know?'

'Where have they gone?'

'Perhaps they're out picking berries.'

'You be careful! Don't try and be funny.'

'What's funny? What's it all about?'

'They wouldn't be out all night picking berries, stupid.'

It was serious, then. The two women had been constant companions, and all their luggage had gone from the hut they shared; since yesterday, someone said. We could talk more or less freely in our own language while the questioning went on. If anyone knew more, she was not saying, even to other Estonians. The four had last been seen early yesterday.

'We know your lot go on shopping trips. You, especially.' Back to me. 'Did you send them off? Which way did they go?'

'Perhaps north?'

'Why north?'

315

'Or maybe south?'

He tired of my help, tried the others in turn, lectured us on cooperation, shouted a bit and then dismissed us.

■

'They've escaped,' said Ivan with certainty. He did not mince words, nor did he seem at all excited about it.

'Nonsense, Vanja,' answered Vilma. She was happy at my safe return. If I had been detained, she would have had good cause to worry – for both of us. She was inclined to brush off the Lagedas. 'They've gone on a buy-and-sell trip, that's all. Good luck to them.'

'With all their belongings?'

'They've parked them somewhere.'

'No, they've escaped.' Ivan had heard about the disappearance earlier in the day. 'Plenty have done it before, but they get them all. They'll soon be back,' he assured us.

■

Vanja proved right. They were back within forty-eight hours, caught on the edge of the marsh. I think it was Kargaja who had followed and found them.

The planning had been good. Last summer, they had hired a man with a horse and sleigh from Schmarkovka, twenty-five kilometres away. From there, it was forty kilometres to the railway across the now-freezing marsh. They would have made it if they had hurried – even boarding the train had been arranged – but they had not been prepared to part with enough goods. They were overloaded, too inexperienced with their borrowed sledge, therefore too slow, and had been caught.

Surprisingly, there was no punishment, not even a harangue. Apart from reasonably good-natured jeering from the locals at their simple-mindedness, both families were not a whit worse off; they had not even paid the agreed three hundred roubles to the man in Schmarkovka.

Another surprise. The inquiry stopped as soon as the escapees were caught. Since that was before they had contacted the man with the horse, it seemed that nobody was bothering about him. This was knowledge worth storing: presumably he was still open for business.

My contact, I had heard, had died in the summer.

∎

A couple of weeks into winter we were bored. We got in Karpovna's and each other's way, moving about restlessly. Conversation exhausted itself in brief spurts, subsiding into moody silences. Paul was the only contented one. He sat on his cot nibbling wheat in his front teeth like a squirrel, one hand moving down and up in slow rhythm, a grain at a time, dull eyes following his mother's aimless wanderings as if pulled by strings.

Vilma was sporadically reading *Narta and Maria* for the fourth or fifth time. It was the only book we had between us, stuffed brand new into the parcel my mother had brought to the carriage in Rakvere. I knew it by heart and was sick of it, having read it even more times than Vilma, and recited it more again in the dark to Karpovna. I could quote it by the page, even now, though the author's name is long since forgotten.

Ivan was about to go out. 'Could I help, Vanja?' I asked suddenly. Lifting dying animals from traps did not appeal, but it would be better than this void.

'*Vot*, I'd take you with me,' he laughed, 'but you don't know how to walk in the forest. You'd frighten a squirrel straight up a tree.'

He was probably right: I had no hunting skills. The skins of squirrel, chipmunks and the occasional hare went to the office for the credit of workdays to him. He would rather hunt alone.

'Well, you could at least bring a carcase or two home for us.'

'What, squirrel?'

'If you can't bring a hare.'

'And if I can't – ?'

'Why not?'

'You're serious?'

'We'll give it a try.'

∎

They looked like skinned rats. Vilma and I avoided looking at each other and gingerly picked up one stiff little body each. We could hardly back down, what with Vanja grinning and holding us to our rash promise.

'How will you cook them?' he challenged.

317

'Anything to boil them with?'

'Only one thing.'

'What?'

'You'll need plenty of it. And to eat them, you'll need more.'

'All right. What?'

'Determination!'

Too true. There was no salt to spare, let alone herbs or spices. We ate them with potatoes, cautiously at first, as stomachs tried to revolt – the meat, if returned, would have been no great loss: we hated to waste an accompanying potato – later almost with relish. Our noses uncrinkled slowly as our palates adapted. There was just one thing –

'Ann?'

'I know. It's like eating a pet cat.'

'The devil will eat heavenly oats if he's hungry enough.'

■

Another runner, another meeting. Although all misdeeds had been accounted for, we suffered customary apprehension at the command. This time there were twelve of us. Which twelve? We made a quick, practised appraisal. To determine the reason for a summons might be to prepare a defence. Ah! All Russian-speakers. Good. We unbent a little. Now, we could calmly await the commandant, who might be anything up to three hours late. He liked to remind us who was boss. Today, it did not matter. This selection meant there was merely some general order to be broadcast to everybody. Not selective.

Alma was there. She worked in the office now. 'An NKVD man came and gave the order,' she said. 'One I've never seen before.'

Pavel Apraskin, the bookkeeper, had arranged the office job for her. After some uncomfortable shuffling Alma had confided the terms to me. 'Ann, I wanted you to know, but nobody else.' I had promised not to tell. 'It's not entirely cold-blooded, Ann. I like him. He's a nice man. And – well – he *is* a man . . .'

Undoubtedly he had been quite reasonable to us at most times: my only quarrels with him were probably of my own making. 'Don't worry, Alma dear. As far as the others are concerned, it's handy you're experienced at bookkeeping; you're a logical choice.' Clever Apraskin: bread buttered both sides! Alma had been the very competent manager of her husband's hotel.

'And he's a deportee, after all.' He had come as a child. I suddenly pictured him as a normal accountant or banker, with a normal intelligent wife, in a normal Ukrainian town. Is this what our young ones, plucked away and dumped here, are headed for? I was doubly glad mine – and Alma's: she had left a boy behind – were not with us. 'Don't worry. Just watch Dusja, she's rocky: she could get you both in hot water.'

The room was warm, with the oven going nicely. Several benches had been arranged around the centre table. More formal than usual: was that significant?

Kalesnikov and a stranger accompanied the commandant, who was on time today, or unusually close to it. The stranger took our attention. He was one of Them. We fell silent, our early relief evaporating. He did all the talking, oily goodwill oozing out of every pore, word and gesture, everywhere except the NKVD eyes.

What was our life like? Was it hard? Were we well paid? Were our living quarters all right? Did we have complaints?

Not perturbed by our silence, as he was not really asking questions, he went on to praise the members of Udarnik for their splendid work. We waited like wooden dolls.

'*Vot*, we have decided to appoint in each *kolkhoz* three *desjatidvorniks*.' A *desjatidvornik* is a monitor or caretaker of ten people. 'A job of honour.' Which meant no bread. 'It will be their duty to check a list of all deported persons every morning and report their whereabouts to the office.'

The Lagedas had been gone a whole day before they were reported missing. Someone had been doing some thinking in the NKVD, and that always meant fresh orders, more restrictions, greater hardship for us at the bottom. The job would be hard, tramping daily through snow to widely spaced cabins in the bitter cold.

'You have all been appointed.' He smiled for us in our good fortune.

The NKVD man was in such good humour that Ronald, the only man in the group, requested news of the men who had started out with us. Ronald Mirt, eighteen, was here with his mother and sixteen-year-old brother. On the occasions the question had been asked before, there had never been anything but evasive answers. We expected no more now, a year and a half since our separation.

'Why not?' he smiled. 'As it happens, I have their papers with me. Just ask!'

A swift buzz of excitement was followed by a moment of fearful silence. Then someone sharply cried out a name.

'Well – and working.'

Name after name was called. He looked up and down the list, with obliging patience and application, stopping somewhere with his pen at each call.

'Alive and well.'

After Lehtmets – 'Well, and working' – I asked about Mikael: Lembit Mikael, husband and father of my erstwhile room-mates.

'Well – and working.'

Mr Mikael had been dying of cancer at the time of his arrest. With the best care in the world, his family had been informed, he could not possibly have lasted three months.

Nevertheless, such are the embers of human optimism, that a puff of the foulest air can stir a glow. Not one of us believed him. But maybe . . .

■

Christmas Eve again. A small tree – leftover symbol of capitalist degeneracy and a crime against the State – with a mutton-fat candle made by Karpovna on top; a meagre feast; a quiet 'Silent Night'. Just Vilma and I and an emotional Karpovna, after Ivan was asleep. A long night of tears, heartache and despair.

25

THE BEAR'S DEN

W ould there be no end? This time the summons came at midnight. I even had to put my signature to the commandant's 'invitation'.

Icicles, shining in the light of a pale full moon, hung from ledges and eaves. The cutting frost slashed at my hands, face and feet. The cold forced its way to my bones, and blood slowed almost to a stop in my vessels.

There was nothing frivolous about this one. A personal subpoena, for me alone. Had somebody told?

■

I had read all sorts of crime fiction in my schooldays: Sherlock Holmes, Pinkerton, Nick Carter, Edgar Wallace. They were my only guides to behaviour under pressure. I had been caught and I was about to be interrogated. I had no doubt of it. I decided that, above all, I must keep calm, weigh each word, answer carefully.

It seemed unlikely that one of ours would tattle, but you never knew how people would react, even in response to what you thought was right. For instance, there had been Mrs Mikael's reaction when I had told her of the NKVD man's report about her husband.

'So now you're a communist messenger!' she had snapped. She had never really trusted me, it seemed. 'You're no longer welcome here – spy!' She had slammed the door in my face.

It had blown over. Her son had come to apologise for her, and I had been asked to join them for Christmas dinner. But there might be others. If she could think that, even in her wildest moment, what about some who knew me less well? Was there some unknown favour-currier?

What else? The *desjatidvornik* business was all I could think of; as far as I knew, I had committed no other crime. Not one to warrant a signed summons. We had been given our rounds, and found them near impossible. Every day, to do our 'job of honour' properly, we would have had to plough kilometres through snow and cold to tick off names of people who could not possibly leave their cabins even if they had wanted to. I – and most of the others – had simply gone to the office with the lists marked all present. A punishable offence, naturally. But who would tell? Had some crazy one tried to escape, like the Lagedas? Had someone not been home? Or, did we simply have one among us sunk low enough to inform?

■

I approached the corner of the Bear's Den. Kersti, one of our girls, was coming out, and she was crying. I slid back behind the corner and took her arm as she passed. It must be worse than I had thought.

'Kersti, what's happening? Why are you crying?'

'Oh, Mrs Lehtmets. You too! I'm sorry,' she whispered between sobs. 'It was awful! I'm sorry! But I mustn't talk, they said they'd – Oh, go in. Go. And be braver than I was. He's waiting.'

As she vanished like a sad little ghost into the pale night, I stood trembling before the door. I had no theory left now: she was not one of the monitors. A strip of yellow light showed under the door. 'Be braver,' she had said. Not a sound was left in the world but Kersti's haunting cry.

The door opened immediately at my knock. I jumped as the light fell on me. Inside, as the pupils of my eyes contracted to it, I could see only a man in black uniform. Another one: shiny hair, shiny boots, the smell of scented hair oil. The shine and smell of trouble.

'You are Anna Ljahmez. We will go into the other room.'

'Ann,' I corrected automatically. I insisted on the 'Ann'. I had long since given up trying on the surname.

'Follow.' He opened the door wider, locked it behind me, walked around the table and sat down. One chair on either side.

Nobody else in the room. I saw him more clearly: metal teeth, nondescript features, the expressionless eyes that were part of the uniform.

I made to sit down. The chair was hard and rickety. His was better.

'No. Take it further away. Three paces back.'

Fighting down a hot surge of anger, I compressed my lips, turned my back on him, measured three paces, and slowly placed the chair. Then I faced him, sitting with arms folded. How would Sherlock Holmes conduct himself?

'Anna Ljahmetz?'

'My name is Ann. A-N-N.'

They would *not* give my name the taint of Russia. I held my breath in case I had gone too far.

'Of no importance.' Wasted. 'Let us talk a little.' The smile was almost ingratiating. It did not become him. 'You speak Russian.'

'Yes.'

'And write?'

'I write it too.'

There was no gun. In all our accounts of interrogations back in Estonia there had always been one on the table. They had waved a gun at us on the night of our 'sentence'. I found him no less menacing without one. He lit a cigarette, then fixed his eyes on me without expression. 'You will write your life story. All of it.'

'All right.' Better than interrogation. I concentrated on ignoring the cigarette. It was poor stuff. It smelled heavenly.

'You will have it back in the *kolkhoz* office by tomorrow evening.' It would take a pretty fast pen! 'Is that understood?'

'Yes.' Something would have to be left out. What? What were they after? I wondered where it was to go, why it had to be written rather than told.

'Very well then.' He puffed, starting my olfactory nerves jangling again. 'Do you know anything about your husband?'

'No.' Other nerves joined in. 'Not since the train at Rakvere.'

He said nothing. I said nothing. I stopped breathing.

'That's all.'

All? After that?

I forced myself to breathe normally and look straight in front.

'You can go. Be back tomorrow night at twelve.'

I was not going to ask questions. *Kurat!* Lips shut tight over clenched teeth, I got up and left.

■

I sat exactly three paces from the table while he read my autobiography. He flipped from here to there, one sheet to another, smoking all the time. He's trying my nerves, I thought. Probably he can't even read. He was certainly not remotely interested in it.

I had begun composing the story on the way home last night: the trivia I thought they would want, the facts I thought they might already know. Schools. Addresses. Committees. Organisations – they'd love those. Guides – what about the nine-pin bowls? – cub scouts? Only the *Naiskodukaitse* seemed dangerous: the Women's Home Guard; I had been in charge of local recruiting campaigns for the two years before Occupation. It would be dangerous to put it in, but possibly more dangerous to omit it. How much did they know?

Vilma and Karpovna had been relieved when I had got back. They had been fearing much worse. Vanja had pen and ink, but no paper, so I had decided to go and see the 'oracle', Mrs Ivanovna, again the next evening. I could ask her advice, unlike Vilma or Karpovna; and she had paper, a good excuse for calling on her. She recommended that I say nothing about the Home Guard. If he should ask directly, she said, admit it and say you'd forgotten: they couldn't punish you for a bad memory. I had doubted that, but had accepted the advice, borrowed some paper – she had everything – and gone home to write.

He lit another cigarette. Would he never finish shuffling those damned papers? Another puff of smoke drifted over. I could stand it no longer.

'Will you give me a cigarette?'

He offered the packet with a smile. I had to rise to get to the table. I suppose he thinks I'm done for now, I thought. I took one as casually as I could. He lit it for me – like a human being! – and I sat down again, drawing deeply. It occurred to me, as it had done many times in the past twenty-four hours, that I still did not know why Kersti had been crying. He watched, with frank interest, as I inhaled.

'Are you a Jewess?'

'No.'

He seemed puzzled. 'Not?'

'No, I'm a smoker. An Estonian smoker. One who hasn't had a cigarette for months.' A little exaggeration wouldn't hurt. I was enjoying this one. As my nerves soaked up the soothing draught, I felt that I could cope with him. And he had helped my resistance, which was gratifying indeed.

'Why not?' he asked.

'*Why* not?' It seemed too silly to answer. Except that he was quite earnest. He just didn't know. 'Because there is no tobacco.'

'What else can't you get?'

'What do you mean?'

'Your living quarters. Do you have a good cabin?'

'Yes.'

'Where?'

Question after question on housing. How long? How much? How many? He evidently knew very little. Equally evidently, he could scarcely care less about the answers.

The flat, hard look came back in his eyes, despite the smile; preliminaries were almost over, I sensed, and my answers became shorter and wary.

'Where did you live before you came here?' How many rooms? What did your husband do? And you? Where did he work? Did you help him?

'And now?'

'I don't know where my husband is.'

'What work do you do here?'

'Whatever I'm told.'

'Is it hard?'

'Yes.'

'Do you work long hours?'

'Yes.'

'Why?'

Why! 'To get the five hundred grams of bread.'

'Is it good bread?'

'Quite good.'

'As good as you used to get in Estonia?'

'Different.'

'Do you always get it?'

'When we've earned it.'

'The storeman is honest?'

'As far as I know.'

'Is he always there?'

'Usually.' I had threatened many times to complain to the director about the storeman's slackness and piggish manner.

'Even when you come in late from the fields?'

'Sometimes not.'

'Do you get your bread in the morning, then?'

'I've never gone without.'

'Does he swear at you?'

'I haven't noticed.'

'And your brigadier?'

'Which one?'

'Skakalkin.'

Kargaja. The Jumper. My friend, whose foul language was a byword, whose face I had torn, who would still do me a dirty trick if he could. Was he behind this?

'What about him?'

'Is he hard on you?'

'Fairly.'

'And does he swear?'

'Perhaps. I don't know the language that well.'

He was trying hard to get a complaint. Well, keep on trying.

'Has anybody else treated you badly?'

'Not too badly.'

'Any of the other deportees?'

'I wouldn't know.'

'Well, you'll be here for some time yet,' he said off-handedly as he gathered papers. Maybe it was nearly ended, I thought. I became even more wary. 'Work a little longer and there may be a good job for you. You speak Russian well, and you know everybody. A good job with extra bread. Sugar. Wheat.' Pause. 'Cigarettes.'

'Thank you.' I kept the edge off my voice as best I could. 'You are very kind.'

'You understand? A special job.'

'I understand.'

'Think it over.'

'I am alone. I don't want much. I have everything I need.'

'Think it over, all the same.'

I didn't answer, beyond a half shrug of assent.

He lit one more cigarette, taking smoke in deeply with an air of intense satisfaction. Very unsubtle; very tantalising.

'I'll give you till tomorrow night. The same time.'

∎

'Have you given it thought?'

'I'm frozen.' I had not yet put my foot inside the door. 'Let me at least get into the warm room.'

Given it thought! I had wondered all the way home where lay the greatest insult. That I should consider becoming one of their agents? That I was thought so obtuse as to need it spelt out for me? Or that a spoonful of sugar and a few cigarettes could sway me?

I took my familiar chair without answering. Given thought? The only thought I needed was to keep my tongue from landing me in trouble. I would have to think of that constantly.

'Do you have friends?'

'Oh no, I'm a very quiet woman.'

'Do you go visiting your neighbours?'

'Seldom.'

'Or go to the communal quarters?'

'I stay at home.'

'With all those others?'

'If they are in.'

'How many in the house? Two women and their young. Apart from yourself.'

He made it sound like a farmyard.

'Yes,' I said.

'Isn't it crowded?'

'We get along very well.'

'And you don't talk?'

'A little.'

'A little? Women?'

'A little.'

'What about?'

'About families and – '

'And at work?'

'Oh yes. I work in the fields and – '

'And talk?'

'We talk sometimes. About our homeland, our children, schooldays – '

327

'Is that all?'

'And food.'

'Only that?' One word, cutting and angry.

'Yes.' Almost as sharp.

The show of politeness had worn thin.

'If your own room is what you want, you can have it. And everything else.'

He pushed over a sheet of paper and a pen. Still well out of reach.

'What is that?' I asked.

'A pledge of silence.'

I stood up to read what was on it. He turned the sheet over, printed side down, holding out the pen with the other hand. I remained standing, hands on the table.

'Sign here.' The blank side.

I took a deep breath. Something would happen soon.

'What's the matter?' He gestured impatiently with the pen. Spots of anger glowed on his cheeks. 'You don't want your own house?'

I shook my head, ignoring the proffered pen.

'Why not?' he shouted.

'I have no furniture.'

My patience was at an end, too. It must be nearly two o'clock in the morning, and I had hardly slept last night, thinking about this interview. I had been keyed up all day. Now, a climax was approaching. He no longer pretended. And Sherlock Holmes and Co. could help me no more. No use putting things off any longer. I must declare myself, and I must do it firmly, but reasonably civilly, or I might get myself deeper in trouble. I was in far enough as it was.

'Nor have I a man to get wood for the fire. I am better off sharing. I am not interested in my neighbours' doings, either. I prefer to stay where I am. Bigger houses are in the village. The edge of the forest is good enough for me. I like it there. It is warm in Karpovna's hut.'

The anger spots blazed. His jaw muscles moved in a furious spasm and a black furrow contracted his eyebrows. He was an animal. How could I ever have thought otherwise? A wild animal, eyes burning, metal teeth bared. He tore open the table drawer and pulled out a gun. 'You'll regret this!' he raved.

My eyes were glued to the weapon, my feet to the floor. He waved it about and beat the table with the butt – I flinched every time, half expecting it to go off in my direction – yelling curses and threats. I waited, paralysed. I wouldn't be the first to simply 'disappear'. What did they do? Shoot us on the spot and dispose of the bodies? Or send us off to die in some hell of a prison camp? For a moment, I felt detached enough to ponder the question.

The gun brought me back to earth. Was he going to fire? If I turned, he might miss. I waited too long.

He threw the gun back in the drawer and reached across the table. Before I could pull away, he grabbed my right hand and wrenched my wrist. A shock of pain ran up my arm. No time even to move. He dropped one hand and jerked at the other. The same pull, the same pain, and I was left staring down at two dislocated wrists. It was all over, and I was still too shocked to cry out.

Quieter but still cursing, he moved around to my side, opened the door, spun me towards it and shoved. I fell on my shoulder in the soft snow, holding my useless hands up out of further danger. They hurt in a numbed way. I tried: I could move my fingers. The door bolts snapped shut. The moon was strong enough to cast a shadow. Slowly, I rolled over, got to my knees, then my feet, finally walked, hands outstretched to the night. I held them high before me in triumph. The crooked black shadows danced grotesquely on the snow. I exulted at them. I think I was a little mad. I didn't sign your paper! And now, with these hands I could not sign if you could change my mind! Whose victory?

In the silence, in the frozen moonlight, I sobered as the pain increased. I knew I must get to the hospital. Home first, then the hospital.

■

I kicked at the door, elated but weak and cold. I could have dropped on the spot. I could have gone on for a hundred kilometres. Vilma came out and cried. Karpovna groaned. Between them, they bundled me inside.

'Get on the sled,' the landlady fussed. 'I'll pull you to the hospital.'

'No.' She could just as easily be pulling herself into trouble, which could only make more for me, too. 'But I'd like some warm clothes.' I was shivering. 'I must go by myself.' For a

329

reason beyond fathoming, it was important. It was part of my victory that I continue alone.

'Please,' Vilma said. 'I'll come with you.'

'No.'

Karpovna helped me into her sheepskin coat and made me change into her felt boots. Vilma, hurt by my rejection, stoically warmed Paul's milk and made me drink.

I knew where one of the first-aid nurses lived, more or less on the way to the hospital. I'd try her first. She was the one who did the tricks with the thermometer.

'Not here. She's on duty.' Bang!

I was not in great pain, but my hands were useless. Work, food, warmth, life itself depended on them. They *must* be put straight. I plunged on to the hospital. At least I didn't have a bullet in me. The hands would recover, provided I got treatment. It had better be quickly, that's all.

I would rather have seen her at home. This place made her official. She took a quick look, and I saw the hesitation in her eyes.

'Please,' I said.

She knew better than to ask the cause. To know would be to become involved. And I knew better than to volunteer explanation, as she would be obliged to report and get permission before attending me. My eyes held hers, and she nodded. It was understood.

She turned, and led me to a small room with the only bright light in the hospital. She had seen wrists like these before. Taking them in turn, she pulled and twisted while I bit on my lip, holding tight to consciousness, the heavy breath of the secret police between us and speech. Then she rubbed in some liniment, bound each joint with rags and splinted them with wooden slabs. I dried my eyes on my shoulders.

She switched off the light. 'Go now,' she whispered. Her first words. 'Don't use them for four or five days. Keep out of sight. Come again next week, same time, and have them re-bandaged.' It was close to dawn.

■

A week of pain – of being handled by Vilma, handfed, toileted like a baby – and they were much better. Only some weakness and swelling remained, puffing up after heavy work; and forever after a reliable ache at the first change of weather.

26

MRS BALTER

There were two good reasons for a *prasnik*. New Year's Eve and New Year's Day were major holidays. That was one reason. The other was the 'premium', the winning of the *kolkhoz* competition.

People in the office were planning on a grand scale. A yearling bull had been slaughtered, women were baking and cooking. A walk along the village roads surprised with all kinds of unaccustomed smells, sending the salivary glands into frenzy, making hands into fists of self-control. We were not included.

It would be the best *prasnik* for years. A couple of weeks late, but who worried about dates? A New Year was a New Year. A premium? – *a vot!* – why not combine the two?

The certificate hung proudly in the office above the director's desk, and there was an air almost of gaiety among staff and Russian callers. However, we deportees had no desire to view the document and clap each other's backs. We went to the office to talk about food rations, work credits, the promised pay for our year's work. And, as we had not been invited to celebrate the premium we made a point of ignoring the certificate – to irritate the Russians, of course, which it did very satisfactorily – just as we were ignored in our claims for food and invitations to the *prasnik*.

Dusja made us feel better about missing the feast. 'You should have seen the place after the last one,' she said glumly. 'It looked like a brothel. There was spilt *braschka* – beer – all over the tables, and the floor was littered with scraps, bones and *schweinerei*. Tchah! The steps were slippery with vomit. Half the men had black eyes or bloody noses, and some of the ladies – huh! ladies! – were missing tufts of hair.'

She shook her head slowly. 'A real good feast though. Eating. Drinking. You never saw so much. Then the fights.'

'Is that usual? Fighting?'

'Never known it otherwise. But last year . . .'

'What about?'

'*Vot*, the men over the women, women over the men. They're always the first ones, the small fights.'

'And the big ones?'

'*Vot*, over the year's totals!'

Let them have their *prasnik*.

■

Our Karpovna was one of the cooks in her own *kolkhoz*. No premium did not mean no New Year celebration. She brought home a couple of pies, a piece of meat and a half bucket of *braschka* from their New Year party, the food concealed under her jacket. The *braschka* was nearly black, brewed from burnt bread with hops and sugar. A devil's drink, tasting deceptively like sweet ale.

Karpovna would not join us in our private *prasnik*. 'You go ahead,' she said. 'I've had mine.'

'Why not another?'

'That stuff has a kick.'

'Estonians have hard heads and leather stomachs.'

'Good for them! For me, one's enough, thanks.'

'Remember we offered,' we sang.

'Make the most of it while I'm away.'

'You can be sure of that!'

Two mugs each of the *braschka*, and Vilma and I had frills on for the evening. Two brown holes in the snow and two thumping heads in the morning testified to the power of the brew.

■

In desperation, I asked Dusja when her husband was likely to return. It seemed that he was the only hope.

The bookkeeper had gone to Novo-Vasjugan with all his notes and the year's reports. The office files, for want of a better word, were a shambles. The girl assistant for most of the year was hopeless, the bookkeeper himself little better. None of them – bookkeepers, clerks, timekeepers, foremen – had any real education: therefore they had neither the wit nor the skill for convincing 'cooking' to cover their deficiencies. It was still midwinter and, without the books, the storekeeper was unco-operative. We went to the office many times: no documents. The director shrugged his shoulders: nothing to do with him. The girl could not even find my name on a pay sheet: not her fault. The storekeeper shook his head: no papers, no rations. Even Alma could not help without the bookkeeper's records, which was small consolation.

Dusja promptly burst into tears. 'I don't know,' she wailed. 'Devil take him,' she cursed through the flood. 'He's done it before, *vot*. He's got another wife in Novo-Vasjugan. I think she's even got a baby!'

I shot a glance at Alma. She was suddenly busy over a desk. Pavel Apraskin was more of a man than we'd thought. 'We're just beating our heads against a wall,' I muttered.

Eventually, he came back. The *kolkhozniks* lined up, one after the other, and went away with their bags of wheat, peas, flax, wool and roubles. A few arguments, but mostly they were satis-fied. Dusja was happy, the bookkeeper surly as, aside from any personal discontent at returning, he had probably been rapped over the knuckles in Novo-Vasjugan.

Then us. No wool, no hay, no flax, no money. We had 'eaten' it in advance. My total was seventeen kilograms of wheat and three of peas to last the rest of winter. Five months. I took it, too tired to argue. We were all in the same boat. Thank God for the reserves. And God help those who had none.

■

'Will you come with me to Malinovka?' Enn asked. 'I must get some more things for Mother.'

I wondered if Mrs Balter had held on to her money too long. We had made the trip earlier in winter, to visit Gerda and Eda and do some exchanging but, at her request, had bought little for her. She had starved herself, hoarding resources, mainly to keep something for Enn, many times giving readily to others. I was not the only one indebted to her. Now, she spent nearly all the day on her bed, too lethargic to care, too weak to refuse her son money that, a week or two ago, she would have.

'Yes, I'll come. Nothing to do here, and I've friends to see.'

■

Eda still lived on her oven. Her asthma was no better, she confessed, but she was busy learning office work, for the director had half-promised her a job in the *kolkhoz* office in spring. I hoped she would get it; she could not keep going on physical labour. It was becoming the regular thing to have an Estonian handling the bookwork. Eda felt that she was lucky. Not even strings attached, she said, that was how much they needed her.

■

Gerda lived in a warm house now. I sought her at the old lock-up in the potato field, but it was deserted. The friendly nightwatchman's wife directed me to the storeman's kitchen. 'I was asked to move in,' Gerda said, with all her old zest. Whether that meant an arrangement with the storeman, or an order from the director, to keep her from stealing potatoes, I did not know and thought it prudent not to ask. 'I tell fortunes from cards and palms and I have a job as the horseman's assistant. We won't get into trouble this summer.' She was irrepressible. 'My son will be the shepherd's offsider and I'll be groom,' she laughed.

'How did you manage it?'

'I didn't get much for my workdays, so I had to do something!' A neat sidestep. 'We've retired from the vegetable business, now we're in meat and transport. You must take life as it comes. Come on, have something to eat.'

'Potatoes?' I smiled.

'What else?'

'Silly of me to ask.'

'Next year, we won't have to crawl. Remember?'

How could I forget!

Gerda knew where to find us a hunter who was 'not all that wrapped up in the "State first" business'. Enn was a hundred roubles poorer as we scuffed our way home under parcels of bear's fat, butter, meat, bread and milk. We had not borrowed a sled as it would have invited requests, refusals, troubles.

I regretted that Vilma could not come with us. We could have done with help and she had wanted to come. But she was house-bound, and would be for the next couple of months, as she had no winter clothes. I must see to mine soon, too; the *tscherkis* were wearing thin, the *fufaika* and coat not thick enough.

■

Enn called again. This time, to ask if I could sit with his mother. He had to go carting logs, and the landlady had left a week ago on a two hundred and fifty-kilometre trek, with supplies for people working deep in the forest. The temperature was –42°. I went because I agreed she could not be left alone, and stayed two days and nights.

Mrs Balter wanted a companion more than a nurse. She wouldn't eat, drank reluctantly, refused attention. There was little I could do for her but listen. She talked of home, Enn, his father and older brother. They had both been taken. She talked between long pauses – sometimes so long that I thought she had slipped away – of the fragile hopes she had had for her family, of the ambitions that were dust, of a mother's secret lost dreams.

'Look after Enn when I'm gone, Ann,' she whispered after one of her silences. 'I know how much he thinks of you. Soon he will be the only one left.'

I could only hold her hand and look away. It was dark in the room, the thin light through the frosted window silhouetting a row of jars on the sill. Milk. Berries. One of butter.

'I had dreamed of having as much bread and milk as I could wish for.' She lifted a weak hand. 'Now I can only look at them.'

I could not contain my sobs, remembering how Mrs Balter had comforted me in the carriage, helped me since, and given me food and money when I needed it most. And I could do nothing to repay her.

'Don't cry. You were a good child to come, Ann. I wanted someone with me, to say all I had on my mind. I've said it now.' Her hand squeezed mine. The pressure was barely perceptible. 'I've left instructions for Enn to do what has to be done. Don't be too upset, I'm not afraid of death.' Her voice wavered for a moment. I thought we would break down together. 'Only I didn't want it to come here.'

There was nothing to be done but to fight back tears and hold her hand tighter. I felt that I would not hold it in life again.

'I am tired, dear. You must be, too. When Enn comes, go on home. Please come again in the morning.'

In the morning, Enn came to me. I was not needed. It was Sunday, which was appropriate.

■

There were no men and few tools. Those we had – an old pick and a spade – produced only jarred hands and a mocking ring from the frozen earth. We just had to get through the crust, however. Alma, Eha, Helga and I gathered twigs from the forest, acquired some wood from the kolkhoz stables, and began our long softening-up task. Fire was not to be wasted; so we warmed ourselves as well as the ground. Nor was effort to be wasted; we dug slowly, one at a time, through the ashes. The storeman from Eha's kolkhoz gave us a few potatoes, which we baked during the alternating defrost and scrape operation, relishing the extra sustenance despite our gloom.

By Saturday, we were down a metre, almost to unfrozen earth. The coffin was ready, and a few of the others free to lend a hand.

'Oh take me by the hand, my Lord.' Mrs Balter's own choice. The Lord's Prayer. The Estonian National Anthem. Recited silently, heads bowed: there were a couple of doubtful guests at the funeral.

■

Back in autumn, a few with special skills from the four Maisk *kolkhozes* were told to prepare to go to Novo-Vasjugan. Probably from other *kolkhozes*, too: there was Tiia, my very good friend of the *klopkas* – kegboards – who worked in Red May office now, and Elma, who had learned sewing and milli-nery at home. I had not applied, as I did not possess any skills.

While digging the grave, it turned out that Alma and Helga were going.

'But what qualifications do you have?' I could not keep envy out of my voice. When volunteers had been called, I was not dismayed at being ineligible as it skirted a problem: the devil or the deep blue? Who knew what awaited them there? Now, I sud-denly wished I were one of the travellers. Winter here was like living in a vacuum; I was fairly safe for the season, but safe only for existence, nothing more. No contact with any but the closest of neighbours. Now, with Mrs Balter gone, free of obligation in Maisk, it was worth taking a chance to get closer to life. A 'city' must have some heart, even here. Novo-Vasjugan: our Tallinn, Berlin, Paris, London. Eda and Gerda now had jobs, Alma had had one and was leaving it. I had nothing. I felt left behind, back-watered even in this back-water, and the urge to leave was suddenly strong.

'None,' Helga smiled. 'I'll see what it's like and line a nest for you if you wish.'

I wished. Vehemently.

'It's a promise, then,' she said.

She had had the remainder of her husband's clothes to exchange for provisions. Alma's reserves were low.

I helped them cut and dry slices of bread, and make frozen balls of mashed potato in preparation for their journey. We did a lot of talking while we worked; for my part, vacillating on whether or not I really envied them. I concluded positively that I did, and would snap up an opportunity to follow.

They were due to go in March, when the days were longer, before the thaw. I asked early for permission to go as far as Malinovka, to see them off and to pay another social and perhaps business call at the same time. It was granted.

'Your turn will come, Ann,' Alma said.

I believed it. 'We'll get you off first, then.' It was only a matter of time.

■

There was a little fresh snow on the track, a couple of centimetres only; good and slippery, firm under foot. It was a fine, cold morning, perfect for travelling. But the sleds still made hard work, with one pulling, one pushing. I was a spare, able to oscillate between the two main sleds, relieving on each in turn, first the one with the harness in front, then the one with the pole behind. Tiia and Elma took the lead sled and navigated. Tiia's son came next in the tiny caravan, with his own special miniature sled and harness, stepping out firmly behind his mother like a young foal. Helga and Alma, bringing up the rear, needed the most help. Theirs was the heaviest sled, laden with their own belongings

337

and most of the provisions for the journey: a bag of dried bread, a smaller one of frozen potato balls, a big bag of 'chips' – sliced and dried potato – and one of sliced frozen milk. A few extra edible treasures were concealed about their persons. Some further hoarded supplies had had to be eaten or converted to currency for fear of discovery and confiscation.

We used the winter track: it was shorter. In two or three places we could shorten it further by leaving the path through the forest – the same path we had cut as one of our early tasks – to go directly across the frozen marshes; doubly good, as it was not only a short route but a flat one. The hills were the real difficulty. None very high, all were Everests in our state of nutrition. Later in the trek, they were to become too much.

For footwear, the leaders had good warm sheepskin *tscherkis* with double soles. The lad had a pair of old felt boots cut down. What Alma and Helga wore, I did not know and didn't ask; all I could see were two pairs of lumpy feet covered in pieces of sacking tied with string. Every step looked hard work. I went from one to the other to give them a breather, wondering how they would make the hundred and fifty kilometres. I did not know the road beyond Malinovka, whether it was easier or harder than the twenty kilometres from Maisk. Probably much the same: tough. I did not feel like expending energy in discussion on it. And I did not know how familiar I would one day become with it.

■

When, eventually, I did cover the full distance – without a load, and in reasonable footwear – I marvelled at those four women and the boy. They had made it in seven days and nights, which I was to discover was a very good time. One section had a whole series of steep hills, up and down, for three kilometres. Bad enough without impediment, soul-destroying to do some hills twice, even thrice, a sled at a time, halving the load. And then, fifty kilometres before Novo-Vasjugan, where there had been a partial thaw, the runners would not glide through horse manure on the tracks; it was like pulling string through wax, they said. Alma and Helga had to leave their heavy bag of dried bread with some Estonians for safe-keeping; the weight was just too much. And later, when Alma took a boat back up river to collect it, it had gone. Eaten by the children, she was told. She went back empty-handed. No blame was laid. How could there be? Alma said later that they had been literally starving; the bread had been a gift of heaven. The reason? No ration cards had been issued to the whole area through a bookkeeping error, and their stored food had run out. They had had absolutely nothing. In this incredible system such an error might take years to counter, and no amount of commonsense or humanity could intervene; a deportee – or a hundred deportees – simply did not exist if there were no name on some bookkeeper's list. So the bread had gone.

■

We lived as if we were tied in a bag. A rare news item might come from someone travelling past, perhaps someone from hospital, where contact was made with people outside our collective. Even then, the horizon was only fractionally widened, the news remarkable for its triviality. Yet some form of postal connection must have existed, because the *kolkhoz* seniors received directives from somewhere. They seemed, however, not to get word of important events. If they did, they kept it to themselves. There were no newspapers and no radio; and, though the communicating sleigh came and went more or less regularly, no visitors. You would have thought the driver would be a source of information, but he never had more than a shrug and a surprised look that anything beyond a few kilometres away should interest anyone. He did not read, nor did he talk about things he did not understand, which imposed severe limits on his range of conversation.

'Almost feel I'd welcome a summons from the commandant,' Vilma grumbled, 'or summer would come and we could go to work.'

'They'll come soon enough. Both.'

I had had my trip to Malinovka to send the party off to Novo-Vasjugan. My erstwhile cub friend, Leo, and his family – mother Asta and brother Eric – had joined it there and gone on with it. I had said my goodbyes and done my visiting. Word for word, all details had faithfully been reported to Vilma. I had called again on Eda, whom Vilma knew. She still wheezed, and was down to little more than rags, but she had a job working as an 'apprentice' office girl, reckoning *kolkhozniks'* workdays. This was done at home, by pencil, on three-year-old newspapers, for seven kilograms of flour, paid in advance. She was happy. And Vilma was resentful.

339

'It's all right for you! Marching off as if you're on holidays. And Lia! Strutting around the neighbourhood like a peacock in her warm green trousers and her yellow boots. All she needs is a tail. But she won't come over here to chat with me. Oh no!' Her eyes flashed when she was excited. 'Tied down here. She knows I can't get over to her.'

'She'll come.'

'Now, even Eda's got a job.'

I would lend her some clothes when she got like that, and promise to mind Paul while she went off to visit some friends. She would take the whole day. It was worth it for the several days' peace that followed in the house.

On one of these days Vilma came back with real news. We had been waiting for word from Novo-Vasjugan, but none had come. Then, like a stroke of lightning through the Estonian population – via Vilma to me – flashed the report: Mrs Gayeva has had a letter from the men's camp! I did not know Mrs Gayeva well, seldom saw her. She worked with Vilma, with whose cooperation I managed to waylay the lady at the store, as the word was that Lehtmets had been named in the letter, and that hundreds of Estonians were with him.

Mrs Gayeva confirmed that this was so. However, she would not produce the letter and, to my mind, was oddly evasive about so astounding an event. The one thing she did volunteer, on my demand to see the missive, was that it was not in her husband's handwriting. My only conclusion was that, possibly with her acquiescence (she was desperate for food for her two children), the whole thing was a fraud to boost our morale and hence our work potential; else, I reasoned, why mention the handwriting? She could not freely admit to deception, or her own head was on the block, but her admission and her lack of enthusiasm about the whole event were intended to convey this message. We decided to accept it as such – quietly, to avoid trouble for Mrs Gayeva.

27

THE CONCERT

A love of music and dancing is one of few traits common to all Soviet citizens; free or slave, from the Arctic to the Caucasus, from Mongolia to Europe, the scores of cultures embraced share an age-old passion for their traditional songs and dances.

Ronald Mirt had his accordion. As the freeze relaxed, he would take it to the office in the evenings. Melodies from opera and operetta, popular songs and folk tunes attracted us there as soon as we were able to get out and about freely. He was versatile: Estonian songs vied with the old Russian romances, favourites with locals and deportees alike.

We gathered in the office to talk. Sometimes we would sing. The Russians were also out of hibernation, having meetings, making plans for the May Day celebrations. The music drew them to the office, too. After the recent 'work victory', this year's May Day was going to be particularly lavish, with great ideas about eating and drinking through the night, which happened to be a Saturday. We had no part in the discussions, but they made no secret of them. They would finish their business, shout requests to Ronald, sing their own songs, listen to ours, and talk freely about the coming feast. We even got to singing in each others' language, which came as something of a surprise. The evenings were easily our most convivial so far.

One night, it was made clear that their plans were strictly for Russians only. No Estonians at the May Day party.

'What?'

'*Nyet.*'

'Why, didn't we put in our share to the work victory?'

'*Nyet.*'

'You couldn't have done it without us!'

'Regular *kolkhozniks* only.'

'What do you call us?'

'Bloody foreigners.'

Incensed, we stopped going to the office.

■

Ronald came by within a couple of days. 'There's a meeting in my quarters tomorrow.'

'What about?'

'Tell you when you get there. Eight o'clock.'

■

'A concert?' we howled as one. 'For them?'

'On Saturday night, May the first.'

'Their May Day celebration? You're not serious!'

'Very.'

'And we're not even invited to the party! You tell them what they can do with their concert!'

Ronald was embarrassed. There were fifteen of us, all women, mostly of the younger group. Only Mrs Tareke and Mrs Vosu represented the *babushka* brigade. They were the most vehement of all, very explicit, if crude, about where that concert could be put.

'Well, actually, the director had asked me before we found out about that,' he said.

'Too bad.'

'And I agreed.'

'Well, now you can damn well disagree.' Hell hath no fury . . . and there were fifteen . . .

'Well – really – he didn't so much ask me. It was practically an order.'

'Well, we'll order you to put the accordion where you put the rest of the concert. The director can then play his own music.'

Ronald was a good musician. Though quailing before fifteen angry women, he showed he was an even better talker. 'Listen. Just for a minute. You say how can we have a party, let alone perform for a concert – especially for Russians – when you're all starving – when every one of you has a husband or son, father or brother, also starving – in a slave camp – or dying – or dead.' We were listening. Yes, that is just what we are saying . . . Very firmly, we are saying. And will keep on saying . . . 'I have a father there, too. I understand how you feel. And I try and understand how *they* would feel. Do you think they would condemn us if we created a little diversion – for ourselves, for others – in this hard life we have of our own?'

We shouted a bit, but had no real answers.

'My father wouldn't,' he went on. 'I know he wouldn't. He would think the same as I. And I believe your relatives would, too. Give it thought, as I have. Moping and complaining doesn't make things easier. We're all witness to that. Getting on our high horses won't either.'

'But for *them* – '

'If director Kalesnikov was tactless – if his wish seemed more of an order – don't be too hard on him . . .'

'We hard on him? Now you *must* be pulling our legs!'

'He has been a just boss. You know that. He's much fairer than a lot of others we've heard about. You can't expect royal manners out here in Siberia. He was deported here himself – '

'He must have forgotten.'

Dear Jesus! Once a deportee, now a director . . . Could we – could an Estonian – finish up like that? If we were here half a lifetime? Become part of the system?

'He's grown up here. He's asking a favour of us, for the welfare of all.'

'All?'

'Everyone.'

We huddled. We were being logical, reasonable. I was one of many who could see no reason to change my mind. What nerve!

'I know,' Ronald said, 'that you wouldn't be influenced – in a matter of principle like this – by an extra ration of bread.'

We tried to ignore him.

'Mari Lohk-Lepik,' he added casually, 'has promised to help compose the program and teach the songs.'

'Really?' Mrs Vosu was impressed. Until now, she had kept her nose in the air, lips tight, ears shut, and slowly shaken her head in an unchangeable 'No.'

'Who's she?' one of the young women asked.

'She was music teacher at Narva High School,' said Ronald.

'A good one at that,' Mrs Vosu admitted. 'And popular.'

'A fine musician.'

'Well – ' She was wavering.

'She's going to do the translations as well,' Ronald added.

'She is a very dedicated patriot,' Mrs Vosu observed.

'You're sure?'

'Oh, absolutely.'

'Well – in that case – '

Within half an hour, we had almost put together a program.

'Just what,' Mrs Tareke then asked, 'did you mean by Mari doing translation?'

'Er – all items have to be in Russian.'

'Now wait – '

'I can't help it. It's their national holiday, after all.'

'Yes, but – '

'Russian language. Russian style,' he said firmly.

Cunning fellow! Said earlier, we might have vetoed the whole thing. By now, we were carried away.

'Russian-style, eh?' It was the pensive Mrs Vosu. 'Where do we get the shod louse?'

'Where else but from Tuula?' came the shouted chorus.

The burst of laughter settled all argument.

Two or three were puzzled.

'It's an old story. Of a Russian delegation invited to the English royal house. They had to take a gift. A truly Russian gift. "A samovar," one said, "from Tuula, where they make the best samovars in the world." "But the English don't use samovars," said another. "They're crazy about animals," one said, "the horse is the national idol. We should give a living present." "But our gift must be truly Russian," was the objection. "And it must be a technical achievement," said yet another, "to show our sophistication." So they nailed Tuula's shoes on a louse!'

■

Apart from Mari and Ronald, we had Narva's former *prima donna* in operetta, Marju Kadajas, and Ines Seppre, who had studied ballet for many years. Ines even had a tutu and toeshoes in her suitcase. When she produced them, I was reminded of seeing her in *Silva* at home. From the shadows, from this collection of Siberian criminals, emerged several lesser talents, particularly singers.

344

Ines and I decided to do a gipsy dance. Clothes would thus be no problem.

Kalesnikov, at a meeting, had promised two kilograms of bread for each artist.

'That's all right, then. We wouldn't dance for potatoes.'

'Why is that?'

We let him worry about it.

■

Days were lengthening. Though the cold still lingered in the mornings, and descended swiftly with the sun, the afternoons were warm and bright. The earth's surface softened, soaking up the last of the snow. Crop fields were already tinged green. The sky stayed blue to spite our concert preparations; an early spring meant extra work.

The first artistic benefits came. We were given easy tasks while the main work force trudged bitterly to the forest every day. No time off, right to the last minute, so there had to be another way of awarding the perks.

Even on the first of May, the very day of the performance, we had no holiday. The foreman, however, singled out Marju and me – the only two performers in his brigade – and led us to the edge of a large field. I felt vastly important. The concert was the most exciting *kolkhoz* event for years; the participants were entitled to bask in their moment of adulation.

'I'll be back after lunch,' he warned, 'to measure the area you've cleared.'

Where grain grew, so did weeds. Weeding was a long and thankless task, which none of us had ever done without accumulating a deficit of at least a day for every two worked. It would usually be far easier to take out the grain and leave the rest. Today, a surprise!

'You mean this field?'

'Measured after lunch.'

Only thistles, few and far between, and the odd lonely, yellow-flowering thing we knew as the 'curse of Rakvere'. The cleanest field I had seen.

Done local fashion – thorough cleaning of the strip near the road, removal of tall growth and visible flowers deeper in – we finished early. The rest of the time we lay on a gentle slope in the sunshine in sweet-smelling grass, listening to the singing of free-flying birds and the buzzing of insects. We talked little of home and husbands. Marju had no children.

'Well, finished, I see.'

We scrambled up.

'What have you done?'

Marju waved her hand in a majestic half-circle.

'Good girls. Well done! A whole workday! Go home and get ready for the concert.'

■

The big schoolhouse was full and overflowing. Karpovna and her son had been in the front row for a couple of hours: I had secured prize 'tickets' – there might be value in that favour some time – and she was not going to lose those seats. Her eyes, and Ivan's and a hundred others, I saw through the cracks, were fastened on the blanket curtains, as though they might at any moment fly off like magic carpets. We behind were cautiously optimistic. The dress rehearsal had been dismal, and Marju and Mari had assured us that that meant a successful performance. The director was there; foremen, storekeepers, office workers; wives, children; almost everybody. Not the commandant, I noticed; nor the executive committee man, nor the man in black. No party member, Ronald observed. Such notable absentees must be policy: applauding of the decadents was probably 'not permitted'.

The curtains were drawn. Marju drew long gasps as she stepped on the stage. I felt my own breath catch. Her pale blue and silver evening dress shimmered in the soft flickering light, a vision from another world. Her voice had lost something in its two years in the wilderness, and her Russian was far from good, but arias from *Silva* and *Countess Maritza* drew tremendous cheers. She lifted us out of Siberia, audience and players alike. We could not look back.

Ronald played medleys of Hungarian and Estonian tunes, arranged by Mari. A roaring success. Meeri, who had been a full-time student with operetta experience, sang romances in a mellow contralto to Ronald's accompaniment. Soft, full of feeling. She was a lively girl, dark, her Russian diction perfect; but she was singing to her own home land. Her *U Kamina* – 'By the Fireside' – had to be repeated. A Russian, but also a universal, favourite. They wanted it yet again, emotion charging the applause that shook the building.

Then it was my turn, and I was as much stirred by Meeri as any of the audience. The gipsy dance with Ines. I had never danced the part of a boy, but was not concerned about that. Ines was the main part and she was beautiful: naturally dark – dark hair, dark eyes, olive-skinned – and fortunately even smaller than I: she needed no props to be the perfect gipsy girl. She had a floral skirt that had been the lining of a quilt, a white blouse, beads around her neck, and a string of frozen rowan-berries threaded on cotton in her hair. My costume was a pair of half-mast pantaloons, borrowed from a Ukrainian boy, and a Ukrainian embroidered shirt. I had to tie up my blonde hair with a red kerchief, which went against the grain; but I found a red flag, and took great joy in ostentatiously tearing it up for the purpose. To further salve my patriotic conscience I buckled on Marju's Estonian belt. Charcoal for moustache and eyebrows, a few slaps on the cheeks, and my make-up was complete.

Our *czardas* went smoothly, until near the fiery end. It was too much for my much-repaired faithful brassiere. One strap gave up the ghost, and the unexpectedly freed breast joined in the jumping rhythm. Perhaps it was not too obvious, I thought desperately. There was nothing to do but 'go on' in the true tra-dition of the theatre . . . Can I turn my back? . . . Ines, stifling giggles, would not allow it.

Kihin (Lord help us, the only translation is 'titters'!) came from several spots in the darkened hall. At least, I thought des-perately, none but a few friends will recognise me. They won't laugh me off, they can be depended on.

Not long now . . . Ines kept a straight face.

Karpovna's excited voice floated up loud and clear from her vantage point. Oh Lord, why oh why did I get her those seats? 'Look, Vanja, look! It's not a boy at all! *Batjuschki*! – Dear father!' I faltered. She even called Stalin to witness! 'Look, it's *our Njura*!' she cried at the top of her voice, as bare feet pounded our climactic finish.

No producer could have done better. The half-time curtain jerked across, to cheers, applause, and laughter. Never remotely considered in the program, but oh! so rare and welcome.

■

After the heart-stir and release of the first half, the second was never in doubt. Morale, both sides of the curtain, was sky high. And we knew our best was to come.

For our Gipsy Camp we had permission to use live coals. Young firs and pines back-dropped the stage. Flickering 'juniors', behind and above, gave a beautiful moonlight effect. We sat by the fire, a pan of glowing charcoal surrounded by stones, while Gipsy Mother threw on an occasional twig to cause a momentary blaze of flame and a whiff of clean wood smoke. Ronald was the Old Man of Music, complete with beard, knee boots and kaftan adorned with a huge-buckled broad Estonian belt. Aita, one of the few dark-haired Estonians, led the singing, soloists and choir ending in *Black Eyes* with the whole audience participating. It had to be sung again. The dances, too, had calls for encores; but these had to be ignored. We were exhausted.

Finally, Ines danced her solo from *Silva*. Many remembered her in the same role at home. I had to steel myself to watch. Now, surprisingly, so far away, in such a setting, it was ecstasy to see her again. In her flowing, white costume she moved gracefully through the whole dance, face serene, body liquid, faultlessly executing the difficult *pas* on her toes, finishing in perfect balance. The stage and Russia dissolved. There was only Ines.

In the storm of clapping, stamping and shouting we worried about the schoolhouse roof.

28

ANNA DENISOVNA

'Njura! The office! In a hurry!'

That damned stranger, I thought immediately. I should have known better.

'What's it this time?' Vilma asked the messenger.

'How would I know?' He was off, like a startled rabbit.

'What, Njura, again?' Karpovna's reproach meant concern; for me or for her, I could not tell which. 'I'll have to toss you out, like Ustinja did.'

I should keep my opinions to myself. Especially with strangers around. It's time I learned.

'Hurry up,' my landlady went on. She did not mean it about putting me out; she really worried for me. 'And come back with your bones intact this time.'

■

It was my own fault. Last night, in the shop, there had only been the storekeeper, talking to the stranger. I had got in very late – every day I'd been getting later – to pick up my bread. I hardly noticed him: he was like anyone else.

'Hello, Njura,' the storeman had said. 'A bit later and you'd have had to go hungry.'

'A bit later and I wouldn't have had time to call before starting again!'

It was a new job, beginning the day after the concert. So far, it had probably lost me more than it had gained. Except, perhaps, for keeping me alive, which at the moment seemed of purely temporary and rather doubtful benefit.

We had heard during the winter of a logging project for young women and boys, four or five kilometres up river. It was paying bread, and I had not let the chance slip by. A lot of women had been forced to pass up the opportunity for lack of work clothes. That did not stop me, for I had had time during the winter to do repairs, even to add to my wardrobe. I felt that I was adequately equipped. The weather was quite mild, although there was still snow in the forest. I would need my skiboots. Too bad, I had hoped to keep them in reserve.

Ronald was to call as my guide, the first morning. He failed to appear. Fearful of losing my place in the team, I waded to the village and ran to the brigadier's – Lenkov, a sensible man, with a limp, a sharp-eyed wife and a reputation for fairness – and caught him as he was leaving. He laughed when I swore at Ronald.

'He's not thinking about you today, Njura.'

'What then?'

'Not what. Who. But no matter, I'll get you there.'

We cut through the forest, and found Ronald on a tree stump with Ljuba, the same girl who had dallied with the shopkeeper after berry-picking. One for business, one for pleasure; she was smart as well as pretty. Lucky Ronald, he had better things to do than call for me. Even so, I was cross with him, as his oversight could have cost me dearly.

The women's job was to cut finger-thick willow branches, the longer the better. These we warmed over a fire until they were soft enough to twist together into ties for lashing logs. Several logs formed a raft for carrying more logs. The only tools we had were *keens* – heavy things like machetes – and axes. By the first night my hands were blistered, Ljuba's little better.

'Bloody lily-handed intelligentsia,' was the limit of sympathy.

By the time we had made ourselves gloves, and learned to work without pain, we were given a new job, rolling logs onto the rafts. Each log had to be worked into precisely the right place on the bank, from where an extra push at the correct second would drop it where it belonged. If it slipped into the water, we had to haul it back up again, using long sticks with bent ends like boathooks. If it dropped incorrectly onto the raft, there was work for the men below on the pontoon, straightening it up. They didn't thank us for that.

It was there that I lost the boots. I used to hide them during the day and work in bare feet so as not to wear them out; under a bush at the end of the field, well off the track, marked with a fir twig. One day, when I went to look for them, there was no fir twig. My prized skiboots, carefully nursed for nearly two years, gone!

'You were silly leaving them out of your sight,' scolded Vilma.

I had to agree. 'But no-one else goes there.'

'Who but Lenkov?'

'He's not a bad fellow. He's friendly to us.'

'What the hell does that have to do with it? Those things are priceless.' As if I didn't know. 'Worth more than a fur coat. You were a fool!'

The same night I had one of the sudden stomach storms that were a part of life. Knowing I could not make it outside, I grabbed my coat in the lobby, and emptied myself into it, throwing the filthy thing into a puddle outside before crawling back to bed. In the morning I went to retrieve and wash it, but it, and all in it, had gone.

'You're a double fool,' said Vilma.

I agreed, again. A triple, a quadruple fool. A sick fool. First boots, now coat . . .

'Probably that gaolbird down the road,' she said.

'I can't think of anyone else . . .'

'Well, why don't you go and tackle him about it?'

I thought of the evil look of the man, and was afraid, even though the coat had taken hours to make from scraps.

'You're a fool.'

'Oh, shut up!'

Two more long days of log-hauling without boots, Vilma not talking to me, and then the storekeeper's nagging with the stranger looking on. 'You don't like the job, Njura? Then why didn't you go to Novo-Vasjugan with your friends?'

'I'd have gone gladly,' I said bitterly. Out of habit, I kept a close eye as he weighed the daily half kilogram for me. 'But I can't sew, or impress the right people. My specialties are only the saw, axe, *keen* and boathook.'

'Would you go? Really?' the stranger had then asked quietly. He looked like any other villager. There was nothing menacing

351

about him. Just another *kolkhoznik*.

'Tomorrow. On foot.' I spoke to him as if he were one of us. Recklessly. 'Anything to get out of this nest of thieves and rogues.' To say nothing of moody room-mates, thoughtless lovers, hectoring foremen. I had had enough of all of them.

'I see.'

'Life there is supposed to be for humans. Not just for crooks and chumps. And workdays are shorter. And you get paid full measure.'

Neither had said a word as I picked up my bread and left, giving the episode no more thought.

■

'So you want to move to Novo-Vasjugan?'

There was only the foreman, Lenkov, and the same man who had been in the store yesterday. The foreman looked stern and remained respectfully silent. My eyes would not stop straying to his boots. Maybe his wife was wearing mine. He wasn't.

The stranger spoke quietly. I had not noticed before, but his voice was no peasant's. He was educated and appeared genuinely polite. Beyond that, I could tell nothing from his expression or his eyes. I could only wonder what I had let myself in for.

'Is that so?' he asked mildly when I remained silent.

He was patient, too. If he was NKVD, he was very different. Did that make him more, or less, dangerous?

I nodded. Wherever it may lead, there was no point denying it: I had been vehement enough in his presence last night. I had criticised the system. I had made wild, though vague, accusations. And not just to anybody, that was now certain.

'Yes.' The tongue that had put me here clung dryly.

'If you still wish to go, you must be ready by four days' time.' Days of the week – Monday, Tuesday, and so on – were rarely mentioned, they meant so little. So many days ago, or counting days hence, was the common reckoning. 'A boat will leave at nine and you may draw three days' bread for the journey.'

It was not my tongue alone that ceased to function now. I think even my heart stopped. My stunned silence seemed no less than he expected, however, as he switched off me and turned to some papers.

I closed my gaping mouth, stared at his back, shook my head

and moved to rush out.

'Anna Denisovna!'

It was Lenkov. I stopped in mid-movement, left shoulder to him, not daring to turn. 'Anna Denisovna, would you call at the office again tomorrow – see the director – clear your papers – figure out your workdays?' It must be a dream. So now it's 'Anna Denisovna' and 'would you'. And Novo-Vasjugan.

Who is this man whose presence makes the foreman almost a gentleman? who talks and acts like a real one himself? who overhears me spouting complaints and waves a magic wand? What a pity that Ustinja wasn't on hand to observe such Chinese courtesy! She wanted so much to impress the right people.

Our hut was deserted when I got back. No-one to tell my good fortune to. Good fortune? It must be good fortune: there could be no possible evil purpose. But I couldn't help worrying.

■

I decided to skip work for the rest of the day. I would need time to sort my belongings. Whatever was happening in the longer view was more important than the evening crust. It could well be the turning point of my life in exile.

Working clothes first. I had a pair of skirts made of heavy jute sacking, well patched. And an equally well-patched blouse or shirt. Two sets of underwear made of sheets. A pair of acquired canvas gloves, that I could wear when there were no overseers about. A pair of stockings, of pink floral quilting. Sheepskin *tscherkis* and mittens. Two pairs of cotton socks. An old kerchief. And my fur coat, eaten down to a jacket. Not bad. Not good.

I was rather better off in Sunday bests. A pair of fine wool beach slacks, a yellow lacy patterned knitted blouse, the silk underwear that had strayed and returned, a blue woollen skirt I had been unable to sell as it was too short and too narrow. A pale-blue, apple-blossom-print summer dress, one pair of silk stockings and a pair of sandals of woven patent strips, otherwise useless items, remained as my reminder that I was going home one day *not* as a Russian peasant.

I still had my long yellow chenille beach robe. Elli Seppre, Ines' mother, had offered to make this into a jacket and slacks if I was ever in dire need. And, during the winter, I had turned Vilma's white and my own pale-blue woollen swimsuits into

353

several lined caps – Red Riding Hood style – white with blue applications, and blue with white. We had 'eaten' some and kept one each. Mine, by choice, was blue.

Bedding and household needs were the problem areas. One old sheet, my quilted eiderdown – or what was left of it, after most of the stuffing had been filched for clothing, the silk for patching and lining – one small tablecloth and a worn pillow with no slip. One *kateljok* – gained by exchange for the carriage saucepan – one silver and one wooden spoon, a handleless knife, half a comb and my manicure scissors. My fortune.

How I could have done with my skiboots and lost jacket! Stolen only in the past few days, too. But what's gone, wailing won't win back.

I took my robe to Elli, the dressmaker. She was happy for me. Two days was all she would need. I was pleased about that. I washed, mended, and could hardly wait for evening, to tell my 'family'. We had been together for a long time – one crowded Siberian winter equals an age anywhere else – and, despite a few flare-ups, had become very close. Vilma was overjoyed for my sake, though I noticed later how she kept looking, moist-eyed, to my corner of the hut. She had often been impatient with me, but from worry, I think, like a devoted sister. I had been short with her, too, for reasons that did me less credit. And Karpovna said miserably that she and Vanja would miss my stories.

I would miss them, no doubt, wherever and with whomever I might end up in Novo-Vasjugan. But I was determinedly elated. *Kurat!* This was what I had wanted, I was not going to let anything spoil it. To the devil with sentiment!

■

The director was not in the office in the morning. Nor in the evening. I began to worry as, without his clearance, I would be unable to leave. Not that I anticipated difficulties – at worst, no more than the usual red-tape ones – even though I had been steering clear of him. Since the ribbing about romance, and Ott's funeral, we had been no closer than a passing nod. I was ridiculously unsure of my own thoughts about him.

'When will he be in?'

'Who knows?' the girl in the office shrugged. 'But he might be in the bookkeeper's hut now.'

I went to Pavel Apraskin's, the bookkeeper's.

'He's just gone.'

And so had the best part of a bottle of vodka on the table – with two glasses. I accepted a glass from an over-friendly Apraskin and finally caught up with the elusive Kalesnikov on the way to his office. We walked along the edge of the ditch, the director in front, I behind, according to local custom. He was working hard at keeping steady.

'Njura,' he said over his shoulder, 'if you were to go back to Estonia, would you take me with you?'

Shocks were coming too frequently. It was a good thing that I could not look him in the eye. 'Well – '

'I suppose you wouldn't want me,' he went on in a melancholy tone, 'in a *fufaika*.'

I could only imagine he was referring to nationality. Which, oddly enough, did not seem to matter at the moment. 'And you?' I wasn't above a little coquetry, if only to avoid a direct answer. The vodka had put him off guard; my single glass had, perhaps, emboldened me. 'Would you want me?'

'Ah, I see you wouldn't.' He weaved on, shoulders hunched.

We were at the door of the office, now empty. I felt on the verge of a triumph, but it gave me no satisfaction. He was a good man, an attractive man, and water had passed under the bridge since the day of the funeral. I had a brief argument with myself.

Finally, I had to admit I was disappointed. I had wanted to hear him say yes. I did not dare consider what might have followed. Of course, I had given him no reply either, so it was a stalemate. I hoped he would not pursue the matter, as there was no satisfactory ending.

There was no trouble with my papers, and I was allowed pay for my workdays: four kilograms of wheat grain. I asked if I could have flour instead of wheat. Perhaps I shouldn't have, should have left well alone. The director gave me a long, steady look from under his eyebrows. I felt my heart beat faster. Silently, he bent and pencilled an order to the storeman.

Now, it was up to me. I had to say or do something, to thank him. There were only the two of us in the building. He was still far from sober, I reminded myself. A Russian man. I had rejected him, teased him a bit, had now been a mite cheeky, asking that last favour.

'Thank you,' I said, adding in the Russian manner, 'don't think too badly of me,' and offered my hand.

He did not stand, as I had expected. He reached up, slowly at first, then, with a quick tug, pulled me off balance and threw his arms around me. Surprised, I felt his breath on my face. I struggled – I wonder just how strongly? – and his lips touched the corner of my mouth. Then I was out on the steps, trembling. And not, I realised at once, from outrage or anger. It had all been so quick, so unexpected, my action instinctive. I wondered: had circumstances been different – if he weren't drunk – had I had time to consider . . .

Any other man in Maisk would have felt my fingernails. This one was *not* a party member; he *had* given his old trousers and felt boots to the boys in the forest; he *had* thrown us some of his own planks for Ott's coffin. His language was moderate; he had never pawed women in searches, not even when they were bulging with peas or potatoes. I discovered other things only later – perhaps fortunately, as they might have influenced the office skirmish – such actions as his defending me against some who wanted me sent away, and others who blamed me for stealing from the *kuljstan*. I heard about these in Novo-Vasjugan. I thought of all his good points – how he had treated us, his neat appearance, the way he looked at me from under his eyebrows – and fingered the warm spot on the corner of my mouth.

I confessed my sin to Vilma, for I felt more than slightly guilty.

She laughed. 'Why create worries for yourself over half a kiss?'

But it was not that half kiss that disturbed me.

'What then?'

'The other half.'

■

I saw the director once again, in 1946, in the Novo-Vasjugan canteen. We talked in a corner about *kolkhoz* happenings, without the old look. He told me, with a broad grin, that there had never been such a good potato harvest as the one after Lia and I had dug the field over with our fingers. We laughed together like old conspirators, not mentioning the Maisk farewell.

■

When the time came to go, Vilma was at work and Paul in the 'day-care centre'. I was almost glad, as I was feeling the pangs of leaving. It was early morning, and I was tired. It had been a late night, a long round of goodbyes. I would miss Vilma, Paul, and Enn. Others too, but them the most. And Karpovna, Vanja . . . the director? I was not sure . . . all the other Estonians. On the other hand, I was getting away from Skakalkin, Ustinja, sundry foremen, the gaolbird next door, the storekeeper, reminders of Mrs Balter. Perhaps it balanced. Dusja: Gerda. Marusja, Natasha: Tiia, Lia. At least I was going from a collective farm to a city: from the sticks to the hub.

They had wished me well last night. 'A good journey, see you back soon.' I spat three times over my shoulder on the cold way home, and wished pepper on their tongues for, all things considered, having made the break, I had little wish to see Maisk again.

■

The landing was crowded, with even some local hierarchy present. I looked around stealthily. No director. Karpovna stood, shaking her head and wiping the corner of her eye with her knuckle. It was a fine morning, still fresh. It would warm up later.

The shopkeeper was a fellow passenger. So were several others, whose luggage was piled in the sun near the edge of the landing. The vessel itself consisted of engine and carriage. The engine: a four-oared boat. The carriage: a small barge, already sitting deep in the water under a load of boxes, bags, bundles, and six big barrels of *pihta* oil.

The shopkeeper had been in great good humour last night, telling me he would be going, and of my exceptional good fortune to be travelling with him.

'You know who that was?' he had asked. 'That man who spoke to you in the shop?'

'No.' I determined to be blasé. 'Should I?'

'He is the director of forestry in the province of Novo-Vasjugan. The whole province! A very high position.'

I was impressed, despite myself. I wondered . . . and need not have. I was about to be told.

'His name is Jelski. You really are very lucky, you know. He told me he had lived for five years in Narva – you know

357

Narva? in Estonia? – and had gone to the Russian high school.'
I nodded. Of course I knew Narva. On the Baltic Sea, nearly on
the Russian border, in my own county of Virumaa. 'He knows a
lot about Estonia, and Estonian affairs and' – he sounded a little
puzzled about this – 'seems to have a high regard for Estonians.'

'Director of forestry, is he?' I mused. 'And I didn't even thank
him.'

'Guess you can do that when you get there. He's a *ladna*
man – a good fellow.'

A burst of extra shouting signalled 'all aboard'. Karpovna
came close to me, and furtively made the sign of the cross over
my chest.

'Good luck, Njura,' she whispered, 'good health and keep
your mouth tight.'

She stepped back again, forcing a smile. I was moved. Her
gesture could easily get her into trouble. I could have hugged
her, but that might not be good for her, either. I had to say what
I wanted with moist eyes, as my tongue was dry. For once, her
perceptive advice was unnecessary.

■

The sheltered spots had all been taken. As usual, I had been too
slow. I needed Enn to manage me, I thought with a pang; I really
would miss him, my co-traveller over so many journeys. The sky
was clear except for thin, high cloud. What wind there was came
from the north-west; it shouldn't matter too much being in the
open, it shouldn't rain.

Elts Kepi, the quiet wife of Narva Primary School's dedicated,
if unobtrusive, headmaster – naturally they had had to be deported:
what a dangerous pair of villains! – Elts had been slow, too. We
decided to set up house on the barrels. Several planks across
them, covered by a handy tarpaulin, folded in quarters, did the
trick. A comfortable floor. And Elts surprised me. Not a talkative soul – rather, I had thought her a bit serious-minded – she
calmly rummaged in her bundles and spread a snow-white sheet,
pillows, eiderdown on top, patting them smooth before forty
startled eyes. 'Let them beat that,' she murmured.

Besides the two of us and the shopkeeper, there were twelve
others aboard the barge. Ronald Mirt and his mother, the
Sillas, and the three Kesa women – wife, mother, and daughter

Vaike – were some we knew well. Captain Kesa himself was already at Kuntika, a village on the river just this side of Novo-Vasjugan. He was reputedly a brigadier. His mother, with us now, and father, were the original targets of the round-up, though it is beyond comprehension why; they were, and always had been, farmers, with no interest in anything beyond their small holding near Rakvere. The irony was that the Captain (permanent army) was not on the list, but bundled in as a 'child' with Mrs Kesa senior. Presumably, his own wife and child accompanied him because the arresting officer did not know what else to do with them.

■

'What is the stuff in these barrels?' Elts asked.

'*Pihta* oil.'

'So I've heard. What's that?'

I had had to gather larch branches for it in the winter. Perhaps some of it was my own pickings from the forest. Now I had to ride the river with it. 'They use it to make fuses or detonators or something. It's going to Tomsk. It's an explosive.'

Elts stared. 'No wonder they went quiet when we were banging planks around on it!'

I had not given it a thought. I did now, and felt goose-bumps. 'Perhaps it needs heat to set it off,' I suggested weakly.

'There won't be much danger in that direction,' Elts said dryly. 'Not from what our skinny bodies would generate.'

We were obliged to travel with the stuff on this, its first journey. I fervently hoped not to accompany it on its last.

'We should be comfortable enough on top here.'

'As long as it stays put.'

'And if it doesn't?'

'Boom!'

■

The pilot called, 'Cast off.' And did it himself.

At exactly nine we left the harbour of Maisk, a narrow three-metre-long jetty, with two slim piles sticking up at the corners, with rings through them. Our ropes slid through the rings and dropped free as we drifted off downstream to a thin chorus of farewells from the bank.

One hundred and eighty kilometres, the pilot had said. Clear weather. A fair current. We should be in Novo-Vasjugan by tomorrow evening. Elated – only two days and a night – I faced down river . . . The way you're behaving, Ann Lehtmets, you'd think we were heading for Paris!

'Two to an oar. Come on now.' The pilot held the boat to the barge, for us to clamber across. We drifted slowly sideways, then backwards, a length or two from the shore. If we had been going upstream we would have lost ground already. 'Get us out into the stream. Hurry it up.' Elts and I sat courageously at one of the front oars.

'Let me sit at this oar with Ann.' Mother Mirt had climbed in beside us. 'You go over to that one, Elts. Take it with Eedi.'

Why on earth? Perhaps they know nothing about rowing and want our help. Elts and I looked at each other – after all, Mother Mirt was not young: we did not want to be disrespectful.

'Shift over, Ann.' I shifted. 'Now hold it like this . . . So . . . Forward like this . . . So . . . Together now . . . Pull . . . two, three . . . Dip the wrists . . . Forward . . . Up . . . One, two, three, together now . . .'

Mother Mirt, who looked as though she had wielded nothing heavier than a knitting needle, had been born by the sea. Frail as she was, she had us performing smoothly in no time. A couple of changes, and the engine had its carriage rolling steadily downstream in the middle of the Vasjugan. A fast walker would have been left far behind.

It was near midsummer, the river on its way down, the hectic rush of winter's ice and snows almost done. In a month or two, cows would be able to cross in places. The flow was steady, no longer dangerous, still ice cold, the banks up to two metres high. For the most part, the stream, averaging about thirty metres wide, ran through flat marshy land, with straggling shrubby growth stretching away either side for kilometres. In the distance, we could see forest-clad low hills, occasionally closer clumps of alders, birch and cedar. Thorns and rowan and blackcurrant, with early berries showing, were everywhere. A few birds sang. There was no evidence of animal or human life.

We were to use all available daylight. Which left only three or four cold hours for rest. Elts and I decided we would sleep in clothes, under bags, with the eiderdown on top.

■

I woke shivering, curled myself tighter to no avail, and lifted my head above Elts'. In the frosty light of midnight, I made out the figure of the shopkeeper stamping on the shore. My back was freezing. It would get colder yet before the sun rose on our first-class outdoor cabin. I prodded my bedmate till she squirmed. 'Elts! Elts! Shall we ask the shopkeeper to sleep here? There's plenty of room.' We certainly didn't use much, huddled as we were.

'Is he a party member?' A natural enough question, the first thing to know about any Russian. If Elts were properly awake, however, she would not have asked. I would never have con- sidered him if he were a member, and she would know it. We would as soon share with a skunk.

'Of course not.'

'Huh.' Part doubt. Part apology.

'I know he's not. That's definite.' I shivered, coiled up tighter. 'You know, we are using his tarpaulin and bags.'

'His?'

'Well, he is the storeman.'

'If you like, then. But keep him on your side.'

I had every intention of doing so.

'And you do the asking,' she added.

I pondered a little longer – Shall I? Shan't I? Would it be worth it? What will he try to make of it? – before I got out.

He was astonished, but quick enough to accept. And he wasted no time putting an arm around me. I was ready, how- ever, and, without a word, took it up firmly and placed it away. He was snoring before I drifted off.

When the pilot woke us my bed partner was already at the wheel. He grinned. I looked away. He had served his purpose; I didn't know him.

It was our turn to row. We climbed stiffly to our stations, an unlikely crew of eight. 'God, my fingers! They're numb. Oh for a pair of gloves!'

'My toes are icicles.'

'Look at that damned shopkeeper – grinning away – '

'Don't know how he does it. Last I saw of him, he was stand- ing on shore like a brass monkey.'

I took my place among the grumbling rowers. I had slept

beautifully, warm back and front. Elts caught my eye, and winked.

I had many dealings with the shopkeeper after that, and was amply rewarded. Though he recalled our encounter with the bear many times, he never once reminded me about the night on the barge. And he never again put his arm around me. But odd small favours . . . What do you expect from a man you've slept with?

About midday a solid bump threw us all in the boat. We had had small bumps before, from floating logs. This one stopped us dead, a jolting thump, followed by another as the barge hit from behind, grinding up over our stern to come to a halt, bearing down on us with a slight list.

We picked ourselves up, shaken more than hurt, and waited apprehensively while the pilot cursed, the vessels creaked, and water gurgled scornfully past. I looked over, and judged the bank to be just inside my swimming distance. The water was not for swimming if it could be avoided. But I could see no reason for our sudden halt.

While the pilot jumped back and forth, peering over the sides to find the obstruction, the barge slowly turned with the tide. Gracefully detaching itself, it swung free and away downstream, gaining momentum until the rope tautened with another jerk. Still, our engine did not budge.

He found it: a huge tree trunk, embedded on the bottom, with us jammed firmly in one of its forks. Eventually, after two hours of the men attacking the stump through the water with an axe, the women rocking the boat to and fro and pushing with boat-hooks, we were free.

'Good work,' the pilot said. 'We'll have to blow up that snag. Look, it's holed the boat.'

The rest period went in bailing. The sun, that had shone pleasantly on an open-air cabin, beat hot on our sweating backs. We had a tiring time before us. We would be late, too.

■

Kuntika. Still eighteen kilometres from Novo-Vasjugan.

While in Maisk, I had swapped my enamel saucepan for the *kateljok*, a heavy cooking pot with a handle, like an outsize billy can. And, at our last meal stop, I had gathered and stored aboard some dry sticks. As we approached Kuntika, an Ostiak village, I

362

could see a few huts in the distance and the crossed stakes of a cooking place on the high bank above the landing. Elts and I already had some of Karpovna's potatoes peeled. I was off the boat before it touched, and had the pot of potatoes over a dancing fire almost before the others had landed.

A tousle-haired boy shuffled up from behind the corner of the nearest hut. He must have watched us come in.

'What are you doing here?' he asked.

'Cooking potatoes.'

'I can see that. Why did you land here?'

'Our boat has a hole in it.'

'This is my cooking place.' He was quite pleasant about it.

He was about sixteen, pure Ostiak: dark-haired, dark-eyed, smooth-skinned. 'My name is Anashka and I'm an idiot.'

'How an idiot?' I replied. 'You don't look the least bit silly to me.' I appreciated how Alice felt in Wonderland. 'And silly people never know they are.'

'Who are you?'

'My name is Ann Lehtmets.'

'Where are you going?'

'To Novo-Vasjugan. To work in the forest.'

'That's if you get there. You've got to get through the devil's cauldron first.'

'What's the devil's cauldron?'

'Ljah-mets. That's a funny name. Listen, I don't think you're Russian.'

'I'm Estonian.'

'And you used "you" to me, not "thou".'

'I'm sorry.'

'*Vot*, it's good you are Estonian. There are lots of Estonians here, lumbering. You will probably come here too.'

'Where are they now?'

'Ljahmets, give me a rouble and call me "thou".'

The boy must be crazy, after all. In a bright sort of way.

'Look, I have no money with me. But next time I'll call thee "thou" and I'll have a rouble for thee.'

Elts came up and Anashka disappeared.

'Who was that?'

I told her.

'A self-confessed idiot?'

363

'Who recognises an Esti and likes money.'

'He's no idiot if he can stay alive in this ante-room to hell. Without even working!'

'It might help if he were.'

'Now then!' Elts laughed. 'None of your cynicism.'

'How long have we got here?'

'Not long.' Elts laughed again. A real laugh. 'Just as well you couldn't hear him.'

'I did hear him!'

'Not that one.' She jerked her thumb at Anashka, then at the boat. 'Him. One of the bosses from Kuntika came down while you were lighting the fire. He pointed at you and said, "*Vot*, that woman won't be the first to peg out, others haven't even got off the boat and the whore's already cooking!"'

'Well, he knows what – '

Like 'bastard' in English, the word was used in everyday conversation. It could even be a term of affection, though it took some getting used to. 'Oh, why worry,' I muttered. 'He doesn't mean anything.'

'The others might think twice about that – ' Elts blew over a mouthful of hot potato. 'If I should ask . . . whuh . . . if anyone noticed . . . whuh . . . where the shopkeeper . . . whuh . . . slept last night . . . whuh . . . whuh . . . whuh . . . '

'Elts, you wouldn't!'

■

'There it is! Get us out into midstream!'

We had been keeping close to the left bank.

'Quick now! Nikolai, come take the oars. And pull!' The pilot stationed himself in the bow, boat-hook poised. 'Elts and Njura, you take the tiller. And keep her straight!' he yelled.

'There's the devil coming up already!'

Nothing seemed amiss. We were simply going a bit faster.

The pilot cursed. 'There's a damned log in the way. Over to the right bank! Right! Come on there, closer!'

We leaned on the tiller and gasped as a jagged log flashed past. Then another on our left. Suddenly we caught his urgency. On the right, water churned in a wide arc leading to a swirling circle. As if pulled by a magnet, boat and barge headed for the eye. A few of the women cried out. Elts and I had no breath left for that; we were lying horizontally, feet braced against the side timbers, pushing a tiller that pushed back like a live thing to take us into the silent cauldron.

'Push!' the pilot yelled. 'Shove!' He jabbed at a log with brown water creaming up it like an ocean breaker.

'Stop your bloody cackling, women!' roared the shopkeeper. 'Grab a boathook and push us back into the middle!'

The tiller lunged this way and that, the whole boat shivering under the strain; the barge behind kicked, bucked, twisted and jerked, trying its hardest to tear free of us into the whirlpool. Then the sucking eddy rushed past and it was over, the devil's cauldron left behind. The warm afternoon sun watched us glide smoothly on as though nothing had disturbed those languid waters.

Elts and I crawled stiffly on hands and knees back to our cabin on the barge; our muscles – or was it shaken nerves? – refused to carry us upright.

We had time to recover. The sun would set at least an hour before we could reach Novo-Vasjugan, the city I had been building hopes on. I had already begun to wonder why I'd left Maisk.

29

LAKE LEHTMETS

'You'll be sleeping in the stables for a while,' the brigadier mumbled. He did have the grace to sound apologetic.

'Stables!' Elts muttered. Usually philosophical, her disappointment broke through.

'For a few days, at least. The communal living quarters are being renovated.'

'Get the horses in first so we'll feel at home, won't you?'

It was all the same to me. I was too weary to complain. The goat shed would have done.

The brigadier didn't hear. He led us on through the dark.

The stables were properly built. Solid logs and doors. Windows. The front was a separate roomy barn for housing carts, harness and accessories. In a back corner was a big bin of oats, vaguely visible in the lantern-light, and a crude ladder heading to a loft.

'You can sleep on the cart,' said Nikolai, the guide, 'under the tarpaulin. Or, if you want to wait a while for a bed, I'll unharness the horse first, and take him for a drink.'

Why wait? I climbed to the loft, found hay, and threw down several armfuls. It was clean enough, I conceded. Too tired to consider anyone else, I kicked it into a heap and sank. From a vast distance, I heard the brigadier talking to me about tomorrow. I was to meet a bookkeeper named Karlovna. Karpovna? No, not my Karpovna, I registered in the middle of a yawn. She was going to do something for us, but I was asleep before I heard.

■

367

Pleasant surprise. Tiia was shaking me awake. The sun was well up as I stretched luxuriously across my soft bed. The shed was almost empty.

'You look well, Tiia.' Much better than when we had dragged *klopkas* together through the ice-cold mud of Maisk.

'I waited hours for you last night. And you didn't get my message?'

'What message?'

'They said you did.'

'Oh, are you the bookkeeper? Karlovna?'

'That's me. It's patronymics all the way here.'

'I was nearly asleep.'

'Not like back in the *kolkhoz*. I work as bookkeeper in the forestry office, and live with my son and Margo Niilsen in the little hut over there – see? Let's go quickly. The others are already in the office and the director's waiting.'

Tiia rattled on. I gave up trying to edge a word in.

'The director's name is Piotr Pavlovich Jelski. He's nice.'

'Nice?'

Tiia had not changed. She was still an optimist.

'For a Russian,' she conceded.

'Huh.' Obstinacy would not allow me to agree. I did not mention the Estonian connection.

'Come on, we'd better get in there for the meeting. Afterwards, we can go straight to my place. Then we'll pick up your things and move them over. Tonight we'll have time to talk.' We neared the office. Her voice dropped lower. 'The fat madam in the silk dress in there is Jelski's secretary and wife, Elena Ossipovna. He's all right, but' – we were at the office steps and Tiia's voice fell to a whisper – 'she's a party member. Be careful.'

The forestry director was as polite and courteous as he had been in Maisk. He was a countryman at heart, despite his grey coat, tie and white shirt. The woman at the desk did not enter into the business of the meeting. She eyed us with the same mistrustful curiosity that we eyed her. She looked sharp and mean. Tiia's warning was timely. I knew I was going to have trouble with her before long.

The director, to our surprise, rewarded our efforts at the devil's cauldron – 'You were acting helmsmen, I believe' – with fifty roubles each. His wife asked me to tell her all about our 'brave efforts', and listened with a supercilious smirk. She resented our windfall.

I did not like Ossipovna. I did not like her cold eye and frosty superiority. Jealousy, I wondered? She was attractive except for the hint of hardness, a bit plump (as I would like to have been), hair done (which mine had not been for ages), wearing a silk dress (which I could have worn better). I thought about that dress as I finished my story. It was certainly not from the boutiques of Russia . . . What poor soul had had to trade it? In what circumstances? What had she got? Enough? Her life, maybe? I hoped so: she had had good taste . . . And now it was Ossipovna's. Then I thought no, not jealousy: the antipathy I felt for her was a deeper emotion, a more general one, involving that previous owner – hundreds, thousands of previous owners . . .

'Is that all?'

'That's all.' I kept my voice level.

'You'd better report to the commandant,' she said shortly.

Nor did she like me, that was plain.

■

Tiia's office was like an office anywhere, if you accepted local architecture and could ignore used-newspaper documents. There was a typewriter on a desk under one of the three windows, and potted plants in two corners: one a rubber-tree, the other, I thought, a hibiscus. I inspected it. 'Rose of China?' I asked Tiia. The Estonian term. She nodded, pleased.

The head bookkeeper was a Latvian woman I remembered from the boat on the Ob. She remembered me, too, though a little distantly, as it was her husband I had quarrelled with in the queue for hot water. She was a widow now – at least she knew: among the thousands who could only suspect – greying, though still attractive, and ‡ la mode from hair to shoes. I wished I had changed; I felt dowdy in their world.

It was some comfort to finger the crude documents. As in Maisk, they were cut-up old newspapers with writing over the print, mainly in ink, a few typed, some pencilled.

Margo Niilsen awaited us at Tiia's place with food. Elts was already there. I was glad to leave the office, not least because my stomach was complaining at unfulfilled promise. Another pleasant surprise! Margo was no stranger: I had known her, too, in

369

Maisk. She had come down in the season's first mail boat with her daughter Kersti, who was away in Kuntika, lumbering. I had not known about it. Kersti had been the frightened girl outside the hut the night I had had my hands hurt. She had often asked about me, I heard now, and Margo was pleased that we would soon meet again. So was I. I never did hear what had made her cry. Margo was ill, and unable to work, but was paid three hundred grams of bread a day to mind Tiia's son and to housekeep.

'You mean that?'

'Yes, I mean that. Paid for baby-sitting. Tiia draws extra for me.'

Tremendous news, the best yet. No work-or-starve dictum. Almost like civilisation: you could be ill – and survive!

We ate, tidied, and stored our few things in Tiia's attic, as we still had to spend nights in the stable. Elts and I at last agreed that we were ready to formally report our arrival.

■

For the second time in a few hours, I recalled knocking at that midnight door in Maisk. First Kersti, now that sign: 'Commandant'. Prods to memory. My skin prickled once more, though there was nothing to fear now.

'Enter!'

Elts went ahead without hesitation. She had not had the Maisk experience. There it was again: the raised desk, the uniform, the cold eyes looking not quite at us. Different, yet the same. How many more times would there be?

The familiar, supercilious air of boredom. Another man, younger, also in uniform, stood near the window, watching with some interest. Perhaps he was new to it, learning. I stepped forward, a fraction behind Elts, not wishing to appear afraid. Neither was I eager.

'Be seated.'

We stood. He did not care.

'Name? Age? Where from? Where going?'

He filled a sheet for each of us, and pushed the two papers across the desk.

'Sign here. This says you will not leave the region of Novo-Vasjugan. And you will report regularly to this office. Once a month.'

I reached forward to pick it up. I should have been prepared. A soft hand slammed down on the paper.

'Just sign. Here.'

I had not read a word.

Elts and I glanced at each other. What was the difference, anyway? We signed and left.

'I suppose we'll get used to it,' Elts sighed.

'I hate to think so.'

■

Novo-Vasjugan was no collective farm village. It was the biggest town I had seen in two years, and I was reasonably pleased with what I had found so far.

I had decided early, on our return from the commandant's office, to take a look at the town, and parade myself in case some unknown friend might spot me. Elts preferred to sleep – she had not made as free with the straw last night as I, and had decided to take advantage of the horse's absence – so I strode off alone.

Margo's directions to find an erstwhile Maisk citizen named Elma led me to the shoe- and dress-making factory where I indeed found Elma. She was using a pair of dress-maker's scissors, which I recognised instantly as having belonged to Elli Seppre. Elli, while converting my beach robe, had lamented their loss some months earlier; they had been stolen from her cabin, which we all knew at the time because such a fuss had been made. They were the only good scissors in the whole *kolkhoz*, and dark things were said about how they would be used when we found the Russian who had taken them. I could not conceal my surprise.

The warm reunion I had anticipated turned sour. Elma knew where the scissors belonged, and their value. There could not possibly be a satisfactory explanation, despite her confused story of having bought them from a Russian girl.

Saddening. I had not thought we had regressed so far.

I sat on a pile of stacked timber behind the office. Alone now, I could take time to study Margo's map, rough as it was. It had been a busy morning, and I was glad of the short rest, but there were still people, mainly from Maisk, I wanted to look up, on my own and others' accounts. There might not be many opportunities. Two, at least, were working in the *Selpo* – consumers' cooperative – which should not be hard to find. Others could take longer. Some, I might happen across.

From the woodheap, I turned into Sovietskaja – Soviet Street. People seemed to be rushing, as in a real city, moving with purpose and speed along the unpaved dusty right-of-way. There was no cover, kerb or sidewalk, simply a very straight line of timbered fronts bordering the broad thoroughfare on either side. It was lunchtime, I guessed. This was confirmed within a few steps by a strong smell of cabbage coming from an open doorway atop a wide staircase. As the smell and hubbub from within poured out, so did people converge and pour in. A communal eating house. I joined the stream, and entered through a screen of buzzing flies.

Ten or twelve long, bare, wooden tables were spaced across the bare board floor. Most places were occupied by people eating soup from black tin bowls, using wooden spoons. Some had pieces of bread beside the plate, most none. There was little conversation. Inside the door, on the left, was a long counter where workers, and, judging by their clothes, functionaries too, milled into a queue. When the queue leader presented a card, a square was cut from it with a pair of scissors – *Kurat!* scissors again! – the square was dropped in a box, a piece of bread handed out and a slip of white paper given. The majority were without cards; they were given the strip of paper only, no bread. The paper, presented at the window at the end of the counter, bought a bowl of soup and spoon. A somewhat puzzling method, but the girl with the scissors and paper strips was fast, as was the older woman at the soup window. The line kept moving. I wondered about my chances.

Under the window, near the front, on my right, apart from the rest, was one big table covered with a white paper 'tablecloth'. Four men in black uniforms sat wielding knives and forks over bacon and eggs and meat patties, served direct from the kitchen. One caught my eye for a moment as he surveyed the hall, picking his teeth with a fingernail. My eyes strained forward; my nostrils revived a forgotten fragment of the past; an instant cavity bored into my stomach.

I decided against trying my luck; I thought I could not bear a rebuff. Not now, after that tantaliser. I had reached the top of the steps heading back to the street when my young friend, Leo, greeted me. The boy had grown noticeably since Malinovka. Not only physically, either. He bowed ceremoniously, and

372

respectfully invited me to dine with him. I accepted his arm, matching his mock courtesy. He with his soup ticket and forty kopeks, and I with my bread ration and seventy-five kopeks, took turns with our one wooden spoon – 'No soup ticket, no spoon. You ought to know that' – looking wryly at the white-clothed table as we ate. Leo laughed; I pretended to. He could dismiss inequality; I still could not.

Leo told me that he and his mother worked in the commune stables. Asta, in the stables? I must tell Gerda! 'And I'm a water carrier,' he added proudly. Alma, Helju and Leo's brother, Erik, were felling trees some three kilometres away. 'They're exceed-ing the quota, too,' he said. All lived together in one hut. Would I like to visit them? Yes. Tonight? Yes. What time? As soon as my own accommodation was sorted out. I could only pray this visit would be more satisfactory than the last, when Asta had annoyed us with her flawed priorities.

Meal over, bowl and spoon returned, we walked along the middle of the now quiet road; past an apothecary, *Selpo* shop, the office of the committee and party room; under a Victory Arch of brown-painted wooden planks; past a warehouse, *milits'* headquarters, gaol, 'clubroom'-cum-school. This was Soviet Street. Behind, and parallel, was Kolkhoz Street with post office, kiosk, and a 'closed' shop, for party members only. Next to the shop was a well.

'There are three wells in Novo-Vasjugan,' Leo explained. Again, there was a note of boastfulness. Truly this was the voice of innocence: proprietary pride bragging about a town of three wells. This child, who should be at school soaking up knowl-edge and getting the best of everything, could find importance in carting water and exceeding norms; and saw nothing amiss in others – his captors – scoffing food he used to take for granted, should now be getting regularly, and would likely never have again. 'Another for the hospital. And I think some of the bosses have a well of their own. They never have to come here, anyway. All the rest comes from water-holes in the marsh or the lakes. I'm a water carrier, you know.'

I looked down, but I couldn't see the bottom. There was a wooden pail attached to a chain wound fully up to its spin-dle. I let out the handle a couple of turns – it moved freely enough – thought better of it and wound it up again.

Farther along Kolkhoz Street we came to the flourmill on the river. Next to it was a fish store with old nets, pots and bags, the earth shiny with scales. A pervasive smell drowned that from the mill a hundred metres away. There was open, dusty ground between the two.

'You know all the important buildings and the wells, Leo. Do you know how many people live in Novo-Vasjugan?'

'Ah, the residents. The souls of our city. Two thousand and one, now you're here.'

The hut, with its poorly patched window, and its door hanging askew on rusted hinges, looked as miserable as the stables alongside. Thank goodness we hadn't been billeted in these!

Leo looked in. 'No-one home,' he reported, and led me next door. The whole complex could do with attention. The stable roof had holes in it, the supporting walls tilted to one corner like an old cardboard box. It was a wonder it didn't collapse. Yet, once inside, I had to alter my opinion. It was cared-for. Perhaps Asta had not changed.

'Don't rouse at me, Mum, I've brought a visitor.'

Asta looked up, opened her mouth, closed it again, smiled uncertainly, cried 'Ann,' and dropped her birch broom to throw her arms around me. She had been sweeping between partitions, and the dust from the dirt floor settled around us as we hugged.

I cut our greetings short when a man, who had been bending over a feed box, straightened up. He was unmistakably Russian – stolid, grim, and purposeful. Though Asta was unperturbed, even amused, I watched warily while he advanced at a steady walk, eyes fixed on me.

When he stopped a metre away, I held my breath. When he extended his hand I took it, too surprised to think of an alternative. 'Aleksei Voronin,' he introduced himself gravely.

'Our brigadier,' said Asta.

'Anna Denisovna,' I said, automatically. Good God, what's happening to Ann Lehtmets? Am I going native?

'*Vot*, Asta,' he said seriously, 'if we have a visitor from Maisk, we should go and sit inside.'

This was no more nor less than old-fashioned local custom. However, we deportees, war-mongers and blood-suckers, were not used to consideration at all, let alone the courtesies of a bygone era. My heart warmed to the city. Just compare this to

Skakalkin's greeting!

He knew Maisk well, knew people there, promised to visit and take messages, finally saw me to the gate. Asta had slipped quietly to second place; she knew what cultivating him might mean to me. I waved to her over the Russian's shoulder. We would catch up later. It was becoming more obvious that she was not the same introspective complainer we had worried about in Malinovka. I wondered if she still had her fine clothes and silver and cutlery, and was suddenly sure she had not – she had her health and her boys instead.

'*Vot* you have friends at the stable here – you can speak the language – you're a *ladna* woman. If you don't like it in the forest, come back, and I'll make you stableman – that is, if you're not afraid of horses.'

'Horses?' I scoffed. 'Scared? Shaft horses, draught, anything. Harnessing, grooming, driving – I wouldn't know how to be scared of them. I'm no stranger to the axe and the saw and the shovel, either. Perhaps I shall come and work for you, you're a kind and reasonable boss.'

I laid it on thick in response to the '*ladna* woman'. At least the last part was sincere, if not the confidence with horses.

■

At six o'clock, as nearly as we could judge, Elts and I knocked at Tiia's door. 'Not earlier,' she had said, and had seemed quite agitated about it.

'Come in.'

Tiia nervously ushered us inside. There was a blanket over the window, even though it was not yet dark; when the door was quickly shut behind us I could barely see across the room. I blinked, feeling closed-in, as though thrown in a dungeon.

Perhaps town life was not for me, after all. Not that I had imagined drums and trumpets but, except for Leo and Asta and the brigadier in the stable, our welcome, so far, had not come up to scratch. Tiia was oddly ill-at-ease. Margo explained, 'The director's wife told Tiia on her first day that for office workers in the forestry department it was not recommended they have visitors.'

'We'll be yours, then,' Elts said. 'Where's the problem?'

No response. Not a joking matter.

'What did she mean by that?' I asked. Unnecessarily, as

'visitors' obviously meant other deportees. Having been semi-Russified by promotion, Tiia was to cut off old connections. They both looked uncomfortable.

'One of the Estonians here warned me early in the piece,' Margo went on. 'Madam goes around personally looking into windows.'

I began a few words on Madam, but checked myself under Elts' warning glare. Elena Ossipovna was enemy enough. We needed friends. Tiia already looked acutely embarrassed, while Margo busied herself at the rough centre table.

'Well, let's have all the Esti news then.'

It seemed I was wrong: Tiia had changed, perhaps as much for the worse as Asta had for the better.

I had half a wish to be back in Maisk where we were all sprats together. The bigger the pond, it seemed, the wider the range in fish. This was a big pond. A lot of fish. And we were still the sprats.

■

We were just back at the stables when visitors arrived.

'Forgive us being late, but we heard there were new arrivals and had to see who they were.'

The young couple came from county Virumaa. In their late twenties, they were cheerful, good-looking, and lively. We quickly established rapport. The man had been a correspondent for the *Virumaa Herald* and had known my husband. 'If you're not going till tomorrow, why not come and spend the night at our villa in the woods?'

'Both of us?'

'There's plenty of room.'

'You mean you have your own cabin?'

'Our very own. Just ourselves, the two children and their grandmother.'

'You think we should?'

'Why not?'

Elts declined. She was tired.

'I'd love to,' I said, and promised Elts I would be back early in the morning.

Twilight was fading as we went through the town. About two kilometres past the *Selpo* we left the main road for a track into the woods. My companions were talkative and apparently popular. They knew everybody. As we walked, we went through the deportees' routine: swapping names and news of people from home, from the carriage, the barge, our various destinations since. In the gathering dark, beyond a line of birch trunks, I made out the sullen twilight shine of water, flat and forbidding under a thickening blanket of fog.

'Cranberry Lake,' said my guide. His voice dissolved into the mist. It sounded eerie. 'It always steams at this time. This is the end of a cranberry marsh that goes on' – he waved over the sinister water – 'oh, a couple of hundred kilometres. The drier patches grow mushrooms, too, and bilberries.'

I shivered.

'Past the villa,' he laughed, 'there's a really beautiful little lake surrounded by deciduous trees. The forest lake. We'll have to call it your lake now: Lake Lehtmets.' My name means 'leaf forest'. Even his laughter was damped in the fog.

'I like that.'

'Lake Lehtmets it is, then.'

The path turned sharply left and I gasped. Over a few low bushes, framed between small trees, was the 'villa'. It was a picture: walls of logs and sawn timbers faced with birch bark; roof of sods of mossy turf, tiny window of patched glass with a 'junior' flickering welcome in the middle. All in a grassy clearing, surrounded by marsh birch and willows. A fairytale house. A merry fire crackled in front, smoke curling into the darkening sky. Instead of the wicked witch, a white-headed little woman cradled a fair-haired child in her arms, while a boy a year or so older stood by, gravely watching our approach.

'Ah, I see Mama's planned supper for us by the fire.'

And what a supper! A mug of milk each – no trouble to get an extra one for me! – a couple of potatoes baked in the ashes, a big piece of real butter for each potato. 'Good heavens, do you run a dairy?'

'Oh yes,' Mama answered. 'We have a forest full of cows, a pair of milking machines and an underground butter factory.'

I joined politely in their mirth. There must be a story behind this affluence.

■

The morning was a rush. The couple had to be at the fish-works by eight.

Mama called from the door, '6.30.' And for me, 'It'll be 7.30 when the sun gets to the top of that birch. Time for them to leave. Come on.' She had promised me a treat.

She led me to Lake Lehtmets, a towel over my shoulder and a block of home-made soap in my hand. I bathed in cool, clear water, Mama watching benignly. I left reluctantly when she called me out.

'That was beautiful,' I puffed. It was more than that; I just could not find the words.

I dried with a real towel, standing on clean grass among the birch and aspen. Ancient firs and pines, huge and tall and straight, looked austerely overhead at their counterparts across the water. My ripples died; the silent lake returned to the mirror it had been. Below the shivering aspen, deer-moss and cranberry sprouted from the forest floor, hugging the trunks. Climbing hops curled higher to drop their prolific yellow-green runners. The wine-like air was undisturbed but for the dash and twitter of small birds.

I sighed, marvelling at the ways of the Creator. Such grandeur; such serenity. He made Siberia. So seldom did He let us know it.

'We have a call on the way home.'

We skirted Lake Lehtmets. I was attached to my lake, with its water-weeds, reeds, its yellow and white flowers: 'Waterlilies,' I exclaimed. My favourites. I wanted to pick some.

'The bottom's deep out there. Muddy. We've had to pull cows out of the middle and it's taken hours, even with ropes from the village.'

I allowed myself to be dissuaded.

I was not to fully understand the 'dairy business' until later years. It was simple. A few cows wandered the woods, more or less wild; there were no fences. So did the occasional bull. They all belonged to the *kolkhoz* or the bosses, of course – hence the ready assistance when in trouble – but if you lived in the forest, and made friends with a wanderer at the right time, when she was full, or in calf . . .

'Here's the cellar.'

Mama lifted a sizeable sod from an otherwise ordinary piece of turf, took a bottle from the exposed cavity, showed me the urn made from a hollow log, sliced off a piece of butter, replaced the sod and patted it back in place.

'They barge in and have a look through the huts every now and then. So . . .'

■

I rushed out my adventures to Elts.

'Oh, that swim! It was divine! In Lake Lehtmets, isn't that marvellous?'

'I'm glad you've had a good time.' Sarcasm did not really become her. 'If you'd been here, all you could have caught was a boat to Kuntika.'

'Who wants to?'

'Well, I'm going. You'll have to, too; that's where they're sending us. You'll have to wait till tomorrow, now.'

'I'm in no desperate hurry.'

'By *oblasok*.'

'Oh!'

'That's different, isn't it?'

'How did that come about?'

'The boat came down this morning, with two Russian girls. They're picking up supplies and going back to Kuntika this evening. I'm on it. So are a couple of others from here. You would have been, too, if you'd been around.'

'There's still plenty of time.'

'But there's no room left.'

'Well, that's my bad luck.'

'Ann, I'd have waited with you, but I've never been in an *oblasok*.'

'Don't worry, Elts dear.' The dear soul was torn between loyalty and fear. 'I've often paddled kayaks at home, an *oblasok* doesn't scare me at all.'

'Really?'

'Really.'

The *oblasok* was a notoriously lively canoe. And, in truth, I had had little experience in kayaks. What's more, I was as terrified of going through the devil's cauldron again as she was. The only thing I could see as an advantage was that I had become a most facile and apparently convincing liar.

Elts was plainly relieved.

379

'Oh well, if you're sure,' she said. 'But Tiia won't be there to see you off, because August the first is the day the controller comes to inspect the books.'

The date gave me a shock.

30

UP AND DOWN THE VASJUGAN

T he wind was stronger at the river front. The water looked dirty and rough. Angry little waves slopped irregularly against slippery banks. The two *oblasoks*, tied to pegs in the ground, rocked and snorted. The trees across the stream waved and creaked. The bare grass on this side was wet from gust-whipped wavelets.

I was feeling sorry for myself. I had suddenly realised last night that today was my birthday. I had felt miserable then, and saw no cause for improvement now. I remembered my first workday in Maisk and how I had been let off. And my fit in the fields last year, with exemption again. Perhaps something nice would happen on this one, too? But no. The weather was foul, the *oblasoks* were ready, daunting in their violent movement; there was no escape. No amount of tears or tantrums would change a thing.

A young woman stood near the smaller of the two canoes. She was tall, aloof, darkly pretty, striking in a floral silk dress. She was holding a *kateljok* and a couple of bundles, probably clothes, for loading. Juhan Kesa, the Estonian army captain who had been so morose on landing at Maisk, now a lumber brigadier at Kuntika, was bent over the other, carefully placing a sporting rifle and a pair of rubber boots among the bags. The dark girl and I had time only for nods.

'These we have to look after like our own eyes,' he said. 'They're the director's.'

Finally, satisfied, he climbed in.

'Right. Your turn.'

Bravely, I waded out, handed him my small bundle, threw in

my *tscherkis* and stepped over the side while he steadied the craft with a paddle. After an initial wobble that nearly pitched me straight over the other side, I settled on the seat behind him and clamped my hands around a paddle.

'Sit still and relax.'

I sat still. He took a few strokes. My heart shivered.

'For God's sake relax!'

The nose of our eggshell swept back and forth at an alarming rate. It tipped sideways. Water poured over. I screamed and clutched the sides. The water looked terribly rough.

'I said sit still, devil take you!' He went on swearing, whether at me or the river I didn't know, and took a few more dips. We shipped water on the other side. '*Kurat!*'

A deep voice called from the bank: 'What are you performing about? Be calm.' It was Silk Frock. I silently damned her. 'It's a simple enough thing!'

A few more hair-raising metres, and a gust of wind turned our nose toward the shore. Kesa, still swearing at each stroke, helped it in, no more than twenty steps from where we had begun. I grabbed my things and jumped into thigh-deep water.

'No good trying more today,' Kesa said as he towed the *obla-sok* back. 'This river's bucking like a wild horse. Wait here while I go and find out what we do next.'

I sat on my bag and spread my saturated skirt, still expecting wrath despite his apparent control.

'You're a smoker, aren't you?'

I nodded miserably.

'Here, light yourself a *pabeross*. I'll be back soon.'

I smoked. As soon as his back was turned, I cried. Self-pity, frustration, gratitude for Kesa's tolerance, anger at Silk Frock and her unsolicited advice: all poured out in a hot flood.

I sat a long time. No Kesa, no message. The floral silk dress moved into the corner of my eye. I dried tears surreptitiously without turning my head. Who needed her?

'Why do you cry?' said the deep voice.

'I cry for sheer joy – '

'I hope I didn't upset you.'

' – because it's my birthday.' And I'd not even given it a thought until last night.

'I didn't mean – '

382

'I'm forty years old. Not because of you and your – '

'I am Latvian. Nina Schmelis, from Riga. Forgive me if I upset you – '

'Yelling at me like a – '

'Many happy returns for your birthday.'

' – like a – '

'August the first, is it?'

'Yes.'

'From the bottom of my heart.'

'Oh!'

'I, too, will turn forty this month. Isn't that a coincidence?'

I'm told I have a temper like a gipsy's shotgun: a crack and a bang and it's all over. She was dark-haired, brown-eyed, anxious. We shook hands and laughed. I would have thought her much younger than she said.

By the time the message came, we had sorted out lineage and status. It was easier with a total stranger of different nationality; no overlap of acquaintances, or toes to avoid treading on. We could ask direct questions and give direct answers. We were friends in five minutes.

The journey would be abandoned today, reported Kesa. We would start at nine on Monday.

Perhaps I was born under a lucky star.

■

'Dance?' I said incredulously.

'In your best clothes. Hair up. No arguing.'

It was Nina's idea, and we had no trouble coopting Ronald – also awaiting movement orders – and his accordion.

The Novo-Vasjugan cultural rest hut was nearly full when we arrived, mostly with young Russian women. They too danced, but kept open-mouthed distance from the high-spirited ladies of fashion stepping out on a Saturday night to celebrate their birthdays. The few men present gave us an even wider berth, frankly over-awed.

One couple out-shone us. Tall, striking, impeccably dressed, they danced beautifully. Early in the evening, the man spoke to his partner, crossed the floor and asked us in turn to dance. Having observed the courtesies, we spent the rest of the evening together. They, too, had something obviously very personal to ommemorate; we did not hear what. They were Romanian, from Chernovtsy, where both had been high-school sports instructors. In the course of conversation, it emerged that the man had been a medallist in gymnastics at the Berlin Olympics.

Criminals all, we allowed capitalist decadence out of its cage for the night.

■

Monday morning, back to white mice and pumpkin. It had been nice to pretend.

'You watch the boat for a minute,' Kesa said. 'I have some business to do.'

'Fetching the slipper?'

'*Kurat!* What the – '

'Never mind.'

One more to the ranks of those who thought me crazy.

Nina had already gone in the larger *oblasok* with Ilse Veskimaa and Ilse's five-year-old son, Peet. They had left in calm water, the sun climbing through trees across the river into clear blue sky. I had thought we would follow immediately. Not so the brigadier, who seemed to have been wasting time.

I watched the other canoe head steadily upstream, keeping close inshore to minimise the current. They looked steady and efficient. I hoped I wouldn't make Kesa angry again.

'Here, take one.' He was back with two loaves of bread under his arm. So that was why he had dithered. 'Share it with Nina if you like, but don't tell the others.'

I hesitated.

'It's all right. No coupons. Just deliver a letter for me.'

Who wanted a golden slipper!

We soon fell into easy rhythm, paddling in companionable silence. The river was mirror-smooth. The shore, a couple of metres away on our right, changed constantly. For a time, the scene would be low and marshy, the reeds whispering, the occasional agitated waterbird flap-dashing away at our approach. Then the bank would rise sharply and trunks of trees would spread to the sky, roots exposed, foliage hovering over us, glistening, cooling, blotting out the sun. On the other side, twenty metres across the stream, heavy needle forest grew on the lowlands, grass on the heights behind showing softer green through

384

the occasional chinks. Birds called. Invisible creatures rustled the ground cover.

Kesa pointed out sights and sounds to me. I think he loved the country. I could narrow my view and share his joy in God's world as I half-listened to the sound of his voice, the dip of the paddles, the ceaseless chatter of birds, the muted racket of a myriad frogs.

'See in there? Bear tracks. Listen! Waterfowl. See the shape of that pine? Those berries, they're poisonous. A nest, see? Trunk all of a couple of hundred years old.'

A shudder, a quick twist, and we were in the water. The load, too. Gasping and spluttering, we surfaced, to find the river was only waist-deep. It was also cold. Fortunately, the bottom was firm and flat, and such was the speed of our capsize, I hadn't time to be frightened. I grabbed at my paddle, then Kesa's as it floated past, and my bag and his, as he struggled to right the canoe and tow it ashore. Up on the bank with them, then back in the chilly water. I caught a boot as it was about to sink, and helped Kesa gather clothes as they spread gently over the inno-cent expanse. Having rescued them, it took the two of us all our time to land a big sailcloth heavy with Vasjugan.

We stood, panting, to survey the serene stream that had quietly thrown us in. The only visible evidence of disaster was a small barrel of tasty salted tomatoes floating smoothly back toward Novo-Vasjugan. 'Whore of a river,' Kesa muttered. 'Must have been a hidden eddy.'

There was nothing for it but to strip to our underwear. Further would have been more comfortable, but modesty saw only outer-clothes and rescued gear hanging on the bushes. The sun was pleasant, the breeze negligible.

'*Kurat!*' Kesa's shout, as he leapt for the water, startled me. 'The director's gun!'

'*Kurat!*' I echoed, following at the double. 'And we've only got one of his boots!'

'*Kurat!*' for good measure.

The great Estonian swearword simply means Devil. Yet, such is its native popularity, its versatility, the variety of expression any Estonian worth his salt can put into his *Kurat!* that it has become almost a universal favourite.

My bare foot found the boot.

Kesa, wading deeper, shouted, 'Give me a hand, I think I've got it!'

The water was up to my armpit. I held on, while he edged his foot further.

'Let go.'

He dived, and came up with the gun first try. The boot moved easily to my toes.

'Doesn't getting it wet do some harm?' I asked, as he laid the weapon on the turf.

If you keep your mouth shut, his threatening scowl assured me, he's not going to find out, is he!

'Look!'

The little tomato barrel was bobbing in towards the shore, only a hundred paces down. Like children, we splashed to the rescue, shouting like a pair of crazy fossickers striking gold. From disaster, one hundred per cent recovery.

Because of the gun, the capsize had to remain our secret. So did our near-naked dance of victory while we waited for things to dry.

'This has been a very interesting trip,' a more sedate Kesa promised, as we clambered up the Kuntika landing. 'I'll enter it as one full day.'

■

Kuntika was another Maisk. After two weeks of the same life in a different location I had new friends in Nina, Elts, Kesa and Vaike, Margo's daughter Kersti, Ronald, and Silva the cook, who was having an ill-disguised affair with director Jelski; otherwise, except for a hundred-odd kilometres of river, Novo-Vasjugan was as far away as ever.

We knew some of the Russian girls had been stirring trouble. One in particular, Siina, had threatened to report us for every minor misdemeanour, real or imagined.

Most times we could have ignored such talk. But not from Siina, she was not one for idle threats; she had promised torment for the whole *schweinerei*: Silva the cook, Peet and his mother Ilse, Nina and Elts and me, Kesa and Vaike. She was sick of felling her quota while we stood about and loafed but were always first in the bread queue. And Kesa the foreman favouring us. And Silva giving us bigger rations – and thinking she'd get away with it because she was on with the director. And our being too stuck-up to talk to the Russian girls.

So when a snap after-work meeting was called, we were not surprised. And snap meetings, in my experience, always meant trouble. However, we still had optimists in our midst.

'Now we'll get a roasting,' I muttered.

'Don't worry,' Nina said. 'He'll treat us right.'

'We're really for it,' Elts fretted. 'They saw me make an awful botch of dropping a tree. Nearly on them. What will he do? I couldn't live on any cut in my ration.'

Vaike Kesa said, 'Don't you believe it. Dad says Silva has done some good groundwork to protect us.'

One way of putting it, I thought. Good luck, Silva.

The meeting began in friendly enough fashion.

'Are you satisfied with your quarters? – any sickness?' No diatribe, I noticed; a point in director Jelski's favour. 'Receiving your bread regularly? – tools adequate? – sharp enough?'

We waited uneasily. There must be more than this banality to fetch the director and *kolkhoz* chairman here.

'Any complaints?'

Siina rose to her feet. She was a pretty enough girl, in her early twenties, medium-haired, dark-eyed, firmly built. She was hard-looking, though, tonight more so than usual, as she flashed a triumphant glance at us and a conspiratorial one at the director. We've got them, the message blinked, let's give these uppity foreigners a poke in the eye. She opened her mouth and took a deep breath.

The director's fist hit the table. 'Sit down, Siina! I have not yet finished talking. And before you say anything, listen!'

Siina sat as though shot, mouth still open.

'*A vot* – ? – Well – ?' She closed it.

'Now listen, and don't forget. Estonians and Latvians are orderly, industrious people. They are not used to us and our ways, and they won't ever get used to us if we are underhanded.'

It was our turn to sit with mouths open while the Russian girls burned. Siina, in particular, was the picture of mortification.

'They are staying, like it or not. That is not your decision, nor is it mine. I might add it is not theirs, either. Those of you who don't like to stay in the same work parties with them may pack bags and report for transfer.' Since transfer would probably be off the face of the earth, it was unlikely to attract applicants. 'The meeting is over,' he finished abruptly.

Siina and friends departed wordlessly, eyes down, hackles up.

The presence of the slightly surprised *kolkhoz* chairman, our new and typical man in black, prevented us from openly applauding. Jelski had gone out on a limb for us; we had no idea how sound a limb, so we must not embarrass him. There was a misgiving, too: however courageous, voicing his sentiments might have been unwise in the presence of the chairman. I wondered if harm would come of it.

I found out three days later, when I came across Anashka sitting on Kuntika's office steps, grinning broadly.

'Good day, Ljahmets. Got a rouble for me?'

When in trouble, think of your friends.

'So you remember, do you?' I called him 'thou', and sat with him.

'Why not? You promised me a rouble next time we met.'

I handed over the note.

'It's a fine day. Why did you come looking for me? I was right, wasn't I? There are lots of Estonians in Kuntika.'

Within two days of our 'victory' over the Russian girls the daily bread allowance had been decreased. We thought it unlikely the two were connected, though we considered the possibility that Jelski might be face-saving or, perhaps, being over-ridden. Probably, we had concluded, the drop was general, though, of course, it hurt us more than those who could match the norms.

'Yes. I have found some friends here.'

'Aren't you all friends?'

Interesting observation. 'Mostly.'

'I knew it.'

'And I look to thee as a friend, too. Do you know where I can buy some potatoes and peas?'

'They've cut your kitchen rations, haven't they?'

'Yes, we need – '

'You didn't think I'd know, did you?'

'No, I didn't. We – '

'Potatoes aren't ready. Peas are still too young. You were nice to me. Sit behind that bush and wait.'

He was back in a matter of minutes, shirt front bulging.

'Here, quick. Put them in your head-scarf.' A thick bunch of earth-fresh carrots. 'Tell me when they're finished. There's more.'

I was curious, but forbore from asking where they came from.

'You know it's only your brigade they've cut,' he said. 'Did you do something wrong?'

■

Kesa brought the great news.

I was sitting on his doorstep with Elts and Vaike, munching the last of the carrots. The reduction in food, from base subsistence level to below, was serious. We simply could not live without augmentation, and my self-styled idiot friend could not be relied on indefinitely. If starvation to death was their aim, one way or another we would have to find a way to cheat them. So far we had no plan.

'Ann, you're to be ready for the morning boat to Novo-Vasjugan!'

'Why? What else can they want?'

'I think nothing bad. Else the invitation would have come from the *milits*. This was from the director.'

I got up quickly. 'Oh! I'd better see him, then.'

'He's gone. He told me to tell you. The mail boat leaves at nine.'

Perhaps it was not bad, as Kesa thought; after all it was why I had left Maisk, it was what I had been waiting for: the big city, away from the nit-picking of a backwoods collective. I was excited, but fearful as well, despite Kesa's reading of my orders.

I was again torn between the two worlds: the city, and the opportunity for knowledge and communication, possibly with easier work and regular sustenance; and out here where I could achieve a measure of peace in a time-slot – providing I survived! Here, too, were the people I would rather be with. Always – always – in the background was that other world, the real world, the dream world, where my children might be alive, needing me, missing me, as I needed and missed them. Novo-Vasjugan was that one step nearer, so there was no contest.

'I'll be ready.'

'Come on, Vaike,' Kesa said. 'Let's go to the office and write a letter to your mother. Ann can deliver it.'

■

The boat left sharp at nine. Kesa, true to his word, saw me off. I would miss his reliability. As Elts hugged me goodbye – an unusual show of emotion between us – I realised it was not only her I wanted to have with me on my venture. I was acutely disappointed that Nina, the Latvian, was not to join me in my assault on Novo-Vasjugan; we had clicked so quickly.

The boatman-postman was a one-legged *kolkhoznik*. He was an Ostiak, sixty, talkative, and as active as a two-year-old. He skipped into the boat, cast off, hopped to his seat and pulled out into midstream as if he could row all day. 'Just as well you don't row with your legs, eh?' he grinned, glancing down at his stump.

The banks slid steadily past. Our little boat, laden with the two of us plus my luggage and a few canvas bags, rippled through the water in a pleasant breeze. The Ostiak waited courteously for me to speak next.

I had seen much of it by now, and felt a strange intimacy with this land I had certainly never wanted to know. Though at times I would hate, resent, fear it, I could never tire of it. River, sky, banks, trees, space. God's world. God's, not the Russians'. Whatever else they did – to me, to others, to the earth itself – they could not enslave *it*; it was here long before they were, and would be here long after they'd gone. I was fascinated by it: its beauty, permanence, total indifference to Russian occupation. I sensed the same contentment in my shipmate.

'Does all this mail come from Kuntika?' I asked companionably.

'From all over the place. From one *kolkhoz* to another. Some of this stuff starts from Schmarkovka. I take all I collect to Novo-Vasjugan and pick up there for the return trip.'

I had heard of mail going backward and forward, up and down the river, sometimes for months. And of letters lost in the sorting systems – or more likely the censors' offices – of Novo-Vasjugan: wherever from or to in the area, it all went through there. I was to have my own experiences in due time –censors, KGB, long delivery, non-delivery – but that was to come. So far, mail was not a part of my life; I could only hope that some day it might be.

'At Schmarkovka, the postman from the next stop up, Metvetka, takes everything for beyond. And so on, about once a week; depends a bit on the current. In the winter it's carted by horse. That's a lot more trouble.'

'Do you do that, too?'

'I'm a boatman. But I could,' he grinned. 'You don't need two legs on a horse either.'

He would not say how he had lost the leg, but informed me proudly that he had been a hunter and fisherman in the *taiga* – the forest regions of the north, as far as trees would grow – before he was wounded.

'What did you hunt?'

'Everything.'

'Bears?'

'I've shot any number.'

'Shot and killed?'

'Stone dead!' What else? his amused look implied: you wouldn't want to miss!

'And other animals?' Now we had common ground. He loved his subject – the wild – as I loved to hear about it.

'*Vot*, there are still plenty of hares, squirrels, chipmunks, weasels, lynxes, foxes.' He shrugged away those he couldn't recall offhand. 'Mink too. Sable. Ermine. But not many. They bring a good price if you're lucky enough: twenty roubles for a first-class skin. And out in the deep forest there are elks, reindeer – '

'Reindeer?'

'Aye. Forest reindeer. They're shy creatures. They come down from the *tundra* in the autumn. Winter up there's too hard. No feed.'

'The others come down too?'

'Some of the birds do. The little animals – the burrowing creatures – they can't live up there at all. They can't dig.' I remembered trying to put a spade through frozen earth. 'Wolves. I've seen a few.'

'Did you hunt the reindeer?'

'I've shot a couple. As a young man. We cooked their meat over open fires – delicious – and dried some for later. They're protected now. Get shot yourself, if you're caught. No more reindeer steaks, not worth it.'

So there was fauna conservation. A point in totalitarian favour. And a surprise to me. A pity they didn't extend it to people!

'You know,' he reminisced, 'the innards were particularly good, baked on those coals.' Ugh!

He rowed automatically, eyes focused thirty-five years back, nodding appreciatively at his memorable meal, while I stared in disbelief. Eating innards when the pick of the beast was available!

'Those were the days, *vot*. I've still got his antlers.' He returned to the present, and me. 'Hanging on my hut wall. If you ever happen back this way, come and have a look.'

'Surely.'

I asked what fish there were in local streams and lakes, and if there was any chance of catching some.

'You could catch them with your hands once. Now there are government quotas to be filled by *kolkhozniks*. They are too big, those quotas. Much too big. And, if they ever happen to get filled, they make 'em bigger. Short-sighted. Fishing it out.'

At sixty, and out on the open river, such criticism was probably safe. Even so, I felt momentarily disturbed – how you become conditioned! – and let his observation pass. You could never be really sure.

'In the Vasjugan River you can still get pike or perch or – ' – a name I did not know – 'and in the lakes some *linask*.'

I knew *linask*. A good table fish, caught in the shallow lakes at home. A real prize. Fresh fish! My stomach sighed.

I could have listened to more of the old hunter, but the journey was soon over. Once again I was on the river bank, this time alone and with mixed feelings of dread and anticipation.

'If you're ever back this way I'll show you those antlers and we can talk some more.'

'I probably shall be.' Although, at this moment, I felt I could do without the river and Kuntika and lumbering forever. 'Thank you for the pleasant trip. Yes, I'd like that.' Like a cruise ship acquaintance. We were both sincere, both knew it would not eventuate. And, all the time, I had the sense that something momentous was about to happen.

31

THE BRIGHT LIGHTS

Elena Ossipovna was not downright unfriendly. She looked me up and down before gesturing me to the inner office. She preceded me, walked behind the desk, seated herself, scrutinised me thoroughly . . . She should have seen me half an hour ago, when curiosity had steered me here straight from the boat! Sweaty, in travelling clothes with the smell of the boat still on them, hair a mess, bare feet covered in thick river mud with a topcoat of fine dust from the road . . .

It was just as well I had taken Tiia's advice and gone to see Margo at the laundry before reporting in; Margo, she had told me, did the director's washing, and had access to clean water and soap. 'Our new office worker must not look like a peasant.'

■

'Anna Denisovna, do you have a change of clothes?'

'I have, Elena Ossipovna.'

'And do you have some footwear?'

'I have, Elena Ossipovna.' A lie.

Hessian skirt and bare feet, though clean, were not fit attire for office workers. Agreed. A little more cordiality would have been welcome, even so.

'You may sit.'

May I indeed!

'Fill in this application.'

It was a simple enough form. They already had my life's details.

'Pick up your bread ration card for this month from the office, and settlement for your work in Kuntika. Fifteen roubles.'

'Fifteen?' Less than it was worth, more than expected.

'Your quarters, bread and soup for the three weeks have been deducted. Now, here you will be in the office by nine tomorrow morning. Your immediate superiors will be Irma Janovna' – the Latvian head bookkeeper – 'and Tiia Karlovna. The workday is from nine till six, with an hour for lunch. Sundays are off, unless there is extra work to be done. The salary is seventy-five roubles a month less quarters, heating and light. The stableman will give you a mattress and straw, and you will be allotted a cot in the communal quarters. Iida Andrejevna is in charge there.'

Clear, concise instructions, I thought. Elena Ossipovna is no fool. If I wanted to keep my cushy job, I would have to stay on the right side of her.

'Thank you,' I said.

She bent her head to the desk. I was dismissed.

'Tiia,' I asked on the way out, 'who is Iida Andrejevna?'

'Mrs Kesa,' Tiia said. 'You've met?'

'I know her husband and daughter.' I carried their letter for her.

'Poor soul. She's on sick leave for a few days. Mrs Kesa senior lives there, too. She's partly paralysed. Come to lunch, I'll tell you more.'

'Are you sure you're allowed out?' I could not resist an acid touch.

'Who are you, Anna Denisovna, to question your superiors?'

We left the office. Tiia had not changed that much, I conceded. She still had the ability to turn a sour word into a joke.

'That being the way the things are, Madam Superior, what do I do now?' I retorted with a laugh.

'After lunch, which will not today – nor will it usually – take an hour to eat, as you might well imagine, you can get your living arrangements in order. In the meantime I'll put you in the local picture.'

Tiia rattled on, and I could not help a secret smile; her attitude, changed overnight, showed I was distinctly more acceptable since I had joined the staff. Among other news, she had seen reports that Silva, our Kuntika cook, had been posted hurriedly to a not-too-close *kolkhoz*. And director Jelski had been called away on unspecified business. It was today's mystery, the office buzzing with it. Punishment and reprimand, I suggested, with Tiia agreeing after hearing of the startling meeting in Kuntika.

Lunch over, I went to inspect my new home: a big, square, log-walled building, with seven or eight well-scrubbed steps outside leading up to a solid door. It looked cared-for, and quite pleasant. I knocked and stepped into a big, open room with two cheery windows, a floor bleached clean white, and a large stove, with four iron cooking holes, against the door wall. Near the stove was a long trestle table holding a remarkable array of cooking and eating utensils, no two alike. Cots, about twenty in all, arranged in rows against the remaining three walls, pointing into the centre, virtually completed the furniture. The beds varied in size, height and shape; even more in construction and covering. A patchwork, but tidy and clean.

Margo squatted cross-legged on a frail-looking stool between beds against the far wall, sewing. An elderly woman with swollen and discoloured legs lay near the open window. Mrs Kesa senior. Her daughter-in-law, the Iida Andrejevna who was in charge of the hut, was at the stove. I made myself known to her, passing over the letter and parcel from Kuntika.

'Are they all right?'

'They're both well.'

'Thank God for that,' she whispered.

'Which cot do I take?'

Margo called, 'You can come next to me if you like. There's a spare one here.'

The empty bed was a crude affair, rough-sawn legs and frame supporting slats of small timbers green enough to have a little give in them. My mattress was stuffed, sewn and put in place in short order. The bedclothes came out – 'I'll sneak them in with the director's next laundry day,' Margo promised, 'and give them a good wash' – and my tattered suitcase wardrobe was pushed under the bed with some difficulty, as there was less than arm's distance between cots. All it needed now was the pure linen tablecloth – a present from my mother-in-law, one of the more perplexing discoveries in the luggage my mother had packed – and my bed was complete. It promised to be the best for many a night.

■

I began the new job with enthusiasm, sitting at my office table in clean clothes, ready and willing to write all day. How much better than bending to a spade or axe.

Disillusionment was quick in coming. Disappointment number one: instead of a pen I was handed a pot of glue, a reel of linen thread, a large darning needle and a bundle of papers of varying sizes, shapes and textures, all second-hand and frayed. My job was to make this bundle of tatters into a book, putting numbered pages in order, numbering those unnumbered. I was to find missing pages, of which there were plenty, searching everywhere myself before troubling the bookkeeper. For a whole week I searched, glued and sewed; and, by the Saturday evening, I had the whole lot quite neatly between covers, as motley an assortment of applications, request forms, pay slips, accounts, bills and reports as anyone ever saw, mostly written over old newspapers or used circulars and documents. Why anyone might ever need to refer to them puzzled me; *how* anyone would ever find a wanted page was incomprehensible.

I was given 'important work' as our load increased, holding a real pen, using real ink in rewriting some of the more official reports – pay lists, requisitions, inventories, trading and production figures – on clean paper. Pen, ink, paper. Real writing! Even though it was in Russian, largely fabricated, and likely never again to see the light of day, the thrill was beyond my own anticipation. I was getting somewhere!

Where, Ann? Don't think about that.

One evening, while handling a pay list from Volkolva, I saw the name Elli Ranna. I had last seen Elli in Aipalova trying desperately to sustain her three small children. I collared the brigadier from Volkolva, a decent Ukrainian, who promised to deliver a letter in which I pledged to keep her a few kilograms of wheat if she could somehow collect it. It was fortunate that I was in the office to hear of her; more so, that I had the reserves to help. My new job *was* an advance, there *were* still blessings to be counted.

Osvald Pedusoo, as well as being knowledgeable, was discreet and reliable. Osvald, last seen at a railway station predicting an early end to the war, had been a high-school teacher, presumably forgotten in the separation of the sexes, and had gained a reputation in Novo-Vasjugan as a gatherer of intelligence. Where he got his astonishing flow of information was a mystery, as nobody else ever had any. Now that I was white-collar, I must keep up-to-date – why else was I here? – so I cornered him over a bowl of soup to ask what was new from the front. Surely there was something in that avenue to give some satisfaction.

Politics, and the war itself, were never discussed in the office, seldom in quarters. News was practically non-existent anyway. The few times we talked – among ourselves of course, as no serious topic could safely be broached near Russians – nobody knew anything. We could only guess. What surprised me in my new surroundings was not so much the lack of information, as that so few seemed to care. Even my good friends, Tiia and Margo, were reluctant to talk freely, while others quite pointedly closed up. Perhaps, I granted, they had families and jobs to protect. Or perhaps, I thought grimly, and as seemed more likely, they were simply resigning from the world. I found myself getting impatient with them. I had not come to Novo-Vasjugan, and taken an office job, to be more cut off than I had been in the wilderness of the *kolkhoz*.

'It appears the Russians are winning,' Osvald said, in his calm, friendly manner.

'Oh no!'

'My local-yokel workmates are hoping for a happy ending quite soon.'

'It can't be!'

'That's what the news is, Ann.'

That they could win, that communism and all that went with it could come out on top, was absolutely unthinkable. To even consider it was to shake the foundation, as far as I was concerned, of the will to survive. Was this what had happened to the others? Had they begun to doubt? And, losing faith, were they losing heart?

'No!'

We *must* have something to hang on to! Russian victory meant never leaving here, never being home again, never seeing . . .

'It's what I hear.'

'How would they know?' I demanded. 'Do they ever read papers, ever hear a radio?'

'Probably not, my dear Ann. Probably not.' He smiled over his wooden spoon. 'And please keep your voice down.'

'If they did, it's only propaganda!'

'Very likely.'

'Then why – '

'It's what they say. They seem quite cheerful about it.'

I trusted my worries to Tiia, and soon wished I hadn't, for this brought on disappointment number two.

'I've heard the same rumours,' she said airily. 'Maybe you're right, Ann, they're just trying to placate their own people. Maybe not. But don't you worry, I have some news for you. Really *good* news. When you've finished your two weeks in the office, you can take Kersti's place. Isn't that lucky? She's got a sick certificate, there's a vacancy.'

Back to her old sprightliness. Perhaps I should be pleased. But was this a new Tiia? this now the full width of her view?

I longed for Nina's deep voice, her intolerance of meekness and small-mindedness: the very traits, I thought wryly, that had angered me at our first meeting. She had no family to consider – her son had died soon after reaching Novo-Vasjugan – she was staunchly patriotic (albeit Latvian), straight-forward, as unbendingly set on outlasting this exile as I. Some of our own number seemed to have forgotten the skies beyond the prison bars. We thought alike, Nina and I, and I needed her strength. After such terrible intelligence from Osvald, my flagging optimism needed reinforcement, not Tiia's blithe submission.

■

My two-week stint of pen-handling saw the director off to Kargasok loaded with reports, Ossipovna the boss, and me the temporary office cleaner. Kargasok, where the Vasjugan River joined the Ob, was the next link in the administrative chain to Novo-Sibirsk, Omsk, and Moscow.

Even by the end of the third day I knew I would not last. And this was disappointment number three: the dashing of my hopes in the Bright Lights. The office was easy to clean, and cleaner's pay was better than a clerk's. 'Real work' must be more honourable than sitting at a desk.

The work was no trouble. The difficulty was Elena Ossipovna.

On the second day, the windows were not sparkling enough, and there was dust on top of the oven. The next, she did not like my coming to work in slacks. Then, I must not move my desk without permission. I must always be either in the office or the barracks during working hours, not out so often; I must not talk to people; I must not question superiors; I must be quicker to answer. At the end of a week, although the job was child's play compared with lumbering, I longed to be back where the trials of survival were easier by far than controlling myself under the snide malice of Her Niggling Majesty.

No sooner yearned than done. In my fourth week in Novo-Vasjugan, I was told I must return to Kuntika. Orders. The director had come back and seen my finished files and, although he was pleased at first, it seemed, after consultation with Elena Ossipovna, that neither clerk nor cleaner was now required in his department, and I could leave by the next boat, three days away.

I shed no tears.

■

Meanwhile, I could mark time hoping to see Elli. She had had my message, and promised to come as soon as possible. It would be a shame if I had to leave Novo-Vasjugan before she got here, for I desperately wanted to see her. Elli was more than a hometown acquaintance, she had been a very dear friend.

In our present community-within-a-community, subtle gradations of intimacy had developed. Siberia was a world of its own, its inhabitants a race – or rather races – apart, isolated as few places on earth are. Our group of deportees, strangers to each other in varying degrees, had been dumped on an existing, though struggling, society. We were unwilling; they were hostile. We newcomers thus became instant comrades, allies with a common foe, bonded as only those who have shared extreme adversity can ever understand. Fellow-sufferers of differing language and background were thus united by definition; fellow nationals, with the added tie of language, became immediate boon companions; old acquaintances, instant intimates; friends, virtually kin.

Elli was in the closest of the latter bracket. Few at home had been closer. I looked forward to her visit wholeheartedly, praying she would come before I left for Kuntika.

■

Another diversion. And further illustration that some good can come of anything.

A salt barge arrived. Late one afternoon, it pulled quietly in, unannounced, from the mysterious mines that were never mentioned without a catch of fear or a shiver of sympathetic horror for the poor devils at the other end. Nobody questioned its port of origin now, and no word was offered – only that the salt had to be unloaded in a hurry. Every spare hand – storeman, clerk, office boss, even children – had to report for work. Voluntary work, this, for the common good. No pay. No compulsion, but if you didn't go, watch out!

The salt, from fine gravel to brick-sized rock, sharp on the feet, glary on the eyes, murder in cuts and scratches, was to be shovelled into sacks, about ten kilograms a time, carried from the open hold and dumped on large canvasses spread on the bank. This meant a loaded journey over the barge, across the crude board gangplank, and about a hundred paces up a fairly steep slope; then back for more. From high above, we must have looked like a colony of ants swarming over the shelving bank between moored barge and waiting tarpaulins, all on the move, crisscrossing, weaving, bumping into each other; checking, stopping, starting, carrying; all confusion, yet achieving the transfer with astonishing speed. The barge emptied, the heaps grew, and all between was twilight activity, to the discordant music of screams, shouts, swearing in Russian, retorts in other tongues, even occasional laughter. Orders were yelled; people stumbled, fell, got up, muttering, to carry on. In charge was the director of the fish factory – Dobrovolsky – in neat working dress plus inevitable knee boots. He was a powerful fellow, with a back and neck like a bull, pleasant enough, though a bit of a show-off. He hoisted a bag, all of one hundred kilograms, trotted it up, went back for another, dumped that and squatted high on the bank. 'Now, you lot,' he roared, 'I've filled my norm. Get on with yours! I want all this stuff ashore by midnight.'

It was done. Better that than slaving all night.

Shortly after finishing, I and another 'barefooter' – a term used regularly now, contemptuously by the Russians, with a certain perverse smugness by ourselves – slunk along the bank in the dark, resting frequently, soles of our feet burning, hearts in mouths, half-dragging a bag containing four shovelfuls of salt. The woman was from Riga; we had never met, yet we were soul companions, tacitly risking spending the rest of our lives together in the dreaded camps. It would be too bad if all that 'voluntary work' fetched nothing, though; there had to be recompense; the thought had occurred to us simultaneously, half-way up with this, the last load.

Dividing the precious stuff, we whispered good-night and went our strangers' ways.

I had the next day off. Margo, Mrs Kesa and the Pedusoos were rewarded with a couple of handfuls of my booty, and I did some trading. Customers were easy to find: they found me.

Salt was normally quite unobtainable, except in the special shop reserved for party members. As some of these illustrious citizens were not above indulging in a spot of capitalist enterprise, there was a limited though well-known black market, at six roubles or two litres of milk to a small glass of salt. I was happy to undercut them for my special clientele.

■

Elli arrived, as a messenger from her *kolkhoz*. We adjourned – with Elena Ossipovna's permission, no less, this being my last day – to the communal quarters, before falling into each other's arms, laughing and crying. I did not know I had so much emotion left.

With many of my new friends, there had been links with the past; we had talked of friends and families until we felt we knew each others'; we had discovered mutual acquaintances, been to the same places, done the same things, sometimes even discovered we had met before. We had become close, occasionally very close. But nothing like this. Elli and I did not need to introduce ourselves or describe our pasts. We knew without talking. We had *shared*. Our reminiscences weren't reminders, they were memories. We talked, and sat in silence.

Elli no longer hoped for her eldest son's survival. He was ten, would not see eleven. She had sold or exchanged everything she had brought with her, laboured all day in the *kolkhoz*, sewed and knitted for the Russians at night, nursed a semi-paralysed old woman. Her goal, now, was the lives of her younger two. I wondered at her resilience, at whether or not I could have kept her sanity, her sense of humour, her tenacity. Her boy, her own darling son, dying . . .

'You'll manage, Elli, I'm sure. Having got this far – '

'And yours, Ann. I pray for them, that one day you will have news.'

'There's some wheat here I don't need. I kept it for you, when I heard you were near.'

'Thank you, Ann. No. It wouldn't save my family. It may cause trouble. But the offer itself will give me strength.'

'Well, salt? Look, I have plenty.'

'That I shall take!' She was overjoyed. 'Salt! How nice. The children won't know what it is!'

'Truly?'

'Yes.'

'Take it, and my blessing.'

We hugged farewell.

■

Tiia was petulant. 'Didn't I try to help you to a greener branch?'

'Forgive me, Tiia. I suppose I should have been more submissive with her.'

'I understand that. I don't find her easy to get on with either. Still –'

'I think perhaps I'll be safer at a distance.'

'Why?'

'You, too.'

'What, you want me to go? Leave here?'

'No, I mean you'll be safer if I do.'

'I had hoped the two of us in the office –'

She was pensive, the old effervescence gone.

'I'm sorry. Really I am.'

'You're to go with the postman tomorrow. Back to Kuntika.'

■

I sat on the bank to wait, not minding the dampening grass, their boat not expected for some time yet. My own voyage back to Kuntika, in the tiny *oblasok* with the young Ostiak postman, had been uneventful; I had reported to the brigadier, made up my bed – not as comfortable as the last one, I noted ruefully, though the gain in privacy compensated – and now sought only peace while awaiting my friends.

The thirst for town life was truly assuaged. I had wanted information on the outside world; and the nearest approach to genuine news had been shockingly, incredibly bad. I had hoped for easier work, found it, tried it; and could not stomach its conditions. I had made contact with one old friend, Elli, and wept myself to sleep at her plight and the reminder of my own. Russians were everywhere, which was galling enough; some of my own people were accepting their state – on the way to *becoming* Russian – which was devastating. On the whole, Novo-Vasjugan had been a resounding failure.

Staring into the water, I could only employ my trick of blotting out those thoughts ever on the verge of consciousness . . . Tiiu, Tiit. Two years older now – would I know them? They me? Was there a normal life out there? . . . Elmar. A chance he was alive? . . . The children. Could they be not? Dear God . . .

Stop. Concentrate. Think of the present . . . the sunset . . .

A lone black bird circled high in the sky, slowly. A hawk, perhaps. Or a vulture . . . Vulture? The bird of death? . . . *Kurat!*

I went to the water's edge and dipped my feet. It was cold; flowing gently, calming to the nerves, soothing to my suddenly disordered system. That's better. I must keep in the slot.

The breeze was dropping, the water smoothing. The beauty of trees and sky was breath-taking, now doubled in the reflection. The vulture down there, up there . . .

Kurat again!

The boat rounded the bend. Elts, Nina, Ronald and Vaike appeared. I heard their shouts, and responded to their waves.

'Ann! How good you are back!'

Last day in Novo-Vasjugan: 1957. The aircraft is a converted war-plane, carrying five passengers. Ann's travelling rug was sent by Tiiu in Australia. Ann flew to Tomsk, then went by rail to Moscow and Estonia.

THE LETTER

Another winter: the sixth. 1948. Another day. How was I to know it would be one of the most glorious days of my life?

Back in Novo-Vasjugan, I was now the indispensable general factotum for the Administrative Centre: office cleaner, messenger, occasional scribe, maker of the sweets when sugar came in. Elena Ossipovna was no longer in charge; life was relatively peaceful.

Lunchtime, and it was usually worth the effort to walk the kilometre or so to my own cabin, shared with my old friend Elli Ranna, built by our own hands last summer with the aid of the Estonian boys. It was the last in the row, on the edge of the forest. Close enough; far enough. Out of harm's way, yet handy for the boys to throw in some sly wood on their way home. Elli would have a fire going, perhaps some company. She had come in from Volkolva to join me three years earlier, with her two remaining children. There was no doubt now about their survival.

There had been heavy falls this winter, and the hut, built as low as comfort would permit, would have been completely buried but for the regular clearing of the front. Fresh snow had fallen last night: helping Elli clear it was one reason for my lunchtime trek.

With two hundred metres still to go, I looked up. There would be no clearing, for punched in huge letters in the pure, white bank was the message: LETTER FROM YOUR SON.

My brain whirled. Tiit! My darling boy. Alive!

What about Tiiu? She too?

Six years! Not my little boy any more. My son. Nineteen years old. A man! And Tiiu – God willing – sixteen! Oh, Elmar.

Crying, laughing, praying, I pushed on through the powder snow. No weariness could slow me now; no fatigue, no cold, no famine stop me. My hands shook as I pushed open the door, brushed aside tears and saw the letter propped on the centre table.

'Tiit,' I cried aloud. 'I'm coming.'

POST-POSTSCRIPT

Ann's last fifteen years in Siberia were in conditions marginally better than those detailed, almost entirely due to adaptation and experience in handling them — plus, perhaps, the high attrition rate of fellow deportees.

She was finally permitted to return to Estonia, provided she could raise the expense of travel. This was achieved at a cost of trading clothing and 'luxury' goods sent from Australia — and the 400 thus-gained roubles placed in the conveniently opened drawer of a Russian official.

■

The first trickle of mail between Siberia and the western world began in 1947. Of the succession of letters sent by Ann over the years, one found a friend in Sweden. A newspaper advertisement placed by the friend ultimately reached Tiit, at that time stateless at sea, and Tiiu, in a displaced-persons' camp in Germany. Their letters – Ann's first indication that they were alive – reached Novo-Vasjugan in 1948, via International Red Cross.

Erratic correspondence continued between Tiit, now settled in New York, Tiiu, who had migrated to Australia with Ann's sister and family, and Ann.

Persistence from Australian, British and American diplomatic services during the Khrushchev 'de-Stalinification' era in 1956, and Ann herself, resulted in her return to Estonia – still in the

USSR – in 1957. This was in two stages: by air from Novo-Sibirsk to Tomsk, and train on to Moscow and Tallinn. The stolen bolt, kept seventeen years for the purpose, was thrown from the train window near Pihkva (Russia's Pskov).

With the aid and experience of the Lutheran World Federation, further persistence through almost unbelievable obstructions – refusals of exit visa, 'loss' of Australian entry visa, passport holdups, 'difficulties' in train travel from Estonia back to Moscow for the flight out, insistence on prepayment in foreign currency to cover flight costs (it was eighteen months between payment in American dollars and boarding) – saw Ann reunited with her daughter in Adelaide in 1960, after nineteen years' separation.

■

Ann lived to be 96 years old and died in October 2000 after a short illness.

She had lived to form an extremely close relationship with her daughter Tiiu, and to win the love and admiration of her four grandchildren, Martin, Ann, Robert and Linda. She had arrived in Adelaide in time for Linda's first birthday and in years to come found happiness in welcoming eight great-grandchildren into the world

Ann was able to visit her son Tiit in the USA on three occasions. On the first, she spent almost two years on invitation travelling and speaking to Estonian communities in North America at a time when the world was ignorant of the unimaginable hardships suffered by Baltic and other deportees to Siberia. Tiit also came to see her in Australia, as the photograph on one of his visits testifies. Sadly, he predeceased his mother, dying of cancer in the USA in 1999

Although increasingly frail in body, she retained a sharp mind — even a wry sense of humour — until near the end of her shattered life. Her chief regret, other than the loss of those 20 years of family, voiced occasionally on watching contented elderly couples, was growing old with no partner to share their later joys and sorrows.

*On the road from Maisk to Malinkova,
a path trodden many times by Ann*

A cross erected to the children who died at Aipolova

Ann on her 70th Birthday

*Tiit, Ann and Tiiu at ESTO '88 — The Free Estonian
World Festival at Melbourne, December 1988.*

412

DOCUMENTS

Rehabilitation certificate as passed by the Supreme Presidium of Soviet Socialist Republics on January 19, 1989, restoring civil rights to the victims of the repressions of the 1930's, '40's and '50's, issued to:

Lehtmets, Elmar Alexander: restrained 14.6.1941 under article 58-13 (relating to civil nonconformity) found guilty and sentenced on 17.06.1942* and punished by shooting to death 17.06.1942* at Sosva. *i.e. the same day.

ii) Lehtmets, Ann: Deported on June 1941 without court trial to the Oblast of Tomsk, region of Vasjugan, until November 15, 1957.

Rehabilitated on December 7, 1988, by order ot the Estonian SSR along with the victims of the mass deportations of the 1940's and '50's.

iii & iv) Lehtmets, Tiit (then aged 13) and Tiiu (then aged 9): Deported by administrative order on June 14, 1941, but sentence not carried out.*

*Only because they were not at home

Eesti NSV Siseministeerium
Informatsioonikeskus

200101 Tallinn, Pikk 61
Tel. 663-711

Nr. 25113

« 16 » märts 19 90. a.

ÕIEND

Kod. _____ LEHTMETS, Tiiu Elmari t., _____ sünd. 1931 a.

kuulus 19 41 a. juunis _____ Eesti NSV Virumaalt

_____ administratiivkorras väljasaatmisele,

kuid otsus tema suhtes jäi täitmata.

Kod. _____ LEHTMETS, Tiiu Elmari t. _____ on Eesti NSV

7. detsembri 1988. a. seaduse «Kohtuväliste massirepressioonide kohta Nõukogude Eestis 1940—1950-
___ aastail» alusel rehabiliteeritud:

Pitsat

Ülem _____ V. Kamõnin

ENSV S.M. tr. 1989 66 t. 3000 nr. 634

Eesti NSV Siseministeerium
Informatsioonikeskus

200101 Tallinn, Pikk 61
Tel. 663-711

Nr. 25111

« 16 » märts 19 90. a.

ÕIEND

Välja antud kod. _____ LEHTMETS, Ann Tõnise t., sünd. 1904 a.,

kes oli kohtuväliselt välja saadetud Eesti NSV Virumaalt

ja viibis asumisel atates « 14 » juunist _____ 19 41 a kuni

« 15 » nov. _____ 19 57. a. Tomski obl., Vasjugani rajoonis

on Eesti NSV 7. detsembri 1988. a. seaduse «Kohtuväliste massirepressioonide kohta Nõukogude Eestis 1940—1950-ndail aastail» alusel rehabiliteeritud.

Pitsat

Ülem _____ V. Kamõnin

ENSV S.M. tr. 1989 65 t. 30 000 nr. 632

Eesti NSV Siseministeerium
Informatsioonikeskus

200101 Tallinn, Pikk 61
Tel. 663-711

Nr. 25112

« 16 » märts 19 90. a.

ÕIEND

Kod. _____ LEHTMETS, Tiit Elmari p., _____ sünd. 1927 a.

kuulus 19 41 a. juunis _____ Eesti NSV Virumaalt

_____ administratiivkorras väljasaatmisele.

kuid otsus tema suhtes jäi täitmata.

Kod. _____ LEHTMETS, Tiit Elmari p. _____ on Eesti NSV

7. detsembri 1988. a. seaduse «Kohtuväliste massirepressioonide kohta Nõukogude Eestis 1940—1950-
ndail aastail» alusel rehabiliteeritud:

Pitsat

Ülem _____ V. Kamõnin

ENSV S.M. tr. 1989 65 t. 3000 nr. 634

Also by Douglas Hoile

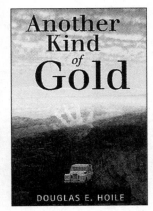

Thomas Coburn is running away from his past. A disastrous marriage and a ruined career as a surgeon have poisoned his taste for city life. He seeks refuge in the small township of Port Gordon, close to the sea and the magnificent Flinders Ranges.

Upon purchasing a vacant medical practice, he finds himself at the centre of intrigue. His predecessor died in suspicious circumstances and there is talk of a mysterious and rare mineral deposit in the Ranges. Land rights are at issue, and Thomas becomes involved in a struggle between developers and aboriginal elders. He also must come to terms with his feelings for an attractive female geologist.

An exciting tale of murder, morality and passion.